JOHN CAMPBELL

PISTOLS
AT DAWN

Two Hundred Years of Political Rivalry,
From Pitt and Fox to Blair and Brown

JONATHAN CAPE
LONDON

Published by Jonathan Cape 2009

4 6 8 10 9 7 5 3

Copyright © John Campbell 2009

John Campbell has asserted his right under the Copyright, Designs
and Patents Act 1988 to be identified as the author of this work

First published in Great Britain in 2009 by
Jonathan Cape
Random House, 20 Vauxhall Bridge Road,
London SW1V 2SA

www.rbooks.co.uk

Addresses for companies within The Random House Group Limited can be found at:
www.randomhouse.co.uk/offices.htm

The Random House Group Limited Reg. No. 954009

A CIP catalogue record for this book
is available from the British Library

ISBN 9780224080668

The Random House Group Limited supports The Forest Stewardship Council (FSC), the leading
international forest certification organisation. All our titles that are printed on Greenpeace approved
FSC certified paper carry the FSC logo. Our paper procurement policy can be found at
www.rbooks.co.uk/environment

Mixed Sources
Product group from well-managed
forests and other controlled sources
www.fsc.org Cert no. TT-COC-2139
© 1996 Forest Stewardship Council

Typeset in Sabon by Palimpsest Book Production Limited,
Grangemouth, Stirlingshire

Printed and bound in Great Britain by
Clays Ltd, St Ives plc

For Kirsty, with my love

Contents

Illustrations

March 1926: reproduced by kind permission of Solo Syndication/British Cartoon Archive, University of Kent, www.cartoons.ac.uk)

14. Aneurin Bevan speaking at the Labour party conference, 1957 (© Getty Images)

15. Hugh Gaitskell with his 1951 budget (© Getty Images)

16. Gaitskell arrives at the 1959 conference in front of Bevan and leaves behind, as drawn by Vicky (taken from *Evening Standard*, 30 November 1959: reproduced by kind permission of Solo Syndication/British Cartoon Archive, University of Kent, www.cartoons.ac.uk)

17. Harold Macmillan and Rab Butler, 1959 (© Getty Images)

18. 'Well, so long, Rab': Vicky's view of the long-suffering Butler, 1958 (reproduced by kind permission of Solo Syndication)

19. Butler ultimately stabbed in the back by 'Mac the Knife' (Vicky's cartoon taken from *Evening Standard*, 17 January 1964: reproduced by kind permission of Solo Syndication/British Cartoon Archive, University of Kent, www.cartoons.ac.uk)

20. All smiles: Thatcher and Heath at the Conservative party conference, 1970 (© PA Photos)

21. Thatcher as Boadicea by Stanley Franklin (taken from the *Sun*, 27 November 1974: reproduced by kind permission of NI Syndication/British Cartoon Archive, University of Kent, www.cartoons.ac.uk)

22. The future leader carries off her predecessor, 1973 (© Getty Images)

23. Joined at the hip: Brown and Blair at the Labour party conference, 2005 (© Getty Images)

24. Blair and Brown as seen by Dave Brown (taken from the *Independent*, 19 November 2001: reproduced by kind permission of Dave Brown/British Cartoon Archive, University of Kent, www.cartoons.ac.uk)

25. Blair and Brown as seen by Steve Bell (taken from the *Guardian*, 11 June 2003: reproduced by kind permission of Steve Bell)

Introduction

Politics is inescapably about power: the drive for power, the exercise of power and the struggle to retain power. Of course it is also about ideas, conflicting ideologies, class and group interests and deep economic forces. But the enduring fascination of democratic politics lies in the dependence of these ideas and forces on the ambitions of competing individuals. No great cause can be advanced except by the genius of an inspirational leader; conversely no leader can succeed but by hitching his fortune to some cause which catches the *Zeitgeist* of his age. Ideas prosper only through the flawed men and women who champion them. It is easy to deplore today's excessive emphasis on personalities at the expense of political content. Yet the clash of contrasting personalities has always been the driving force of progress.

The unique continuity of the British parliamentary system has provided an unparalleled stage for political theatre over the past two hundred years. During the two centuries which separate the age of William Pitt from the age of Gordon Brown the conduct of politics has been transformed almost beyond recognition. The electorate has grown from a few thousand well-born men to include the entire adult population – forty-five million men and women at the last election. Debate that was once conducted in elaborately rhetorical speeches, often lasting several hours, in the chamber of the House of Commons is now concentrated into thirty-second soundbites on television, replayed infinitely on the internet. Governments come and go; parties rise and decline; the issues and ideologies which form the content of political controversy change over time – liberty or order; the prerogatives of the Crown or the House of Lords; tariffs or free trade; capitalism or socialism (or the particular balance between the two); above all, peace or war and the morality and cost of foreign interventions, whether in colonial America, continental Europe or the Middle East. Yet through all these changes of style and substance, the rivalry of ambitious individuals competing for the highest offices – the same offices, for the most part – has remained a constant, and the conduct of politicians merely adapts to different contexts. There is in every age a small number of dominating personalities who embody the contending philosophies of the moment; the clashing egos and the human strengths and weaknesses of these key individuals shape the arguments and determine the historical outcome. These are the leaders who define their age.

They tend to come in pairs. In an adversarial political system every significant shift in ideas throws up its opposing champions. Sometimes – like Pitt and Fox in the late eighteenth century, or Gladstone and Disraeli in the middle of the nineteenth – they are the leaders of rival parties, disputing openly across the floor of the House of Commons, and on the hustings. Increasingly, however – like Asquith and Lloyd George in the early twentieth century, or Bevan and Gaitskell in the 1950s – they are the leaders of factions within the same party, contending for supremacy. In the House of Commons your real enemies are not on the benches opposite but beside and behind you. Often – like Castlereagh and Canning in the early nineteenth century, Macmillan and Butler in the twentieth, or Blair and Brown at the beginning of the twenty-first – they are outwardly good colleagues jostling for the same prize. Some of these feuds start in an approximation to friendship; almost all end in personal antipathy – though only one pair has gone to the length of fighting a real duel and taking shots at one another. But in every case it is the rivalry of these personalities which grips the public imagination. Very often they are contrasting temperaments – one cool and calculating, the other temperamental and impulsive; one ascetic, the other self-indulgent; one idealistic, the other cynical. These personal characteristics are reflected in their politics, and their opposition affords not merely individual dramas but – repeated down the generations – a timeless opposition of 'classical' versus 'romantic' archetypes, 'Roundhead' against 'Cavalier': Pitt, Gladstone, Asquith and Gaitskell on one side against Fox, Disraeli, Lloyd George and Bevan on the other. These contrasts are the very stuff of politics. Time and again, indeed, it is the rivalry which drives individuals to take up opposing causes, rather than opposed beliefs which makes them rivals.

This book traces eight of these epic contests, treating each as a narrative in its own right but also attempting to draw parallels and contrasts to demonstrate not only the transformation in the outward forms but also the inner continuity of the political process. What was once the preserve of a privileged social caste has been gradually prised open to give us the mass democracy of today; yet elections had to be won even in the eighteenth century, and the money spent on winning or fixing them was as disproportionate and corrupting as it is today. The so-called 'nightwatchman state', concerned only with law and order, the regulation of trade and the defence of the realm, has grown into the suffocating leviathan of the welfare state, assuming responsibility for the nation's health, education and safety from the cradle to the grave; yet the arguments over the burden of taxation and the rights, duties and liberties of the citizen *vis-à-vis* the overweening government are essentially unchanged. Britain has acquired and surrendered an empire, declining from the global superpower of the late nineteenth century to a medium-sized regional power still nursing international pretensions beyond its realistic reach; yet questions of peace and war – and the denial of liberty justified by the threat of war – are as contentious today as in the time of Pitt and Fox.

Above all, the conduct of political debate itself has been revolutionised. In the eighteenth and early nineteenth century it was almost exclusively conducted within Parliament – both Lords and Commons – though already amplified by a lively culture of newspapers, pamphlets and caricatures which fed an embryonic public opinion. Parties, factions and 'connections' were inchoate, personal and shifting: patronage was all-important. Power was won and exercised primarily through oratory: speeches were judged as much for their theatrical effect as for their argument. Yet this almost private disputation among a tiny elite at Westminster was always tempered by awareness of the voteless mob outside. Fox was an aristocrat to his fingertips, no democrat by any modern standard, yet he constantly appealed to an idealised concept of 'the people'. Through the middle and later nineteenth century the franchise was steadily extended, first to the professional middle class, then to respectable elements of the working class; the railways and cheaper newspapers carried full reports of parliamentary debates quickly to the whole country; party organisations, Conservative and Liberal, were formed to fight elections and carry the message of rival leaders – pre-eminently Gladstone and Disraeli – who began to address the electorate directly at public meetings. But Parliament remained central, with the Lower house gradually displacing the upper as the chamber in which power resided.

This pattern endured for the first third of the twentieth century – the age of Asquith and Lloyd George – until broadcasting inaugurated a third age. First the wireless from around 1930 and then, in the 1950s, television transformed the way politicians communicated with the nation and increasingly with each other. At first Parliament held its own: in the 1960s and into the early 1980s the newspapers still reported debates, reputations were still made in the chamber and authority derived from command of the House: Roy Jenkins was the last major figure to make his name in this way. But already, in the age of Macmillan and Butler, 'image' was becoming as important as substance. The balance tilted decisively in the last decades of the century – the age of Thatcher and Blair – when Jenkins, returning in 1982 to the area he had dominated in the 1960s, found himself a fish out of water. Today politics is an activity that takes place almost wholly on the airwaves and in the ether. Parliament is largely ignored, even by MPs themselves, except for the weekly pantomime of Prime Minister's Questions which is aimed primarily at the electronic audience. Ministers are held to account not in debate by their elected opponents, but on radio and television by celebrity presenters who are far more famous than the mere politicians they interrogate. By the first years of the new century any substantial difference between the parties has been eroded almost to nothing and the business of government reduced to a game show on which the public is invited to make instant judgements of approval or disapproval. Point-scoring has replaced argument; conspicuous ability is a liability; likeability and perceived 'ordinariness' have displaced knowledge, experience and ideas.

It may be an illusion to imagine that modern politics has declined from some golden age. Every generation thinks its own politicians pygmies compared with the giants of the past. But there has surely been a measurable loss of quality. If not a golden age, there was a period in the middle of the two-century span – lasting roughly from the last third of the nineteenth century to the middle of the twentieth – when the forces of democracy and media were in some sort of balance. The late eighteenth/early nineteenth century was still a predominantly aristocratic age in which party lines, reflecting clear differences of political philosophy, were only beginning to be drawn; the frank venality of patronage and place-seeking was gradually replaced by Victorian standards of public conduct; a new cadre of middle-class politicians arose, reflecting the replacement of agriculture by industry and commerce as the main source of the national wealth, though for some decades yet the great landed magnates still held disproportionate sway. From about 1870 improved communications helped to create a clearly defined two-party system which engaged the loyalties of most of the expanded electorate and endured for about a hundred years, evolving relatively smoothly from a Conservative–Liberal to a Conservative–Labour duopoly. Most clearly in the decade before 1914 and in the two decades after 1945, the public was offered a choice between two well-organised mass-membership organisations representing opposed visions of society, passionately supported by their respective followers, which nevertheless accepted – with a slight wobble around 1911 – the legitimacy of the other view and alternated in government without excessive acrimony or wild swings between extremes. They were led by a predominantly upper-middle-class political elite who mixed socially with one another in the clubs of London and great houses around the country, but at the same time took the business of government very seriously – albeit with a generous helping of hypocrisy – and felt an obligation to communicate seriously with what they still imagined to be an informed and interested public opinion. They operated in a media culture which equally believed in its responsibility to inform and educate the electorate – from the heavyweight newspapers (including important provincial papers) which printed lengthy reports of parliamentary debates and extra-parliamentary speeches, through the popular titles which still – up to the 1960s – covered politics far more fully and fairly than the supposed 'quality' press does today, to television which in its early years was still controlled and presented by journalists brought up in the print tradition.

Between them, the politicians and the media created an electorate which followed politics, was assumed to read the reports of debates and attended political meetings in large numbers, at least at election time. Of course there was an element of self-deception here. Up till the mid-1950s, when television took off, there were many fewer alternative sources of entertainment: people attended meetings because there was not much else to do, they often provided good sport, and they were free; just as they read the political news because that was what newspaper editors thought it was their job to give them. Politicians in turn treated the electorate with respect because they imagined the public to be more interested than it really was. This may have been an illusion, but it was a healthy one, which gave structure and discipline to the national debate.

The rot set in with increasing affluence, bringing an explosion of alternative distractions. Sophisticated market research and the publication of ever more detailed opinion polls revealed the shallowness of public interest in politics, and the media – both print and broadcast – began to give the public what it wanted, not, as previously, what they thought was good for it. Of course there were deeper forces: the loss of empire and great power status, the interconnectedness of the global economy, the growing revelation of the powerlessness of national governments to control events and the withering of any serious distinction between 'left' and 'right' have all contributed to a trivialisation of the content of politics and a consequent loss of respect for politicians, who are no longer seen as statesmen representing great interests or causes but rather as self-seeking careerists, representative of no one but themselves. The demands of the 24-hour media have become so intrusive that the best minds and potential leaders in the universities no longer, as in all previous generations, aspire to a career in government: the life of politics has become almost intolerable, as well as intellectually unrewarding. Thus in a curious way the triumph of mass democracy has brought politics full circle. Though Parliament is no longer the cockpit, in other respects we have returned to a narrow eighteenth-century world of patronage, self-promotion and mutual back-scratching where there is nothing at stake but the achievement and retention of office and the opportunities for personal enrichment that it brings. Politics today is little more than a childish game played out by a small and introverted political class, largely ignored by a cynical and alienated electorate except when it throws up some titillating scandal. It was always a game, of course – that was the fascination which kept players like Fox, Disraeli and Macmillan at the table and the audience riveted by every throw of the dice; but it was once a great game, played by serious-minded people for serious causes and high stakes.

Yet one should not be too pious about the past. The eight duels described in these pages reveal that human nature does not change, however much the level at which the game is played has been debased. The skulduggery – and downright lies – by which Pitt contrived to do down Fox, and the restless scheming by which Canning undermined Castlereagh are echoed in the calculated manoeuvring by which Macmillan repeatedly denied Butler, and by Brown's obsessive briefing against Blair. Spencer Perceval feared the effect of Canning and Castlereagh's duel on the government's popularity exactly as if he was worrying about modern opinion polls. Disraeli's undisguised delight at having 'climbed to the top of the greasy pole' was matched by Macmillan celebrating with oysters and champagne at the Turf Club, while Gladstone's contrasting belief that he was the humble vehicle of the Almighty's will anticipates Mrs Thatcher's righteous sense of destiny a century later. Few political opponents have loathed each other as openly as Gladstone and Disraeli; but Asquith and Lloyd George, Bevan and Gaitskell, Heath and Thatcher and Brown and Blair were all turned from colleagues into bitter enemies by the accidents of achieving or not achieving the supreme office. Almost all of them experienced extraordinary reversals of fortune – from the heights to the depths and back again – in the course of their careers, precisely mirroring the success or failure of their rivals. Most of those who made it to the top finished up with some degree of disappointment; the reputation of some who did not make it stands higher today than some of those who did. The kaleido-scope of politics remains intensely dramatic – as no one knew better than Shakespeare:

> There is a tide in the affairs of men
> Which, taken at the flood, leads on to fortune;
> Omitted, all the voyage of their life
> Is bound in shallows and in miseries.[1]

In Brutus's case it led only to defeat and suicide at Philippi. Most political careers, as Enoch Powell caustically observed, end in failure. Nowadays they end, not on the battlefield or the block, but in electoral defeat and the 'shallows and miseries' of the House of Lords. But the impulse to compete for power, and the import-ance of timing, nerve and luck in determining the outcome, remains the same – even in a decadent age like the present. The eight dramas recounted in this book offer extraordinary testimony to the richness and continuity of the British political tradition.

Charles James Fox
and William Pitt

Charles Fox and William Pitt were born rivals. Their fathers had been rivals before them, though theirs was an unequal contest. The elder William Pitt was the great war leader who inspired the serious of glorious victories over France in the Seven Years War which established Britain's colonial supremacy in India and North America. Ennobled as the Earl of Chatham, he was one of that handful of commanding figures – Gladstone, Lloyd George, Churchill, Margaret Thatcher – who dominate their generation and are spoken of with awe by their successors. Henry Fox by contrast was no more than a wily political operator whose most enduring claim to fame was the acquisition of a vast private fortune while serving as Paymaster-General of the Forces. His reputation as the most mercenary politician of an exceptionally venal age may have been unfair: he was 'the most unpopular statesman of his time', one contemporary wrote, 'not because he sinned more than any of them, but because he canted less'.[1] Lack of cant was one attractive quality he passed on to his more famous son. Nevertheless his notorious venality contrasted with the elder Pitt's rare reputation for financial probity. Henry Fox was furiously jealous of Chatham's earldom, while he had to settle for a mere barony (as Lord Holland). Fortunately their rivalry was carried forward by their younger sons, whose careers were not inhibited by inheriting their father's titles.

Young Fox, born in 1749, was ten years the elder, a boy of precocious gifts, explicitly raised to fulfil the expectations which his father's career had not quite realised. As a child he was spectacularly

9

spoiled. Henry personally acted as his son's pimp and bookmaker, introducing him to the delights of women, wine and gaming at an early age, repeatedly paying his debts and sending him on the Grand Tour at the age of seventeen. In France, while sowing wild oats on a scale which amazed even the French, '*milord* Fox' met everyone who mattered from Voltaire to the duc d'Orleans and became a life-long Francophile. Before Charles was even formally of age Henry bought him a seat in the Commons, and he rapidly emerged as the foremost young orator in the House – 'the meteor of these days', as Horace Walpole called him, 'and barely twenty-two'.² Yet already his mother was worried by a rising threat to his prospects. 'I have been this morning with Lady Hester Pitt,' she wrote to her husband in 1767, 'and there is little William Pitt, not eight years old and really the cleverest child I ever saw . . . *Mark my words*, that little boy will be a thorn in Charles's side as long as he lives.'³

Lady Holland could not have known how right she was. Young Pitt was as sober, studious and single-minded as Charles Fox was reckless and dissolute. 'I am glad I am not the eldest son,' he announced at the age of seven. 'I want to speak in the House of Commons like Papa.'⁴ He too was duly found a seat at the age of twenty-one, became Chancellor of the Exchequer two years later and then in extraordinary circumstances Prime Minister at twenty-four – replacing a short-lived ministry in which Fox had been, though not Prime Minister, the leading figure. He held office, with one short interruption, through peace and war for the next twenty-two years, condemning Fox to two decades of frustrated impotence. Only after Pitt's death in 1806 did Fox enjoy another brief taste of power before his own death eight months later.

In those twenty-two years during which they faced each other across the House of Commons, Pitt and Fox between them defined the shape, the conventions and the rhetoric of British politics for the next two centuries. If Pitt was the first modern Prime Minister, Fox unwillingly created the role of Leader of the Opposition. There was still no organised party system. The words 'Whig' and 'Tory' were used as terms of sentiment or abuse; but they were badges of family or tribal connection, not clear distinctions between opposed ideologies, still less parties whipped to vote in the same lobby. A hundred years after the 'Glorious Revolution' of 1688 – the bloodless coup by which the Catholic James II was forced off the throne to be replaced, at the invitation of Parliament, by the Protestant William of Orange and his wife Mary (James's daughter) – almost everyone who aspired to government called himself a 'Whig'. Yet long before the terminology – imported from France in the 1790s – was generally adopted, Pitt came to embody all the attributes later associated with the 'right' – allegiance to the Crown and empire, strong defence, economy and law and order; while Fox embodied all the attributes of the dissenting 'left' – peace not war, internationalism, human rights, 'liberty' and a romantic exaltation of 'the people'. Modern politics and the twentieth-century party system effectively began with Pitt and Fox.

Yet they started out on the same side – as rivals usually do. Though temperamental opposites, they differed at first about very little. But in the intimate cockpit of eighteenth-century politics they were drawn to different groupings, and circumstances quickly forced them apart. Soon they were leading followings of their own and the logic of events drove them to define themselves in opposition to one another. We shall see the same process again and again in later chapters. It is not opposed views which create rivalry, but rivalry which leads to the adoption of opposing views. Pitt and Fox set a pattern that has been followed repeatedly for the last two hundred years, down to the present.

Charles Fox was a phenomenon.* He was an ugly little man – short, swarthy, unkempt and often unwashed. In an age of unbridled excess he drank, gambled and womanised harder than anyone in London, piling up enormous debts which he never paid. Politics was only one of his interests, and he treated it, like all the others, as a game. Yet he was the most brilliant speaker in the House of Commons and leader of his own party by the age of twenty-five. Above all, he was extraordinarily popular. His friends were devoted to him, and even his opponents had scarcely a bad word to say of him. 'Let him do what he will, I must love the dog,' wrote the

---

*Fox was never in his lifetime known as 'Charles James'. The use of both Christian names was a Victorian affectation. To his contemporaries he was always 'Charles' or 'Charlie'.

historian Edward Gibbon. 'Perhaps no human being was ever more perfectly exempt from the taint of malevolence, vanity or falsehood.'[5] Edmund Burke called him in 1777 'one of the pleasantest men in the world, as well as the greatest Genius that perhaps this country has ever produced'.[6] Years later, after they had quarrelled irrevocably over the French revolution, Burke still called his old friend 'a man born to be loved'.[7] Some observers – Horace Walpole among them – regretted that Fox's dissolute lifestyle prevented the full flowering of his gifts; but most marvelled that he could stay up all night gambling at Brooks's, spend the day at Newmarket then come down to the House and make a brilliant two- or three-hour speech before going back to Brooks's. 'He was seldom in bed before five in the morning, nor out of it before two at noon.'[8] When a Frenchman asked Pitt – during Fox's brief tenure of office in 1783 – how 'a country so moral as England can submit to be governed by such a spendthrift and rake as Fox', Pitt replied simply: 'You have not been under the wand of the magician.'[9]

By the time Pitt entered the House in January 1781 Fox was already its acknowledged master. 'Charles Fox,' wrote Walpole, 'has tumbled old Saturn' – that is Chatham – 'from the throne of oratory.'[10] He had twice held junior office under Lord North but twice resigned, on grounds generally regarded as quixotic. After a false start as a conventionally conservative young sprig – during which period he made several lofty assertions which would later embarrass him, such as declaring in 1771 that 'I pay no regard whatever to the voice of the people' – he had found his true voice as an opponent of the war against the American colonists. As British forces were driven to humiliating surrender first at Saratoga and then at Yorktown, he abandoned his pocket borough and stood successfully for Westminster – the largest popular constituency in the country with an electorate of 12,000 – as a self-proclaimed 'Man of the People' and champion of parliamentary reform. Since the heads of the other two principal Whig groupings, the Marquess of Rockingham and the Earl of Shelburne, both sat in the Lords, Fox was the effective Leader of the Opposition in the Commons. There he mounted a violent assault on North's now floundering ministry which, he alleged, was kept in office only by royal favour and the King's stubborn refusal to accept the loss of America.*

All eighteenth-century politicians held it as axiomatic that the 'Glorious Revolution' had achieved a perfect constitutional balance between Crown, Lords and Commons. A century later all their disputes were still about whether one side or another was threatening that balance. The opposition Whigs believed that George III – largely because unlike his two Hanoverian predecessors he spoke English and spent all his time in England – was seeking to restore the power of the throne at the expense of Parliament. In April 1780 the House of Commons passed by 233 votes to 215 the famous motion that 'the influence of the Crown has increased, is increasing and ought to be diminished'; and henceforth this belief was the cornerstone of Fox's politics. He was not anti-monarchist, far from it, nor in any modern sense of the word a democrat. He merely wanted some reform of Parliament to make it less corrupt and marginally less unrepresentative, to restore the independence of the Commons against the abuse of royal patronage. Everywhere he detected what he called 'the monstrous influence of the Crown'.[11] This by itself would have been enough to earn him the enmity of the King. But George also blamed Fox for leading the Prince of Wales into dissolute ways; there was some justice in this view, though 'Prinny' – the future George IV – needed little leading. The cartoonists regularly portrayed Fox as a seedy Falstaff to the Prince's impressionable Hal. The King was practically the only person in England impervious to Fox's charm. It was his determination never to have him back in office – and the extreme lengths he resorted to in order to exclude him – which made the lasting breach between Fox and Pitt. Their dispute in turn went to the heart of the emerging conventions of constitutional monarchy.

Fox initially welcomed Pitt as a youthful protégé. 'Fox was charmed with Pitt . . . and loved him,' Walpole wrote. 'Had not Pitt so early aspired to be his rival, Fox would have cherished Pitt as his friend and disciple.'[12] But Pitt attached himself to

---

*North's title was a courtesy title which did not prevent him sitting in the Commons. In 1790 he succeeded his father as the second Earl of Guilford (so spelled).

Shelburne – leader of his father's old connection – while Fox leaned rather towards Rockingham. Fox proposed Pitt for membership of Brooks's. But Pitt – a shy young man whose only vice was heavy drinking – preferred the company of his own friends; he attended Brooks's only once, then joined a smaller club, called Goostree's, 'for young men of the opposition, very nice in their admissions, discouraging gaming as far as possible'.[13] Already one observer noted his precocious determination to be his own man, as well as the threat his cool ambition posed to Fox:

> Young Pitt will not be subordinate; he is not so in his own society. He is at the head of a dozen young people, and it is a corps separate from . . . Charles's; so there is another premier at the starting post . . . He seems to hold prudence in much higher estimation than Charles does, and in this respect has an advantage over him; in all others he is nearer in equality with him than anyone I ever saw.[14]

Fox was characteristically generous in praise of Pitt's maiden speech in February 1781. Pitt spoke in support of a bill introduced by Burke to limit government extravagance.

> Mr Pitt's first speech, brilliant and wonderful as it was, was scarcely more remarkable than the warmth and generosity with which Mr Fox greeted the appearance and extolled the performance of his future rival. Incapable of jealousy, and delighted at the sudden display of talents nearly equal to his own, he hurried up to the young Member to compliment and encourage him. As he was doing so, an old Member of the House . . . passed by them and said: 'Ay, Mr Fox, you are praising young Pitt for his speech. You may well do so; for excepting yourself, there's no man in the House can make such another; and old as I am, I expect and hope to hear you both battling it within these walls as I have done your fathers before you'.

Fox was embarrassed; but Pitt turned the compliment gracefully.[15]

From the moment he entered Parliament Pitt was recognised as Fox's equal – if not already his superior. Only Fox seemed unconcerned. In May 1781 he and Pitt rose simultaneously, but Fox gave way to let the young prodigy make his second speech. Displaying 'paternal oratory', Pitt tore North 'limb from limb'.[16] 'If Charles

Fox could feel,' Walpole wrote, 'one should think such a rival, with an unspotted character, would rouse him. What if a Pitt and Fox should again be rivals?'[17] The prospect had connoisseurs of parliamentary oratory licking their lips:

> The warmth of the House of Commons is prodigiously rekindled . . .
> the two names of most *éclat* in the opposition are two names to
> which those walls have been much accustomed at the same period
> – Charles Fox and William Pitt, second son of Lord Chatham.
> Eloquence is the only one of our brilliant qualities that does not seem
> to have degenerated rapidly.[18]

At the end of 1781 Pitt made another very short but devastating speech on the American war, in which he 'took to pieces Lord North's pretended declarations . . . and exposed them with the most amazing logical abilities, exceeding all the abilities he had already shown, and making men doubt whether he would not prove superior even to Charles Fox'.[19] Still Fox continued to be generous, saying that 'he could no longer lament the loss of Lord Chatham, for he was again living in his son, with all his virtues and all his talents . . . He is likely soon to take precedence of all our orators.'[20]

In March 1782 North, having lost his Commons majority, finally persuaded the King to let him resign – an important assertion of the supremacy of Parliament which George was very unwilling to admit. He was reluctantly obliged to accept a new ministry headed by Rockingham in which Fox and Shelburne were the two Secretaries of State. Though Pitt had been in the House barely more than a year he was offered the vice-treasurership of Ireland (a position his father had once held, which carried a salary of £5,000 a year). Astonishingly, he refused it. A few weeks earlier he had foreshadowed his decision by announcing that he 'could not expect to form part of a new administration; but were my doing so more within my reach, I feel myself bound to declare that I never would accept a subordinate situation'.[21] Horace Walpole commented:

> So arrogant a declaration from a boy who had gained no experi-
> ence from, nor ever enjoyed even the lowest post in any office . . .
> proved that he was a boy, and a very ambitious and a very vain
> one. The moment he sat down he was aware of his folly, and said

he could bite his tongue out for what he had uttered; but though he lamented his imprudence, it was of his frankness that he repented. In very few months he showed that he had neither corrected his vanity or ambition.[22]

Fox was a surprisingly good minister, as Walpole was quick to acknowledge. 'Mr Fox . . . already shines as greatly in place as he did in opposition . . . He is now as indefatigable as he was idle.'[23] He was scarcely seen at Brooks's but 'at once gave himself up to the duties of his office [and] displayed such facility in comprehending and executing all business as charmed all who approached him'.[24] By a new division of responsibilities Fox was effectively the first Foreign Secretary, Shelburne the first Home Secretary; but home affairs included the colonies – a division which immediately led to friction over the terms of peace with America. Fox took American independence to be a *fait accompli*; Shelburne – a cold, secretive man, widely distrusted – did not. Fox suspected Shelburne of scheming with the King to undermine him. Within three months he was already on the point of resigning.

Meanwhile Pitt, from the back benches, proposed a select committee on the reform of Parliament. He denounced 'the corrupt influence of the Crown' and invoked his father's view that 'unless a more solid and equal system of representation were established, this nation, happy and great as it might have been, would come to be confounded in the mass of those whose liberties were lost in the corruption of the people'.[25] Fox naturally supported him, paying 'a variety of compliments to Mr Pitt for his steady attachment to liberty'. The motion was only defeated by 161 votes to 141 – the closest the reformers would get for another fifty years. Ten days later Fox and Pitt both supported a bill to shorten the duration of parliaments which was defeated by a much larger majority. The next month found them on opposite sides, however, when Fox opposed, but Pitt supported, a bill to curb election bribery. Fox defended bribery with the wonderfully eighteenth-century argument that 'he was all for cultivating the connection between the elector and the elected, by all possible expedients'. It was by 'intimacy', he argued, that 'character, virtue, property . . . had their natural influence'. The right to be bribed was one of 'the very few privileges the electors of Great Britain retained'.[26] It was an important moment, as Pitt's friend and first biographer, Bishop Tomline, later recalled:

> This was, I believe, the first question on which they happened to differ before any separation took place between them. I must, however, remark that although they had hitherto acted together in Parliament, there had been no intimacy or confidential intercourse between them.[27]

At the beginning of July Rockingham suddenly died. Fox tried to insist that the King should appoint the Duke of Portland in his place; but George refused to be 'dictated to by Mr Fox'[28] and appointed Shelburne. Fox promptly resigned, as he had been about to do already; but his resignation now looked personal and petty, and seemed to betray a lack of judgement. He sought an ally in Pitt, whose speech two months earlier had suggested that he shared Fox's suspicion of royal influence. He tried to dissuade Pitt from throwing in his lot with Shelburne and the King. 'They look to *you*,' he argued. '*Without* you, they cannot succeed; *with* you I know not whether they will or no.' Pitt dissembled: 'If they reckon upon *me*, they may find themselves mistaken.' But Fox told his friends: 'I believe they *do* reckon on Pitt, and I believe they will *not* be mistaken.'[29] He was right. A few days later the boy wonder accepted office as Chancellor of the Exchequer.

This was a decisive moment – the moment when Fox left office and Pitt entered it for the first time. They now sat on opposite sides of the House, where they would remain for most of the rest of their lives. On 9 July Fox launched an intemperate attack on Shelburne, charging that he 'would abandon fifty principles for the sake of power' and predicting that he would soon make a coalition with North: 'In order to maintain himself in power he would be capable of that extremity of baseness.' Pitt sarcastically threw the charge of unprincipled ambition back at Fox:

> The Right Honourable Secretary assures us that it was with the sole view of preventing dissensions in the Cabinet that he resigned from office. I believe him, because he solemnly declares it; otherwise I should have attributed his resignation to a baulk in struggling for power. If, however, he so much disliked Lord Shelburne's political principles or opinions, why did he ever consent to act with that

nobleman as a colleague? And if he only suspected Lord Shelburne of feeling averse to the measures which he thought necessary to be adopted, it was his duty to have called a Cabinet Council and there to have ascertained the fact before he took the hasty resolution of throwing up his employment.[30]

First blood to Pitt. The parliamentary duel that was to last the next two decades was now fully joined. Their next clash came after the summer recess when Parliament reassembled in December. Fox commended the government for having finally agreed peace terms with America, but tried to claim the credit for the previous ministry and mocked Shelburne for having done the right thing despite himself. He quoted a line of doggerel from 'a ludicrous poet':

> You've done a noble turn in Nature's spite,
> For tho' you think you're wrong, I'm sure you're right.

But again Pitt trumped him, with an impromptu parody of his own:

> The praise he gives us in his Nature's spite;
> He wishes we were wrong, but clearly sees we're right.[31]

In truth this was a duel which Pitt was always going to win. Fox was a wonderful orator – witty, rhetorical, hyperbolic, capable when roused of whipping up a magnificent storm of indignation. But Pitt, while equally fluent, was cool, logical and deadly. It was the difference between a 'born minister', as North called Pitt,[32] and a natural Leader of the Opposition. Contemporaries fell over each other to draw the contrast. 'Mr Pitt conceives his sentences before he utters them,' the classical scholar Richard Porson wrote; 'Mr Fox throws himself into the middle of his, and leaves it to God Almighty to get him out again.'[33] (Or, as Fox himself admitted, while he was never at a loss for *a* word, Pitt 'was never at a loss for *the* word.')[34] Sir Francis Baring confirmed this:

> Mr Pitt always spoke with a regular flow of expression, never requiring to go backward to correct himself, but proceeding with an uninterrupted stream of delivery. On the contrary, Mr Fox went *forward* and *backward*, not satisfied with his first expression. He would put

it another way. The *undertone* of Mr Fox's voice was agreeable, almost musical, but when to give force and energy to his delivery he raised his voice it became squeaking and disagreeable . . . Mr Fox occasionally had flashes of genius beyond Mr Pitt . . . [but] Mr Pitt had the ascendancy.[35]

Significantly, Fox did not like his speeches to be printed, maintaining that if a speech read well on the page it was not a good speech.[36]

His admirers still preferred Fox, with all his faults. The Irish leader Henry Grattan wrote that 'Pitt would be right nineteen times for once that Fox would be right; but that once would be worth all the rest.'[37] But even Pitt's critics could not deny his mastery. Richard Rigby – a follower of Lord North – wrote in 1787:

You know that I am not partial to Pitt, and yet I must own that he is infinitely superior to anything I ever saw in that House, and I declare that Fox and Sheridan and all of them put together are nothing to him; he, without support or assistance, answers them all with ease to himself, and they are just chaff before the wind to him.[38]

Horace Walpole, finally, summed up the difference as one of temperament and application:

The one [Fox] trusted to his natural abilities and, whenever he wanted, never found them fail. Pitt, on the contrary, attended to nothing but the means of gratifying his abilities . . . Fox seemed to leave pleasure with regret, and to bestow only spare moments on the government of a nation; Pitt to make industry and virtue the ladders of his ambition. Fox's greatness was innate; and if he had ambition, it was the only passion which he took no pains to gratify.[39]

In fact Fox *was* ambitious. When he turned his attention to politics he wanted office as keenly as the next man – as his next move in the winter of 1782–83 dramatically showed.

Six months after charging that Shelburne might be capable of such 'extremity of baseness' as to make a coalition with Lord North, he did exactly that himself. The parliamentary arithmetic was admittedly difficult, since there were three mutually antagonistic groupings in the House none of which could muster a majority on its own. Shelburne, with the so-called 'King's friends' who

almost always backed the government of the day, could call on
140 votes; North still commanded about 120; while Fox's friends
numbered about ninety. Some form of coalition between former
enemies was unavoidable if any sort of stable ministry was to be
formed. In practice North held the key to a Commons majority
for either of the other two. But the combination that seemed most
implausible was Fox and North. For the past six years Fox had
been denouncing North as a royal puppet – 'void of honour and
honesty . . . the most infamous of mankind'; it seemed inconceivable that he could now make common cause with him. Yet such
was his loathing of Shelburne that he was willing to forget everything he had said about North, on the ground that the only thing
that divided them had been the American war, which was now
over. Even an age accustomed to switches of political allegiance
was shocked by the speed of this abrupt reversal.

Before either finally committed himself Fox made another attempt
to detach Pitt from Shelburne; while Pitt, with Shelburne's blessing,
made at least a show of trying to recruit Fox. Each was trying to
assert primacy over the other. Pitt called on Fox at his house in
South Street. But Fox declared that it was 'impossible for him to
belong to any administration of which Lord Shelburne was the head'.
In that case, Pitt replied, there was nothing more to discuss, since
'he did not come to betray lord Shelburne'. According to Bishop
Tomline, this was 'the last time Mr Pitt was in a private room with
Mr Fox; and from this period may be dated that political hostility,
which continued throughout the remainder of their lives'.[40]

In the Commons Fox defended his *rapprochement* with North
with characteristically disarming candour. 'It is not in my nature
to bear malice, or to live in ill-will,' he explained. 'My friendships
are perpetual, my enmities are not so.' He now cast Shelburne as
the royal placeman who must be opposed in the name of the
people. But he frankly admitted an element of ambition in his
desire for office:

> I shall not disavow my having an ambition to hold such a situation
> in office as may enable me to promote the interest of my country . . .
> I flatter myself that I am not inadequate to the importance of such
> a situation; nor do I think that I gave, during the short time I held

a respectable place in administration, any reason why I should not offer myself a candidate for a share in [a] new arrangement.[41]

Pitt on this occasion made a poor reply. Condemning the 'unnatural alliance' of Fox and North in his most priggish style, he suffered a withering put-down at the hands of Fox's friend Sheridan – author of *The Rivals* and *The School for Scandal* – who compared him to the character of the Angry Boy in Ben Jonson's play *The Alchemist*. Four days later, however, Pitt bounced back with one of his most powerful speeches denouncing North and Fox separately, the one for his incompetence in losing America, the other for his opportunist criticism of the peace terms. North he savaged mercilessly for his 'utter incapacity to fill the station he occupied'. Fox by contrast he still treated with exaggerated flattery: 'Revering as I do the great abilities of the right honourable gentleman who spoke last, I lament . . . when these abilities are misemployed . . . to inflame the imagination and mislead the judgement.'

Like Fox, Pitt did not deny the promptings of honourable ambition; but he claimed loftier principles than his rival:

High situation, and great influence, are desirable objects to most men, and objects which I am not ashamed to pursue, which I am even solicitous to possess, whenever they can be acquired with honour, and retained with dignity. On these respectable conditions, I am not less ambitious to be great and powerful than it is natural for a young man, with such brilliant examples before him [that is his father], to be. But even these objects I am not beneath relinquishing, the moment my duty to my country, my character, and my friends renders such a sacrifice indispensable.[42]

Though one excited MP considered this 'the finest speech that was ever made in Parliament',[43] it was not enough to save Shelburne's ministry from defeat by 207 votes to 190. Shelburne now advised the King to send for Pitt, on the ground that his very youth would make it hard for anyone to oppose him. But Pitt, with extraordinary self-possession, declined to form a ministry that would be dependent on North's goodwill. Over the next month he twice refused George's pressing invitation, preferring to preserve his independence and bide his time. George threatened to abdicate rather than accept Fox;

but North steadfastly refused to desert his new ally, and in the end the King was forced to give way. On 30 March 1783 – bridling, it was said, like a horse submitting to a hated rider – he appointed a coalition ministry nominally headed by the aged Duke of Portland, but in reality led by Fox with North as his (sometimes literally) sleeping partner. In the short term, the satirists noted, 'King Fox' appeared to have triumphed over King George.

Even now Fox and North pressed Pitt to throw in his lot with them and continue as Chancellor of the Exchequer. 'It rested with him to have composed one of the new triumvirate,' wrote one of his nineteenth-century biographers; yet 'aided by a judgement far beyond his years', he rejected 'the seductive proposition'.[44] Pitt refused to be subordinate to Fox or anyone else. He calculated that if he held aloof the whole game would eventually fall into his hands – as indeed it did.

The life of the Fox–North coalition was destined to be short – not because it was really any more cynical than most eighteenth-century combinations, but because George III was determined to be rid of it as soon as he could and because Pitt was willing to lend himself to the King's purpose in order to dish Fox. George hamstrung the government from the start by refusing it the normal lubricant of royal patronage – in particular by refusing to create any new peers. Nevertheless Fox was initially optimistic that the coalition would survive, since the opposition was too divided to pose any threat. 'The only source of weakness,' he wrote, 'is the idea of the King's dislike . . . But, on the other hand, our lasting out the summer will prove that his dislike is not such as to proceed to overt acts.' The only danger lay in the ministry's determination to grasp the overdue nettle of reforming the government of India – a 'very delicate' undertaking which was bound to stir up a lot of vested interests. But he expected this to be out of the way by Christmas, after which he hoped 'things will go as smoothly as possible in a House of Commons where there is so able, so indefatigable and so little scrupulous an opposer as Pitt'.[45]

Even now Fox would rather have had Pitt on his side. In September he wrote to his brother-in-law that 'If Pitt could be persuaded (but I despair of it) I am convinced . . . he would do more real service to the country than any man ever did.'[46] While acknowledging his ability, however, Fox still underestimated Pitt's determination to be his own man. The India Bill, introduced in November, afforded boundless opportunity for unscrupulous opposition.

No major piece of legislation was ever so traduced by its opponents as Fox's India Bill. Framed by his friend and mentor Edmund Burke – who conceived it as 'the Magna Charta of Indostan'[47] – it was inspired by the most elevated ideals. No one disputed that the unchecked maladministration of the East India Company had become a scandal. The 'rapacity' of the Company's servants, in Fox's words, had spread 'confusion and anarchy' across the subcontinent: it was widely admitted that something must be done. Burke's solution was to remove political power from the Company and vest it in a commission appointed by the government in London and accountable to Parliament, leaving the Company as a purely commercial enterprise. In the next century this would come to be seen as the normal and proper approach to colonial government. But in the eighteenth century India was all about loot, and the government of India was all about access to that loot – in other words the control of patronage. Fox's critics saw his bill first as a monstrous attack on the property rights of the Company, enshrined in its charter, and second as a scam cynically designed to place all patronage in the hands of himself and his friends. 'It is the boldest and most unconstitutional measure ever attempted,' Pitt wrote to his friend the Duke of Rutland, 'transferring at one stroke, in spite of all charters and compacts, the immense patronage and influence of the East to Charles Fox, *in or out of office*.'[48]

Accordingly – realising that the Bill offered the best opportunity to destroy the coalition – Pitt directed his attack at Fox personally. 'Was it not the principal and declared avowal of this bill,' he demanded in the Commons, 'that the whole system of the India government should be placed in seven persons ... under the immediate appointment of none other than the minister himself? ... The minister would then virtually be the governor of India.' The proposal amounted to 'absolute despotism and ... the most gross corruption'.[49] In a later debate, stepping up the hyperbole another notch, he called the Bill 'one of the boldest, most unprecedented, most desperate and alarming attempts at the exercise of tyranny that ever disgraced the annals of this or any other country'.[50]

Unfortunately for Fox the suggestion that he was intent on grabbing the wealth of India for himself was all too plausible. This was, after all, how his father had made his fortune and Fox himself – though not in fact personally corrupt: he was too careless of money for that – was a notorious libertine. The cartoonists had a field day: the most damaging print portrayed him as 'Carlo Khan, the Great Potentate of Leadenhall Street' riding in triumph through the City, mounted on an elephant with the face of Lord North. It was also a mistake to name as the first commissioners seven of his own supporters, all better known at Brooks's than in India. Yet Fox believed that he was acting from the purest motives. 'I have the weakness of disliking abuse,' he wrote to his mistress Elizabeth Armistead, 'but that weakness shall never prevent me from doing what I think right.'

> I never did act more upon principle than at this moment, when they are abusing me so. I am not at all ignorant of the political danger which I run by this bold measure; but whether I succeed or no, I shall always be glad that I attempted [it], because I know that I have done no more than I was bound to do, in risking my power and that of my friends when the happiness of so many millions is at stake.[51]

In the Commons he put forward the enlightened argument that Parliament's duty was to the welfare of the governed.

> What is the end of all government? Certainly the happiness of the governed. Others may hold other opinions, but this is mine, and I proclaim it. What are we to think of a government whose good fortune is supposed to spring from the calamities of its subjects, whose aggrandizement grows out of the miseries of mankind? This is the kind of government exercised under the East India Company upon the natives of Indostan; and the subversion of that infamous government is the main object of the bill.

He admitted that his bill violated the Company's charter; but the charter was a trust, and the Company had betrayed its charter by neglecting this trust.

It matters not whether dominion arises from conquest or compact. Conquest gives no right to the conqueror to be a tyrant; and it is no violation of right to abolish the authority which is misused.[52]

Here is the essence of a debate which still resonates two hundred years later, between liberal regulation on the one hand and Tory freedom on the other. Fox was arguing for government intervention to protect the governed, Pitt for the untrammelled rights of property. In the debate on the First Reading of the bill, Pitt gave his argument a ringing libertarian twist which is still quoted to this day:

The Bill is said to be founded on *necessity* . . . Is it not *necessity* which has always been the plea of every illegal assertion of power or exercise of oppression? Is not *necessity* the pretence of every usurpation? Necessity is the plea for every infringement of human freedom. It is the argument of tyrants; it is the creed of slaves.[53]

But in the Second Reading debate a few days later Fox responded with an alternative definition, invoking the hallowed precedent of 1688:

Necessity is said to be the plea of tyranny – it is also the plea of freedom. The revolution which established the rights and liberties of these kingdoms, was undertaken and accomplished – nay, was justified at the time, on the plea of necessity: a necessity that superseded all law, and was the glorious means of giving liberty to England.

He denied that the proposed commission vested all patronage in himself. The seven commissioners would all be Members of Parliament, appointed by Parliament, and 'like himself and his colleagues, constantly under the eye and attack of the House'. Thus the scheme would be open and accountable – the very opposite of tyranny. 'It was the character of despotic governments to be dark,' he added; 'of popular governments to love publicity.' Herein lay 'their beauty and their basis'.[54]

Of course Fox did not mean by 'popular government' what later generations came to understand by it: he was a thoroughgoing eighteenth-century aristocrat, not in the least a democrat. Nevertheless, this was the sort of language that made him the darling of Victorian Liberals. Pitt's reply, by contrast, was classic Toryism:

> The right honourable gentleman, whose eloquence and whose abilities would lend grace to deformity, has appealed to your passions, and pressed home to your hearts the distressed situation of the unhappy natives of India: a situation which every man must deplore, and anxiously wish to relieve. But ought the right honourable gentleman to proceed to the protection of the oppressed abroad by enforcing the most unparalleled oppression at home? Is the relief to be administered in Asia to be grounded on violence and injustice in Europe?[55]

Pitt had hoped to defeat the bill in the Commons. In fact it carried its Second Reading by a margin of nearly two to one (229–120). It then immediately passed into committee, where the confrontation of the two champions became still more pointed. Pitt repeated his charge that the bill gave too much power to ministers, and incidentally accused Fox of betraying parliamentary reform.

> He charged Mr Fox with acting with men, avowed enemies to those principles which the right honourable gentleman had so gloriously exerted himself in defending and enforcing when he [Pitt] had first begun his political and parliamentary career, and had the honour of fighting by his side in the same cause: a cause which he never would abandon.

It was true that North was an opponent of reform; but governments in those days were not expected to be monolithic, and Fox had supported a modest reform bill which Pitt had introduced earlier that year. In fact Fox never abandoned the cause of reform: it was Pitt who would very soon turn into a rigid defender of the status quo.

Fox rose to reply at 2.30 a.m. He repudiated Pitt's interpretation of the bill and accused Pitt of deliberately twisting his arguments:

> The right honourable gentleman has misrepresented me tonight again: he has an evident pleasure in it, which indeed I cannot

prevent; but I can prevent the House and the country from believing him. He prefers the authority of his own conception . . . of what I said to my own repeated declarations of my own meaning.

Pitt had promised to come up with a better bill of his own. Fox mocked the young pretender's inexperience:

But there is no limit to a youthful and vigorous fancy. The right honourable gentleman just now, in very serious terms, and with all his habitual gravity, engages, if the House will join in opposing us tonight, that he will digest and methodise a plan, the outline of which he has already conceived. He has nothing new to offer; but justly confiding in the fertility of his own imagination, and the future exercise of his faculties, he promises that he will bring a plan, provided the majority of the House will join him tonight. Now, if ever an idea was thrown out to pick up a stray vote or two in the heel of a debate . . . the idea given a while ago by the right honourable gentleman is precisely such.

Then Fox teased Pitt for 'pronouncing a brilliant eulogy upon me' one minute and the next moment declaring him 'the most dangerous man in the kingdom'. When Pitt interjected 'Dangerous only for this measure', Fox seized on the admission that he had no other ground of disagreement with him. 'I shall not press the advantage he gives me, further than leaving to himself to reconcile his practice and his doctrine in the best measure he can.' In these exchanges one can see the older man almost playing with the younger. Finally Fox defended his alliance with North, asserting that no government could be formed at all without the reconciliation of former opponents, and turned the argument sharply against Pitt, whom he already suspected of scheming with the King's party.

If the coalition be disgraceful, what is the anti-coalition? When I see the right honourable gentleman surrounded by the early objects of his political, nay his hereditary hatred, and hear him revile the coalition, I am lost in astonishment how men can be so blind to their own situation, as to attempt to wound us in this particular point.

Presciently he warned that governments were changed by the vote of the House of Commons, not by the King, before throwing down a challenge to Pitt:

> He says he will stake his character upon the danger of this Bill. I meet him in his own phrase, and oppose him, character to character. I risk my all upon the excellence of this Bill.[56]

Horace Walpole had no doubt that Fox won this contest, and thought that Pitt had tripped himself up on his own impatience.

> Mr Pitt's reputation is much sunk; nor, though he is a much more correct logician than his father, has he the same firmness and perseverance. It is no wonder that he was dazzled by his own premature fame . . . Had he listed [enlisted] under Mr Fox, who loved and courted him, he would not only have discovered modesty, but have been more likely to succeed him than by commencing his competitor. But what [have] I to do to look into futurity?[57]

The Bill passed the Commons easily, and Fox was confident of winning by similar margins in the Lords. But now the King took a hand. Some leading opponents of the India Bill – Earl Temple and Lord Thurlow – urged him that he could not veto it after it had passed both Houses, but could use his influence to defeat it in the upper House. George therefore let it be known that 'whoever voted for the India Bill was not only not his friend, but would be considered by him as an enemy'.[58] On 15 December Fox and Pitt both watched the critical debate from the bar of the House. Fox still confidently expected a majority of about 25; but around two dozen peers switched sides and the Bill was defeated by 87 votes to 79. Two days later the House threw the Bill out a second time by a slightly larger majority, 95–76.

Fox raged at the King's 'treachery'.[59] But at the same time he and North believed that George had played into their hands. By intriguing with the opposition to defeat a bill passed by the Commons he had violated the central constitutional convention that the King must follow the advice of his ministers, who commanded a majority in the Commons. Fox quickly moved a resolution declaring it a 'high crime and misdemeanour' to try to influence debates by reporting the King's opinion, and calling on the House to assert its dignity and independence 'in the instant of their danger'.

> We are called upon to sanctify or oppose an absolute extinction of all for which our ancestors struggled or expired . . . The deliberations of this night must decide whether we are to be freemen or slaves; whether the House of Commons be the palladium of liberty, or the organ of despotism; whether we are henceforth to possess a voice of our own, or to be only the mere mechanical echo of secret influence.[60]

Fox actually read out a copy of the King's letter authorising Temple to use his name in canvassing against the India Bill. And here was the second part of the royal coup: for Temple, not coincidentally, was Pitt's cousin. George had not moved to defeat his ministers' flagship measure without first ensuring that he had an alternative ministry in waiting. Previously Pitt had declined to come to his rescue. But during the passage of the India Bill through the Commons he had shifted his ground. In early December George secretly consulted him through an intermediary, Lord Clarendon, who was sent to find out 'the sentiments of him, who must from the superiority of his talents and the purity of his character be a leader in this important business'.[61] Pitt added his voice to those who were advising him to use his influence to sway the vote in the Lords and indicated that he would be prepared to take office in defiance of the Commons, pending a dissolution of the present House and fresh elections which – with the help of royal patronage – his party managers reckoned he could win.

Fox knew what had been going on; and in his speech of 17 December – without naming him – he pointed the finger unequivocally at his young rival. No *man* – he emphasised the word – would consent to take office as the creature of those he called 'reptiles who burrow under the throne'.

> Boys, without judgement, experience of the sentiments suggested by knowledge of the world, or the amiable decencies of a sound mind, may follow the headlong course of ambition thus precipitately, and vault into the seat while the reins of government are placed in other hands: but the minister who can bear to act such a dishonourable

part, and the country that suffers it, will be mutual plagues and curses to each other.

To doubt Pitt's sanity was below the belt, given that Chatham's mind had failed towards the end of his life. But Fox went on to draw a clear distinction of principle between himself and his former protégé who aspired to replace him.

> If, however, a change must take place, and a new ministry is to be formed and supported, not by the confidence of this House or the public, but the sole authority of the Crown, I for one shall not envy the honourable gentleman his situation. From that moment I put in my claim for a monopoly of whig principles. The glorious cause of freedom, of independence, and of the constitution, is no longer his, but mine. In this I have lived; in this I will die.

He predicted that Pitt would live to regret taking office as the puppet of 'secret influence':

> It is undoubtedly the prerogative of the sovereign to chuse his own servants; but the constitution provides that those servants should not be obnoxious to his subjects . . . The honourable gentleman had there-fore better consider how much he risks by joining an arrangement thus hostile to the interest of the people; that they will never consent to be governed by secret influence; and that all the weight of his private character, all his eloquence and popularity, will never render the midnight and despotic mandates of an interior cabinet accept-able to Englishmen.[62]

Fox's resolution was carried by 153 votes to 80. But the next day the King dismissed Fox, North and Portland without even an audi-ence, merely instructing them to return their seals of office. 'I choose this method,' he wrote to North, 'as Audiences on such occasions must be unpleasant.'[63] Then he invited the twenty-four-year-old Pitt to form a government; and this time Pitt accepted. His position was to all appearances almost hopeless. He could count on no more than 150 Commons votes against 230 for Fox and North; the House laughed when his appointment was announced. Several senior figures declined to serve, so he formed an undistinguished cabinet of just seven members of whom only one – Pitt himself – sat in the Commons, and filled the junior positions with his young friends. One critic dismissed them as 'a set of children playing at ministers', another as 'Old men and Boys', while a leading society hostess, Mrs Crewe, famously told Wilberforce that 'he [Pitt] may do what he likes during the holidays, but it will be only a mince-pie administration' – meaning that it would not last beyond Christmas.[64] More generously, Fox took bets that the ministry would last at least a week.[65] When Temple resigned after just a few days – allegedly fearing impeachment for his part in the backstairs plot – Fox wrote complacently to a colleague in Ireland: 'What will follow is not yet known, but I think there can be very little doubt but our administration will again be established. The confusion of the enemy is beyond all description, and the triumph of our friends proportionable.'[66] 'Depend upon it', Gibbon predicted, 'Billy's painted galley must soon sink under Charles' black collier.'[67]

Deceived by the support of his own untypical constituency, Fox was initially confident that public opinion was with him. One cartoon showed Pitt riding the white horse of Hanover battling with Fox astride the British lion.[68] But other widely circulated prints were much less flattering: many of these, portraying Fox as fat, greasy, venal and ambitious, were paid for from the King's secret service fund. There was always a strong tendency throughout the eighteenth century for the central mass of uncommitted MPs to back whatever government was in power. Now many of these country gentlemen preferred Pitt's high moral tone to Fox's 'Venetian' corruption; others – including many of North's supporters – were increasingly alarmed by Fox's radical language and backed the King's right to choose his own minister. Pitt meanwhile displayed great nerve in the way he grasped power and set about holding it. First he excluded his former leader, Shelburne, in order to show who was in charge. 'This young man,' commented Henry Dundas, 'does not choose to suffer it to be doubtfull who is the effectual Minister.'[69] Then – with the King's help – he dispensed patronage on a lavish scale: the very weapon George had denied to Fox and North. With most seats controlled by local magnates, one judiciously granted peerage could turn six or seven Commons votes. In the first weeks of 1784 Pitt created eleven new peers and promoted another eight: Walpole wrote that they were 'crying peerages about the streets in barrows'.[70] The result was that Fox's majority steadily eroded.

When the House first reassembled after the New Year Fox carried by comfortable margins a series of motions against the new government condemning the way the King's name had been abused to defy the Commons. Defending himself, Pitt coolly denied any knowledge of secret intrigues.

> I came up no back stairs. When I was sent for by my Sovereign to know whether I would accept of office, I necessarily went to the Royal Closet. I know of no secret influence, and I hope that my own integrity would be my guardian against that danger . . . Little did I think to be ever charged in this House with being the tool and abettor of secret influence. The novelty of the imputation only renders it so much the more contemptible. This is the only answer I shall ever deign to make on the subject.[71]

This was, as one twentieth-century historian has written, 'the lie of a master, perfect of its kind, superb in its insolence and totally successful: its very unctuousness carried the war into the enemy's camp, smearing them as the purveyors of shabby slanders and cheap rumours'.[72] Nevertheless it was – as his most recent biographer William Hague admits – a brazen lie. Pitt was not merely the beneficiary, but an active participant in the intrigue which led to the dismissal of the Fox–North coalition; yet he flatly denied it and shamelessly boasted of his 'integrity' in order to refute the allegation. It is no wonder that Fox felt ever afterwards that he had been cheated out of office by a hypocritical liar.

At this stage Fox did not believe that Pitt could get away with it: he might be the minister of the Crown, he reminded him, but he was not 'the minister of the House of Commons'. Not since 'the miserable family of the Stuarts' had a ministry with a majority in the Commons been dismissed in this way by royal whim. He denied that there was a 'trial of strength' between the parties.

> It is no trial of strength between the present ministers and those on this side of the House. If it be a trial of strength, it is whether this country is in future to be governed by a ministry supported by this House, or by the secret advisers of the Crown? This is the question at issue, and I trust it will be very soon decided.[73]

In repeated debates in a packed and noisy House during January and February Fox raged in vain against Pitt's defiance of the House. But Pitt simply ignored repeated motions carried against the government, sitting calmly in his place while the opposition bayed for him to resign. Unable to combat 'Mr Fox's invincible powers of reasoning', Walpole wrote, 'the immaculate Master Billy . . . has prudently adopted an arrogant sullenness, and literally finds that contemptuous silence will govern the House of Commons better than paying court to them'.[74] Pitt acknowledged that the situation could not last, but in the meantime coolly justified his action as necessary 'to save the country from the India Bill, which threatened the destruction of its liberties', confident that 'the world would understand and applaud it'.[75] And increasingly it seemed that he was right. Primed by the Treasury purse, more than two hundred 'loyal addresses' poured in from all over the country supporting the King and his chosen servants against the pretensions of his former ministers; while at Westminster waverers were being successfully 'turned' so that from one debate to the next the opposition's majority steadily dwindled. By 1 February Pitt could claim that Fox commanded only 'a small majority of this House against the loud and decided voice of the people'.[76] The obvious solution was a general election. But with the tide flowing in his favour Pitt was biding his time until he was sure he would win; whereas Fox, fearing he would lose, was placed in the unheroic position, for the self-proclaimed champion of the people, of opposing an early dissolution. He needed to resolve the issue in the present House, yet was helpless to force Pitt's hand: he dared not take the ultimate step of refusing to vote money to the government for fear of precipitating an election.

As always at moments of political deadlock there were well-meaning calls for a coalition. One elderly peer suggested that Pitt and Fox should be invited to get 'gloriously drunk' together and settle their differences.[77] Both dismissed the possibility, Fox calling the idea 'indecent', Pitt 'fallacious'.[78] Charles Jenkinson, the future Lord Liverpool, wrote that they were 'two young men, both of great parts and great ambition, and from their different tempers and characters, I am afraid irreconcilable'.[79] The King was willing to consider a combination of Pitt with North or Portland, so long as Fox was kept in a subordinate position; but Fox was not prepared to serve under Pitt, and Pitt was not prepared to serve under anyone else. So the deadlock continued, which suited Pitt.

Meanwhile, as he had promised before Christmas, Pitt introduced his own much less contentious India Bill, which left the Company's charter and the powers of the Governor-General untouched, with merely a general oversight vested in a board in London appointed by the Crown. Fox complained that this failed to address the problem of corruption and lack of political accountability. In principle this was true: but the reality was that India could not be ruled from London when communications took months to travel in each direction. Fox's bill, though idealistic, was in truth impractical. Pitt's Act, when it was eventually carried, formed the basis of the government of India for the next seventy years.

During February their exchanges grew still more personal. Fox professed to believe that Pitt was the 'dupe' of those who were using his youth and his illustrious name for their own ends and warned that once they had achieved their object 'they will make you nobody'.[80] Pitt in return taunted Fox with his lack of support in the country and boasted of his superior integrity. Each accused the other of overweening ambition. By the end of the month things were turning nasty. After receiving the Freedom of the City of London on 28 February, Pitt was attacked in his carriage in St James's Street – right outside Brooks's – by a Foxite crowd; his carriage was nearly demolished, and he was only rescued by members of White's coming to his assistance and taking him there for safety. Fox's characteristic alibi – that he was in bed with Elizabeth Armistead at the time – did him little good. Finally on 8 March a motion for Pitt's dismissal carried by just a single vote. In a desperate attempt – it was assumed – to prevent a dissolution the Great Seal was stolen from the Lord Chancellor's house in Great Ormond Street: Fox and Mrs Armistead were said to have been seen creeping about with lanterns and crowbars! But a new seal was made overnight, enabling Parliament to be dissolved on 25 March.

There followed what William Hague has called 'the extraordinary mixture of democracy, bribery and skulduggery' which comprised an eighteenth-century election.[81] This was an unusual election, however, since instead of the usual multiplicity of local contests, deals and stitch-ups there was a clear ideological divide across the whole country, provocatively framed in terms that harked back to the Civil War. While Fox and his friends invoked the shades of Pym and Hampden fighting Charles I, his opponents portrayed him as Cromwell or Guy Fawkes, while Pitt – playing on his youth and spotless reputation – was 'Master Billy' or 'the Infant Hercules'.[82] The result was a clear national swing towards the latter. Though Fox tried to ascribe the opposition's loss of around a hundred seats to the effect of patronage in pocket boroughs, the swing was actually greatest in those seats with a large popular electorate. The truth was that outside the circle of his adoring acolytes the self-proclaimed 'Man of the People' was not in fact very popular.

Even in his own Westminster constituency – unique in giving the vote to every householder – he had a tremendous fight, marked by the most scurrilous campaigning and rampant bribery on both sides. One leaflet called Fox – not inaccurately – 'the high priest of drunkenness, gaming and every species of debauchery'.[83] Another Pittite gambit was to bet the voter five guineas that he would not vote for Fox: if he did not – and of course there was no secret ballot – he got his five guineas![84] On his side Fox created a sensation by wheeling out the great Whig ladies to exercise their charms on his behalf. The beautiful young Georgiana, Duchess of Devonshire, was said to have bribed tradesmen with kisses: she denied it but, true or not, the cartoonists made it so. Other ladies canvassed from door to door wearing a fox's brush in their hats; even the Prince of Wales – always ready to enrage his father – drove through the constituency wearing Fox's blue and buff colours. One handbill commented satirically:

> Sure heaven approves of Fox's cause,
> Though slaves at Court abhor him;
> To vote for Fox, then, who can pause,
> Since angels canvass for him.[85]

Polling in those days went on for several weeks. The figures fluctuated daily, but eventually Fox crept ahead. He was finally declared elected by 236 votes over the government candidate, Sir Cecil Wray.*

---

*Fox actually came second in a two-member constituency, with 6,234 votes to Wray's 5,998. Admiral Hood, a hero of the Seven Years War, topped the poll with 6,694.

But Wray refused to accept the result and demanded a scrutiny. Having achieved a sweeping majority in the new House, it would have been magnanimous for Pitt to let his rival's election stand. It was a measure of the bitterness that now infected their relationship that, on the contrary, he vigorously supported Wray's challenge in the hope of having Fox 'thrown out'.[86] In fact Fox was not excluded while the scrutiny proceeded, since he had taken the precaution of getting himself returned simultaneously for Orkney and Shetland – a fallback which allowed Pitt to congratulate him sarcastically, saying that his fame now extended to 'the remotest corner of Great Britain'.[87] When Fox, in a virtuoso performance, complained of 'ministerial persecution', Pitt wondered whether 'a gentleman who had the liberty of speaking three hours at a stretch on his own cause' could really be 'a persecuted man'.[88] Pitt abandoned the scrutiny only when his own supporters decided that enough was enough. After eight months Fox was finally allowed to resume his old seat; but this small victory was the last he would score for many years.

The fact was that Pitt had now comprehensively routed his rival. He had defied the Commons, bent the constitution almost to breaking point and lied outrageously, but he had played a weak hand with exceptional composure and he had been vindicated. 'Public opinion', however defined – both the narrow political class which returned the great majority of MPs and the wider sentiment of the country – had decisively endorsed the popular King and his cool young minister against the radical allegations of the rackety Fox. To the amazement of Europe the boy Prime Minister was now secure in office for the foreseeable future, while his former mentor was condemned to a lifetime of increasingly frustrated opposition.

After 1784 Fox failed either to lead his group properly or retire fully from politics and leave opposition to others. Although from this time on he put his youthful high living behind him, and settled down to a life of surprising domesticity with Mrs Armistead at her house in Chertsey, coming to London less and less frequently, he could never forgive the way that Pitt had worsted him and never missed an opportunity to get back at him whenever an opening arose. On the substance of government policy over the next five years he had little to say. While Pitt was transforming the nation's finances according to the free trade principles of Adam Smith he offered no criticism because he did not pretend to understand the new economics; he was stuck in the age of mercantilism. He did not even bother to oppose Pitt's India Bill, absenting himself with the feeble excuse that 'to be present at the daily or rather hourly equivocations of *a young hypocrite* is at once so disgusting to observe and so infamous to tolerate, that the person who listens to them with forebearance [*sic*], becomes almost an accomplice in them'.[89] Yet he never ceased to claim that he embodied a great constitutional principle, the supremacy of Parliament, which Pitt had breached.

> I stand . . . upon this great principle. I say that the people of England have a right to control the executive power, by the interference of their representatives in the House of parliament. The right honourable gentleman maintains the contrary. He is the cause of our political enmity.[90]

Fox's great chance came unexpectedly in November 1788, when George III appeared to lose his wits. He was actually suffering from porphyria, a nervous disease which produced many of the effects of madness; but doctors at the time did not understand this. The assumption was that the King had gone mad. If he did not recover there would have to be a regency, presumably headed by Fox's old companion in debauchery, the Prince of Wales, who by the conventions of eighteenth-century politics would be expected to dismiss Pitt and bring back Fox and Portland. In this crisis arguments of principle – on both sides – went out of the window. The fact that Pitt had a large Commons majority did not stop Fox believing that the Regent would quickly restore him to office: the newspapers confidently printed lists of those who would be in his cabinet. Unfortunately he was travelling in Italy when the King fell ill, out of all contact with home. When he was eventually traced to Bologna he was so desperate to get back quickly – leaving Mrs Armistead to come on later – that he completed the 1,100 mile journey, over rough roads in an open chaise, in just nine days. As a result he arrived both exhausted and ill; then when he was well enough to attend the House he made a disastrous speech which did his cause no good at all.

Like everyone else, Pitt seems to have accepted that he would be dismissed the moment 'Prinny' was declared Regent. His only policy was delay, in the hope that the King would recover. He therefore set up a search for historical precedents, going back to Henry VI, to try to limit the powers of the Regency, or maybe entrust them to the Queen instead. Fox treated this as sheer time-wasting. There was no relevant precedent, he declared: 'In the present condition of his Majesty, his Royal Highness the Prince of Wales has as clear, as express a right to exercise the power of sovereignty ... as in the case of his Majesty's having undergone a natural demise.' But this unqualified assertion of the royal prerogative contradicted everything Fox had previously said about the supremacy of Parliament. On hearing it Pitt delightedly slapped his thigh and exclaimed, 'I'll *unWhig* the gentleman for the rest of his life.' He in turn now deployed the opposite argument:

> To assert the inherent right in the Prince of Wales to assume the government, is virtually to revive those exploded ideas of the divine and indefeasible authority of princes, which have so justly sunk into contempt and oblivion ... To assert such a right in the Prince of Wales, or any one else, independent of the decision of the two houses of parliament, is little less than treason to the constitution.[91]

This could have been Fox speaking five years earlier.

Both Pitt and Fox drew criticism for the breathtaking reversal of their previous positions. Pitt's 'declaration ... the day before yesterday, that the Prince of Wales had no better right or claim to the Regency than any other subject, gives as much offence and alarm as Fox's assertion that he was of right entitled to it,' one Foxite supporter wrote.[92] But a few days later the same writer realised that his man had come off worst. 'Fox's declaration seems to have done more harm even than I imagined, and Pitt's mountebank speeches suit the nonsense of many.'[93] Once again Pitt was playing a cool hand while Fox's impatience seemed only to confirm his lack of judgement. In subsequent speeches Fox tried to row back from his extreme position, still affirming that the Prince had a 'right' to the Regency but conceding that his appointment required Parliament's 'adjudication'. But over-confidence still led him astray. He believed that the King was 'perfectly mad' and that his condition could only get worse. 'I think it certain that in about a fortnight we shall come in,' he wrote in mid-December. 'The Prince must be Regent, and of consequence the Ministry must be changed.'[94]

As in 1783, an virulent pamphleteering war broke out in support of the two sides. While the opposition attacked 'PRINCE PITT! . . . Greater than the HEIR APPARENT! who, having already destroyed the People's Rights by an undue Exertion of the Prerogative of the Crown, is now willing to raise himself above the Prerogative by seizing on the Sovereignty of these Kingdoms',[95] government propaganda equally denounced Fox's unscrupulous hunger to get his hands on power. The great cartoonists of the day, headed by Gillray and Rowlandson, gleefully satirised both contenders. Meanwhile the two rivals traded insults like schoolboys. Fox charged that Pitt had been in power so long that 'he cannot endure to part with it'. Pitt retorted that this was 'unfounded, arrogant and presumptuous' and accused Fox of prematurely declaring himself the new minister.[96] Helped by the death of the Speaker, Pitt managed to spin out the crisis into the New Year; when he did introduce a Regency Bill it imposed humiliating restrictions on the Regent's powers, particularly of patronage. He still had comfortable majorities, even though a trickle of defectors switched to what they thought was going to be the winning side. The bill passed the Commons at the beginning of February, and seemed certain to pass the Lords before the end of the month. At the very last moment, however, George miraculously recovered. Again the cup was dashed from Fox's – and the Prince's – lips. The Regency Bill was hastily abandoned, and Pitt's supremacy resumed. When a thanksgiving service was held at St Paul's in April Fox was hissed by the crowds, while Pitt enjoyed a hero's reception.

The final breach between Pitt and Fox was caused by the French Revolution which broke out later that year. Most British observers initially welcomed the convulsions across the Channel, in the hope either that they would transform France into a constitutional monarchy on the British model, or – less idealistically – that they would fatally weaken the traditional enemy. Exemplifying this cautious optimism, Pitt told the House in February 1790 that while greater liberty might make France more formidable, 'it might also render her less obnoxious as a neighbour'.[97] Up to 1792 he maintained a carefully balanced position of wary neutrality. Fox by contrast had no such doubts. He had always loved France, while loathing the Bourbons. His friends were the liberal aristocrats who drove the early stages of the revolution, which he confidently expected to be the French equivalent of 1688. 'It is I think by much the greatest Event that has ever happened in the world,' he exulted soon after the fall of the Bastille, 'and will in all human probability have the most extensive good consequences.'[98] In 1791 he hailed the new French constitution hyperbolically as 'the most stupendous and glorious edifice of liberty which has been erected on the foundation of human integrity in any time or country'.[99] At this stage only Edmund Burke warned presciently of the actual outcome, leading to the painful severing of his friendship with Fox.

1792 changed everything. The abolition of the French monarchy, the declaration of revolutionary war against Austria and Prussia, the execution of Louis XVI and the spiralling descent into ever bloodier forms of terror forced British Whigs to choose between extreme democracy or renewed despotism. Pitt's unequivocal response was to commit Britain to the side of reaction while stamping on any sign of revolutionary unrest at home. 'England never will consent that France shall arrogate the power of annulling at her pleasure . . . the political system of Europe.'[100] This was the traditional British policy of intervening on the continent to preserve the balance of power. Fox instinctively took the opposite course, condemning the resort to war in what he called 'the cause of kings'.[101] He held that Louis deserved to be deposed because – like James II – he had blocked the road to constitutionalism; he hoped that by attacking the revolution the Prussians and Austrians in turn would 'risque the existence of their monarchies & so much the better'.[102] 'The people are the sovereigns in all countries . . . They might amend, alter or abolish the form of government under which they live at pleasure.'[103] Naturally he deplored the Terror, but he blamed the conservative powers whose 'unexampled and infamous conspiracy not against France but against Liberty in general' had driven the revolution to extremes.[104] He regretted the Jacobins' excesses. 'And yet, with all their faults and all their nonsense,' he wrote to his nephew, 'I do interest myself for their success in the greatest degree. It is a great crisis for the real cause of liberty, whatever we may think of the particular people who are to fight the present battle.' It would be so much easier, he admitted, if they were like 'our old friends the Americans'.[105]

Fox believed that war with France – like the American war before it – was being deliberately used by George III, with Pitt's help, to extend his own power and complete the *coup d'état* he had begun in 1783. Fox claimed that the government was exaggerating the threat of a French invasion as a pretext for the suppression of traditional liberties. 'We have no invasion to fear,' he argued, 'but an invasion of the constitution.'[106] When the King's Speech in December 1792 declared that 'acts of riot and insurrection' necessitated firm action to restore order he dismissed the suggestion as 'an intolerable calumny on the people of Great Britain . . . used only to cover an attempt to destroy our happy constitution'. He went on to make a classic defence of freedom under the law which still rings resonantly in 2009, when a Labour government is determined to monitor private emails and detain suspected terrorists without trial.

> We are come to the moment when the question is, whether we shall give to the king, that is to the executive government, complete power over our thoughts; whether we are to resign the exercise of our natural faculties to the ministers for the time being, or whether we shall maintain that in England no man is a criminal but by the commission of overt acts forbidden by the law . . .

'Under the pretext of guarding [the constitution] from the assaults of republicans and levellers,' he warned, 'we are led insensibly to the opposite danger: that of increasing the power of the crown and of degrading the influence of the Commons.' Repeatedly and personally he charged 'the minister' – that is Pitt – with conspiracy to subvert the constitution. 'This I call a crisis more imminent and tremendous than any that the history of this country ever exhibited.'[107]

The same month Fox proposed a toast at the Whig Club advocating 'equal liberty to all mankind'.[108] Such inflammatory language strained the patience even of his own supporters. Cartoons portrayed him as a wild Jacobin eager to set up a guillotine in Downing Street, while his opposition to the war was widely seen as unpatriotic, if not actually treasonable. The majority of more conservative Whigs followed the Duke of Portland in backing both the war and the suppression of 'sedition' at home. Fox was supported in the lobby by just a rump of his own friends. But he was now set on a path of total condemnation of the government, declaring that there was 'no address at this moment that Pitt could frame, he would not propose an Amendment to, and divide the House upon'.[109] Privately he affected to see little difference between Pitt's measures and those of the Committee of Public Safety which was sending thousands of Frenchmen to the guillotine. 'I do not think that any of the French *soi-disant* judicial proceedings surpass in injustice & contempt of the law those in Scotland,' he wrote to his nephew, Lord Holland, after four quite moderate reform campaigners were sentenced to fourteen years' transportation by the High Court in Edinburgh.

> At home we imitate the French as well as we can, and in the trials and sentences of Muir and Palmer in particular, I do not think we fall very far short of our original, excepting inasmuch as transportation to Botany Bay is less severe . . . than death . . . Good God! That a man should be sent to Botany Bay for advising another to read Paine's book, or for reading the Irish address at a public meeting![110]*

In 1794 Pitt introduced a bill to suspend Habeas Corpus – 'to empower his majesty to secure and detain such persons as his majesty shall suspect of conspiring against his person and government' – and rushed it through all its stages in two days. Furiously Fox denounced what he termed 'the complete extinction of liberty'; but in fourteen divisions he never mustered more than thirty-nine votes. As always in time of war or national panic, Pitt's assertion that the radical clubs and corresponding societies at which the bill was aimed fomented 'anarchy, sedition and treason' swept aside Fox's warning that 'our pretended alarms were to be made the pretexts for destroying the first principles of the very system which we affected to revere'.

---

*The charges against Thomas Muir and Thomas Palmer included circulating Thomas Paine's best-selling book *The Rights of Man* and reading out a fraternal address from the United Irishmen. Paine himself had already been convicted (in his absence) of sedition.

It was precisely the absence of Habeas Corpus in France, he argued, which had led to the revolution there. Again his criticism was sharply personal: he specifically deplored 'the tone of exultation' with which Pitt described a measure which, 'if actually necessary, should be considered by all a serious calamity'.[111] But the temper of a frightened House was overwhelmingly with Pitt.

Two months later the Portland Whigs joined Pitt's government, leaving Fox almost entirely isolated. He was deeply hurt by their defection, but consoled himself that 'though weak, we are right, and that must be our comfort'.[112] From now on he increasingly withdrew from politics and attended the House less and less frequently, preferring to spend his time with Mrs Armistead at Chertsey, reading, writing and gardening: a remarkable transformation from his former life. In 1795 he secretly married his 'dearest Liz', though the formalisation of their relationship was not revealed until 1802.*

Meanwhile the war was going badly. Pitt might command the House, but he was not delivering the sort of victories against the old enemy that his father had done thirty years before. On the contrary, the French revolutionary armies were rampaging across Europe, knocking Britain's allies one by one out of the coalition. Popular unrest was exacerbated by a sequence of poor harvests; and 1795 saw rioters in London and other cities demanding peace, reform and cheaper bread. Pitt responded by introducing still more draconian legislation: a Seditious Meetings Bill and a Treasonable Practices Bill. Once again Fox roused himself to oppose them – not only in the House, where he argued that 'If you silence remonstrance and

---

*Pitt by contrast never married. He once appeared to court Lady Eleanor Eden, daughter of Lord Auckland, but withdrew pleading an 'insurmountable obstacle'.[113] Modern biographers think he was probably gay; and the same rumour circulated freely in his lifetime, as in this scurrilous verse from 1784:

> 'Tis true, indeed, we oft abuse him,
> Because he bends to no man;
> But Slander's self dare not accuse him
> Of stiffness to a woman.[114]

stifle complaint, you then leave no other alternative but force and violence',[115] but also at big public meetings, where he defiantly proclaimed 'the right inherent in freemen to resist arbitrary power, whatever shape it may assume'.[116] 'This is a great Crisis,' he wrote to Lord Holland. 'I am convinced that in a few years this Government will become completely absolute.'[117] Pitt, conversely, claimed to be defending the supremacy of Parliament against the mob. He carried his legislation by huge majorities; and a general election the following year confirmed his unchallenged authority.

On the Westminster hustings Fox's denunciation of Pitt's government scaled new heights of hyperbole:

> They have been the cause of squandering more of the public money and of spilling more of the blood of human creatures than any other Government or Power that ever was in this or any other country in Europe whatever. With the words of religion and Humanity in their mouths they have destroyed more of God's creatures, and spilt more human blood, than any Prince, Emperor or Despotic Tyrant in the annals of History. They have spilt as much blood as the greatest Conquerors, and lost as much as those conquerors have obtained . . . They have sent men out of their country, contrary to law, to Botany Bay, after trials conducted in such a manner that every lover of justice shudders when he reads them.[118]

He was comfortably re-elected with none of the excitement of 1784; but his magnificent outrage had no practical effect.

In 1797 the demoralised opposition made another doomed attempt to promote a measure of parliamentary reform. It was introduced not by Fox, but by Charles Grey, who thirty-five years later was the Prime Minister who finally carried the Great Reform Bill of 1832. Fox made a moderate speech denying, as he always did, any sympathy for universal suffrage but proposing to enfranchise 'the greatest number of independent votes'.* 'The strongest building,' he maintained, 'stands on the broadest basis, and nothing would tend to

---

*This, he pointed out in passing, by definition excluded women, much as he enjoyed their company and support. 'The reason why the other sex is excluded is certainly not on account of any inferiority of understanding, but because of their dependence on ours.'

strengthen the constitution more than to make the people of England parts of it, and to make them feel an interest in its preservation.' The motion stood no chance, however, since Pitt – the same Pitt who as a young MP had promised that he would never abandon the cause of reform – now, as a thoroughly conservative Prime Minister, equated reform with Jacobinism and set his face adamantly against 'principles which aim at nothing less than the total annihilation of the constitution'. 'Was the House,' he demanded, 'in compliance with the visionary schemes of absurd speculatists, to abandon the polar star of English Liberty?' Cruelly he mocked Fox's claim to represent mounting public clamour for reform:

> The right honourable gentleman, the House will recollect, was accustomed to assert last session of Parliament, with equal boldness and vehemence as now, that the sense of the country was against the system of ministers. Good God! Where can the honourable gentleman have lived? In what remote corner of the country can he have passed his time?[119]

Grey's motion was duly defeated by 256 votes to 91. For Fox this was the last straw. A few days later he announced his intention to withdraw from Parliament altogether, rather than waste any more of his time in 'fruitless exertions and . . . idle talk in this House'.[120] 'I am convinced that in these times I can do no good,' he wrote to a colleague, 'and therefore think that I have a right to consult my ease.'[121]

But he could still get under Pitt's skin. Speaking at the annual dinner in honour of Fox's birthday in 1798, the Duke of Norfolk – one of his improbably aristocratic radical allies – coupled his name with a toast to 'Our Sovereign's health: The Majesty of the People'. For this seditious sentiment the Duke was stripped of the Lord-Lieutenancy of the West Riding and the command of his militia regiment. But soon afterwards, at another dinner, Fox provocatively repeated the offence. Pitt considered prosecuting him, or expelling him from the Commons. 'We might send him to the Tower,' he wrote to William Wilberforce, but thought better of it, for the fear that 'at the end of three weeks he might be led home in procession, and have the glory of breaking windows'.[122] Instead it was decided to expel Fox from the Privy

Council: *The Times* reported that the King 'with his own hand ran his pen through Mr Fox's name'.[123]

In fact Fox had already effectively expelled himself from Parliament: from April 1798 to February 1800 he did not attend at all. He did not come to town even to oppose Pitt's introduction of income tax to pay for the war. But Prime Ministers introducing unpopular policies – even with huge majorities – need opposition to help them rally their supporters. Pitt soon found that he missed his sparring partner.

> Mr Pitt earnestly laboured to draw his opponents back to Parliament, and . . . sometimes taunted and attempted to exasperate the absent Members, and at others studiously magnified the talents and importance of those who were left behind . . . He is also said to have found, that the want of opponents in Parliament deprived him of the readiest weapon which he could hold up *in terrorem* to the King, to force his compliance with any unpalatable measure, or to deter him from insisting on unreasonable objects.[124]

Fox returned to Parliament in 1800 to condemn the government's rejection of a peace feeler from General Bonaparte (or Buonaparte, as his name was then normally spelled) who had now seized power in France. For some time Pitt had been seeking to make an honourable peace, confessing privately that it was 'his duty as an English minister and a Christian to use every effort to stop so bloody and wasting a war'.[125] This had been Fox's view for years. But Bonaparte's rise to power – initially as First Consul – had dashed Pitt's hopes. More accurately than Fox, Pitt recognised the boundlessness of Bonaparte's ambition. Fox, deceived by admiration of the Corsican's genius and his own lingering faith in the revolution, persuaded himself that 'peace upon good terms' was now on offer. In one of his most brilliant speeches he likened Bonaparte variously to Cromwell, Caesar Augustus and the once-reviled but now admired George Washington, dismissed the possibility of restoring the Bourbons and ridiculed Pitt's argument that Bonaparte must prove himself trustworthy before peace could be considered.

> Gracious God, sir! Is war a state of probation? Is peace a rash system? Is it dangerous for nations to live in amity with each other? . . . Must

the bowels of Great Britain be torn out – her best blood be spilt – her treasure wasted – that you may make an experiment? . . . Cannot this state of probation be as well undergone without adding to the catalogue of human suffering?[126]

Pitt won this debate by 265 votes to 64. The next day Fox confessed that his speech had probably changed no more than three votes. His eloquence was magnificent; but his willingness to trust Bonaparte was soon shown to be naïve. Within months Bonaparte had resumed the career of conquest that would soon make him the master of Europe; and Pitt was once again asserting the necessity of continued war. When challenged by one of Fox's associates to state the object of the war he replied with a single word which – like so much in these debates – uncannily anticipates the arguments for another 'war on terror' two centuries later:

I can tell him that it is security: security against a danger, the greatest that ever threatened the world. It is security against a danger which never existed in any past period of society.[127]

Yet within a year, to general amazement, Pitt had resigned. The ostensible reason had nothing to do with the war; rather it was his failure to persuade the King to accept a measure of Catholic emancipation, as a concomitant of the Union with Ireland which the government pushed through in 1800. This was one of two progressive causes on which Pitt and Fox were still agreed. (The other was abolition of the slave trade.) George, however, saw it as a betrayal of his coronation oath and would not hear of it. Fox's withdrawal had deprived Pitt of the hold he had hitherto exerted as the one man who could save George from his hated bogeyman. After seventeen stressful years in office Pitt was glad of an excuse to take a break. For one thing the boy Prime Minister was now over forty and in increasingly poor health; for another he had become an obstacle to the peace which the country was now crying out for. Fox initially could not believe that Pitt would resign 'merely because he can not carry an honest and wise measure', and thought it all 'a mere juggle'.[128] When he realised it was true he was delighted. 'Pitt was a bad minister,' he wrote to Grey. 'He is out – I am glad.'

He wished only that 'some strong expression of popular joy could take place upon Pitt's going out'.[129] Pitt was succeeded by the former Speaker of the House, Henry Addington (giving rise to Canning's famous jingle that 'Pitt is to Addington as London is to Paddington'). Though for some time Fox had protested that he had no remaining interest in office for himself, he thought it prudent to lie low while Addington's ministry was being formed, and did not go up to London: 'I am sure my going at such a time would be subject to imputations and sneers.'[130] At this moment, however, the King's wits failed again, leading to renewed rumours that the Prince of Wales might recall his old favourite. In the event George soon recovered and another glimmer of an opening passed Fox by. Since Addington was pledged to try to make peace, Fox felt obliged to support him. Pitt too endorsed his successor. Thus for the first time in twenty years the two rivals found themselves on the same side – both supporting a minister in whom neither of them had any confidence.

Addington did succeed in negotiating the Treaty of Amiens, which was signed in March 1802; but it provided only a breathing space before war was resumed not much more than a year later. During the interval Fox was able to visit Paris for the first time for many years. He was fêted as a prominent Francophile; but two meetings with Bonaparte cured him of some of his illusions regarding the First Consul's pacific inclinations. Nevertheless when war broke out again – ostensibly over Malta – he still blamed the British government. 'It is entirely the fault of our Ministers and not of Buonaparte,' he wrote to Grey.[131] Since he could not blame Pitt, he blamed George III. 'I always thought it was the K, & the K. alone, & I think so still.'[132] But Pitt supported the renewal of war. Overcoming illness, he came to the House for the first time for more than a year to deliver – from a back bench – one of his greatest oratorical efforts, denouncing Bonaparte's insatiable ambition and summoning the whole resources of the nation to fight 'the liquid fire of Jacobinical principles desolating the world'. Unfortunately the speech was barely reported; but the diarist Thomas Creevey described its impact: 'In the elevation of his tone of mind and composition, in the infinite energy of his style, the miraculous perspicacity and fluency of his periods outdid . . . all former performances of his. Never, to be sure, was there such an exhibition: its effect was dreadful.'[133]

For once Fox did not reply immediately, as the House decided to adjourn early that night; but the following day he too made one of his greatest speeches (which *was* reported). He was satirical about Pitt's high-flown rhetoric, which 'Demosthenes might have envied', but likened it to a delicious dinner whose enjoyment is spoiled by the bill.

> In the beginning of the last war . . . there was no want of imagery, no want of figures of rhetoric, no want of flowers of eloquence – eloquence seldom equalled and never surpassed by man, and all exerted to support the war. We know how that war ended, and the damp which was cast upon our ardour at the sight of the bill when it came to be paid. So now, when I hear all these fine and eloquent philippics, I cannot help recollecting what fruits such speeches have generally produced, and dreading the devastation and carnage which usually attend them.

Fox denied that Malta was worth a war; he denied that Malta was essential to the security of Egypt, or that Egypt was essential to the security of India; he even denied that India was 'essential to the vital interests of Great Britain'.[134] Nevertheless three days later, since the country was 'actually at war' again, he promised to give it 'the best support in my power'.[135]

The unspoken question raised by Pitt's speech was how soon he would be recalled to lead the national effort again, since Addington was clearly unequal to the task. There was much talk of a 'Ministry of All the Talents' to include both Pitt and Fox. But that was still as impracticable as it had been for the past twenty years. While Fox 'did not think it at all likely he should ever be Minister himself . . . he was determined, if possible, to prevent Mr Pitt ever again being so'.[136] Claiming to 'lay aside all personal prejudices', he considered it 'completely demonstrated that Pitt, with all his great talents, is wholly unfit for it'.[137] Pitt, for his part, was once again biding his time until he could return on his own terms. 'I do not see how under any circumstances I can creditably or usefully consent to take part in any Government without being at the Head of it.'[138] Though now as critical as anyone of Addington's incapacity, he would take no part in a combined opposition to bring him down. He was 'a low, mean-minded dog', Fox raged. 'What a man! . . . Oh, he is a sad stick.'[139] Lord Grenville – Pitt's Foreign Secretary for the whole of the previous decade – was so exasperated by his attitude that he joined up with Fox – a reversal as startling as the Fox–North combination of 1782–83. Now Pitt professed himself willing to include both Grenville and Fox in a new government; but he was safe enough, since George III still refused point blank to accept Fox, expressing his 'astonishment that Mr Pitt should one moment harbour the thought of bringing such a name before His Royal notice'.[140] Fox was willing to stand aside while his friends and Grenville joined the government; but Grenville would not abandon his new ally. So when Pitt eventually returned to office in May 1804 – the same day that Bonaparte – now calling himself Napoleon – proclaimed himself Emperor of France – it was at the head of a narrower ministry than before. Fox believed that he had 'surrendered himself up entirely into the hands of the Court'.[141]

The government's majority was too uncertain to give it any security. The first major test came on a bill to improve recruiting to the army. Pitt was forced to make an uncharacteristically defensive speech, insisting that it was 'the prerogative of His Majesty to choose his ministers' and declining to say that he would resign if the bill were defeated.[142] In fact it passed, in an exceptionally crowded House, by 265 to 223; but the opposition was jubilant. 'Nothing could have fallen out more to my mind than what has happened,' Fox crowed to Holland; 'the party revived and strengthened, Pitt lowered, and, what is of more consequence in my view, the cause of *Royalism* . . . lowered too.'[143] Those who still hoped for a dream coalition were disappointed again. 'One thing we may collect from the debate,' wrote one Grenvillite, 'is that the mutual antipathy of Messrs. Pitt and Fox exists as strongly as ever, and that no Cabinet negotiations can at present be in agitation.'[144]

The following summer Pitt, his health failing, made another show of willingness to include Fox and Grenville. But Fox would still not serve under Pitt, Grenville would not abandon Fox, Pitt would still not accept a lesser post, while the King would still not admit Fox, 'even at the hazard of a civil war';[145] so this overture was as stillborn as all the others. Fox as usual put the worst interpretation on Pitt's motives:

> I presume the intention is to endeavour to put us in the wrong . . .
> and in this way, if Pitt were to manage dextrously, I should fear he
> might have some success. I have strong dependence, however, on his
> temper and character: and suspect he will be more anxious to keep
> himself clear of the imputation of what I should call modesty, and
> he humiliation, than to fix upon us that of unreasonableness.[146]

In truth, pride prevented either submitting to the other. But where
Pitt's was a pride of *place* which forbade him, after so long as
Prime Minister, to contemplate a lesser position – Asquith took
exactly the same view in the middle of another war 111 years later
– Fox's was rather a pride of *person*: he had cultivated, over twenty
years, such a contempt of Pitt's character, based on his resentment
at the way Pitt had cheated him out of office in 1783 and a principled objection to most of his policies ever since, that he could
not bear the thought of serving with him in any capacity. One
observer noted that in private Pitt never spoke abusively of Fox,
while Fox frequently did so of Pitt.[147] Fox's deepest desire, from
1783 onwards, was to see Pitt out of office again, and he judged
events by whether they contributed to that result. Even at the end
of 1805, when the news came in of Nelson's victory at Trafalgar,
his reaction was ambivalent. 'It is a great event,' he wrote to Holland,
which 'more than compensates for the temporary succour which it
will certainly afford to Pitt.'[148] On this occasion he was patriot
enough to welcome the victory, because he thought it would hasten
the end of the war, even though it might help Pitt. Six weeks later,
however, he frankly welcomed Napoleon's crushing defeat of the
Austrians and Russians at Austerlitz on the same grounds, though
this mortal blow to Britain's continental strategy was widely held
to have destroyed Pitt's will to live. He died just over three weeks
later on 23 January 1806, exhausted and heartbroken, of gastric
ulceration brought on by years of heavy drinking, at the age of
forty-six.

Even when Pitt was dying Fox still distrusted him. 'As to your
News,' he wrote, 'I must know Pitt's Resignation is certain before
I believe it. Even if he is dying the ruling passion will prevail.'[149] 'I
should be very sorry,' he told another correspondent, 'to have Pitt
escape in such a manner from the complete disgrace that must at

last befall him.'[150] When his rival's demise was confirmed he felt cheated, rebuking a friend who rejoiced at it:

> How can one rejoice in the death of any man? Death is a thing without a remedy. Besides, it is a poor way of getting rid of one's enemy. A fair good discussion that turns him out is well – but death – no![151]

He declared himself 'very, very sorry' – but only because 'one feels as if there was something missing from the world – a chasm, a blank that cannot be supplied'.[152] Pitt's death, he said, 'would render every debate flat and uninteresting . . . I hate going to the House. I think I shall pair off with Pitt.'[153] Eight months later he did exactly that.

Meanwhile he refused the usual tributes to the dead. When a motion was proposed to give a public funeral to the man who had led the country in war and peace for most of the past quarter-century, Fox opposed it. 'It cannot be expected that I should so far forget the principles I have uniformly professed, as to subscribe to the condemnation of those principles by agreeing to the motion now before the House.' He was happy that the state should pay Pitt's debts; but he could not subscribe to an endorsement of his record.

> No man can be more desirous than I am to bury in oblivion those contests in which we were so long engaged; but I never can consent to confer public honours, on the ground of his being 'an excellent statesman', on the man who, in my opinion, was the sole, and certainly the chief supporter of a system which I was early taught to consider as a bad one.

It was painful to take this view, which he knew would be misrepresented; but 'my public duty calls on me, in the most imperious and irresistible manner, to oppose the motion'.[154]

Was this refusal mean, or honest? Principled or petty? Whichever it was, Fox was not alone. Several other speakers echoed his objection, and 88 Members joined him in voting against the motion. With 258 in favour, however, it was easily carried; and Pitt was buried with full pomp in Westminster Abbey, close to his father.

Meanwhile his friends could not sustain the government without their leader. It was symbolic of how indispensable Pitt had been that the moment he was dead the King was obliged to lift his veto on Fox. He had no choice but to accept a so-called 'Ministry of All the Talents' headed by Grenville, with Fox back as Foreign Secretary – the office from which he had been abruptly dismissed twenty-two years earlier. The ministry did not deserve its name, since the Pittites were excluded. Its only *raison d'être* was to try to make peace, as Fox had been urging for so long. After such a long absence he threw himself into the task, imagining that he could quickly agree terms with his friend Talleyrand. But it rapidly became clear that Napoleon did not want peace. Everything Fox had maintained since 1792 – that the war was all George III's fault, not due to French aggression – was cruelly disproved. The war dragged on for another nine years before Napoleon was finally defeated.

Fox did achieve one longstanding ambition in his last brief period as Foreign Secretary. On 10 June he moved the resolution by which the House of Commons finally conceded William Wilberforce's long campaign to abolish the slave trade. Ironically this was one issue on which Fox and Pitt had remained united down the years. Both had expended some of their greatest oratory in the cause; but even their combined eloquence had failed to overcome the entrenched majority of the slave-owners and their supporters. Now, after Pitt's death and within weeks of Fox's, abolition slipped though anticlimactically in a House barely a quarter full, by 114 votes to 15. It passed the Lords a week later by 41–20.

But Fox too was already terminally ill with dropsy, hugely overweight and swollen up like a balloon. In his last illness the doctors drained sixteen quarts of fluid from his body in one day. He refused to ease the burden of the House of Commons by taking a peerage, as he wrote to Lord Holland. 'The peerage, to be sure, seems the natural way, but that cannot be. I have an oath in heaven against it; I will not close my politics in that foolish way, as so many have done before me.'[155] He died on 13 September 1806. He was not awarded a state funeral like Pitt's; but the crowds were at least as large and more emotional. He too was buried in Westminster Abbey, just a few feet away from his lifetime's nemesis.

They were closer in death than they had ever been in life, which inspired Walter Scott to pen a mawkish ode – entitled 'Patriotism'

– mourning the loss of three great British heroes – Nelson, Pitt and Fox – within a year. Its final stanzas squeezed every drop of sentiment from the proximity of the two politicians' monuments:

> With more than mortal powers endow'd,
> How high they soared above the crowd!
> Theirs was no common party race,
> Jostling by dark intrigue for place;
> Like fabled gods, their mighty war
> Shook realms and nations in its jar;
> Beneath each banner proud to stand,
> Look'd up the noblest in the land,
> Till through the British world were known
> The names of PITT and FOX alone . . .
>
> Drop upon Fox's grave the tear,
> 'Twill trickle to his rival's bier.
> O'er PITT's the mournful requiem sound,
> And FOX's shall the notes rebound.
> The solemn echo seems to cry,
> 'Here let their discord with them die.
> Speak not for those a separate doom
> Whom fate made Brothers in the tomb;
> But search the land of living men,
> Where wilt thou find their like agen?'[156]

Unquestionably Pitt won their political duel in their lifetimes. He was Prime Minister for a total of nineteen years, whereas Fox managed less than two years as Foreign Secretary, spread over three brief spells. At two critical moments – the confrontation over Fox's India Bill in 1783–84 and the Regency crisis of 1788–89 – Pitt decisively outmanoeuvred his opponent, first to obtain power and then to keep it. He lied shamelessly in the first instance, and was lucky in the second; but on both occasions his cool management contrasted tellingly with Fox's impulsiveness. While even his enemies loved Fox, they could not deny that Pitt was the shrewder politician. Moreover, though there were only ten years between them, Pitt far better represented the changing *Zeitgeist* of late Georgian England and matched the new challenges of the time. Pitt's more sober lifestyle – though he actually drank as much as Fox – reflected a growing puritanical backlash against the unbridled hedonism of the previous generation. Above all, Pitt understood – as Fox did not – the nation-transforming energy of the industrial revolution, and the boundless military ambition of revolutionary France. In all these respects Pitt, and not Fox, met the needs of their time.

Pitt left an enduring legacy in four areas. First, though he was not militarily successful in his lifetime, he embodied for more than a decade the national resolve to defeat Napoleon which ultimately culminated in victory at Waterloo. Second, his far-sighted financial reforms, enacting the free trade principles of Adam Smith, helped create the wealth which enabled Britain to support the twenty-five-year struggle with France, laid the foundations of the great nineteenth-century expansion of British trade and paved the way for the further reforms of Peel and Gladstone. Third, in his single-minded ambition, his professionalism and his reputation for personal integrity – a view of politics which saw office as a public responsibility rather than just an opportunity for personal enrichment – he pointed the way to a less venal, more 'Victorian' approach to the business of government than had been normal in the eighteenth century. Finally, though he started out like Fox as an opposition Whig, circumstances and temperament combined to make him a Tory: a resolute opponent of revolution abroad and reform at home, and thus one of the founding fathers of the modern Conservative party.

Fox by contrast achieved very little in his lifetime. His private life embodied the excesses of the aristocratic past. He had no conception of the needs of the industrial revolution or understanding of the new economics. He was consistently wrong about the French Revolution and the threat posed by Napoleon. He failed to achieve parliamentary reform, or Catholic emancipation, or any of the other progressive causes – except the abolition of the slave trade – that he espoused in his lifetime. The only piece of legislation he ever carried into law was a liberalisation of the law of libel. His career was on paper a complete failure. Yet Fox left a different legacy. By his eloquent support for all those lost causes – religious toleration, freedom of speech, Habeas Corpus, parliamentary reform, the enlightened government of India, even freedom for Ireland – he made his name an enduring symbol of resistance to oppressive government, and posthumously became the hero of

Victorian liberalism and the Whig interpretation of history. Only Fox, G. M. Trevelyan argued in the 1920s, had stood between Britain and a revolution of her own:

> The fifty MPs and half a dozen peers who stood disarmed and help-less beneath Fox's tattered banner were constituting the party destined to reform England and govern her during the best half of the coming century.[157]

> If the whole of the privileged class had joined Pitt's anti-Jacobin bloc . . . the constitution could not have been altered by legal means and change could only have come in nineteenth century Britain along the same violent and blood-stained path by which it has come in continental countries. It is 1832 that justifies the action taken by Fox forty years before.[158]

Today the Whig interpretation of history is out of fashion. Confidence in the inevitability of progress has taken too many knocks since Trevelyan's day. Modern historians are more impressed by pragmatism and hard achievement than by noble rhetoric. The facts of life are perceived to be Tory. With the triumph of Thatcherism, it was Pitt whose reputation rode high at the end of the twentieth century – as patriot, war leader, champion of the free market, and now as the precursor of a 'war on terror' that defends the curtailing of ancient liberties in the name of preserving freedom. A best-selling biography by a former Tory leader made him a hero for our times, while Fox is written off as an irresponsible sensualist, lovable perhaps but fatally flawed. Thus do reputations rise and fall. But still the classic duel of Pitt and Fox – government versus opposition, conservative versus liberal, patriot versus internationalist, right versus left – remains the archetype of political opposition down the succeeding centuries.

Viscount Castlereagh and George Canning

On 21 September 1809, at the height of the war against Napoleon, the two senior cabinet ministers most responsible for the conduct of the war fought a duel on Putney Heath. One was wounded, both resigned and the government fell. Neither held office again for several years, though both resumed their careers and eventually sat again in the same cabinet.

The rivalry of Lord Castlereagh and George Canning is on a different level from any other in this book. They are the only pair to have actually tried to kill each other. But their duel was only the high point of a political antagonism which lasted the whole of their political lives. Their careers ran parallel from the moment they entered Parliament at almost the same time in 1794 and remained uncannily interwoven for the next twenty-eight years. Between them they held the position of Foreign Secretary for a total of seventeen years. In the end it was only Castlereagh's death, by his own hand, at the age of fifty-three, that resurrected Canning's career when it had seemed to be finished. He went on to become Prime Minister, very briefly, before dying himself at fifty-seven.

Political duelling was not uncommon in the eighteenth and early nineteenth centuries. Both Fox and Pitt fought duels over harsh words spoken in the House of Commons – though not with one another. Pitt was Prime Minister when he was called out by an opposition MP whose patriotism he had questioned. On that occasion neither man hit his target: eighteenth-century pistols were mercifully inaccurate, and both were content that honour had been satisfied.

George III was understandably furious that he might have lost his first minister in such circumstances; but the practice – though supposedly illegal – did not die out. The last Prime Minister to fight a duel was Wellington, as late as 1829. Nevertheless the armed meeting of two members of the same Cabinet in 1809 remained a unique event. What had brought these two colleagues to such a pass?

Castlereagh and Canning had certain things in common. They were almost the same age (born in 1769 and 1770 respectively) and were both of Irish family; both started out politically as Foxite Whigs, but under the impact of the French revolution became protégés of Pitt and rivals for his mantle. They both supported Catholic emancipation and opposed parliamentary reform. In every other respect they were utterly different. Castlereagh was well-connected, conscientious, dull but trusted; Canning was a brilliant meritocrat: arrogant, ambitious and widely distrusted. As in Aesop, Castlereagh's plodding tortoise regularly beat Canning's hare for most of their lives. In this case, however, the hare won in the end.

Castlereagh sprang from one of those Scottish Presbyterian families planted in Ulster by James I. His father, Robert Stewart of Newtownards, sat for some years as a member of the Irish Parliament before being created Baron Londonderry (in the Irish peerage) in 1796: Viscount Castlereagh was the courtesy title borne by the heir, which did not prevent him sitting in the Commons. After an Anglican education in Armagh and Cambridge, young Robert began his career in Ireland, regaining his father's seat in the Irish Parliament (at a cost to his father of around £60,000); but in 1794 his obvious promise brought him to the attention of Pitt, who quickly found him a seat at Westminster and soon made him Chief Secretary for Ireland. In this role he showed his capacity first by taking tough measures to suppress the rebellion of the United Irishmen in 1798, and then by forcing through the Act of Union, inducing the Dublin Parliament to vote itself out of existence by means of lavish bribery and the promise of Catholic emancipation, which Pitt was not able to deliver. From then on Castlereagh was an archetypal insider, rarely out of office – except after his duel – and had a knack of holding the key job at critical moments: not only Ireland at the time of the Union, but the War Office at the beginning of the Peninsular War and the Foreign Office after Napoleon's final defeat. 'No-one can deny that his talents were great,' Charles Greville wrote, yet 'perhaps he owed his influence and authority as much to his character as to his abilities. His appearance was dignified and imposing; he was affable in his manners and agreeable in society.'[1] By the standards of the day he was a poor speaker, and the House sometimes laughed at his tortured syntax; but he was a safe pair of hands, well liked and respected by his colleagues, though unpopular in the country where he was regarded as a cold fish. If he had a vice it was a streak of vanity.

Canning's beginnings, by contrast, were the poorest of any man to reach the top of British politics before Ramsay MacDonald in 1924. Though his family too had been settled in Ulster since the time of James I, his father was a dissolute wastrel who came to London, lived a bohemian life among actors and writers, was disinherited and died when George was one year old. His widow – an Irish girl of good family but no money – went on the stage, not very successfully, and lived with a succession of down-at-heel actor-managers, one of whom she married. For the first eight years of his life young George was trailed around the provincial theatres of England, receiving only a scratchy education until providentially – like Oliver Twist – he was saved by a wealthy uncle who took him under his wing and sent him to Eton and Oxford, where he enjoyed a dazzling career as a debater, satirist and wit. He read for the Bar but was always determined – despite his lack of wealth or family – to go into politics. He was initially taken up by Fox and Sheridan; but in 1792 – from a shrewd mixture of conviction and calculation – he ostentatiously defected and offered his services to Pitt, who found him a seat in the Commons the following year and gave him office in 1796 – two years before Castlereagh. Canning was outstandingly clever, but he was impatient and too blatantly ambitious, handicapped by his poverty and lowly origins. In 1799 – with Pitt's help – he married an heiress whose income supported his career; but twenty-eight years later, when he finally reached the highest office, there were still those who thought it inconceivable that the son of an actress could be Prime Minister.

In a political world still dominated by the aristocracy and gentry, Canning was widely seen as a pushy parvenu with a sharp tongue and a knack of making enemies: 'a frothy, unfeeling imposter,' in the words of the diarist Thomas Creevey, 'full of words and epigrams and without any solid reasoning or a bit of heart'.[2] As a result, despite his acknowledged gifts and the valuable debating strength he could bring to any ministry, he was in office for only just over half of his parliamentary career.

A precursor of such twentieth-century adventurers as F. E. Smith and Michael Heseltine, Canning set himself the ambition to be a Privy Councillor by the age of thirty, and he just achieved it. He gained his first experience of office at twenty-six when Pitt made him an under-secretary at the Foreign Office under Lord Grenville. Pitt at this time was keen to explore possible peace negotiations with France: Grenville was less keen, so Pitt used Canning as an intermediary behind his Foreign Secretary's back; in this situation he could be loyal to his mentor only by disloyalty to his immediate boss. The negotiations came to nothing, but the experience left Canning with a reputation, and perhaps a taste, for intrigue. After three years he asked to be moved to a less exposed position. Nevertheless he was already recognised as the most brilliant of the younger orators in a House still dominated by Pitt and Fox; he was also an accomplished writer of light verse, the most prominent contributor to a Pittite satirical magazine, *The Anti-Jacobin*, dedicated to exposing the unpatriotic loyalties of the anti-war party; and he was gathering around him a small party of his own which gave him some independent weight. Meanwhile Castlereagh had been making a different sort of reputation as an effective Chief Secretary in Dublin.

The two men reacted in characteristically different ways to Pitt's resignation in 1801. Pitt left office ostensibly because he was unable to overcome the King's rooted opposition to Catholic emancipation, which he (and Castlereagh) had seen as an essential accompaniment of the Act of Union; but he may also have been glad of an excuse to let someone else make a short-lived peace with Napoleon, and initially gave his support to Henry Addington – the former Speaker – as his successor. Castlereagh uncomplainingly resigned with his leader, but soon – with Pitt's approval – joined Addington's cabinet as President of the Board of Control for India. Canning by contrast, though he too supported emancipation, thought Pitt wrong to resign over it; he refused office under Addington, whom he despised, and mocked his government – 'Pitt is to Addington as London is to Paddington' – thus making a lifelong enemy of Addington and irritating all those who had joined him. 'His saucy manners . . . satirical songs and indiscreet epigrams,' one diarist wrote, 'have already indisposed almost all of Pitt's friends . . . His conduct has opened many mouths of friends and foes, which had been kept sealed by the knowledge of Pitt's favour or the dread of his own wit.'[3] Instead – more Pittite than Pitt himself – he devoted himself to trying to promote his hero's return. In 1802 he recited an adulatory poem lauding 'The Pilot who Weathered the Storm', at a dinner in his honour; he even christened his second son William Pitt Canning. But his efforts were too transparently self-serving. Pitt himself, who was in no hurry to come back except on his own terms, spoke of his 'ungovernable ambition and impatience of idleness and obscurity';[4] while Creevey wrote scathingly of 'the indignant, mercenary Canning, who wants again to be in place'.[5]

When Pitt did return in 1804 – after an interruption of just over three years and the resumption of war – Castlereagh continued in the same office while taking on much of the burden of leading the House of Commons in order to relieve the Prime Minister, whose health was already failing; aside from Pitt himself, he was the only other cabinet minister in the lower House. The following year he added the War Office (with the Colonies) to his existing responsibility for India. If not exactly deputy Prime Minister he was certainly the government's indispensable man. Canning, by contrast, who had hoped to be Foreign Secretary, had to be content with the minor post of Treasurer of the Navy, and very nearly lost that when he infuriated the Home Secretary, Lord Hawkesbury, by gratuitously sneering at his role in the previous administration. Hawkesbury (the future Lord Liverpool) offered his resignation; but Pitt made it clear that he would rather lose Canning. To his wife Canning wrote condescendingly of Castlereagh ('I do assure my own love his continuing where he is, is not considered a mark of high consideration') and contemptuously of Hawkesbury, an

Eton contemporary who was supposed to be his friend.[6] But worse was to follow. When the Foreign Secretary, Lord Harrowby, resigned through ill health in late 1804 Canning was again passed over; and soon afterwards Addington (now Lord Sidmouth) rejoined the government as Lord President of the Council. Canning felt so humiliated by these accumulated slights that he considered resigning. In July 1805 he poured out his grievances in a candid talk with Pitt, which he transcribed in detail for his wife's benefit. While repeating his bitter jealousy of Hawkesbury ('a liar and a coward'), he claimed to feel no similar animus against Castlereagh; but he still resented his preferment ahead of himself:

> I must mention, but with very different feelings, another person in your Government – Castlereagh – for whom I have never at any moment entertained any thing of dislike, & whom upon nearer intercourse I grow to like, as much as the difference of our natures admits, very cordially. But you cannot suppose that standing in the situation in which I do stand in the H. of C. I can very patiently bear the accumulation of two efficient offices upon him – as if there were no-one else capable of executing either of them.[7]

Pitt indicated that Castlereagh would relinquish the Indian job soon; but he did not think Canning would want that. He then – if Canning can be believed – promised him the next cabinet vacancy that arose. But he died before he could honour his promise.

Despite this signal lack of advancement, when Pitt died in January 1806 Canning fancied himself the rightful heir. Unfortunately for him, no one else thought so. In fact there was no obvious successor, but four pretenders, all around the same age. Canning was unquestionably the best speaker of the four, with his own party of around sixteen followers; but the other three all had more experience of office. Castlereagh had been Chief Secretary for Ireland and President of the Board of Control for India, while Hawkesbury had been both Foreign Secretary and Home Secretary; the fourth man, Spencer Perceval, one of the leading barristers of the day, had been Attorney-General since 1802. As colleagues in government over many years they trusted each other more than they did the carping, restless Canning. When Grenville formed, with Fox, the misnamed

'Ministry of All the Talents', they determined to go into opposition. After the death of Fox, Grenville tried to split them by making overtures to Canning, and possibly Perceval – but not the other two. Canning wisely declined to jump ship alone. But he overplayed his hand by trying to bargain as though he were the acknowledged leader of the bereaved Pittites.

Writing to his wife, to whom he invariably recounted the vicissitudes of his career with guileless candour, Canning listed those colleagues – including Castlereagh but not Perceval or Hawkesbury – whom he might try to bring over with him and marked them according to various criteria, five positive and three negative:

(1) Who would carry most of Pitt?
(2) Who would bring or satisfy most people?
(3) Who would feel the most obliged to *me*?
(4) Whom would the King like best?
(5) Whom would Lord G. like best?
(6) Inefficiency
(7) Unpopularity
(8) 'Mischievous intrigue'

Castlereagh was awarded no positive scores at all on the first five questions (where none of the others scored fewer than three), but two negative ones (unpopularity and intrigue).[8] Whatever his protestations to Pitt six months earlier, it is clear that Castlereagh was now Canning's *bête noire*.

Before anything could come of these manoeuvrings, however, Grenville, like Pitt six years earlier, fell foul of George III's refusal to countenance any measure of Catholic relief and was effectively dismissed. George now turned to the elderly Duke of Portland (the same whom he had dismissed back in 1783 over Fox's India Bill, but who had subsequently defected to Pitt in 1795), to lead a purely Pittite cabinet. But Portland was little more than a figurehead for the rivalries of his ambitious colleagues: in the three years of his premiership, he never spoke in the House of Lords and rarely attended the Treasury. In the allocation of offices Castlereagh returned to the War Office and Hawkesbury to the Home Office, while Perceval was persuaded to give up his practice at the Bar to take the then lesser job of

Chancellor of the Exchequer. The Foreign Office was initially intended for the Marquess of Wellesley (elder brother of the future Duke of Wellington), while Canning was to have the Admiralty. But after much swithering Wellesley withdrew, allowing Canning to leapfrog into the vacant place. This was a substantial promotion; but Canning's sense of entitlement was higher still. He insisted that if he and Castlereagh were both Secretaries of State he could not concede Castlereagh the leadership in the Commons: he would refuse office rather than serve under Castlereagh. For his part Castlereagh was happy to give up the leadership, but was not willing to let Canning have it; they eventually agreed that Perceval should combine it with the Exchequer. 'Perceval's precedency,' Canning wrote later, 'was . . . the result of a compromise between Castlereagh and me.'⁹ With his eye fixed on Castlereagh, he failed to see Perceval as an equally dangerous rival.

With the allocation of offices finally settled, the King agreed to new elections: the ministry increased its majority and appeared to be secure for some years ahead. But the combination of four jostling rivals under a largely absentee Prime Minister was inherently unstable – still more so when the government's main business was fighting a war which was going badly. Austria and Prussia had already been knocked out of the latest coalition put together by Pitt before his death; now the Treaty of Tilsit signed between Napoleon and Tsar Alexander I of Russia in July 1807 removed Britain's last continental ally, while Napoleon's 'continental system', extended to Spain and Portugal in 1808, threatened to strangle British trade. Britain had never stood more alone. The Portland cabinet was torn, as Pitt's had been throughout the 1790s, between a continental strategy of trying to build a new coalition to fight Napoleon on land and the naval strategy of relying on command of the seas. Maintaining naval superiority was vital to prevent a possible French invasion of southern England. To this end Canning took the lead in promoting a daring pre-emptive strike – in breach of international law – to seize the Danish fleet before the French could lay hands on it; he then persuaded the Portuguese to surrender their fleet into British keeping too. The Foreign

Secretary got the credit for these two decisive coups; but Castlereagh as War Secretary fully supported them, and provided the men and *matériel* for the Copenhagen expedition. Up to this point the two ministers were working well together – though Castlereagh was ill for several weeks towards the end of 1807, prompting the first suggestion that he might need to be replaced.

Early in 1808, however, Spanish resistance to Napoleon's imposition of his brother Joseph Bonaparte as King of Spain opened a third strategic option. Again Canning took the lead in swiftly promising support for the rebels; and in June the cabinet decided to send the relatively junior Arthur Wellesley – the future Duke of Wellington – to Portugal to support the Spanish – and Portuguese – revolt. At first Canning and Castlereagh shared responsibility for this Iberian strategy; but the conduct of the Peninsular campaign soon opened a serious rift between them.

Wellesley quickly defeated a superior French force at Vimeiro, just north of Lisbon, only to be superseded by two more senior generals appointed over his head. This confusion of command was Castlereagh's responsibility: he allowed his own preference for Wellesley to be overborne by the insistence of the Commander-in-Chief – the King's younger brother, the Duke of York – who was more concerned with hierarchy than efficiency. Sir Hew Dalrymple, previously Governor of Gibraltar, had not seen active service for fifteen years. He promptly concluded an excessively generous armistice which allowed the French free passage to withdraw most of their troops, equipment and loot back to France. When news of the Convention of Cintra reached London it provoked outrage right across the political spectrum – the ballad-makers sang of 'hewmiliation' – and there were demands that the generals involved – including Wellesley – should be recalled, if not court-martialled. For a week the cabinet debated whether to repudiate the convention. Canning would have yielded to this popular clamour, which might have ended Wellesley's career. But Castlereagh, as the minister departmentally responsible, fought for him and at last convinced his colleagues – Canning excepted. Dalrymple was recalled, and never held another command; but Wellesley was exonerated by a court of inquiry and sent back to Spain to pursue the campaign which led to Napoleon's eventual defeat.

In the meantime, while Wellesley was in London defending himself, Sir John Moore was sent out in his place. Canning had no faith in Moore either. Once again Castlereagh acquiesced in his appointment only in deference to the King: he was not encouraged by Moore telling him, before he left, 'Remember, my Lord, I protest against the expedition, and foretell its failure.' When Castlereagh reported this to the cabinet, Canning allegedly exclaimed: 'Good God; and do you really mean to say that you allowed a man entertaining such feelings with regard to the expedition to go out and command it?'[10] There was force in his objection, which was tragically borne out by the sequel. Though the final rearguard action which allowed the bulk of his army to be evacuated from Corunna was heroic, Moore was indeed slow to join up with the Spanish, allowing Napoleon to pour troops into Spain to rout them, leaving Britain's whole Peninsular strategy in ruins. Once again Canning would have made Moore a posthumous scapegoat, while Castlereagh honourably defended his general. Yet arguments in cabinet were not reflected in Parliament. Castlereagh's defence of the Corunna campaign was typically pedestrian, whereas Canning launched a powerful counter-attack – described by Perceval as 'one of the best, most eloquent and most commanding speeches that was ever heard'[11] – which saved the day for the government.

Even if he did not always get his way in cabinet, the Foreign Secretary was now the dominant personality in the government. Rather like Lloyd George in 1916, or Churchill in 1940, Canning seemed to be the only source of energy in a floundering administration. He was not Prime Minister, yet he increasingly acted as if he was – or should be. Following the humiliations of Cintra and Corunna, he complained to Portland on 2 April 1809 that the government was paralysed by 'a spirit of compromise' and gave notice that he would have to resign unless there were changes: 'The Government as at present constituted does not appear to me equal to the great task which it has to perform.'[12] He regarded several members of the cabinet as 'dead lumber'; but when he was invited for talks at Portland's country house a few days later he specifically demanded Castlereagh's removal from the War Office. Portland was in a fix. He did not want to lose Castlereagh, but he could not afford to lose Canning. He consulted his senior colleagues – Earl Camden (Lord President of the Council) and Earl Bathurst (President of the Board of Trade). They agreed in principle that Castlereagh should be given another job and sent to the Lords, but not just yet.

All that summer complicated discussions continued, involving the King and a widening circle of ministers, about how to satisfy Canning without sacrificing Castlereagh. The King – horrified when Portland himself threatened to resign – proposed splitting the War Office, leaving Castlereagh with responsibility for the colonies but transferring conduct of the war to Canning. Canning reluctantly accepted this, out of deference to the King: but still nothing happened. Camden – who happened to be Castlereagh's uncle – was deputed to tell his nephew, but could not bring himself to do it: the result was that most of the cabinet knew that Castlereagh was to be moved, but not Castlereagh himself. Meanwhile, at regular intervals, Canning renewed his threat to resign. Unluckily Castlereagh was involved in a minor corruption scandal dating from his time in charge of India five years earlier. Dutifully, Canning defended his colleague in the House; but behind the scenes he used this additional embarrassment as a further reason for his early 'retirement'. At the same time he far exceeded his authority by promising Lord Wellesley the War Office as soon as Castlereagh could be removed.

It is not clear whether Canning was targeting Castlereagh because he saw him as a drag on the vigorous prosecution of the war, or as the biggest obstacle to his own ambition. His sensitivity over the leadership of the House in 1807 shows that he did see Castlereagh as his rival; this led him to exaggerate his failings as a minister. In so far as he really thought Castlereagh was not up to the job, his conduct can be defended in the public interest: to the extent that he was pursuing a private vendetta it cannot. On public grounds he was entitled to make known his criticism of Castlereagh, and even to tell the Prime Minister that he would resign if Castlereagh remained in place; but Portland and most of his colleagues regarded Castlereagh as a perfectly good minister and a valuable member of the government. By arrogating to himself the right to dictate who should be in the government and who should not, Canning was overreaching himself. But it was Portland and Camden – and the King – who let the crisis fester by failing to act decisively. A strong Prime Minister would either have given Canning what he wanted or slapped him down. Portland merely prevaricated, while the King insisted on secrecy.

One excuse for Portland's inaction was that on 21 June the cabinet decided to send an expedition to Holland to capture French shipping in the Scheldt, occupy the island of Walcheren and destroy the dockyards at Antwerp and Flushing. This ambitious plan, involving thirty-five ships of the line and 40,000 troops, was primarily Castlereagh's idea; but it was approved by the whole cabinet. Canning would have preferred to concentrate resources on Spain, but he went along with it and was therefore bound by collective responsibility. Once the expedition was decided upon, however, there was a good case for maintaining that Castlereagh could not be moved until it was concluded. Perceval, who was increasingly emerging as a pivotal figure, protested to Canning at the 'extreme hardship, not to say injustice' of a reshuffle while the expedition was being prepared and refused to be a party to forcing its architect out against his will. More generally he was alarmed that what was happening to Castlereagh 'might happen to me or any other of the King's servants when they least expected it' if ministers were allowed to scheme against each other.[13] All sorts of compromise arrangements were proposed – both Liverpool and Camden offered to give up their own positions to accommodate Castlereagh; but all except Canning agreed that nothing could happen, and Castlereagh should not be told, until Walcheren was over.

The expedition sailed on 28 July: Castlereagh, Canning and Perceval were at Deal to wave it off. Flushing was quickly captured; but by the beginning of September it was clear that the expedition had failed. There was a hopeless lack of communication between the naval and military commanders; the element of surprise was totally lost; and most of the troops succumbed to swamp fever which was entirely predictable at that time of year. Now it was not unreasonable that Castlereagh

should carry the can. On 2 September Canning wrote again to
Portland demanding that he should be replaced immediately.
But the crisis was finally precipitated not by Walcheren but by
the Prime Minister's health. Portland had just agreed to bite
the bullet when he suffered an epileptic fit. He recovered, but
it was obvious that he could not continue in office. His retirement seemed to offer an opportunity to move Castlereagh as
part of a general reshuffle without his ever knowing that the
axe had been poised over his head for months. 'I am satisfied,'
Perceval wrote, 'that at this moment, he has not the least suspicion upon the subject.'[14] But Canning now openly pressed his
own claim to the premiership, insisting first – contrary to what
he had argued three years earlier – that the Prime Minister must
be in the Commons and, second, that he would neither serve
under Perceval nor expect Perceval to serve under him. In other
words he must be Prime Minister or he would not serve at all.
Having dispatched Castlereagh, he was now trying to clear
Perceval from his path as well. Perceval replied with cunning
modesty that he had no wish to be Prime Minister, but would
be happy to find an acceptable candidate in the Lords; in other
words anyone but Canning.

On 6 September Portland announced his intention to resign
as soon as a successor was agreed. Canning promptly announced
that he would resign at the same time: he evidently believed that
the King would have no choice but to turn to him. Portland
pressed him to withdraw his resignation and attend cabinet the
next day. But Canning stayed away. His absence caused
Castlereagh to ask what was going on; and on 7 September
Camden finally told him. At first he took it 'firmly and reasonably';[15] he resigned immediately and withdrew to his house in
Kent to consider his options. Prematurely Canning crowed that
he had disappeared 'as through a trap-door'.[16] But the more
Castlereagh learned of the summer's goings-on the angrier he
became. Ironically, he had learned the truth only when it no
longer mattered.

The search for a new Prime Minister continued. On 13
September Canning had an audience with the King and repeated
his view that Portland was 'the last of his species': the next Prime

Minister must be in the Commons.* He would not serve under Perceval but declared himself ready to form a government himself if Perceval could not do so. The King declared this interview 'the most extraordinary' of his long reign. Castlereagh's Under-Secretary, Edward Cooke, called it 'the most insolent proposition that was ever obtruded upon a Monarch by a presumptuous Subject';[17] while Eldon, the Lord Chancellor, fumed that Canning was 'vanity in human form'.[18] In one respect Canning was in a strong position, since it was widely assumed that 'without him the business of Parliament could not be carried on'. But his too-evident ambition had alienated his colleagues. 'The holding together the present Administration seems impossible,' the political fixer Charles Arbuthnot concluded, 'for Canning . . . has pretensions which his colleagues will not agree to.'[19] On 18 September, rather than submit to Canning, the rest of the cabinet decided to approach the opposition Whigs to try to form a coalition.

For twelve days, however, Castlereagh had been nursing his wounded honour. On 16 September he wrote bitterly to Edward Cooke:

> I consider that I have been sacrificed to a colleague, both unjustly and ungenerously, and under circumstances of concealment the most unjustifiable. It is impossible for me to disguise . . . the extent to which my confidence in my colleagues has been shaken by what has passed.[20]

He accepted his share of responsibility for the military setbacks in Spain and Holland, but refused to be made a scapegoat. Above all, he was determined to vindicate his private honour. Three days later he sent Canning a stiffly worded challenge, some nine pages long. ('By God,' Canning is said to have exclaimed with Wildean insouciance, 'I'd rather fight than read it.') He admitted Canning's

*In fact nine of the next sixteen Prime Ministers were peers (eleven if you include Russell, who became a peer before his second premiership, and Disraeli, who was elevated while in office). Not until 1923, when Stanley Baldwin was preferred to Lord Curzon, was the convention established that the Prime Minister must sit in the Commons.

right, 'as a public man . . . on public grounds', to demand his removal, but not 'at the expense of my honour and reputation'. It was the deception he objected to.

> You continued to sit in the same Cabinet with me, and to leave me not only in the persuasion that I possessed your confidence and support as a colleague, but you allowed me, tho' thus virtually suspended, in breach of every principle both public and private to originate and proceed in the Execution of a new Enterprise of the most arduous and important nature, with your apparent concurrence and ostensible approbation.
>
> You were fully aware that if my situation in the government had been disclosed to me, I could not have submitted to remain one moment in office, without the entire abandonment of my private honour and public duty. You knew I was deceived, and you continued to deceive me . . .
>
> Under these circumstances, I must require that satisfaction from you to which I feel myself entitled to lay claim.[21]

In truth, it was not Canning who had kept him in the dark. Canning had all along protested at the secrecy and delay. Castlereagh's bitterness was equally directed at Portland and Camden, as he made clear in a letter to his father, Lord Londonderry:

> I was by the infatuation and folly of those who called themselves my friends, allowed to remain in total ignorance of my situation – to plunge into ever heavier responsibility after my death warrant was signed, and further, I was to be kept in profound ignorance of this until the moment should arise, namely, the close of the expedition, when I was to be equally dismissed in the event of failure, or success, unless Mr Canning in his mercy should be disposed to spare his victim, being made absolute master of my fate.

He was concerned that unless he took steps to clear his name it would seem that he had clung to office after his colleagues had decided to remove him:

> How small a portion of the world would have believed that I was not privy to my own disgrace, it being more generally credible that

a public man should be guilty of a shabby act to keep himself in office than that his friends and colleagues would keep him in the dark.[22]

In this respect Castlereagh could be said to have been challenging the wrong man. To try to appease him, Canning's friend Charles Ellis, whom he had appointed as his second, sent Castlereagh's second, Lord Yarmouth, copies of letters demonstrating that Canning had warned Portland of the danger of concealment. In July he had expressly requested, 'in justice to himself, that it may be remembered, whenever hereafter this concealment shall be alleged (as he doubts not that it will) against him, as an act of injustice towards Lord Castlereagh, that it did not originate in his suggestion'.[23] With some justice Ellis wrote later that his friend had been 'fighting the poor old Duke's duel, or Lord Camden's, or Hawkesbury's, or almost anybody's but his own'.[24] Yet while sore at his 'supposed friends', Castlereagh was right to identify Canning as his real opponent. 'It was . . . your act,' he wrote, 'and your conduct which deceived me.' No head of government could bind a colleague in such a matter: Canning should rather have resigned himself than be a party to such deceit. So he refused to be appeased. Canning – though he had never fired a pistol in his life – had no choice but to accept with as much defiance as he could muster.

> My Lord,
> The tone and purport of your lordship's letter, which I have this moment received, of course preclude any other answer on my part to the misapprehensions and misrepresentations with which it abounds, than that I will cheerfully give to your lordship the satisfaction which you require.
> I have the honour to be, my Lord,
> Your Lordship's most obedient humble servant,
> Geo. Canning.[25]

Not so insouciant now, he made his will and wrote a touching farewell to his wife:

If anything happens to me, dearest love, be comforted with the assurance that I could do no otherwise than I have done. God bless my own best and dearest love – a better and a dearer never did God give to man . . . I hope I have made you happy. If you have been a happy wife – and if I leave you a happy mother, and a proud widow, I am content. Adieu, adieu.[26]

The duel took place on Putney Heath at 6 a.m. on 21 September. On the way to the meeting-place – 'just beyond a cottage on the left of the road to Roehampton'* – Castlereagh calmly discussed a fashionable opera singer of the moment and hummed snatches of her arias. Indeed both principals seem to have conducted themselves with exemplary coolness: only Ellis – so Yarmouth told the diarist John Croker – 'was so nervous for his friend's safety that he could not load his pistols [so that] Lord Yarmouth either loaded Mr Canning's pistols for Mr Ellis, or lent one of his own, I forget which, but I think the latter'.[27] Very often in these affairs both men would aim to miss, honour being thereby satisfied. But on this occasion one at least did not fire in the air. Both missed with their first shots; but Castlereagh, unusually, insisted on a second round, and this time he hit his opponent 'as neatly as possible . . . through the fleshy part of his thigh'.[28] Some reports claim that Canning also shot a button off the lapel of Castlereagh's coat;[29] if so, that sounds more nearly fatal than Canning's wound. As it was, however, neither man was seriously hurt. Canning actually offered a third round; but the seconds firmly intervened. Castlereagh went forward to take his opponent's arm, and Canning was able to walk to Yarmouth's house nearby, where a surgeon was waiting.

Assuring family and friends that he was unharmed, Canning told one couple – with the bravado that comes of a near escape – that if they had never been shot through the thigh

you can hardly conceive how slight a matter it is – provided (that is) that it passes through quite clean, carrying only a little bit of your nankeen breeches so big O with it – and comes out on the other side, without turning to the right or to the left to any of the arteries,

*The duel took place, ironically, within sight of the house where Pitt had died three years before.

bones, etc., the which lie thereabouts. If you have a mind to try the experiment, I would recommend Lord Castlereagh as the operator.[30]

The political world was agog when the news leaked out. While satirists had fun with the quarrel between 'Mr Canting' and 'Lord Castaway', government spin doctors tried to play down the incident as having originated 'in some official misunderstanding'. *The Times* attempted to provide a little more detail – plausibly enough, but actually wide of the mark:

> That little cordiality has at any time subsisted between these two Members of the Cabinet is well known in the political circles; but the point that was the immediate cause of the quarrel is stated to have been some strong terms of unqualified censure which were applied by Mr CANNING to the expedition to the Scheldt. He is said to have charged the Noble Lord with the whole blame of the defects in the plan of the Expedition, and of whatever there was of misconduct in carrying it into execution.[31]

While government papers hoped that the existing ministry could somehow be reconstructed – both Canning and Castlereagh, as well as Portland, having now resigned – the opposition *Morning Chronicle* insisted that this was impossible following the two ministers' 'disgusting exhibition';[32] while one independent Whig MP, Charles Western, wrote jubilantly to Thomas Creevey:

> The *duel*! By Lord, this surpasses everything . . . I have no doubt Canning was the aggressor, for the fellow is mad – evinced his insanity more than once last year. I delight in this duel. It is *demonstration* of the EFFICIENCY of our Councils . . . It is really too much to bear.[33]

Perceval meanwhile wrote gloomily to the Speaker:

> Castlereagh and Canning have been fighting. Thank God Canning is not severely hurt, and Castlereagh is not touched. Terrible all this, for public impression. What we are to do is not finally settled. It must end in an attempt to form a united Government with our opponents. But it is a bitter pill to swallow.[34]

Some observers thought Castlereagh had over-reacted. Perceval thought that he had 'misconceived the case very much'; while Lord Holland – Fox's nephew – was not alone in feeling that his conduct 'seemed dictated by a thirst of vengeance rather than a sense of wounded honour'.[35] But most shared Squire Western's view that Canning was primarily to blame. Edward Cooke (admittedly a friend of Castlereagh) wrote to Lord Auckland:

What has passed here is very melancholy. You will not believe that Lord Castlereagh was virtually turned out of office above three months ago, on Mr Canning's demand . . . he had been the dupe and victim of Mr Canning's ambition, whilst he had been daily receiving marks of his confidence. This is not credible in a Christian country . . . All which has happened has been from Canning's monkey tricks to make himself premier.[36]

The Whig leader Earl Grey agreed:

For once Castlereagh appears to me to have had the good fortune to have the best of the case. It is impossible to defend Canning's conduct, either in a public or a private view . . . His pretension to occupy the post of Mr Pitt seems modest enough![37]

The King was shocked that 'two persons holding the situations of Secretaries of State, and still in possession of the seals of office, should have been guilty of so total a dereliction of duty as to violate the laws which they were bound to maintain by the authority vested in them'.[38] However, there seems to have been no question of legal action against the duellists. Instead there followed an exchange of letters and articles in the press in which the combatants competed for public sympathy. Castlereagh's side of the story appeared in the *Morning Post* on 2 October; Canning responded on the 14th, seeking to prove that he had not been a party to deceiving Castlereagh. But his defence was handicapped by the death of Portland, which made it difficult for him to lay the blame where it truly belonged. In November he published a second vindication in the form of *A Letter to Lord Camden*, seeking to rebut 'the perversions and misrepresentations of anonymous writers' by which he was abused; but its immense length and lawyerly hair-splitting did him more harm than good. His reputation for intrigue was so well established that the worst was invariably believed of him. His old enemy Sidmouth wrote that 'the intrigue and perfidy of which Lord Castlereagh was to be the victim . . . if practised by Cesar Borgia would have held a distinguished place in the Prince of Machiavel'.[39]

Castlereagh, by contrast, rather benefited from the duel. The spark of Irish spirit which he had displayed served to humanise his previously chilly image. Not so driven as Canning, he was more easily reconciled to losing office. 'I have every reason to be satisfied with the course I have pursued,' he wrote to his brother on 16 October, 'and as it has pleased Providence that I should begin the world again, I need not fret my heart at losing so shabby a set of friends as mine have proved themselves.'[40] In fact he was not out for long, and it is possible that the duel actually rescued his career. Years later Thomas Creevey wrote that 'there was no fact I was more convinced of than that Castlereagh would have expired politically in the year 1809 – that all the world by common consent had had enough of him, and were tired out – had it not been for the piece of perfidy by Canning to him at that time, and that this, and this alone, had risen him from the dead and given him his present great position'.[41] By this time Castlereagh had been Foreign Secretary for six years.

The immediate fallout of the duel was that Spencer Perceval became Prime Minister. Since the Whigs refused to join a coalition, he was obliged to carry on with a cabinet violently shorn of two of its leading members. Liverpool moved from the Home Office to take Castlereagh's place at the War Office; and after a short interval Lord Wellesley became Foreign Secretary. It was not a particularly impressive Cabinet; but at least the new government, unlike the last, had an efficient head. Perceval – a small, neat, well-organised lawyer and devout evangelical – was no genius, but the old King thought him – by contrast with Canning – 'the most straightforward man he had almost ever known';[42] and over the next three years he proved a more than competent Prime Minister.

Canning and Castlereagh reacted very differently to finding

themselves suddenly out of office. Canning felt cruelly cheated of the prize which he had believed to be within his grasp, and bitter at being abandoned by several of his friends whom he had expected to resign with him – above all Wellesley, who had accepted what he still called 'my office'.[43] Grenville wrote accurately that Canning's 'restless intriguing spirit . . . will not rest till somehow or other he shall get his real [red?] boxes again'.[44] He was still acknowledged to be the ablest man in the House of Commons, and he still had around a dozen 'particular cronies' who made up his personal following. But for the moment he was a political pariah, shunned by both government and opposition; he had little money and no interests outside politics, but was forced to try to rebuild his career as an independent. It is no wonder he was said to be 'dejected beyond measure'.[45]

Castlereagh by contrast wrote to his brother that 'Idleness agrees with me marvellously.' He turned to breeding Merino sheep on his estate in Kent, telling a friend that 'Emily says I shall soon bleat and be covered with wool.'[46] But he did not wholly neglect the House of Commons. He was still concerned to vindicate his reputation, and defended his part in the ill starred Walcheren expedition; at the same time he annoyed his former colleagues by supporting an inquiry into its failure, and helped to carry the motion against the government by four votes. His reputation actually rose after the duel. 'Being turned out has certainly done him the world of good,' Canning wrote ruefully to his wife. 'I cannot disguise from myself that pity works for Castgh., and people look upon me with a sort of half-reproachful eye, as the cause of the ruin of the Govt.'[47]

After a year or so Perceval tried to strengthen his team by bringing both the duellists back. He offered a bizarre deal whereby they could share the Home Office and Admiralty, deciding between themselves which should have which. Canning had lowered his sights to the extent that he was now willing to serve under Perceval, but still declared that he would accept nothing less than the Foreign Office. This was immaterial, however, since Castlereagh dismissed the idea out of hand, on the ground that no one would believe that he and Canning were really reconciled; while Perceval had no wish to restore Canning alone. At the beginning of 1812

Castlereagh was still insisting that he was happier and healthier out of office: 'I have no wish but rather the reverse to return soon to office . . . The fact is that I am not playing a game for office . . . My object is to take the necessary part in Parliament which I think becomes me, and I shall leave it to events hereafter to decide my fate.'[48] True to his word, he refused the Foreign Office soon afterwards when Wellesley resigned. Perceval conspicuously did not offer it to Canning. But a few weeks later, when the Prince of Wales was finally appointed Regent on his father's irreversible decline into insanity and confounded his old Whig friends by retaining his existing ministers, Perceval repeated the offer; and this time Castlereagh accepted. It often happens in politics that those who do not press too obviously for office win the prize, while those who do are disappointed.

But then politics was once again thrown into confusion by an event still happily unique in British history – the assassination of the Prime Minister. In May 1812 Perceval was shot in the lobby of the House of Commons by a bankrupt businessman who blamed his ruin on the government. Once again the Prince Regent was faced with the problem of finding a successor. He tried various combinations under Liverpool, Wellesley or the Earl of Moira before he eventually appointed Liverpool. He did not ask either Castlereagh or Canning. Seen initially as a stopgap, and often derided as a mediocrity, Liverpool went on to hold the job for the next fifteen years. Once again Canning paid the price for his overweening pride three years before. 'Had he fairly joined Perceval on the Duke of Portland's death, as Perceval offered,' William Wilberforce reflected, 'he would now have been the acknowledged head, and supported as such.'[49] But still he had not learned his lesson. With the Prime Minister in the Lords it was widely accepted that Liverpool needed Canning to strengthen the ministry in the Commons, where Castlereagh was the government's only effective speaker. Once again, however, jealousy of Castlereagh led Canning to overplay his hand.

The Prince Regent was keen to promote Canning's return. On a purely personal level, he wrote to Castlereagh's half-brother, he preferred Castlereagh's 'solid and useful abilities . . . added to his mild and gentlemanlike manner . . . to anything he felt or could ever feel for the other' (i.e. Canning). Nevertheless Canning's power of debate – 'especially of retort' – made it vital to have him back in the cabinet. He believed that it was up to Castlereagh, as the effective winner of their dispute, to be magnanimous.[50] And indeed Castlereagh was now ready to be reconciled. With Liverpool's mediation the two men met and shook hands. Not only that, but Castlereagh offered to give up the Foreign Office and take the Exchequer – then a much lower-ranking post – to facilitate his rival's return. Years later Canning recognised this as 'perhaps the handsomest offer that was ever made to an individual'.[51] But at the time he would not accept it unless – as in 1807 – he could have the leadership of the House as well; and this Castlereagh – as before – refused to concede.

It was not so much rivalry as pride that prevented either of them giving way. Castlereagh did not value the leadership particularly for itself: had he not already held it he would not have demanded it. But since Perceval's death he had held it; and he thought it – not unreasonably – inconsistent with his honour that he should be asked to give up both his positions. Canning did attach importance to the leadership, but mainly for the symbolism of it: he was happy to serve *with* Castlereagh 'on a footing of perfect equality', but not, as he conceived it, *under* him: this, he claimed, was 'not from any personal feeling towards C . . . but from a sense of humiliation, hard to endure and I think unnecessary to be proposed to me'.[52] Liverpool tried to negotiate a compromise by downplaying the leadership as merely the management of business, or alternatively by sharing the job between them. But the first ploy convinced neither of them, while the second evaded the issue. Castlereagh stubbornly insisted that (as Thomas Grenville put it) 'When two men ride a horse, one must ride behind.' After several days of what Wendy Hinde, the biographer of both men, called 'almost metaphysical efforts to define equality, superiority and leadership in House of Commons terms',[53] Castlereagh was persuaded to write a conciliatory letter virtually conceding the principle of equality. But Canning still thought it failed 'to reconcile *my* claim of equality with his of pre-eminence'.[54] The exasperated Prince Regent blamed Canning for failing to make allowance for 'the blundering expression of so puzzled a writer as Lord Castlereagh', who had been 'ridiculously obstinate and absurd at first', but had become 'quite reasonable, only wishing for a *perfect equality*'.[55] Moreover, he reckoned, a nominal equality would in practice have given Canning 'the lead without the plague of the situation', since 'with his powers poor Lord Castlereagh would stand but a poor chance of being listened to'.[56] But Canning was adamant.

Thus Canning had a return to the Foreign Office on a plate, at a time when the twenty-year war was finally coming to an end and the map of Europe stood to be redrawn by the victorious allies. Yet he turned it down, and cast himself back into the political wilderness for another four years. Never has an ambitious politician so wantonly cut off his own nose to spite his face, spurning the reality of power for the shadow. Within a year he realised his mistake. 'I am alive to the sense of conscious ridicule,' he wrote bitterly to a friend, ' . . . having refused the management of the mightiest scheme of politics which this country ever engaged in, or the world ever witnessed, from a miserable point of etiquette, one absolutely unintelligible . . . at a distance more than six miles from Palace Yard.'[57] He was not merely an impotent spectator of this mighty restructuring: for the next ten years he had to watch Lord Castlereagh striding the European stage in his place.

Canning still saw himself as Pitt's truest disciple and rightful heir. 'To one man while he lived, I was devoted with all my heart and with all my soul,' he declared proudly. 'Since the death of Mr Pitt I acknowledge no leader . . . I have adhered and shall adhere to [his] opinions as the guides of my public conduct.'[58] In the elections of 1812 he broke with his previous dependence on rich men's pocket boroughs and stood successfully for the popular constituency of Liverpool, finding to his surprise that he relished the cut and thrust of the hustings and the added legitimacy he derived from representing a great commercial city – even though he remained, like Pitt in his years of power, firmly opposed to parliamentary reform. ('I deny the grievance,' he told his constituents. 'I distrust the remedy.')[59] His prospects, however, remained bleak, and in 1813 he practically gave up hope of a return to office. That summer he wound up his private party and released his dozen followers from any obligation to him, since 'No proposition of any kind has been or is likely to be made to me.'⁶⁰ 'I am afraid no possible combination of circumstances can place me again where I stood in July last year: and it is no use to reflect where I might have been had the "tide" of that time been "taken at the flood".'⁶¹ He attended the Commons increasingly irregularly, and the following year withdrew from Westminster altogether. Short of money, and anxious to take his invalid elder son to a warm climate, he accepted a posting – flatteringly dressed up by Liverpool – as special ambassador to Lisbon to welcome back the Regent of Portugal, who had fled the country for Brazil in 1807. Though the Regent never did come home, Canning stayed there for two years – on an astonishing salary of £14,000 a year – watching from afar the final defeat of Napoleon which he felt he had done more than anyone to bring about.*

Castlereagh, meanwhile, had found his métier. Following Napoleon's débâcle in Moscow he successfully put together the fourth and last coalition of continental allies – Russia, Austria and Prussia – which saw the war through to its conclusion, then played a leading role at the Congress of Vienna and the subsequent conferences which settled the peace of Europe, more or less, for the next century. He refused to have anything to do with Tsar Alexander's messianic 'Holy Alliance', which he dismissed as 'a piece of sublime mysticism and nonsense', but led the way – in partnership with the Austrian Chancellor, Count Metternich – in trying to establish a permanent structure of international summits known to history as the 'congress system'. The failures of Corunna and Walcheren forgotten, Castlereagh was now, to Canning's chagrin, one of the most powerful and most lauded statesmen of Europe.

The fact that he was abroad so much – as Canning would equally have been if he had been Foreign Secretary – meant that their

---

*A Secretary of State's salary at the time was £6,000 p.a., so the Whigs understandably attacked his appointment as a cushy billet for a disgraced minister; when he stood for re-election in Liverpool his opponent expressed widely shared cynicism in a satirical jingle:

> Fourteen thousand a year is a very fine thing
> For a trip to a Court without any King.⁶²

dispute about the leadership of the Commons turned out to be largely academic. From 1814 onwards Castlereagh was out of the country for months at a time. With the return of peace, the government faced a host of domestic problems, exacerbated by poor harvests. Like Pitt before them in the 1790s, Liverpool and his Home Secretary, Sidmouth, introduced a range of repressive measures to deal with popular unrest; but since both sat in the Lords, the government often lacked a senior minister to carry the burden in the lower House. Once again, little as they trusted him, his former colleagues badly needed Canning back to share the load. When he withdrew to Lisbon, Liverpool had promised him the first cabinet vacancy on his return. In February 1816, a vacancy duly arose when the President of the Board of Control for India, the Duke of Buckinghamshire, died. This was not a senior job: it was the position Castlereagh had held under Addington and Pitt between 1801 and 1806. But two years of exile – seven years altogether in the wilderness – had finally taught Canning some humility. He accepted the offer and rejoined the cabinet.

He still had very little respect for any of his colleagues, who included not only Castlereagh but his old enemies Sidmouth and Camden, the villain (in his eyes) of 1809. There was in fact no one in the cabinet whom he regarded as his equal. Nor was the Indian job either interesting or demanding, since the Governor-General on the spot made most of the decisions, and communication between London and Delhi took months each way. Gloomily he wrote to his wife in November 1817 that he was 'living a sort of postscript after the real volume of my life is closed'.[63] Nevertheless he tried to be loyal; and in Castlereagh's frequent absence he was the government's leading spokesman in the Commons, well beyond his departmental brief. After the 'massacre' of Peterloo in 1819 – when the Manchester yeomanry fired on a crowd of peaceful demonstrators, killing eleven and injuring 400 – he strongly supported the infamous Six Acts by which the government attempted to outlaw further expressions of public discontent; and he continued to resist any concessions to democracy. Quite unfairly, Castlereagh drew most of the odium for the government's harsh measures – a reputation fixed for ever in Shelley's cruel lines:

I met Murder in the way—
He had a mask like Castlereagh.

– but Canning bore at least as much responsibility. In one piquant
debate in 1817, when the opposition raked up old allegations of
brutality and torture dating back to Castlereagh's suppression of
the Irish revolt twenty years before, Canning came powerfully
and generously to his defence. Generally, however, Canning's
dazzling oratory eclipsed his rival's plodding and often painfully
convoluted syntax. After three years of exemplary loyalty, carefully working his passage back to favour, Canning was once again
becoming dangerously frustrated.

He still wanted to be Leader of the House, and thought he
should be; but Castlereagh still blocked his way. By 1820 he was
once again threatening to resign. Liverpool half-offered a move
to the Home Office – a poisoned chalice at the best of times –
but Canning was not interested unless he could be leader as well,
assuming what he called Castlereagh's 'full inheritance'.[64] Liverpool
would have liked to accommodate him; but he could not risk
repeating the fiasco of 1809 by promising anything at the expense
of either Sidmouth or Castlereagh. Seeing no way forward,
Canning began to consider leaving politics altogether and securing
his still precarious finances by becoming Governor-General of
India when the current incumbent retired. But then he was driven
to resign over an entirely different matter: the trial of the unfortunate Queen Caroline, which dominated politics that year. After
years of adulterous exile in Italy, Caroline had returned to England
on her husband's accession to claim her rightful place as Queen.
King at last, however, George IV was now determined to divorce
her, even though his own adultery was no less flagrant. Public
sympathy was with the Queen and there were riots in her support.
Liverpool and his colleagues handled the matter as tactfully as
they could; but Canning was in a peculiarly uncomfortable position. Years earlier, before his marriage, he had been a close friend
of Caroline: he may even have been one of her lovers. This was
probably not the case, but the King believed it, and so it seems
did some of Canning's colleagues, including Castlereagh.[65]
Whatever the truth, Canning felt unable to be a party to Caroline's

83

prosecution, and so at the end of 1820 – for the fourth time in his stormy career – he resigned.

He did not want to resign. He could not afford to lose the ministerial salary, and he was well aware that his colleagues would think he was up to his 'monkey tricks' again; he was desperately anxious not to play his cards badly, as in 1806, 1809 and 1812, fearing that this time the result would be 'total and permanent exclusion from power'.[66] But he felt finally that honour left him no choice. Liverpool – afraid that he might join up with the Whigs – was happy to make it clear that the door remained open for him to return to the cabinet when the Queen's business was out of the way. Meanwhile Castlereagh wrote him a handsome – but subtly disingenuous – letter of regret:

> As the individual member of the Government who must feel your loss most seriously, both in the House of Commons and in the business of the Foreign Office . . . allow me . . . most cordially to thank you for the uniform attention with which you have followed up, and the kindness with which you have assisted me, in the business of the department for the conduct of which I am more immediately responsible.[67]

No doubt he meant it kindly. In view of the way the cards had fallen over the past ten years he could afford to be magnanimous. But Canning must have read these double-edged compliments with bitter irony.

Liverpool did try to bring Canning back almost immediately, now thinking of the Admiralty as a possible berth for him. But now it was the King – still furious over Canning's supposed intimacy with Caroline – who would not have it; and Liverpool's own position was not strong enough to defy the royal veto, especially since his other colleagues were still unenthusiastic. So Canning's thoughts turned again to India. In April 1821 he poured out his bitter sense of failure in further candid letters to his wife:

> What does the reputation of being the first speaker in the House of Commons do for me? Nothing. It only leads people to believe that *fine speaking* is not necessary for carrying on the affairs of the Government . . . but that business can go on very well without

84

it. And so it can. And the more it goes on without me the better. I am weary – and at 51 or thereabouts I cannot afford, either in the common or the moral sense of the word, to hazard new experiments, and new combinations, as I would with the possibility of 20 years before me. The next stage – whatever it be – must be decisive for life – and if it is to be as barren of advantage as all former steps have been I shall have done little for the comfort of old age, and of that of those whom I ought to have thought of long ago rather than of my own etiquette and points of honour.

He refused to 'play second fiddle to the end of my days . . . At 51 one must consider one's last card as being to be played – and with a view not so much to indefinite advance, as to secure retreat.'[68] He would not accept being Castlereagh's 'lieutenant-General' any longer, but said he would rather take up road-making 'upon Mr MacAdam's new principles' for his subsistence.[69]*

For his part Castlereagh was 'quite tired of all the discussion about Mr Canning and the changes in the Cabinet'. He told Mrs Arbuthnot – wife of the Tory party manager Charles Arbuthnot – that 'he wished he could slip his neck out of the collar and have done with the whole thing'.[70] That of course was just what Canning was waiting for him to do; but he had no real intention of retiring. After Castlereagh's death, Mrs Arbuthnot wrote that she used to reproach him for being too forgiving towards Canning, 'who had always caused jealousies and dissensions in the Cabinet'; but Castlereagh told her that 'he had had his struggle with Canning and had left him far behind, and that therefore he had no jealousy about him, and that he thought his talents would be useful to the public'. Mrs Arbuthnot added that Castlereagh 'did not think Canning an upright or honourable man, but still thought he might be made a useful person'.[71]

There seemed to be one last chance for Canning. At the beginning of 1822 Liverpool moved to strengthen his government by healing the nineteen-year-old rift with the Grenvillite group who had abandoned Pitt to join up with Fox in 1803. Grenville himself – Canning's old boss at the Foreign Office in 1796–99 – did not return

*John McAdam revolutionised road-building by his method of crushed stone mixed with tar. He was awarded £2,000 by Parliament in 1825.

to office, but his followers gained one cabinet post and several junior ones. Thus Pitt's old party was reunited for the first time for nearly twenty years, leaving only the old Foxite Whigs in opposition. There was just one exception: Canning, who saw himself above all others as Pitt's heir, was still excluded. By now he had practically made up his mind to go to India. He still rebelled against the idea of exile, however lucrative. But the promotion of the thirty-three-year-old Robert Peel to the cabinet as Home Secretary was the last straw. If Peel got the Home Office, he believed, 'the door is closed against me for ever'.[72] 'I see no imaginable combination of things through which I can ever again be involved in a political negotiation.'[73] Before Parliament rose for the summer recess he made what he thought would be his last speech in the arena he had dominated for so long, and was preparing to leave, when the door was suddenly opened for him again by an event at once shocking and deeply ironic.

For some time Castlereagh had been complaining of overwork. He was still carrying the principal burden of government business in the Commons on top of the Foreign Secretaryship. The previous year he had succeeded his father as second Marquess of Londonderry; but since this was still at this date an Irish peerage it offered no escape from the Commons. Over the summer his family and servants noticed that he was behaving strangely. He developed paranoid delusions, and believed that he was being blackmailed. The King, before leaving on his famous visit to Edinburgh, was worried about him and warned Liverpool that he should not be left alone. His wife locked away his pistols and his razors. But on 12 August, quite calmly, Castlereagh evaded his doctor and cut his throat with a small penknife.[74]

Suicide, like duelling, was not uncommon in the early nineteenth century. Within the last few years two prominent politicians – Samuel Whitbread in 1815 and Sir Samuel Romilly in 1818 – had taken their own lives. But Castlereagh's death was a great shock. He had been in office, with only three short intervals, for twenty-one of the last twenty-four years. He was unpopular in the country – there was an unseemly demonstration at his funeral – but well liked by his colleagues, an excellent manager of the Commons and a conscientious minister who had become, in ten years at the Foreign Office, the embodiment of Britain's standing in Europe. He might well have succeeded Liverpool in due course as Prime Minister. His death left a huge gap. Most obviously it transformed Canning's situation. Yet the initial assumption on all sides was that he would still go to India. 'Now what will come next?' Thomas Creevey asked himself. 'Will the perfidious Canning forego [*sic*] his Indian prospects – stay with his wife and daughter to succeed Castlereagh? I *think* not.'[75] Half the cabinet still distrusted him; the King could not wait to see him out of the country; while Canning had now persuaded himself that he could not afford to stay in England and was quite looking forward to ruling an empire on a salary six times that of a Secretary of State. Liverpool, however, wanted him back; and he was supported by the now immensely influential Duke of Wellington who persuaded the King to lift his veto. When it came down to it, Canning could not refuse: his life's ambition had always been in the House of Commons. This time, finally, he was being offered the leadership of the House as well as the Foreign Office – Castlereagh's 'whole inheritance'. It was ironic that he should achieve it only by his rival violently removing himself from the scene.

He still made a show of reluctance. 'I would that the offer had not come,' he wrote to his aged mother. 'The sacrifice of personal interest which I make to public duty is enormous.'[76] 'Public glory', he protested, meant 'private ruin'.[77] To his wife, however, he was more honest. He knew that fate had given him the chance to repair the disastrous error he had made ten years before.

> Do not let us fall into the traces of 1812 dearest love! The fatal decision which blasted all my prospects – threw away the good-will of the Sovereign, the Ministry and the House of Commons, and forfeited for me the most splendid situation in this country – in Europe – and in history, was founded upon a few cross words, and cold looks operating upon a temper vexed and tired with conflicting discussions.[78]

Thirteen years after leaving it, he had finally got his former job back, he wrote to a friend, 'ten years too late for enjoyment, and perhaps for advantage to the country'.[79] But there was still 'glory' to be won at the Foreign Office; and over the next five years he secured his reputation as one of the greatest Foreign

Secretaries in British history – building on, but also surpassing, the achievement of his predecessor. But he too found the strain too much for his health. When Liverpool's long reign ended in a fatal stroke in 1827 Canning too was dying. He finally grasped the premiership – still in the face of much misgiving and recrimination. But he lasted less than four months before following Castlereagh to an early grave. They are buried within a few feet of each other in Westminster Abbey.

Despite the little matter of their duel, Castlereagh and Canning have gone down in history not as rivals but as the two Foreign Secretaries, spanning seventeen years between them, who laid the foundations of Britain's foreign policy at the zenith of her imperial power in the nineteenth century. The Victorians tended to contrast their reputations, painting Castlereagh as the ally of Metternich who would have committed Britain to preserving the reactionary status quo in Europe, while crediting Canning with asserting Britain's difference from the continental empires and implicitly supporting liberal and nationalist movements in Italy, Spain, Belgium, Greece, Portugal and South America. Canning was Gladstone's hero, as Pitt had been Canning's. Modern historians, however, have seen a much greater continuity in their views. Castlereagh had already kept Britain out of the Holy Alliance. Although in the immediate aftermath of the war he did see value in the victorious powers continuing to work together to keep France in check and secure the basis of a lasting peace, by 1820 he was refusing to join the autocracies in declaring their right to suppress revolutions wherever they arose. In a classic paper which Canning acknowledged as the foundation of his own policy, Castlereagh declared that the quadruple alliance had been forged to combat the domination of Napoleonic France: it was never 'intended as a Union for the government of the world, or for the superintendence of the internal affairs of other states'.[80] When Canning recognised the independence of Spain's South American colonies, declaring in his most famous phrase that he was calling 'the New World into existence to redress the balance of the Old', he was following a course which Castlereagh too, before his death, knew could only be a matter of time. 'The only difference between him and Castlereagh,' Earl Grey noted as early as 1825, 'seems to me that [Canning] can make brilliant speeches.'[81] By the time Canning took over from Castlereagh in 1822 events had moved on seven years since Waterloo. Canning had the easier and more popular task of establishing Britain's stance of lofty distance from continental squabbles, which lasted – the Crimea apart – until 1914. He also articulated the policy better, and mobilised public opinion behind it to burnish his own reputation as the champion of British interests. Essentially, however, as the young Henry Kissinger wrote in 1957, 'The difference between Canning and Castlereagh was primarily a question of emphasis.'[82]

Both men defined themselves during their lifetime as the heirs of Pitt; they spent their careers in government combating the contagion of the French revolution, both at home and abroad, opposed by the straggling remnant of the Foxite Whigs. Hence in modern eyes they count – anachronistically – as 'Tories'. At the very end of his life, however, Canning's brief premiership split Liverpool's 'Tory' coalition, partly on personal grounds but mainly over Catholic emancipation, which he had always supported, but which Wellington, Peel and others still vehemently opposed (though the Duke was forced to concede it only two years later). After his death, most of Canning's followers eventually joined the Whigs, so that he came to be seen – despite his lifelong opposition to reform – as a proto-Liberal (and thus a suitable hero for Gladstone). Castlereagh, by contrast, though he had been equally – ever since his time in Ireland in 1798–1800 – an advocate of Catholic emancipation, and actually differed from Canning, over their long association, on very little except points of military strategy, was for ever associated with the repressive domestic measures of the Liverpool government after Waterloo, and is consequently remembered as a reactionary Tory. Such is the lottery of historical reputations.

So long as he was alive, Castlereagh won his political duel with Canning hands down, just as he did their real duel on Putney Heath. Time and again the tortoise blocked the path of the more brilliant hare. Just as Canning was on the point of giving up the race, however, Castlereagh's suicide gave his career another lease of life. Though he had only another five years to run, it was enough for Canning to win the history books.

Benjamin Disraeli and William Gladstone

Gladstone and Disraeli defined political rivalry in the nineteenth century. There were other powerful figures in the half-century after Waterloo – Liverpool, Wellington, Peel and Palmerston. But none of these had an opponent who was his equal, or captured the public imagination so dramatically as the titanic duel of opposites which improbably pitted a cynical Jewish novelist against a self-flagellating evangelical churchman in a contest to govern the greatest commercial empire of the age. Both were exceptional personalities, quite outside the normal categories of political life, the most unlikely leaders of their respective parties. Yet for nearly thirty years – from 1852 to 1880 – these two exotics alternated in office, first as Chancellor of the Exchequer, then as Prime Minister, loved and loathed in equal measure by their partisans, distrusted by many of their own colleagues, but creating around themselves the modern party system to address the expanding electorate via new media of transport and communication. Starting their careers in the rough but exclusive Georgian world of aristocratic patronage and pocket boroughs, they reached their apogee in the age of the railways, the telegraph, the mass meeting and High Victorian morality. Their images spawned a whole industry of pious commemorative plates and satirical chamber pots. The Queen herself doted on one of them and abhorred the other. And all the time they detested each other with a personal virulence unmatched by any other pair of opponents in British politics before or since.

Like Fox and Pitt, they were as different in habits, tastes and style as two men moving in the same society at the same time could be. Again like Fox and Pitt, they started out in the same party and for many years could have been colleagues had circumstances – and personal antipathy – not driven them apart. More radically than their eighteenth-century predecessors, however, Disraeli and Gladstone confounded the expectations that might have been predicted for each of them at the start of their careers. Whereas the positions Fox and Pitt adopted reflected their different temperaments, the ultimate political destinations of Disraeli and Gladstone seemed – superficially at least – to defy their backgrounds and personal tastes. The young Disraeli was a penniless adventurer who attended neither public school nor university but sowed his wild oats with the abandon of Fox, was baptised at the age of fourteen but never paid more than formal lip-service to Christianity and never ceased to pride himself on being an oriental outsider: yet he became leader of the Conservative party. Gladstone, by contrast, was conventionally educated at Eton and Christ Church, was only reluctantly deflected from taking holy orders and always treated politics as a form of practical religion: famously hailed at the age of thirty as 'the rising hope of those stern and unbending Tories',[1] he claimed Pitt, Canning and Peel as his mentors yet finished as leader of the Liberal party, regarded by many even in his own party as a dangerous radical. Both men traced extraordinary journeys, in opposite directions, across the complex landscape of Victorian Britain. Maybe this is why they hated each other so much.

They met for the first time at a dinner party in January 1835, when Disraeli was thirty and Gladstone twenty-five. Until then they had moved in entirely different worlds. Gladstone's early life was by far the easier. Son of a Liverpool merchant family whose wealth was derived partly from slave labour in the West Indies, he had risen effortlessly via Eton and the presidency of the Oxford Union to enter Parliament in 1832 for a seat in the gift of the Duke of Newcastle and was already Under-Secretary for War and Colonies in Peel's short-lived minority government in 1834–35. Though desperately earnest, and at this stage of his career largely preoccupied with arcane controversies of church politics, it was already obvious that he was destined for the top. At the very end of his life Disraeli began a novel whose principal character was a wicked caricature of the young Gladstone: 'He was essentially a prig, and among prigs there is a freemasonry which never fails. All the prigs spoke of him as the coming man.'[2]

Disraeli, conversely, was an outsider. His father, Isaac D'Israeli, was a naturalised Jewish *littérateur* who converted to Christianity when his eldest son was just entering his teens.* Though his two younger brothers went to Winchester, Benjamin was patchily educated at local schools and in his father's library, where he dreamed of achieving fame as a writer. Modelling himself on Byron, he tried to storm London society as an outrageous dandy, had several affairs with older married women, travelled in the Middle East (whereas Gladstone followed the more conventional Grand Tour of Europe), and published four more or less auto-biographical novels (with a curiously homoerotic undertone) which achieved some *succès de scandale* but made him little money.[3] He stood for Parliament four times between 1832 and 1835, partly to try another way to fame, partly to escape his debts. His luck changed when he became secretary to the former (and future) Tory Lord Chancellor, Lord Lyndhurst – a notorious old roué with whom he allegedly shared a mistress. It was at dinner at Lyndhurst's that he first encountered Gladstone.

Each apparently thought the other 'rather dull' – Disraeli scoffed that the main course, a swan stuffed with truffles, was 'the best company there' – though Gladstone later recalled being amazed by the 'singularity' of Disraeli's clothes.[4] They had nothing whatever in common, and no one present could have guessed that their lives would become entwined. For another few years they still had little if anything to do with one another. In 1836–37 Disraeli published two more romantic novels before he finally – at the general election following the accession of the eighteen-year-old Queen Victoria – managed to get himself elected for Maidstone. Gladstone's more sober progress was epitomised in the title of his first book, published

---

*Disraeli dropped the apostrophe from his name in 1822 – though his opponents continued to use it for many years to emphasise his Jewish origins, and habitually referred to him as 'the Jew'.

the following year: *The State in its Relations with the Church*. They did have one thing in common: both married in 1839. Gladstone finally overcame extreme diffidence with women to marry the daughter of a Welsh Anglican squire who bore him nine children and eventually brought him the substantial estate of Hawarden, in Cheshire. Disraeli by contrast married frankly for her money a widow twelve years older than himself who paid his debts and brought him a town house in Mayfair. They had no children, but he came genuinely to love his Mary Anne.

Politics at the beginning of Victoria's reign was entering a period of exceptional fluidity. The long hegemony of Pitt's heirs and successors – Liverpool, Canning and Wellington – had ended with the passage of Catholic emancipation in 1829 which split the Tories and brought Fox's disciples out of the wilderness at last. The Whig ministries of Grey and Melbourne carried the great parliamentary Reform Bill of 1832 and a number of ameliorative social reforms against a threatening background of poor harvests and Chartist agitation, while the Tories in opposition – as always after a heavy defeat – reinvented themselves under Sir Robert Peel – a middle-class moderniser who reflected the rising industrial and commercial interest. In 1841 Melbourne's government fell and the Tories won the ensuing election. But Peel – like Pitt two generations earlier – was committed to the gradual extension of free trade. In 1846, partly in response to famine in Ireland, he determined to repeal the Corn Laws, which imposed a protective duty on imported corn: this U-turn outraged the landed interest, and the party split again, this time permanently. Repeal was carried with the help of Whig votes, but Peel was defeated immediately afterwards and Lord John Russell took his place, inaugurating a Whig hegemony that lasted for nearly thirty years. In this defining crisis of the mid-century Gladstone and Disraeli took opposite sides.

When Peel formed his government Gladstone was initially disappointed to be offered merely the vice-presidency of the Board of Trade. But he was promoted to the cabinet within two years, was quickly converted to free trade and did much of the detailed number-crunching for Peel's tariff-reducing budgets. 'Gladstone could do in four hours what it took any other man sixteen to do,' one colleague wrote, 'and he worked sixteen hours a day.'[5] In 1845, however, he resigned – over a convoluted matter of conscience concerning the Catholic Church in Ireland – before the Corn Law crisis broke, lost his seat and found himself out of Parliament at the crucial time. Disraeli wrote to his sister that Gladstone's explanation of his resignation was 'involved & ineffective. He may have an *avenir* but I hardly think it'.[6] Meanwhile Disraeli had been passed over, despite begging shamelessly for office. 'All is over,' he despaired to Sarah.[7] In fact there was no reason why Peel should have found room for such a posturing young spark. But Disraeli determined to make Peel pay for his omission. He attached himself to a group of aristocratic rebels who styled themselves 'Young England', began to gain a reputation as a witty performer in the House and wrote two more novels, more political than their predecessors: *Coningsby* (1844) and *Sybil* (1845), in which he satirised Peel as a narrow-minded technocrat lacking in principle and vision.

Disraeli's only principle was self-advancement. The fourteenth Earl of Derby, his leader for more than twenty years, told Prince Albert that 'he did not think Mr Disraeli had ever had a strong feeling one way or the other about protection or free trade'.[8] But by placing his sharp tongue at the service of the largely inarticulate Tory squires who opposed repeal he not only helped to destroy Peel but made himself effectively second-in-command – under Lord George Bentinck – of the protectionist rump that remained when the party split. All the young talent in the party, including Gladstone, followed Peel into the wilderness. The Peelites never forgave Disraeli for his cynical and destructive role in 1846. But when Bentinck died in 1848, he became the effective leader of what remained of the Tory party in the Commons (under Derby in the Lords). Little as they trusted him, they had no one else. With help from the Bentincks he acquired a country seat at Hughenden near High Wycombe; he began to dress more soberly, speak less extravagantly and gradually transformed himself into a respectable, if still unusual, Tory leader.

Gladstone meanwhile found himself at thirty-six out of office, without a party and temporarily without a seat.* His promising

---

*At least he was better off in one respect than Churchill, who found himself in 1922, at the age of forty-eight, 'without an office, without a seat, without a party and without an appendix'.[9]

career appeared to be in ruins. He was tormented by family problems and tortuous religious crises, while for a time his notorious
nocturnal 'rescue work' with London prostitutes seriously upset his
mental balance. When he returned to the Commons (for Oxford
University) in 1847 he concerned himself mainly with church
matters. Russell's Whig government was kept alive for six years by
the mutual antagonism which prevented the Peelites and the protec-
tionists from combining against it. Gladstone's natural political
home was still the Tory party: but Disraeli was an obstacle to co-
operation. 'It is a very unsatisfactory state of things,' Gladstone
wrote to his father in 1849, 'to have to deal with a man whose
objects appear to be those of personal ambition and who is not
thought to have any strong convictions of any kind.'[10]

For his part Disraeli wanted to bring Gladstone back. He quickly
realised that protection was a dead end: it was no good being leader
of a party that had little chance of ever winning a majority. When
Peel died in 1850 Disraeli urged Derby to drop it ('Protection is
not only dead but damned') in order to lure the leading Peelites –
Gladstone and Sir James Graham were the only two he thought
'of first-rate calibre' – back into the Tory fold.[11] To this end he was
even willing to cede Gladstone the leadership of the House. In
February 1851 Gladstone came close to joining a prospective Derby
government; but Derby – unable to ditch his convictions quite so
lightly as his lieutenant – reneged at the last moment. Disraeli was
furious, but Gladstone was probably relieved. By now he had begun
to identify Disraeli as the villain of the sort of high-minded moral
drama he needed if he was to resurrect his stalled career.

Some years later Gladstone wrote an unpublished article
attributing what he saw as the corruption of honest politics to 'the
subtle self-seeking which History will probably impute to Mr
Disraeli'. There was no need, he pronounced pompously, 'to enter
into the moral of his singular career: and no-one would gratuitously
enter upon a task which it would be so difficult to execute with
fairness, at once to him, to the country, and to public virtue'.[12]
Gladstone already had good reason to dislike Disraeli, personally
as a rootless adventurer and adulterer, politically as the unprincipled opportunist who had harried Peel to an early grave. But by
the time he wrote this he had elevated Disraeli into the very

embodiment of evil in public life, whom it was his God-inspired mission to combat. It was a view from which he never departed for the rest of his long life.

The decisive moment occurred in 1852, when Russell's government fell and Derby this time accepted the Queen's commission to form a minority Tory government. (The Peelites again refused to join.) It was an exceptionally inexperienced cabinet – comparable only to Ramsay MacDonald's first Labour cabinet of 1924, or Tony Blair's of 1997. Hitherto only Pitt in 1782 had ever led the Commons with no previous experience of office: but Disraeli had to become Chancellor as well, because there was no one else. Even his chutzpah hesitated at this challenge: but Derby told him airily: 'You know as much as Mr Canning did. They give you the figures.'[13] Gladstone wrote to his wife that 'Disraeli could not have been worse placed than at the exchequer.'[14] But by taking the job Disraeli put himself firmly in Gladstone's sights, since finance was Gladstone's particular forte and he was burning to become Chancellor himself. Within a few months he was giving notice to Lord Aberdeen (the Peelites' leader) that 'I for one am not prepared to accept him as a financial organ, or to be responsible for what he may propose in his present capacity'; he considered every speech Disraeli made 'more quackish . . . than its predecessor'.[15] The Chancellor's 'unscrupulousness and second motives' made him 'at once the necessity of Lord Derby and his curse'.[16]

Inexperienced as he was, Disraeli had an exceptionally difficult financial inheritance to deal with: not only did he seem to face a deficit – actually the Treasury figures were wrong – but his backbenchers expected him to do something to compensate for the loss of protection. His response – in a budget speech lasting five hours, delivered to a hostile House containing three critical former Chancellors – was an ingenious ragbag of improvisations, introducing differential scales of income tax for various favoured interests. Gladstone immediately judged it 'the least conservative budget I have ever known', and one marred by 'fundamental faults of principle which it is impossible to overlook or compound with'.[17] To his wife he wrote that he felt 'a long speech fermenting within me and I feel as a loaf might in the oven'.[18]

On 16 December Disraeli, recovering from flu and somewhat

the worse for drink, wound up the budget debate with another brilliant speech lasting two and a quarter hours, much of it delivered against the background of a dramatic thunderstorm. He began disarmingly by admitting: 'I was not born and bred a Chancellor of the Exchequer; I am one of the Parliamentary rabble.'[19] But he went on to defy the majority opposite with a series of insolent personal retorts which silenced his critics in turn. 'Argument, satire, sarcasm, invective, all were abundant and of the first class,' wrote the radical John Bright. 'He fought for his life and never a man fought more desperately or with more skill and power.'[20] Even Gladstone found it 'grand; I think the most powerful I ever heard from him', though he thought it 'disgraced by shameless personalities . . . I was on tenterhooks', except when his 'superlative acting and brilliant oratory from time to time absorbed me and made me quite *forget* that I had to follow him'.[21]

Gladstone did not have to follow him at all. When Disraeli sat down exhausted at 1 a.m. the House prepared to divide. But then, against all precedent, Gladstone – a mere private member – rose to reply.

> He rose choked with passion, for which he could find no vent in words, and his first utterances were the signal for fresh explosions from each side of the House alternately . . . His usually calm features were livid and distorted with passion, his voice shook, and those who watched him feared an outbreak incompatible with parliamentary rules.[22]

Gradually he gained a hearing – and control of himself. Disraeli's gibes had given him the opening he needed for what was actually a well-planned intervention. Once he had got the attention of the House he spoke for as long as Disraeli – another two and a quarter hours – 'to show the conservative party how their leader is hoodwinking and bewildering them'.[23] First he rebuked Disraeli for his lack of 'decency and propriety' in maligning his predecessors; then he denounced the budget as a betrayal of Peel's legacy of financial probity, of which he had appointed himself the almost sacerdotal guardian. Finally, and most woundingly, he treated Disraeli as a lightweight charlatan who did not understand finance and had fiddled his figures to suggest a non-existent surplus.[24] The whole performance was immodestly designed to advertise his own claim to the Treasury as decisively as it smashed Disraeli. When the House finally voted at 3.45 a.m. the government was defeated by 19 votes. It would probably have been defeated anyway. But Gladstone's astonishing *tour de force* made him appear to be the architect of its defeat.

This was the moment when the Gladstone–Disraeli duel really took off. Contemporaries recognised the epic quality of the scene. 'Like two of Sir Walter Scott's champions,' *The Times* reported next day, 'these redoubtable antagonists gathered up all their forces for the final struggle, and encountered each other in mid-career.'[25] Disraeli's pre-eminent modern biographer, Robert Blake, described its significance with graphic eloquence:

> The artist who wished to immortalize, as if upon a Greek vase, an instant of time that would illuminate the political history of the mid-Victorian era would have done well to choose the moment when Gladstone rose to answer Disraeli at one o'clock in the morning of December 17, 1852; the faces of the members, pallid in the flaring gaslight, contorted, some with anger, some with delight, arms gesticulating in hostility or applause; Gladstone on his feet, handsome, tall, still possessing the youthful good looks, the open countenance which had charmed his contemporaries at Eton and Christ Church; Disraeli seated on the Treasury Bench, aquiline, faintly sinister, listening with seeming indifference to the eloquent rebuke of the orator. It was a scene which was not easily forgotten. It coloured the parliamentary life of a whole generation.[26]

Gladstone's speech was more than just a parliamentary attack: it was a declaration of war. He was geared up to an extraordinarily high state of righteous exaltation. The next day he gloated to Catherine about having been 'able to screw Disraeli up to the mark', and admitted: 'I have never gone through so exciting a passage of parliamentary life.' But then, characteristically, he also tried to pretend that it was nothing personal: 'I am told he is much stung by what I said. I am very sorry it fell to me to say it. God knows I had no wish to give him pain, and really with my deep sense of his gifts, I would only pray they might be well used.'[27] This was humbug. A few days later – the day the Derby government resigned – he was left in no doubt of the feelings he had aroused when he was surrounded by a mob of drunken Tory MPs in the Carlton Club and was lucky to escape without a beating.[28]

Up till that point Disraeli had not seen Gladstone as a personal enemy. Though amused by his Jesuitical religiosity, he claimed that Gladstone was 'the only one of the Peelites between whom and myself there was some inkling of sympathy'.[29] That changed overnight on 16–17 December. When Derby's government fell, the Peelites joined the Whigs in a coalition in which they took all the best jobs: Aberdeen was Prime Minister and Gladstone inevitably the new Chancellor. Privately Disraeli was confident that the new ministry would be 'brief, its end ignominious', and expected to be back in office very soon.[30] Meanwhile the outgoing and incoming Chancellors became involved in a childish spat which perfectly symbolised their new relations. The convention was that the new incumbent paid his predecessor the cost of the furniture in 11 Downing Street. But a new arrangement had recently been agreed by which the furniture would be leased from the Office of Works. Gladstone thought this meant he no longer had to pay Disraeli, and declined to do so. Meanwhile he expected Disraeli to pass on to him the Chancellor's robe, which both believed to have belonged to Pitt. In an increasingly icy exchange of letters Disraeli continued to demand that Gladstone pay him for the furniture, while saying nothing about the robe. In fact Gladstone was in the wrong about the furniture, Disraeli about the robe. But Disraeli skilfully used Gladstone's obstinacy about the furniture to diddle him out of the robe. The correspondence began with cool correctness: 'I remain, dear Sir, faithfully yours, W.E. Gladstone'. 'I have the honor [*sic*] to remain, dear Sir, your obedient servant, B. Disraeli'. But it soon descended into barbed impersonality:

> Mr Disraeli regrets very much that he is obliged to say that Mr Gladstone's letter repudiating his obligation to pay for the furniture of the official residence is not satisfactory ... As Mr Gladstone seems to be in some perplexity on the subject, Mr Disraeli recommends him to consult Sir Charles Wood, who is a man of the world.*

---

* Sir Charles Wood was Disraeli's immediate predecessor as Chancellor.

To which Gladstone retorted:

> It is highly unpleasant to Mr W. E. Gladstone to address Mr Disraeli
> without the usual terms of courtesy, but he abstains from them only
> because he perceives they are unwelcome.[31]

Gladstone did eventually pay for the furniture, but Disraeli kept
the robe, which is displayed at Hughenden to this day.

Disraeli had the better of this trivial dispute; but Gladstone now
commanded the big stage. In April he presented his first budget:
the first of nine over the next twelve years, a magisterial sequence
which still gives him an unchallenged claim to be the greatest
Chancellor of all time.* In another stupendous speech of five hours
he made good his claim to the mantle of Pitt and Peel, cleverly
renewing income tax for seven years – scrapping Disraeli's objection-
able differentiated scales – while still promising its eventual
abolition, abolishing a lot of duties and cutting more; above all
making fiscal policy the instrument of a higher moral purpose and
restoring – as he believed – principle and probity to public life.
Unlike Disraeli the year before, he had the benefit of a surplus to
play with, as well as a Commons majority behind him. But both
men knew that whichever of them solved the income tax problem
would reap a big political dividend for his party: with this budget
Gladstone went a long way towards securing it. Meanwhile he
appeared to have established himself as the pivotal figure on the
political scene for years to come. 'The Budget . . . has raised
Gladstone to a great political elevation,' wrote the diarist Charles
Greville, 'and what is of far greater consequence than the measure
itself, has given the country assurance of a *man* equal to great
political necessities and fit to lead parties and direct governments.'[32]

Disraeli by contrast was thoroughly eclipsed. He tried lamely
to claim that Gladstone had only followed his example. In an
anonymous newspaper article in 1853 he wrote scornfully of the
'monomania of Mr Gladstone, which is always to out-herod

---

*Gordon Brown introduced more between 1997 and 2007, but even before the
'credit crunch' of 2008–09 his greatest admirers would not have put him in
Gladstone's league as a financial reformer.

Mr Disraeli in everything'.[33] Privately he talked of abandoning politics and going back to literature. He had reason to be tempted. The previous year a cheap edition of his novels had sold 300,000 copies. He had also achieved the popular accolade of a place in Madame Tussaud's waxworks. (Gladstone, surprisingly, had to wait until 1870 for this honour.) He might not have made a great success as Chancellor, but he was unquestionably a celebrity. Yet politics was now in his blood. 'His whole soul,' Mary Anne wrote, 'is devoted to politics and ambition.'[34] Having once entered the great game he was determined to win it. In order to rebuild the Tory party as a vehicle capable of lifting him to power, however, he recognised that he must draw Gladstone back to the party, since it was now clear that no strong government could be formed without him. This, paradoxically, was his purpose over the next six years.

The first good opportunity arose in 1855. The Aberdeen government had got itself embroiled in the Crimean War; and the catalogue of unpreparedness and maladministration which the war revealed led to a Commons motion for an inquiry on which the government – despite a powerful speech from Gladstone – was defeated. Derby then tried to form a coalition to include the heavyweights of all three groups – Tory, Whig and Peelite. After fifteen years as a rumbustious Foreign Secretary under Grey, Melbourne and Russell, the seventy-year-old Palmerston had been moved to the Home Office under Aberdeen. There was now popular clamour for him to take charge of the war. Derby also hoped to retain Gladstone at the Treasury. In fact Palmerston refused to serve under Derby. But Gladstone was willing, so long as at least one other Peelite, probably Graham, was included as well. 'A strong sentiment of revulsion from Disraeli personally,' he noted, '. . . was alone sufficient to deter me absolutely from a merely personal and separate reunion.'[35] On these terms he expected to continue in office. But Derby failed to invite Graham, and so lost Gladstone too. Disraeli was again furious. He had believed that Conservative reunion was almost 'an accomplished fact', and looked forward to forming 'a strong Government, which will astonish the world'.[36] But Derby – whose drive for power was never strong – believed the country was crying out for Palmerston. He stepped aside, and Palmerston – still nominally a Whig though in practice thoroughly conservative and effectively independent – eventually became Prime Minister. 'Our chief has again bolted,' Disraeli wrote disgustedly to Lady Londonderry.[37] Gladstone felt equally let down. 'I think that Lord Derby's error in not forming an administration was palpable and even gross,' he wrote years later. 'None of the three occasions when he took office offered him so fine an opportunity as this . . . but he missed it.'[38] For once Disraeli and Gladstone were agreed. Both were equally appalled at the aged Palmerston becoming premier. They had been willing to serve together in the same cabinet. Who knows where that might have led? The next day they chanced to run into each other in the House of Lords. On an impulse, Gladstone offered his hand, 'which was very kindly accepted'.[39] They shook hands; but the reconciliation was momentary.

Gladstone's dilemma was that he disapproved of Palmerston almost as much as he did Disraeli, and for much the same reasons: 'Pam' was a buccaneering old Regency buck who had survived into the Victorian age. Nevertheless, he was persuaded to carry on as Chancellor. After just two weeks, however, he resigned, with his two Peelite colleagues, in protest at Palmerston's acceptance of an inquiry into the war, which he regarded as an outrageous assertion of parliamentary power over the executive. His overweening behaviour during these weeks – he refused to serve not only under Derby but also under Russell and Lansdowne, thereby ensuring exactly the outcome he least wanted – cast doubt on his judgement, not to say his temper: he might be indispensable, but he was also exceedingly difficult to work with. Now he was frustrated at having his great work at the Treasury interrupted. 'I greatly felt being turned out of office,' he told his friend Bishop Wilberforce. 'I saw great things to do. I longed to do them. I am losing the best years of my life out of my natural service.' Yet he added: 'I have never ceased to rejoice that I am not in office under Palmerston.'[40] His problem was that – like Lloyd George in the 1920s – he was a dominant individual lacking the support of a major party. He desperately wanted to get back into office; but the Peelites were too small (and fading) a group to sustain him, while he could not stomach either Palmerston or Disraeli. For the present there was little he could do. He closed his London house and retired to Hawarden to write an eccentric book on Homer in which he tried to reconcile his reverence for the classics with his Christian faith, expending his thwarted energy in strenuous bursts of tree-felling.

Disraeli tried again in 1858. Following their handshake in 1855 there was talk of a 'Gladstone–Dizzy coalition'[41] and renewed speculation that Disraeli might be willing to cede the leadership of the Commons. But Gladstone remained elusive until March 1857, when he came storming back to deliver two powerful philippics – one denouncing Sir George Cornewall Lewis's budget almost as violently as he had attacked Disraeli's in 1852, the other condemning Palmerstonian gunboat diplomacy in China. On both issues Disraeli lent discreet support to Gladstone's fulminations; and on the second the government was unexpectedly defeated. But Palmerston simply appealed to the country and came back with an increased majority. Within a year, however, Disraeli's skilful parliamentary generalship contrived another defeat on a fairly trivial matter. This time Palmerston petulantly resigned, and Derby, showing more mettle than in 1855, formed his second minority administration. *The Times* published a list of the likely cabinet, with Gladstone as Chancellor and Disraeli as Foreign Secretary. But the Peelites again refused to join – Roy Jenkins comments that they were becoming 'a group of vestal virgins'[42] – so Disraeli returned to the Treasury. This time he was careful to frame his budget on sound Peelite principles, and Gladstone gave it his warm approval; so in May 1858, when a vacancy arose, Derby made him another offer. Disraeli was no longer willing to give up the leadership of the House; but Gladstone might have either India or the Colonial Office.

Some of his friends encouraged Gladstone to accept, even though it meant serving under 'D'Israeli'. 'Side by side,' Graham assured him, 'you would soon virtually supersede him . . . and I feel certain that in the Commons pre-eminence would be yours, let the official arrangements be what they may.' He should rejoin his old party before it was too late.[43] Aberdeen's advice, however, was the opposite. In 'this age of progress', he argued, the future lay not with the Tories but with the emerging Liberals.[44] Gladstone agreed with Aberdeen. Behind his pose of righteous humility he had a well-developed instinct for power. Palmerston, now seventy-four, could not be around for very much longer: the leadership of the

Whig–Liberal alliance would then be his for the taking. Disraeli, on the other hand, was only five years older than himself. If he rejoined the Tories they would be jockeying for control of the same party for the rest of their lives.

At this point Disraeli made an extraordinary direct appeal, urging that it was 'of paramount importance in the public interests' that Gladstone should join the Derby government. Its apparently artless candour is so unlike Disraeli's normal style that one has to wonder what he was up to. He admitted that for the past eight years 'our mutual relations have formed the greatest difficulty in accomplishing a result which I have always anxiously desired'. Claiming that 'instead of thrusting myself into the foremost place' he had always been willing to make any sacrifice to secure Conservative reunion, he suggested that it was now Gladstone's turn to be 'magnanimous', modestly citing the precedent of Canning's willingness to serve under Castlereagh in 1809.

> Mr Canning was superior to Lord Castlereagh in capacity, in acquirements, in eloquence, but he joined Lord C . . . when the state of the tory party rendered it necessary. That was an enduring and, on the whole, not an unsatisfactory connection, and it certainly terminated very gloriously for Mr Canning.

'I may be removed from the scene,' he added darkly – almost seeming to hint that he might follow Castlereagh's grisly example – 'or I may wish to be removed from the scene. Every man performs his office, and there is a Power, greater than ourselves, that disposes of all this.' He ended with an almost grovelling assurance that even if 'party necessities retain me formally in the chief post . . . your shining qualities would always render you supreme'.

> If you join Lord Derby's Cabinet, you will meet there some warm personal friends; all its members are your admirers. You may place me in neither category, but in that, I assure you, you have ever been sadly mistaken.[45]

What Gladstone made of this gushing missive – particularly the clumsy reference to a Higher Power – can only be imagined. His reply was stiff and characteristically convoluted, denying any personal animosity but still insisting that 'the difficulties ... are broader than you may have supposed'.

> You assure me that I have ever been mistaken in failing to place you among my friends or admirers. Again I pray you to let me say that I have never known you penurious in admiration towards anyone who had the slightest claim to it, and that at no period of my life, not even during the limited one when we were in sharp political conflict, have I either felt any enmity towards you, or believed that you felt any towards me.

He could not join any government, he explained, on the strength of his party connections, but must consider 'what are the conditions which make harmonious and effective co-operation in cabinet possible ... and what change would be requisite in the constitution of the present government, in order to make any change worth a trial'.

> I state these points fearlessly and without reserve, for you have yourself well reminded us that there is a Power beyond us which disposes of what we are and do, and I find the limits of choice in public life to be very narrow.[46]

In fact Gladstone had already made his choice. But what of Disraeli? Was he genuinely seeking to persuade Gladstone to come over? Or disingenuously trying to ensure that he did no such thing? 'I wish you could have induced Gladstone to join Lord Derby's Government ... in 1858,' he wrote to Bishop Wilberforce four years later. 'It was not my fault that he did not. I almost went on my knees to him.'[47] But nothing Disraeli did was ever straightforward. Most likely he was half sincere: he probably calculated, on the one hand, that the Tories without Gladstone would remain a permanent minority, so it was worth some grovelling to try to win him over; alternatively, as he suggested to the editor of *The Times*, Gladstone's refusing a fair offer might 'work for our advantage in public opinion'.[48] On the other hand, if he could once lure him back into a Tory government Disraeli probably reckoned he could handle him, or outmanoeuvre him, to his own advantage. Gladstone had already resigned from office twice in the past twelve years and might well be provoked into doing so again. By contrast Disraeli was adept at playing a long game.

Within months Gladstone gave a perfect illustration of his capacity to self-destruct. Blocked politically, and obsessed with his Homeric studies, he accepted a bizarre mission to inquire into the government of the Ionian islands, which had been a British protectorate since 1815. The invitation came officially from Disraeli's fellow-novelist Edward Bulwer-Lytton, then serving briefly as Colonial Secretary, who thought it 'a masterstroke';[49] but many saw Disraeli's hand in it. 'I was privy to the plot,' Disraeli admitted, 'but never supposed it wd result in anything but endless correspondence.' Gladstone's friends begged him to decline, fearing that it would marginalise him; but vanity and stubbornness induced him to accept and in November 1858 he sailed for Corfu, where he promptly sacked the High Commissioner and proposed taking the position himself. Disraeli could not believe his luck. 'Now that we have got him down,' he was reported to have said, 'let us keep him down.' The government quickly approved his appointment; but Gladstone had failed to realise that accepting the office would oblige him to give up his seat in Parliament – a detail that had not escaped Disraeli. As soon as he understood the position Gladstone resigned and returned hurriedly to England to secure his re-election. He now saw that Disraeli had made him a laughing-stock, and was heard at a dinner party vowing to be avenged by 'dethroning Disraeli'.[50]

In fact Gladstone played no part in the fall of Derby's second government a few months later. It was widely agreed that the 1832 franchise settlement needed bringing up to date, so in early 1859 Disraeli tried to seize the initiative by introducing a new reform bill. Gladstone supported Disraeli's measure, without enthusiasm but to try to get the question settled. It was defeated, however – as constitutional reforms so often are – by an unholy combination of Russell, who wanted to go further, and Palmerston, who wanted no reform at all. Derby went to the country and gained some seats; but the Tories were still short of a majority, so he resigned. All that the election had achieved was to consolidate the anti-Conservative coalition. In June 1859 the three strands – Whigs, Radicals and Peelites – came together to form the Liberal party. Yet Gladstone's behaviour, at this watershed, was baffling. He did not attend the critical meeting at Willis's Rooms, and then voted with the government on the confidence motion which spelled its defeat. Forced finally to choose, he seemed to be about to rejoin the Tories. He would still have preferred a Derby–Palmerston combination. Yet when that proved impossible he accepted the Treasury again – 'my old office'[51] – under Palmerston. Indeed he insisted on it. His vote seems to have been no more than a gesture to his past – or a way of demonstrating his indispensability. He still had misgivings about Palmerston, but persuaded himself that the old devil's support for Italian independence – one of Gladstone's pet causes – outweighed his other vices; and there was still the reassuring fact of Palmerston's age. So he embraced Palmerston – and Liberalism – and turned his back finally on Disraeli and the Tories.

Now at last the two rivals were definitively in different parties. 'I am afraid that the truce between us is over,' Gladstone wrote to his wife, 'and that we shall have to pitch in as before.'[52] For the next thirteen years, until Disraeli went to the Lords, they faced each other directly across the floor of the House, champions of their respective parties, usually following one another in debate, alternating between government and opposition as the advantage ebbed back and forth between them.

At first it was Gladstone who dominated. Back at the Treasury, he was in his element – and this time there was no war to derail him. Over the next seven years he resumed the sequence of great budgets which established the framework of late Victorian finance which endured well into the twentieth century. Among other landmarks, his 1860 budget finally confirmed income tax as a permanent feature of the fiscal landscape, while he continued to reduce the role of indirect taxation. His relationship with Palmerston was as fraught as expected, and he was constantly on the brink of resignation. Nevertheless Gladstone was – in Greville's words – 'now *the* great man of the day'.[53] His command of detail, combined with his moral earnestness and his torrential eloquence, gave him an awesome power in the House: and he did not hesitate to use it. 'To smash an antagonist across the House of Commons,' he confessed to a female admirer, 'is sometimes not disagreeable.'[54] For the moment Disraeli could not compete, and learned to keep his head down. 'He betrays in the House of

Commons', Greville noted, 'a sort of consciousness of his inferiority to Gladstone, and of fear of encountering him in debate.'[55] Facing growing criticism from his backbenchers, he offered to resign the Tory leadership; but the party still had no one who could do better, so he carried on.

Yet even in these years he scored some minor victories. By contrast with Gladstone's passionate engagement he developed a pose of studied impassivity – not so insolent as in his youth, but languidly sardonic. Like a matador teasing a bull, he could easily enrage Gladstone with his barbed pinpricks. It was fortunate, he once teased, that Gladstone did not yet lead the House since this 'proud post' was not a job for anyone 'who had any regard for his nervous system'. 'From what I have observed of the right hon. Gentleman's temperament,' he suggested, the Treasury gave 'ample opportunity to his eager mind and impetuous rhetoric'.[56] Moreover he was adept at exploiting divisions in the cabinet. In May 1860, for instance, knowing that Palmerston disliked his Chancellor's proposed abolition of duty on paper, he launched a withering attack, mixing fiscal arguments against the loss of revenue with shrewd *ad hominem* criticism of Gladstone's imperious manner, mocking his sometimes impenetrable verbosity:

> ... with all the mysterious dogmatism he knows so well how to assume when it suits him – contradicting himself as he constantly does with rapid incoherence, but covering his contradictions with that robe of glittering phraseology which prevents one from immediately detecting the weakness of his argument.[57]

The government's majority fell to nine, and the Lords – with Palmerston's barely disguised encouragement – threw the proposal out. Gladstone was humiliated but did not resign.

The next year Gladstone determined to prevent such piecemeal defeats by framing his budget for the first time as a single bill, while Palmerston – still feeling no obligation to support his Chancellor – gave his party virtually a free vote. Disraeli sensed an unprecedented opportunity to defeat the budget, which surely would have brought Gladstone's – and possibly the government's – resignation. Both men were keyed up for the crucial division.

But some twenty Tories unaccountably stayed away, allowing the government to win by 15 votes. 'In the very hour of victory,' Disraeli lamented, 'I had the mortification ... to see a division of my own troops march away from the field of contest.'[58] Gladstone conversely celebrated 'one of the greatest nights on the whole of my recollection'.[59] 'The ascendancy of Gladstone is daily more conspicuous,' one Radical MP recorded. 'D'Israeli courted defeat and won it.'[60] It was now the latter's turn to consider resignation, but again he was persuaded to stay on.

In 1862 Gladstone opened a new front in political warfare by making two triumphant speaking tours, first to Manchester and then to Newcastle, where he addressed huge audiences and was acclaimed by enthusiastic crowds. This was deeply shocking to Victorian convention, which held that political debate should be confined to Parliament and deprecated what was called agitation 'out of doors'. But Gladstone's tax-cutting budgets had made him a hero to the rising class of artisans. Having chosen the side of 'the future', he was beginning to realise that there was a powerful new constituency in the great industrial centres which he could make his own. So often frustrated at Westminster, he relished his ability to command a bigger stage in the country. Like most nicknames, the sobriquet 'the People's William' was originally conferred derisively; but it stuck. In 1864 he confirmed his rapid evolution towards the left by suggesting – subject to characteristically tortuous qualifications – that 'every man ... not presumably incapacitated by some consideration of personal unfitness or political danger' was 'morally entitled to come within the pale of the constitution' – that is, deserved the vote.[61] Around the same time he abandoned Tory Oxford before it abandoned him and sought a more popular constituency in South Lancashire. 'He is a dangerous man', Palmerston warned. 'Keep him in Oxford and he is partially muzzled, but send him elsewhere and he will run wild.'[62] Addressing his new constituents for the first time Gladstone duly told them: 'At last, my friends, I am come among you "unmuzzled".'[63] 'Gladstone will soon have it all his own way,' Palmerston predicted, 'and whenever he gets my place, we shall have strange doings.'[64]

Disraeli could not compete with Gladstone's new-found populism, so he deplored his vulgarity instead. But he knew that he had been upstaged, likening himself to 'an actor without an audience'.[65] He was getting old – he turned sixty in 1864 – and seemed to be in failing health. 'He has lost his former vivacity,' Derby's son Stanley noted, 'and sleeps much in his seat.'[66] In truth, politics offered little to arouse him. At the 1865 election the government retained its majority almost undented: Palmerston seemed likely to go on for ever. 'The leadership of hopeless opposition is a gloomy affair,' Disraeli reflected, 'and there is little distinction when your course is not associated with the possibility of future power.'[67] His ambition still burned, but his prospects looked bleak: like Churchill at the same age – but with much less experience of office – he seemed doomed to be remembered as a brilliant failure.

Then Palmerston's death in the autumn of 1865 changed everything. So long as he was alive party lines were blurred and allegiances confused. The moment he died the healthy 'binary' system which had been ruptured in 1846 was restored almost overnight. Gladstone was now liberated – as Palmerston had predicted – to come out as an unqualified Liberal; while the Tories were free to be unambiguously conservative. Although it was not until 1882 that W. S. Gilbert wrote in *Iolanthe* that

> Every boy and every gal
> > That's born into the world alive
> Is either a little Liberal
> > Or else a little Conservative![68]

in practice that era – which actually only lasted until 1886 – began with Palmerston's death. In the short term Russell succeeded to the premiership, fourteen years after he had last held it; but he was seventy-three, and now sat in the Lords, so Gladstone was leader in the Commons at last, as well as the undisputed leader-in-waiting. Russell immediately reopened the question of parliamentary reform, which Palmerston had blocked for the past seven years. In principle this opened up a clear left–right divide, with the Liberals still holding a comfortable majority to push through their legislation. But over the next two years Disraeli – suddenly reinvigorated – contrived by a dazzling feat of parliamentary legerdemain to stand this logic on its head.

First he wooed the substantial minority of old Whigs who, from reasons of Palmerstonian conservatism or naked self-preservation, were opposed to further reform, in order to defeat Russell's bill and bring down the Liberal government. Then he persuaded Derby – reluctant as always – to form yet another minority Tory government and managed to carry a bill of his own that was more radical than the Liberal one. This was a supreme triumph of tactics over strategy, and improvisation over any sort of principle. His motivation throughout was frankly to dish Gladstone, whom he outmanoeuvred at every turn. The whole question was immensely complicated, depending on arcane calculations of how many new voters would be enfranchised by different schemes of registration, and which party would lose or benefit from each. The two parties were equally cynical about seeking their own advantage. But Gladstone had thought deeply about the subject, had mastered the detail and knew what outcome he wanted to achieve. Disraeli, by contrast, was careless of the detail and indifferent to the outcome, just so long as he kept control. His only concern was that a bill should be passed by a Tory, not a Liberal government; and in this he succeeded.

After eight days of debate on Russell's 1866 bill the champions wound up for their respective sides in huge speeches lasting two and half hours each. Disraeli made the traditional conservative case that 'votes should be weighed, not counted' and rejected Gladstone's dangerous idea of a 'moral entitlement' to vote, accusing him of 'introducing American principles which must be fatal to this country'.[69] Gladstone responded testily that enfranchising another 400,000 voters out of five million adult males scarcely amounted to democracy.* Unwisely, Disraeli tried to embarrass Gladstone by unearthing a speech he had made at the Oxford Union against the 1832 bill. Gladstone brushed this aside magnificently:

---

*The idea that women might get the vote was still too outlandish to be taken seriously, though John Stuart Mill did introduce an amendment for women's suffrage. Going beyond Fox, Disraeli boldly suggested that 'if there is to be universal suffrage, women have as much right to vote as men. And more than that – a woman having property now ought to have a vote.'[70] But he did not vote for Mill's amendment.

The right honourable Gentleman, secure I suppose in the recollection of his own consistency, has taunted me with the political errors
of my boyhood . . . He, a Parliamentary champion of twenty years
standing . . . is so ignorant of the House of Commons, or so simple
in the structure of his mind, that he positively thought he would
obtain a Parliamentary advantage by exhibiting me to the public
view . . . as an opponent of the Reform Bill of 1832.

What Disraeli had stated was quite true, as Gladstone confirmed:
'I deeply regret it.' But he – unlike his opponent – was now older
and wiser.

I grant my youthful mind and imagination were impressed with the
same idle and futile fears which still bewilder and distract the mature
mind of the right honourable Gentleman. The only difference between
us is . . . that having these views, I . . . express[ed] them . . . plainly,
forcibly, in downright English, while the right hon. Gentleman does
not dare to tell the nation what he really thinks, and is content to
skulk under the shelter of the meaningless amendment which is
proposed by the noble Lord.

In his peroration Gladstone reaffirmed his conversion and warned
his former party not to stand in the way of progress:

You may bury the Bill that we have introduced, but . . . you cannot
fight against the future. Time is on our side. The great social forces
which move onward in their might and majesty . . . are against you;
they are marshalled on our side; and the banner which we now
carry . . . will be borne . . . perhaps not to an easy, but to a certain
and to a not too distant victory.[71]

This was one of Gladstone's greatest oratorical efforts. But his
vision of social forces too strong to be resisted alarmed not just
Tories but many on his own side. Thirty-five Liberals voted against
the bill and the government's majority of 60 was cut to five. Scenting
blood, Disraeli now harried and harassed the government at every
turn, skilfully exploiting the Liberal back benches' mounting resentment of Gladstone's remote and bullying manner. Used to
commanding majorities, Gladstone could never match Disraeli at
this sort of parliamentary alliance-brokering; carrying the burden

of government business in the Commons practically alone, he was exhausted and exasperated by Disraeli's unscrupulous manoeuvring. On 18 June the government was defeated on a technical amendment which Gladstone rashly made a question of confidence. Russell resigned and Derby formed his third minority government, with Disraeli once more back at the Treasury. They took office on an anti-reform mandate; yet when Gladstone challenged the new government to pick up the Liberals' bill, Disraeli urged Derby to do exactly that:

> Suppose, instead of discharging the order of the day on the Reform Bill, you took up the measure where it stops ... You could carry this in the present House, and rapidly ... It would cut the ground entirely from under Gladstone.[72]

Derby hesitated. But riots in Hyde Park and 'monster' demonstrations in the country, plus Queen Victoria's wish to see the issue settled, finally convinced him that it was necessary to deal with it. Disraeli justified the government's about-face by arguing that a moderate Tory bill was preferable to a more extensive Liberal one. Lord Cranborne (the future Lord Salisbury) and two other die-hards resigned; but in February 1867 Disraeli committed the government to introducing a bill of its own. Gladstone was deeply suspicious. Every previous measure that Disraeli had produced in his career, he wrote, had been 'thoroughly tortuous'.

> The Ethiopian will not change his skin. His Reform Bill of 1867 will be tortuous too. But if you have to drive a man out of a wood you must yourself go into the wood to drive him. That is what I am afraid of.[73]

When Disraeli introduced his bill in February 1867 he presented it as a conservative measure – not a prelude to democracy, but the minimum reform necessary to preserve the constitution – and hoped for all-party support. In its original form it would have given the vote to all male householders in urban seats, with a number of complicated reservations. Gladstone would have been wise to have welcomed it so far as it went and then tried to amend it during its passage through the House. Instead he attacked it root and branch,

with the same sort of pent-up violence that he had exhibited in
1852. 'His manner is sometimes so very excited and so alarming,'
Disraeli mocked, 'that one might almost feel thankful that [we] are
divided by a good broad piece of furniture.'[74] Gladstone's refusal
to see any merit in the bill at all only alienated his own supporters.
Disraeli ridiculed Gladstone's 'cloud-compelling manner' and
charmed the House into passing the Second Reading without even
a division.[75] 'It was the most wonderful piece of acting & the most
extraordinary exhibition of talent I have ever heard,' wrote one
Liberal MP. 'He pitched into everybody, he abandoned all his
principles, & all through he delighted and amused the House.'[76]
'Men who have heard Mr Disraeli throughout his career,' reported
the journalist Edward Russell, 'agree that never did he show such
mastery over his audience.'[77] 'Disraeli's insolent triumph,' a third
writer agreed, spelled the 'entire collapse of Gladstone's attack.'[78]

When the bill went into committee Disraeli made it clear that
he would accept amendments from anyone except Gladstone, whose
only purpose, he asserted, was to wreck the bill.

> The right honourable gentleman is an opponent with whom any
> man may be proud to have to contend . . . But do not let us
> misunderstand the motive or the conduct of the right honourable
> Gentleman . . . It is a party attack.[79]

In fact Gladstone was earnestly trying to improve the bill, according
to his own ideas; but most of his supporters did not understand
the technicalities and wished only to be shot of the issue. On 13
April his most important amendment was defeated by 22 votes,
with forty-five Liberals voting against. While Gladstone reflected
bitterly on 'a smash perhaps without example',[80] Disraeli celebrated
at the Carlton Club, then went home to Mary Anne, who was
waiting up for him with a bottle of champagne and a Fortnum's
pie. 'Why, my dear,' he is supposed to have told her, 'you are more
like a mistress than a wife.'[81]

But the bill was not through yet. With no secure majority, Disraeli
still had to twist and turn, day after day, successfully playing the
middle ground against the two extremes. He still cared less about
the details than about keeping the initiative. In May he pulled off

his most daring coup – without reference to the cabinet – by uni-
laterally accepting a Liberal amendment which added, at a stroke,
half a million new voters. He frankly defended his action as an
opportunity to 'destroy the present agitation and extinguish
Gladstone & Co'.[82] By this amendment the bill was transformed
out of all recognition from the modest measure he had introduced
in February: it now enfranchised more than twice as many new
voters as Russell's bill which he had denounced the year before as
dangerously democratic. Yet his own party was so mesmerised by
his performance that it swallowed even this. Cranborne railed at
'a political betrayal which has no parallel in our Parliamentary
annals'[83] – exactly the charge Disraeli had once levelled at Peel; but
the amended bill was again approved without a division, and Derby
was able to take it through the Lords without difficulty.

Gladstone was so clearly beaten that he did not even speak in
the final Commons debate. One colleague reported him 'quite awed
by the diabolical cleverness of Dizzy'.[84] Bishop Wilberforce, a friend
of both men, described the dramatic reversal in their fortunes:

> The most wonderful thing is the rise of Disraeli. It is not the mere
> assertion of talent. He has been able to teach the House of Commons
> almost to ignore Gladstone, and at present lords it over him, and I
> am told, says that he will hold him down for twenty years.[85]

Gladstone's humiliation was encapsulated in a schoolboy joke. 'Why
is Gladstone like a telescope? Because Disraeli can draw him out,
look right through him and shut him up.'[86]

Up to this point Disraeli and Gladstone, though dominant in the
Commons, were both subordinate to leaders in the Upper House.
Over the winter of 1867–68, however, first Russell and then Derby
retired. In the space of a few weeks both pretenders, one aged fifty-
eight, the other sixty-three, finally scaled the pinnacle of leadership
in their own right. This was a symbolic moment, marking the
dawning of a new age: two hereditary grandees were succeeded by
two commoners of middle-class origins, both born in the nineteenth
century. Moreover Disraeli's accession to the Tory leadership in
February 1868 made him Queen Victoria's seventh Prime Minister.

'A proud thing for a Man "risen from the people" to have obtained!' she gushed to her daughter.[87] Of course she exaggerated. Disraeli was scarcely sprung of 'the people'; Canning's beginnings were poorer, and Peel's father was a cotton manufacturer. Nevertheless it was a remarkable achievement, and Disraeli did not disguise his delight. 'Yes', he famously told a friend who congratulated him, 'I have climbed to the top of the greasy pole.'[88] He celebrated with a lavish party in the new Foreign Office building graced by the cream of society from the Prince of Wales down: even Gladstone felt bound to attend.

Yet his achievement was precarious. He still had no majority in the Commons, and Gladstone wasted no time in reminding him of the fact. Nine years earlier, after the fiasco of his Ionian adventure, Aberdeen had accurately predicted that Gladstone was 'terrible on the rebound';[89] never was this better illustrated than after his discomfiture in 1867. No sooner had Disraeli moved into 10 Downing Street than Gladstone seized on an issue calculated to reunite Liberals, Whigs and radicals – to say nothing of the Irish. The privileged position of the Anglican Church in overwhelmingly Roman Catholic Ireland had long been an anomaly: it was a measure of how far Gladstone had moved from the Erastianism of his youth that he now recognised the grievance and resolved to deal with it. His conversion was sincere: the first step in what was to be the dominating mission of his later years, to 'pacify Ireland'. But his timing was also politically inspired. Disraeli's biographer Buckle thought raising it at this moment 'Gladstone's most brilliant and successful stroke as party leader'.[90] Asked why he had done so, his close colleague the Duke of Argyll replied simply: 'There really was no other way of getting Dizzy out of office.'[91] It worked, though not immediately.

Taken by surprise, Disraeli was obliged to answer Gladstone's powerful case when plainly the worse for drink. He was never at ease with church questions at the best of times and could only bluster that disestablishment of the Church in Ireland was the thin end of a wedge which would endanger 'the Realm of England' and even 'the Crown'.[92] For once it was Gladstone who managed a pointed innuendo, wickedly suggesting that the Prime Minister was speaking 'under the influence of' – here he paused – 'a heated imagination'.[93] (In his diary he wrote that Disraeli was 'tipsy.')[94] With all strands of the opposition voting together, the government was duly defeated by majorities of 60 and 65. Disraeli, however, did not resign. He had been in office less than three months and did not wish to be remembered for the shortest premiership on record. Two things helped him to hang on. First, the Queen was indignant that Gladstone had taken up the church issue without consulting her. She had not yet conceived the violent antipathy for Gladstone that she developed later, but she had already formed a strong preference for Disraeli. That alone might not have signified; but Disraeli had a second argument – that it would be wrong, after the passage of the Reform Bill the previous year, to hold new elections on the old register. It would be months before the new register was ready. With Victoria's approval he therefore promised to resign, but not yet. Gladstone was momentarily furious at his clinging to office in this way: he was 'in a white heat with an almost diabolical expression of countenance'.[95] But in reality the Liberals did not want an election before the enlarged register was in place. So Disraeli remained in office, though scarcely in power, for a few months longer, enjoying the perks and patronage of the position while the Commons witnessed the strange sight of Gladstone acting as if he were already Prime Minister, steering his Irish legislation through the House from the opposition bench.

Eventually Disraeli went to the country in November. The election of 1868 was arguably the first modern general election, pitting two charismatic leaders against each other for the first time, fighting a national campaign with an enlarged electorate. The likelihood was always that Gladstone would win – the Tories had not won a Commons majority in thirty years – but the effect of the new register was unpredictable. 'Confidence in Gladstone seems on the increase throughout the country,' his former (and future) Foreign Secretary, the Earl of Clarendon, wrote. 'On the other hand a demoralised nation admire[s] the audacity, the tricks and the success of the Jew, and the fight between the two will be as personal on the hustings as it has been in parliament.'[96] In fact only Gladstone really campaigned as a national leader with big public speeches at mass rallies, while Disraeli confined himself to more traditional addresses to more select audiences. Derby contrasted his former lieutenant's 'calm, temperate and dignified' campaign with the 'balderdash and braggadocio in which Gladstone has been indulging on his stumping tour'.[97] Though his emphasis on Irish disestablishment cost Gladstone his own seat in staunchly Protestant South Lancashire, forcing him to find another fallback constituency in Greenwich, the Liberals won a majority of over 100. After less than ten months in office Disraeli set a new precedent by resigning immediately without waiting to meet Parliament; and Victoria reluctantly appointed Gladstone in his place.

The contrast between his feelings and Disraeli's on achieving the highest office could not have been greater. Where Disraeli had frankly celebrated his worldly achievement, Gladstone in his diary piously attributed his success to God: 'I ascend a steepening path, with a burden ever gathering weight. The Almighty seems to sustain and spare me for some purpose of His own, deeply unworthy as I know myself to be. Glory be to his name.'[98]

Gladstone's first premiership, which lasted from 1868 to 1874, was the greatest modernising government of the nineteenth century. As well as the promised disestablishment of the Irish Church, and an Irish land reform bill, it introduced universal, compulsory and (for the poorest) free education up to the age of thirteen; competitive examinations for entry to the civil service; the abolition of the purchase of commissions in the army; and voting by secret ballot. Gladstone dominated his government to an extent not seen since Peel, and dominated the Commons, taking much of the government's highly contentious legislation personally through the House. For the first two years of this torrent of legislative activity, Disraeli offered little sustained opposition. Though already sixty-four when Gladstone took office, he declined to retire, but bided his time, following a strategy of masterly inactivity while secretly writing another novel. *Lothair*, published in 1870, was a sensation: the first fiction ever published by a former Prime Minister, it sold 15,000 copies in three months and led to a collected edition of all his novels which earned him around £10,000. At the Royal Academy dinner that year he spoke for literature while Gladstone represented politics. The same year the *Punch* cartoonist Tenniel caricatured the two men as 'the Lion and Unicorn fighting for the crown', from Lewis Carroll's just-published *Through the Looking-Glass*.

Gladstone was the Lion who 'beat the Unicorn' – Disraeli – 'all round the town'.[99] It was reasonable to assume that Disraeli would never hold office again.

Yet he did not entirely give up the game and could still rile Gladstone when he wished. 'Gladstone's . . . temper is visible and audible whenever he rises to speak,' Stanley noted in 1869. 'Disraeli is quite aware of the advantage which he possesses in his natural calmness: and takes every opportunity to make the contrast noticeable.'[100]

Moreover the government soon began to lose its way. While Gladstone focused on his domestic reforms, the international scene darkened in 1870: the Franco-Prussian war, the unification of Germany, the Paris Commune, Russia's unilateral abrogation of the neutrality of the Black Sea and a prolonged wrangle with the United States over compensation for damage wrought by the British-built *Alabama* during the American civil war left Britain looking isolated and diminished: a public raised on the robust simplicities of Palmerstonian foreign policy felt no confidence in a Liberal government apparently in hock to the radicals and the Irish. The mantle of Palmerston was there to be picked up, and Disraeli saw his opportunity. 'I am not sorry to see the country fairly frightened about foreign affairs,' he wrote to Derby. It was time that 'the reign of priggism should terminate'.[101] In February 1871 he emerged from his tent to make a long and powerful speech on the question of the Black Sea which, one MP wrote, 'annoyed Gladstone exceedingly . . . He lost his temper – & Disraeli, who is provokingly calm, actually shone by contrast.'[102] Another described the scene in graphic detail:

> The premier was like a cat on hot bricks and presented a striking contrast to Disraeli . . . For Disraeli cuts up a minister with as much sang-froid as an anatomist cuts up a frog. Gladstone could hardly keep his seat. He fidgeted, took a quire of notes, sent for blue books and water, turned down corners and 'hear-heared' ironically or interrupted his assailant to make a denial of one of his statements, or to ask the page of a quotation so frequently that Disraeli had to protest once or twice by raising his eyebrows or shrugging his shoulders. And when Gladstone rose, you could see that every stroke of Disraeli's had gone home. He was in a white passion, and almost

choked with words, frequently pausing to select the harshest that could be found.[103]

Gladstone was so exasperated that 'some unparliamentary violence was feared'.[104] After two years carrying practically the whole burden of government business, he appeared not only tired but increasingly rattled, losing command of the House, while suddenly Disraeli was again in 'high spirits'.[105] He scored another 'very palpable hit' in May when Gladstone introduced the ballot with an evident lack of enthusiasm for his own measure.[106]

In early 1872 Gladstone persuaded Victoria to end her decade-long mourning since her beloved Albert's death by attending a thanksgiving service for the Prince of Wales's recovery from typhoid. Huge crowds outside St Paul's Cathedral cheered her return to public visibility. More significantly, while Gladstone arrived and left in silence, Disraeli received 'an overpowering ovation . . . The cheers which greeted him from all classes convinced him that, for the day at least, a more popular man did not exist in England.'[107] He began to believe that he might after all be Prime Minister again. Accordingly, taking a leaf out of Gladstone's book, he addressed two big open-air rallies – at Manchester in April and at Crystal Palace in June – designed to re-establish the Tory party as the true 'national' party whose mission was to uphold the empire, maintain the constitution and assert British interests against the 'cosmopolitan' weakness of the Liberals and radicals. So far as domestic issues were concerned he condemned the 'principle of violence' behind the government's restless reformism and deplored the harassment of 'every institution and every interest, every class and calling in the country'; another familiar Conservative complaint down the years. Yet at the same time – in an obvious attempt to reach out to the new electorate – he proposed that government's first duty should be 'the elevation of the condition of the people' and hinted that true patriotism required legislation to provide clean air, clean water and decent sanitation for all. He ended his Manchester speech with a famous passage comparing the government front bench to 'a range of exhausted volcanoes' on the coast of South America.

Not a flame flickers on a single pallid crest. But the situation is still dangerous. There are occasional earthquakes, and ever and anon the dark rumbling of the sea.[108]

With these two wide-ranging speeches Disraeli declared himself the leader of an alternative government in waiting.

Gladstone was scornful of his opponent's sudden interest in social welfare, suspecting that 'the wizard of Hughenden Manor' was up to his old tricks. 'I will say they are quacks,' he wrote to Granville, 'deluded and beguiled by a spurious philanthropy.'[109] But at the same time he recognised the truth of Disraeli's final gibe. 'What am I now?' he wrote wearily to his latest female confidante, the reformed courtesan Laura Thistlethwayte. 'As Dizzy says, an exhausted volcano.'[110]

In December 1872 Mary Anne Disraeli died, aged seventy-nine. She was always likely to predecease her husband, but Disraeli was devastated; moreover he was left without a London house, since Grosvenor Gate where they had lived since their marriage was Mary Anne's only for her lifetime. He had to move into a hotel. Loneliness was now an additional reason to throw himself back into politics; while the lack of a London home was further incentive to try to recapture Downing Street. Meanwhile Mary Anne's death cut the last tie which had maintained tolerably civil relations with Gladstone. Despite their political opposition, Gladstone had always had a soft spot for Mary Anne. During her final illness he brought tears to Disraeli's eyes – a rare event – by expressing his good wishes in the Commons; and on her death he wrote a typically earnest letter of sympathy. But this bond of humanity between them had now been removed.

In March 1873 Disraeli launched a highly personal assault on Gladstone's latest instalment of Irish legislation, a bill to establish a Catholic university which outraged the Protestants without pleasing the Catholics. Though Gladstone for once responded with a graceful speech which almost won back the House's sympathy, the government lost the division by three votes and Gladstone, not without relief, resigned. But now it was Disraeli's turn to keep his rival on the rack. He had had enough of minority governments in 1852, 1858 and 1867–68 and had no wish to form another. He refused to take office until he was confident he could win an election and secure a majority. Though the Tories had won thirteen by-elections in two years, his party managers told him he needed a little longer. 'I decline altogether to take office,' he told the Queen's secretary, Colonel Ponsonby. 'We did not defeat the government. We threw out a stupid, blundering Bill, which Gladstone, in his *tête montée* way, tried to make a vote of confidence. It was a foolish mistake of his.'[111] Gladstone was furious, arguing at length that Disraeli's refusal breached all recent precedent; but in the end he was compelled to continue in office. A few days later both men had to explain their positions in the House. Once again Disraeli ran rings round his opponent: as the radical John Trelawney admitted: 'I think D'Israeli had the best of it.'[112] Privately Gladstone raged against 'the artful dodger'.[113] 'The Conservative Party will never assume its natural position until Disraeli retires,' he wrote in his diary, then added wearily: 'I sometimes think he & I might with advantage pair off together.'[114] In August, obliged to find a new Chancellor, he added to his burdens by taking over the Treasury himself. But Disraeli had the government on the run, until Gladstone tried to regain the initiative by calling an election in January 1874.

This was the second head-to-head contest between the two leaders, but this time Gladstone was on the back foot from the start. After five years of hyperactivity the electorate was ready for a quieter life. The country would be better off, Disraeli declared, with 'a little more energy in our foreign policy and a little less in our domestic legislation'.[115] In fact Gladstone had exhausted his programme and was unsure what to do next. Rather desperately he jogged back twenty years and promised to abolish income tax – an unrealistic suggestion that made no appeal to the new electorate and was widely dismissed as a cheap bribe. Disraeli compared him to a thief who had recently stolen a trinket by throwing snuff in the jeweller's eyes. 'So it is that Mr Gladstone throws gold dust into the eyes of the people of England.'[116] *The Times* deplored 'the personal bitterness and almost vituperation' of Disraeli's language. 'It is going far beyond the bounds of gentleman-like controversy to compare Mr Gladstone to a jewel thief.'[117] But Gladstone could not win. When he retorted with pained dignity that he did not propose to follow Disraeli's example, the paper was disappointed:

'Mr Disraeli sparkles spontaneously with epigram, but Mr Gladstone's wit it must be confessed is somewhat elephantine.'[118] A week later it concluded that the whole election was about contrasting styles rather than competing programmes. 'The contest has been in an unusual degree a personal one . . . The issue to be decided was whether the country should be in the hands of Mr Gladstone or Mr Disraeli.'[119] The result was the first independent Tory majority for half a century.

Disraeli was delighted to have made it at last, especially at the expense of his old rival. 'Never was a man in a prouder position than myself,' he wrote to the new love of his old age, Selina, Countess of Bradford. 'Only those who are acquainted with the malignity of Gladstone through a rivalship of five and twenty years can understand this.'[120] He was Prime Minister at last on his own terms, with a comfortable majority and the prospect of a full term of office if his health held up. But he knew that it might not, and recognised that 'power has come to me too late'.[121]

Gladstone was correspondingly angry, not so much at losing office as at yielding it to Disraeli. 'Is it not disgusting,' Catherine wrote to their son Herbert, 'after all Papa's labour and patriotism and years of work to think of handing over his nest-egg to that Jew?'[122] Rather than stick around to watch his successor dissipate his legacy, he stunned the political world by resigning the Liberal leadership as well. He had not enjoyed his previous experience of trying to oppose Disraeli's slippery manoeuvres in 1866–68. To re-commit for several more years of opposition followed by a return to government at the age of perhaps seventy, he wrote in his diary, was 'not consistent with my views for the close of my life'.[123] In the absence of an agreed successor he was eventually persuaded to stay on as caretaker leader for another year. But then he genuinely intended to retire. 'I deeply desired an interval between Parliament and the grave,' he told his biographer John Morley.[124] It was actually to be another twenty years before he finally retired. His withdrawal in 1875 appeared to leave Disraeli in possession of the field: in fact the climax of their rivalry was still to come.

Some Prime Ministers groan endlessly about the burden of office; others frankly glory in it. Disraeli, naturally, was one of the latter. Conscious of how far he had come, driven all his life by ambition

rather than principle, loving the game of politics for its own
sake rather than for any particular programme he wished to pursue,
he relished the position, the patronage and the respect it finally
earned him from those who had always distrusted him. Above all
he relished the relationship it allowed him to cultivate with Queen
Victoria. Now a widower himself, he could empathise with her
widowhood. He flattered her shamelessly, where Gladstone, as she
famously complained, had hectored her. ('He speaks to me as if I
was a public meeting.')[125] Disraeli treated Victoria as a woman rather
than a figurehead, and wrote her gossipy letters that went far beyond
the usual protocol of Prime Ministers' relations with the sovereign:
privately he called her 'the Faery'.[126] He had no need to poison her
mind against his rival since she loathed him already. Gladstone, she
wrote to her daughter in Germany, was 'a very dangerous and unsatisfactory premier . . . arrogant, tyrannical and obstinate, with no
knowledge of the world or human nature'.[127] She noted the difference between them with characteristic shrewdness. 'When I left the
dining room after sitting next to Mr Gladstone I thought he was
the cleverest man in England; but after sitting next to Mr Disraeli
I thought I was the cleverest woman in England.'[128]

Disraeli's premiership of 1874–80 was another important
reforming administration. But unlike Gladstone, who drove every
detail of his legislation through the House himself, Disraeli did not
pretend to be interested in the small print of what he called
'parochial' business.[129] He let his ministers get on with realising
some of the social measures he had foreshadowed in his two big
speeches in opposition: an Artisans' Dwellings Act, a Sale of Food
and Drugs Act, an important Public Health Act and legislation to
protect the rights of trade unions which, he frankly hoped, 'will
gain and retain for the Tories the lasting affection of the working
classes'.[130] He was more interested in the other side of the vision
he had set out in 1872, the reassertion of British prestige abroad,
and specifically the consolidation of the empire, which was embodied
in two symbolic acts. First he pulled off a brilliant diplomatic/
commercial coup by buying the controlling block of shares in the
recently opened Suez Canal, thereby both thwarting the French and
safeguarding the route to India. Second, by the Royal Titles Act of
1876 he bestowed on Queen Victoria the title of Empress of India.

This was something Victoria had long hankered for, but it had been given new point by the declaration of the German empire in 1870. Disraeli managed to present it as a romantic gesture from the Prime Minister to his Queen. Gladstone thought it 'a piece of tomfoolery'[131] and came back to the House 'in one of his white rages' to oppose it – which further damaged his relations with Victoria.[132] Around this time he read Disraeli's early novel *Tancred*, in which the hero is advised by an eastern prince to 'magnetise' the British Queen by using his 'beautiful' voice to whisper 'fine things' in her ear.[133] Gladstone feared that this was exactly what Disraeli was doing. Quite apart from the question of the imperial title he was afraid that by encouraging Victoria's blatant partiality Disraeli was corrupting the constitution. In principle he was right; but the Crown survived.

The biggest row while Gladstone was still reluctantly leading the opposition was over a bill to outlaw 'ritualistic' practices in the Church of England. Disraeli saw the matter purely in political terms as a sop to his party's traditional Protestantism and an opportunity to exploit Liberal divisions; Gladstone, by contrast, believed that the government had no right to interfere with internal church affairs; he tried to oppose the measure but found himself out of step with his party and had to back down. 'An immense triumph!' Disraeli crowed. 'Gladstone ran away.'[134]

Such confrontations were becoming rare, however, since in 1875 Gladstone made good his determination to retire and withdrew to Hawarden, leaving the Liberal leadership uneasily shared between Lord Hartington (heir to the Duke of Devonshire) in the Commons and Granville in the Lords. This should have left the field to Disraeli. But like Pitt in 1796 when Fox withdrew, Disraeli found himself diminished without his adversary. He seemed to lose interest in the House, lost his touch in managing it, and began to feel his age. He did not wish to give up the premiership; but in 1876 he decided he could lead the government more comfortably from the Upper House, and went to the Lords as the Earl of Beaconsfield. ('I am dead,' he quipped, 'but in the Elysian fields.')[135] Thus ended, anti-climactically, the greatest parliamentary duel of the century. Yet just when it seemed to be dwindling away, their rivalry flared into new life, sparked by events 1,500 miles away in the Balkans.

The Ottoman empire in the eastern Mediterranean had been slowly crumbling for years. British policy was traditionally to try to shore it up, for fear of Russia filling the vacuum; the Crimean War had been fought to keep Russia out of the Balkans. By the 1870s Christian populations in Serbia, Romania and Bulgaria were increasingly revolting against Turkish rule, with Russian encouragement. News of brutal reprisals by Turkish troops in Bulgaria began to reach Britain in May 1876. Disraeli initially treated the news with studied indifference, brushing aside reports of torture with a tasteless joke. 'Oriental people seldom, I believe, resort to torture, but generally terminate their connection with culprits in a more expeditious manner.'[136] Gladstone was at Hawarden, writing a theological disquisition on punishment in the after-life from which he was reluctant to be called away. But public opinion was roused to a ferment of indignation by a high-minded alliance of churchmen, journalists and liberal academics. By late August Gladstone could not resist: if there was a moral crusade in the air he had to lead it. When he heard of a planned meeting of working men in Hyde Park he saw that 'the iron was hot and the time to strike had arrived'.[137] He set aside his work on the next world and in four days wrote a furious 6,000-word pamphlet denouncing Turkish rule in Balkans in the most lurid language. 'Good ends', he wrote to Granville, 'can rarely be achieved in politics without passion; and there is now, for the first time in a good many years a virtuous passion.'[138] Published on 6 September, *The Bulgarian Horrors and the Question of the East* sold 40,000 copies in four days and 200,000 by the end of the month. In his diary he wrote that he had been called back to public life 'by a great and high election of God'.[139] Yet in his own way he was as opportunist as Disraeli. Since his defeat in 1874 he had been chafing at retirement: subconsciously at least he was surely on the lookout for a suitably high-minded cause which would enable him to get his own back.

His pamphlet was way over the top. The Turks, he wrote in one frankly racist passage, were 'the one great anti-human specimen of humanity', whose 'abominable and bestial lusts' drove them to commit outrages so vile 'that it passes the power of heart to conceive or tongue and pen adequately to describe them' – though he did his best, vividly painting for his readers the 'heaps on heaps of dead', 'the violated purity alike of matron, of maiden and of child', and scenes of cruelty 'at which Hell itself might almost blush'. 'No government ever has so sinned,' he asserted; 'none has so proved itself incorrigible in sin.' As 'an old servant of the Crown and State', he demanded that the British government should reverse its policy and 'apply all its vigour to concur with the other States of Europe in obtaining the extinction of the Turkish executive power in Bulgaria'.

> Let the Turks now carry away their abuses in the only possible manner, namely by carrying away themselves. Their Zeptiehs and their Mudirs, their Bimbashis and their Yuzbachis, their Kaimakams and their Pasha, one and all, bag and baggage, shall, I hope, clear out from the province they have desolated and profaned.[140]

Even Roy Jenkins admits that Gladstone was 'stronger on the rhetoric of indignation than on detailed knowledge of what was happening in the Balkans', and allows that 'Disraeli's desire to burst the bloated bladder of expostulations with a sharp pin of mocking deflation is understandable'.[141] Disraeli thought the pamphlet 'quite unprincipled as usual' and 'outrageous', not least because Gladstone proposed, 'for ethnological reasons no less, to expel the Turks as a race from Europe'.[142] Personally he was stung that Gladstone had the 'impudence' to send him his 'vindictive and ill-written' pamphlet, which 'accused him of 'several crimes'.[143] (In fact Gladstone had been dissuaded from criticising the Prime Minister by name.) More seriously Disraeli held to established British policy: he believed that trying to drive the Turks from Europe 'would lead to another Thirty Years War'.[144] Gladstone's emotionalism only stiffened his refusal to acknowledge what was happening. Though it was now clear that around 12,000 men, women and children had been massacred he still dismissed the reports as 'coffee-house babble'.[145] This combination of stubbornness and flippancy further enraged the Liberals and fuelled the agitation.

On 9 September Gladstone made a great open-air speech – in pouring rain, to Disraeli's great delight – at Blackheath (in his Greenwich constituency) in which he backed Russia's right to intervene in defence of the Bulgarians. The public demand for action, he asserted, had attained 'a breadth and a height and a depth that carries it far out of the lower region of party differences, and establishes it on grounds, not of political party, not even of mere English nationality, not of Christian faith, but on the largest and broadest ground of all – the ground of our common humanity'.[146] Disraeli responded eleven days later with a speech at Aylesbury in his own former constituency in which he had little to say about events in the Balkans except to blame the trouble on the Serbs, but explicitly accused 'designing politicians' of exploiting the generous sentiments of the people for 'sinister ends':

> I do not think there is any language which can denounce too strongly conduct of this description. He who at such a moment would avail himself of such a commanding sentiment in order to obtain his own individual ends, suggesting a course which he may know to be injurious to the interests of the country, and not favourable to the welfare of mankind, is a man whose conduct no language can too strongly condemn ... Such conduct, if pursued by any man at this moment, ought to be indignantly reprobated by the people of England, for in the general havoc and ruin which it may bring about it may, I think, be fairly described as worse than any of those Bulgarian atrocities which now occupy attention.

On a lighter note he ridiculed Gladstone's idea of expelling the Turks from Europe:

> If he had gone to the House of Commons and proposed ... to go to the top of Greenwich hill and roll down to the bottom, I declare he would not have proposed anything more absurdly incongruous.[147]

The Times considered the suggestion that Gladstone's speeches were worse than the atrocities themselves 'one of the gravest charges ever made by one eminent British statesman against another'.[148] But Disraeli was delighted with his rebuke. 'I think the Greenwich Tartuffe will have a long face,' he wrote to Lady Bradford.* 'Certain I am ... that before Parliament reassembles he will be one of the most disconsidered public men in England.'[149]

---

*Tartuffe is the religious hypocrite in Molière's play of that title.

Far from supporting Russian action against Turkey, Disraeli and his Foreign Secretary Lord Derby (the fifteenth Earl, the son of his old leader) sought to prevent the war which he accused Gladstone of stirring up. His difficulties, Disraeli wrote to Lady Chesterfield in October, were 'immensely aggravated by the treasonable conduct of that wicked maniac Gladstone'.[150] 'If you have a war,' he added bluntly a week later, 'Gladstone has caused it.'[151] In his speech at the Lord Mayor's banquet at the beginning of November Disraeli actually threatened military action *against* Russia if she did not stem the flow of so-called 'volunteers' into the region. 'Although the policy of England is peace', he warned, 'there is no country so well prepared as our own.'[152]

'The provocation offered by Disraeli at the Guildhall,' Gladstone raged, 'is almost incredible.'[153] Whereas he had hitherto refrained from attacking the Prime Minister personally, he told Granville, it was now *'wholly* unavoidable'.[154] On 12 December he spoke at another great protest meeting in central London attended by a galaxy of celebrated figures of the day from John Ruskin and William Morris to Anthony Trollope; letters of support were read out from Darwin and Carlyle, and the young Thomas Hardy was in the audience. Gladstone's contribution seems to have come too late in the day to be reported: but the resolution of 'this intolerable assembly', as Disraeli called it,[155] was voiced by the Whig historian G. O. Trevelyan: 'No matter how the Prime Minister may finger the hilt of the sword, the nation will take care that it never leaves the scabbard.'[156] In fact liberal indignation did not reflect the nation. Gladstone's crusade did not even have the support of the Liberal party: the official leaders, Granville and Hartington, were embarrassed by his activities, recognising that the wider public positively relished Disraeli's Palmerstonian sabre-rattling. A music hall song of the day precisely paraphrased his Guildhall speech, while adding a new word to the language:

We don't want to fight, but by Jingo if we do
We've got the ships, we've got the men, we've got the money too![157]

After an abortive conference at which the powers tried unsuccessfully to mediate, Russia finally declared war on Turkey in

April 1877 and by the end of the year was threatening Constantinople. Disraeli responded by ordering the British Mediterranean fleet through the Dardanelles and Indian troops to Malta. Gladstone denounced the movement of the fleet into 'forbidden waters' as 'an act of war – a breach of European law', by which 'the great name of England had been debased and degraded'. In a speech at Oxford he unwisely admitted playing 'the part of an agitator', explaining that he was driven to it by the Prime Minister.

> When you speak of the Government you mean Lord Beaconsfield . . . My purpose . . . has been . . . to the best of my power, for the last eighteen months, day and night, week by week, month by month, to counteract as well as I could, what I believe to be the purpose of Lord Beaconsfield.[158]

The Times was shocked by such candour:

> It is not quite worthy of Mr GLADSTONE to announce himself to the world as the opposer and accuser of LORD BEACONSFIELD. The signs are only too apparent that his opposition has done something both to sour him and to distort his judgement of facts. The evil influence of LORD BEACONSFIELD is not so potent and unlimited as he would have us believe.[159]

But once again Disraeli was delighted. 'What an exposure!' he wrote to Lady Bradford. 'The mask has fallen, and instead of a pious Christian, we find a vindictive fiend who confesses he has for a year and a half been dodging and manoeuvring against an individual – because he was his successful rival.'[160] Obliged to defend himself in the Commons, Gladstone denied any personal hostility: he had never made 'one imputation as to the motives of one single man'. There was nothing improper in opposing the government's foreign policy in the name of peace, neutrality and the concert of Europe. On the contrary, he insisted, invoking a surprising precedent: 'I ask what is the brightest jewel in the fame of Fox? Undoubtedly, the resistance he offered to the Revolutionary war.' Canning, Peel and Palmerston had all opposed government policy in their day.[161] Calling for peace, however, is unpopular when the country is clamouring for war. In an echo of the robust street politics of Fox's day Gladstone had his windows broken and he and Catherine required police protection from the London mob.

Yet peace prevailed. Disraeli's sabre-rattling was successful to the extent that Russia backed off and accepted an armistice. The provisional Treaty of San Stefano went a long way towards meeting Gladstone's demands, creating a largely autonomous Bulgaria and confirming the independence of Serbia, Montenegro and Romania. This alarmed Austria, however, so another congress was summoned in Berlin, presided over by the German Chancellor, Bismarck. Though increasingly unwell, Disraeli attended in person – an unprecedented departure for a British Prime Minister which marks the dawn of summit diplomacy. He revelled in the formal ceremonies and balls, formed a good relationship with Bismarck – who famously remarked that '*Der alte Jude, das ist der Mann*' ('The old Jew, he is the man')[162] – and managed to dominate the conference, securing a revised settlement marginally less favourable to Russia. This diplomatic triumph crowned his career. He returned to London to a rapturous reception claiming to have brought back 'peace with honour' – a phrase that had a fine ring to it until another elderly Prime Minister claimed the same for his ignominious Munich settlement sixty years later. Queen Victoria wrote that 'High and low are delighted, excepting Mr Gladstone, who is frantic.'[163]

Gladstone should have been pleased. In the words of his biographer John Morley: 'The treaty of Berlin became in fact an extensive partition of the Turkish empire, and the virtual ratification of the policy of bag and baggage.'[164] Indeed in the Commons he did 'thankfully and gratefully acknowledge that great results have been achieved in the diminution of human misery and towards the establishment of human happiness and prosperity in the east'. Yet in the same speech he complained that 'the voice of England has not been heard in unison with the institutions, the history and the character of England'. He charged that Disraeli and Salisbury (who had succeeded Derby as Foreign Secretary) had spoken 'in the tones of Metternich, and not in the tones of Mr Canning, or of Lord Palmerston, or of Lord Russell . . . It was their part to take the side of liberty; . . . as a matter of fact they took the side of servitude.'[165] 'A work of liberation . . . has been effected,' he conceded in a magazine article, 'but not by us nor with our good will: we have not had part or lot in the matter, except to cavil at it, and to curtail it.'[166]

Gladstone's inability to give Disraeli any credit confirms the extent to which personal animus was now distorting his judgement. For some time he had been finding the explanation for Disraeli's policy in his racial origins. 'Some new lights about his Judaic feeling, in which he is both consistent and conscientious, have come upon me,' he wrote to Granville in November 1876.[167] This was not quite anti-Semitism; but he increasingly felt that Disraeli was essentially un-English. In fact he had come to believe that Disraeli was not so much pro-Turk as anti-Christian. For centuries the Jews in the Middle East had lived peacefully among Muslims – it was the Christians who persecuted them; and it was true that Disraeli in his novels romanticised Islam while his professed concern for the Church of England had always seemed skin-deep. Yet Gladstone suspected that another motivation was old-fashioned British imperialism.

> What he hates is Christian liberty and reconstruction. He supports old Turkey, thinking that if vital improvements can be averted, it must break down; and his fleet is at Besika Bay, I feel pretty sure, to be ready to lay hold of Egypt as his share. So he may end as Duke of Memphis yet.[168]

There was some truth in this. The Treaty of Berlin did accord Britain some rights in Egypt – to protect the Suez Canal – which ironically posed major problems for Gladstone in the next decade; while Britain also acquired Cyprus (another headache in the next century). But Gladstone's fantasies went beyond this. In the original draft of his article for the *Nineteenth Century* he included a wild sentence describing Disraeli as 'that alien', whose purpose was 'to annex England to his native East and make it the appendage of an Asiatic empire'.[169] This libel his editor prudently excised.

When the treaty was signed Gladstone undercut the general rejoicing by denouncing the Cyprus agreement as an 'insane covenant . . . an act of duplicity not surpassed and rarely equalled in the history of nations'.[170] Disraeli delivered a cutting retort at a banquet in Knightsbridge a few days later:

Which do you believe most likely to enter an insane convention, a body of English gentlemen honoured by the favour of their sovereign and the confidence of their fellow-subjects, managing your affairs for five years, I hope with prudence, and not altogether without success, or a sophistical rhetorician, inebriated with the exuberance of his own verbosity, and gifted with an egotistical imagination that can at all times command interminable and inconsistent series of arguments to malign an opponent and glorify himself?[171]

Having delivered himself of this devastating put-down Disraeli followed it up, with no sense of irony, by objecting in the House of Lords that Gladstone had used 'offensive epithets' about himself. Unwisely Gladstone demanded examples, and let himself be drawn into another correspondence from which he came off worst.[172] Gladstone should have learned by now that he could not beat Disraeli at this game.

By now the two men really detested one another. As Lord Granville explained to the Queen:

Lord Beaconsfield and Mr Gladstone are men of extraordinary ability; they dislike each other more than is common among public men. Of no other politician would Lord Beaconsfield have said in public that his conduct was worse than the Bulgarian atrocities. He has the power of saying in two words that which drives a person of Mr Gladstone's peculiar temperament into a great state of excitement.[173]

Disraeli was even more scathing about Gladstone in private:

Posterity will do justice to that unprincipled maniac Gladstone – extraordinary mixture of envy, vindictiveness, hypocrisy and superstition – whether prime minister or leader of the opposition – whether preaching, praying, speechifying or scribbling – never a gentleman.[174]

In his letters he often pretended to endorse Victoria's belief that Gladstone was really mad. But his true judgement was probably expressed in a letter to Lady Bradford in 1879:

What you say about Gladstone is most just. What restlessness! What vanity! And what unhappiness must be his! Easy to say he is mad.

It looks like it. My theory about him is unchanged: a ceaseless Tartuffe from the beginning. That sort of man does not get mad at 70.[175]

Behind the rhetoric, the reality was that Disraeli had once again stolen the credit for what was in essence Gladstone's policy. Over the next twenty-five years the Turks were indeed progressively expelled from Europe, while Disraeli's attempt to fill the vacuum by extending British influence in the eastern Mediterranean, though popular at first, turned out to be unsustainable, bringing with it more burdens than benefits. Already in 1879, as the afterglow of Berlin faded, Disraeli's government, like Gladstone's before it, was running out of steam and luck both at home and abroad. At home a sequence of bad harvests led to a severe trade depression; while abroad the government suffered two severe blows to national prestige: the ambush and slaughter of 1,600 British troops by the Zulus at Isandhlwana in January, and the murder of the British envoy at Kabul in September. Both disasters obliged the government to send increased forces to restore order in South Africa and Afghanistan respectively; and gave fresh ammunition for Gladstone to lambast what he now termed 'Beaconsfieldism'.

Never inspired by suburban Greenwich, Gladstone was in 1879 seeking yet another new constituency – his fifth. Rejecting Leeds, he accepted Lord Rosebery's invitation to stand for Midlothian and embarked on an unprecedented campaign, quite disproportionate to the small electorate. In the space of two weeks, in halls, markets and railway stations around and beyond the constituency he made some thirty speeches, many of them major orations, some accompanied by torchlight processions, and claimed overall to have addressed around 87,000 people: moreover every speech was reported at length and read at breakfast tables up and down the country. He was not even officially leader of the opposition – he was still supposed to be retired; but he felt a powerful moral compulsion to hold Disraeli's government to account for all its 'mischievous and ruinous misdeeds', foreign, imperial and domestic. Abroad he accused his rival, in his usual heightened language, of chasing 'false phantoms of glory' in defiance of 'the dictates of justice', leading to 'suffering, discredit and dishonour'.[176] He condemned the 'most wanton' invasion of Afghanistan which had left that country a 'miserable ruin'; and the unprincipled annexation of the Transvaal – a free Christian republic – against its clearly expressed will, once more charging Disraeli with betraying the legacy of Canning and Palmerston.[177]* By contrast he set out six principles of Liberal foreign policy, which basically amounted to peace and freedom based on the concert of Europe. At home he denounced the Tories' 'mischievous . . . new fangled' social legislation, unprecedented 'innovations' and 'quackery', which he saw as a 'new method of government'.[179] So far as domestic politics were concerned, Gladstone's Midlothian speeches were deeply conservative; but this was disguised by the revivalist passion of his prodigious 'crusade'.

Disraeli claimed not to have read 'a single line of all this row', though he admitted that his secretary had taken notes in case he needed to answer his rival's 'wearisome rhetoric'. 'What a waste of powder and shot!'[180] It amused him that Gladstone's exertions seemed to be predicated on an election in 1880, whereas he had no intention of going to the country before 1881. In fact he changed his mind after an unexpected by-election victory and called a snap election after all to try to take advantage of Liberal divisions. But it did not avail him: the pendulum had swung back and the electorate was again ready for change. Gladstone made another tremendous swing around Midlothian; though still not formally leader, it was clear that he must be Prime Minister again if the Liberals won. Disraeli thought his 'spouting all over the country, like an irresponsible demagogue . . . wholly inexcusable in a man who was a statesman'.[181] He himself, as a peer, was debarred from campaigning, so the contest was sadly unbalanced. The result was a Liberal majority of around a hundred, giving Gladstone a 2–1 margin in the three elections the two champions contested head to head. He did not disguise his jubilation.

*Gladstone still abominated Palmerston, but now believed Disraeli's iniquities were ten times worse. Privately he called Disraeli 'the worst and most immoral minister since Castlereagh'.[178] It is not clear why he thought Castlereagh so wicked – unless it was the whiff of homosexuality surrounding his death. It is an example of the Victorian demonisation of Castlereagh which accompanied the canonisation of Canning.

'The downfall of Beaconsfieldism,' he exulted, 'is like the vanishing of some vast magnificent castle of Italian romance.'[182]

Queen Victoria was horrified by the result. 'She will sooner *abdicate*,' she told her private secretary, 'than send for or have any *communication* with *that half-mad firebrand* who wd soon ruin everything & be a *Dictator*.'[183] Disraeli advised her – quite correctly – to send for Lord Hartington, the Liberal leader in the Commons. But it was clearly Gladstone whom the electorate had voted for; so in the end she had no choice but to appoint him. Despite all his protestations about wishing to retire, therefore, Gladstone became Prime Minister for the second time at the age of seventy – once again taking the Treasury himself as a sort of hobby. Disraeli reluctantly faced the end of the road: he was suffering, he wrote to Lady Chesterfield, 'the most painful passage in political life, the transition from power to obscurity'.[184] In retirement he published yet another novel – *Endymion*, largely completed before 1874 – but he did not cease to rail at Gladstone from the wings, now referring to him in his letters at 'the Arch-Villain'. 'I don't give my mind to politics,' he wrote to Lady Bradford in September 1880, 'but it seems to me that the A.V. has carried everything before him.'[185] 'I fear that he is so unscrupulous a character and is surrounded by such second rate men, that great public mischief may occur.'[186] 'I think the A.V. so wicked a man that he would not hesitate to plunge us into a great war to soothe and salve his maniacal vanity.'[187] 'I see no chances of salvation unless he really goes mad, but he is such a hypocrite that I shall never believe that until he is in Bedlam.'[188]

In his last months Disraeli began to develop his critique in fiction. Only a fragment of this final novel was completed; but it contains an unmistakable caricature of a humourless religious hypocrite named Joseph Toplady Falconet who, it seems, was to become the unwitting agent of revolutionary nihilism.[189] Had he lived to finish it, *Falconet* would have been a unique exhibit in the annals of political rivalry. Sadly, however, Disraeli fell ill in March 1881 and died – in a rented London house – in April. A visitor during his last illness was delighted to find that 'his pleasant spitefulness about "Mr G" was not abated'.[190] Gladstone himself called at the house but was not admitted. 'May the Almighty be near his pillow,' he noted unctuously in his diary.[191]*

Disraeli's death faced Gladstone with the problem of paying appropriate tribute to him. He immediately offered a state funeral in Westminster Abbey. But Disraeli had instructed that he wished to be buried at Hughenden, beside Mary Anne. Gladstone could not decide what he felt about this. On one hand he thought there was 'something very touching' about his wish to be buried with his wife. But on the other he thought it a characteristic pose of pretended simplicity: 'As he lived, so he died – all display, without reality or genuineness.'[193] He caused considerable offence by failing to attend the funeral, unconvincingly pleading a prior engagement. He did attend the memorial service in the Abbey, where he was obliged to listen to the Dean describe himself and Disraeli as the 'Great Twin Brothers' of political life.[194] Finally, after three weeks of sleepless nights and diarrhoea, he managed to deliver a carefully phrased encomium in the Commons. He admitted that he had been 'separated from Lord Beaconsfield by longer and larger differences than, perhaps, ever separated any two persons brought into constant contact in the transaction of Public Business'. He avoided any false praise of Disraeli's contribution to public life, but found several less contentious qualities to celebrate: his 'extraordinary intellectual powers', 'his long-sighted persistency of purpose', allied to 'remarkable power of self-government'; 'his great Parliamentary courage'; his strong sympathies with his race'; and his 'profound . . . affection for his wife'.[195] He was generally thought to have said what was necessary.

To his son Harry he protested: 'I am not and never was his rival, so far as it depended on my will or intention . . . I have been most widely and sharply severed from him, but by something totally different from personal hatred, and I am bound to say I do not think he felt any hatred towards me.'[196] But this was cant. Two days before his Commons tribute, the historian Lord Acton wrote that Gladstone not only thought Disraeli's doctrine false, 'but the

---

*Even on his deathbed, Disraeli was more irreverent. When Victoria asked to visit him he declined the honour, saying, 'She would only ask me to take a message to Albert.'[192]

man more false than the doctrine'.[197] To the very end of his life Gladstone still blamed Disraeli for what he considered 'a distinct decline in the standard of public life'. 'For all this deterioration,' he told John Morley, 'one man and one man alone is responsible . . . He it was who sowed the seed . . . He is the grand corrupter!'[198] 'In past times,' he told another confidant, 'the Tory party had principles by which it would and did stand for bad and for good. All this Dizzy destroyed.'[199]

Gladstone lived for another seventeen years, during which time he formed two more governments and became increasingly obsessed with Ireland, splitting the Liberal party in a doomed crusade to deliver Home Rule. By the end the 'Grand Old Man' seemed more like an Old Testament prophet than a politician, half-terrifying, half-comic. He finally relinquished office in 1894 and died in 1898. Unlike Disraeli, he was buried in Westminster Abbey, near to Pitt, Fox, Canning, Peel and Palmerston, but right at the foot of Disraeli's statue. Eventually Gladstone's own statue was placed not opposite Disraeli's, as was first proposed, but nearby on his left, apparently giving him the cold shoulder for eternity.

Gladstone's later years were curiously dogged by Disraeli's shadow. The one major legislative achievement of his second ministry was another reform bill in 1884, which added two million new rural voters to the register; but this lacked the *éclat* of Disraeli's 1867 Act and probably helped the Conservatives more than the Liberals. Abroad, he was saddled with the legacy of Disraeli's policies in Egypt and South Africa, suffered an embarrassing defeat by the Boers at Majuba Hill and was unfairly blamed – not least by the Queen – for the death of Gordon at Khartoum. Then the Liberal split over Ireland in 1886 allowed the Tory party – now led by the reassuring figure of Salisbury – to become the dominant national party of tradition, patriotism and wealth which Disraeli had always wanted it to be.

Of course Gladstone left a massive legacy of his own. The whole financial and administrative structure of British government, founded on free trade, low taxes and balanced budgets, which lasted well into the twentieth century, was largely his creation. Likewise the Edwardian Liberal party which enjoyed its brief heyday between

1906 and 1915 took its distinctive colouring – moralistic, nonconformist and instinctively (though not always in practice) anti-imperial and anti-militarist – to a great extent from him. Disraeli's career was less obviously successful. He was in government much less, and left a less coherent body of legislation. Yet politically his legacy was almost more enduring. The Tory party which he forged after 1867 somehow united all the most potent symbols of British identity – the monarchy, the Church, the land, the Union and the empire – to create the world's most consistently successful vote-winning machine, which constantly adapted and reinvented itself to stay in power through most of the changing circumstances of the next century, while the Liberal party fractured and faded away. A key element in the party's success, as the electorate expanded, was the appeal to working-class Conservatism announced in Disraeli's Crystal Palace speech of 1872, which in turn harked back to the subtitle of his 1845 novel *Sybil, or The Two Nations*. Cynical, visionary or merely accidental: with Disraeli, who can say? Yet there turned out to be a curious consistency in his apparently unprincipled opportunism which continued to inspire Conservatives – and enrage their opponents – decades after his death.

Both were paradoxical, not to say contradictory, figures: but it was their contradictions which gave their legacies such potency. By their long antagonism, each in important ways helped shape the policies of the other. The young Gladstone was a natural Conservative and still felt himself to be a Tory right up to 1859. But after the Corn Law split of 1846 he was prevented from rejoining his old party largely by his abhorrence of Disraeli, which pushed him reluctantly towards Palmerston and the Liberals instead. He was also driven by a moralistic internationalism, particularly in his deeply felt support for Italian independence, which anticipated his later passionate support for Balkan freedom. But this was greatly sharpened by his detestation of Disraeli, which led him after 1876 to see traditionally pragmatic British foreign policy as irredeemably wicked for no better reason than that it was the policy of his hated rival – in a word 'Beaconsfieldism'. For his part Disraeli, after destroying Peel, coolly ditched protection and from 1853 onwards was content to follow Gladstone's Peelite financial principles. Up to 1870 there was very little in policy content to divide them. The romantic imperialism that he developed from around 1872 was in part an updating of his youthful attachment to the fantasies of 'Young England'. But his Palmerstonian jingoism was also a conscious retort to Gladstone's righteous moralism. The two fed off one another.

Gladstone was clearly the greater Prime Minister, and he beat Disraeli in two of the three elections they fought against each other: in that sense he can be said to have 'won' their lifelong duel. In the longer term he was the embodiment of Victorian financial orthodoxy – the 'Treasury view' which shackled twentieth-century Chancellors down to at least 1940; yet his greatest crusade was waged in opposition to Disraeli's government, and the moral passion of the Midlothian campaign has inspired high-minded protesters from the peace movement of 1920s through CND marchers in the 1950s to opponents of the Iraq war in 2003 (though paradoxically it also inspired Tony Blair). Disraeli's more elusive genius was best displayed in opposition, yet his shrewd fusion of working-class patriotism with 'One Nation' paternalism made the Tories the natural party of government for decades to come. Gladstone's tortured religiosity makes him seem today an archetypal Victorian, a towering historical figure yet almost incomprehensible to modern sensibilities. Disraeli by contrast – witty, cynical and stylish, with a mysterious hint of Oscar Wilde – cuts a far more accessible and attractive figure to modern taste. Dizzy or the Grand Old Man: whichever one prefers, they are unquestionably the two most remarkable personalities who have ever illumined British politics.

H. H. Asquith and
David Lloyd George

For nearly ten years – from December 1905 to the middle of 1915 – Asquith and Lloyd George were good colleagues in one of the most talented governments ever to have ruled Britain. For most of that time they formed the most successful partnership between a Prime Minister and his Chancellor of the Exchequer in the whole of the twentieth century. It was only the strain of fighting the greatest war in history that drove them apart. But then a combination of pride, ambition and the ineluctable logic of events – fanned by the partisanship of their respective followers – transformed them into bitter opponents. As a direct consequence of this internecine rivalry the Gladstonian Liberal party, which had dominated the previous decade, was in the space of a few years practically destroyed.

Both meritocrats of fairly humble origins, they were in every other respect as different as Gladstone and Disraeli: the one a stolid Yorkshireman smoothed by Balliol and the Bar into the epitome of 'effortless superiority', destined from Oxford onwards for membership of the governing elite; the other a mercurial Welshman, raised in rural Caernarvonshire by his cobbler uncle and educated at the local school, polished by no university but determined to storm the citadels of power by his own unaided energy and eloquence. Asquith was ten years older; but they rose by different routes from opposite ends of the Liberal spectrum to reach the two top offices of state at the same time, where they complemented each other perfectly. They moved in different social circles and were never friends; but they respected each other's abilities and balanced each other's qualities. Whereas Asquith was calm, phlegmatic and judicious – the supreme cabinet chairman – Lloyd George was dynamic, imaginative, devious and unpredictable. In peace they worked harmoniously together to leave a legacy of enduring legislation; even in war they still formed, for a time, a powerful combination. By 1914 Lloyd George was widely seen as Asquith's heir apparent, but was in no hurry to grasp the crown. It was the crucible of war which melted Asquith's sterling virtues into liabilities and discovered in Lloyd George the mettle needed in a war leader. If war is the supreme test of leadership, it was Lloyd George – like Churchill twenty-five years later – who rose to the national emergency while Asquith – like Neville Chamberlain – was found wanting. The pity was that Asquith could not accept the fact.

Herbert Henry Asquith was born in 1852, the second son of a Yorkshire wool merchant in a modest way of business, nonconformist in religion and Liberal in politics .* His life, like Canning's, was transformed when he was eight: his father died, and responsibility for his education was taken over by his maternal grandfather and an uncle, who were considerably more prosperous. His invalid mother moved to Sussex, and Herbert and his brother attended the City of London School as day boys, lodging in London. From there he won a classical scholarship to Balliol, where he quickly erased all traces of his provincial roots: he took a first in Greats, was President of the Union and made himself the model 'Balliol man' in the era of its legendary master, Benjamin Jowett. (It was Asquith himself who coined the phrase 'effortless superiority', and he more than anyone else embodied it.) After leaving Oxford his career was initially slow to take off. He was called to the Bar in 1876, but immediately married the daughter of a family friend, who quickly bore him five children: to support this large family he had to supplement his earnings by political journalism. Nevertheless his friend

---

*As a boy, and by his first wife, he was known as Herbert; but his second wife, the formidable but erratic Margot Tennant, whom he married in 1894, always called him Henry. No one outside his family used either name, however, and he always signed himself 'H. H. Asquith'.

R. B. Haldane, another rising young Liberal barrister, wrote that 'from the beginning he meant to be Prime Minister'.[1]

His path into Parliament was eased by the Liberal split over Irish Home Rule in 1886. With Haldane's help he secured the nomination for East Fife, where the sitting Member had joined the Liberal Unionists, and went on to hold the seat for the next thirty-two years. His potential was quickly spotted by Gladstone, who invited him to dinner and gave him some classic advice, attributed to several Prime Ministers down the years: 'If ever you have to form a government, you must steel your nerves and act the butcher.'[2] But it was another six years before the Grand Old Man was in a position to give him his first lift towards that destiny by appointing him Home Secretary in his last ministry. He was not quite forty, with no previous experience of office, but quickly showed himself to be a safe pair of hands.

David Lloyd George had been elected to Parliament two years earlier, aged twenty-seven. His origins were romantic. He was born in 1863 – actually in Manchester, where his father, though thoroughly Welsh, was briefly a headmaster. But William George died before his son was two, and young Di, or Davy, was brought up by his mother's brother, Richard Lloyd, shoemaker and Baptist preacher in the tiny Welsh-speaking village of Llanystumdwy, near Criccieth.* 'Uncle Lloyd' quickly realised his nephew's exceptional talent and encouraged him to fulfil it: from an early age Lloyd George never lacked self-confidence. 'My supreme idea is to get on,' he wrote to his boyhood sweetheart, Maggie Owen. 'I am prepared to thrust even love itself under the wheels of my Juggernaut if it obstructs the way.'[3] Despite this clear warning she still married him. He left school at sixteen and was articled to a local solicitor, passed his exams and set up his own practice in Porthmadog in 1885 – soon joined by his younger brother who selflessly did most of the work while Lloyd George pursued his political career. He made his name in a celebrated case defending the burial rights of nonconformists against Anglican bigotry, and

---

*He combined his uncle's surname with his father's to give the double-barrelled (but not hyphenated) name Lloyd George. Opponents often called him George in a deliberate effort to diminish him.

on the strength of that success was adopted as Liberal candidate for the local constituency of Caernarvon Boroughs which he won – by 18 votes – in 1890.

For his first few years in Parliament Lloyd George operated virtually as a Welsh nationalist, consolidating his local base before launching himself on the wider national stage. Very early he recognised Asquith as a model, writing to Uncle Lloyd a few days after his maiden speech that he did not intend to speak too often. 'Asquith, who of all the comparatively young men has the highest reputation, speaks but once, occasionally twice, during a Session. He has thus acquired a status and always gets an audience.'[4] Writing for a Welsh local paper – he too relied on journalism in his early days to supplement his income – he described Asquith for his readers as 'a short, thick-set, rather round-shouldered man with a face as clean shaven as that of the most advanced curate, keen eyes and a broad intellectual forehead. He is the hope of the rising generation of Radicals . . . and sets out his arguments with great brilliancy and force.'[5] Having opened an office in London he was delighted to be able to brief Asquith in at least one case.[6] There are no more references in his letters, however, until 1895 when he wrote to Maggie of a 'fine duel' between Asquith and Joseph Chamberlain, who 'delivered a tremendous onslaught on the Government . . . Asquith simply smashed Chamberlain up'.[7] Since Lloyd George had a high regard for Chamberlain – and would later make his own parliamentary reputation by attacking him – this must have impressed him. Two years after this he entertained Asquith as the principal speaker at a Liberal rally in Caernarvon and introduced him as a future Liberal Prime Minister.[8]

By then they had crossed swords for the first time when Asquith – reappointed Home Secretary by Lord Rosebery when Gladstone finally retired in 1894 – introduced a bill to disestablish the Welsh Church. This was a measure close to Lloyd George's heart; but it had no chance of becoming law against the entrenched opposition of the House of Lords. Asquith regarded it merely as part of the process of 'ploughing the sands' – that is building up the case for curbing the Lords' veto, which he and Lloyd George would eventually achieve together in 1911. Sixteen years earlier Lloyd George and his Welsh colleagues effectively scuppered Asquith's bill by trying to transform it into a Home Rule measure. In his memoir *Fifty Years of Parliament,* Asquith recalled with characteristic understatement that 'One of the youngest of them, a natural *frondeur,* and already an acute and accomplished debater, Mr Lloyd George, from time to time gave me a certain amount of trouble.'[9] At the time he was a good deal more exercised: he blamed Lloyd George's intriguing with the Tories over disestablishment for helping to bring down the Liberal government in June 1895. Later that year he wrote to the Chief Whip, Tom Ellis, that he had been too generous in defending his Welsh colleague:

> It is not . . . strictly accurate to say we 'accepted' Ll.G.'s amendment, and I think you showed rather too great a tendency to whitewash him, after the underhand and disloyal fashion in which he undoubtedly acted.[10]

With the fall of the Rosebery government the Liberals went into opposition for ten years while Lord Salisbury – the last peer to be Prime Minister – followed by his nephew Arthur Balfour headed Tory governments which in 1899 took the country to war against the Boer republics in South Africa. The Boer war divided the Liberal party, with Asquith and Lloyd George in opposing camps. Asquith followed Rosebery and the Liberal Imperialist section of the party in supporting the war; Lloyd George sided with Sir Henry Campbell-Bannerman and the 'pro-Boers' in condemning the heavy-handed bullying of a small farming community at the behest of greedy adventurers like Cecil Rhodes. There was an echo here of Gladstone's denunciation of the Bulgarian atrocities. Though by no means anti-imperialist, still less pacifist, Lloyd George by his courageous opposition to the Boer war established himself as the leading figure on the radical wing of the party. In June 1901 Asquith wrote that it was time for those Liberals 'who are not willing that the [party] should be captured by Lloyd George and his friends to bestir themselves'.[11] In a speech the next day he firmly answered Campbell-Bannerman and, by implication, Lloyd George. The latter nevertheless insisted that he was 'happily on terms of absolute personal friendship with Mr Asquith', adding pointedly: 'My policy has never been to attack any section of my own party.'[12]

When the war ended, the two wings were quickly reunited, and the Tories split, by Chamberlain's campaign for tariff reform, which challenged another part of the Gladstonian legacy, free trade. In May 1902 Lloyd George ran into Asquith at Crewe station and travelled with him to London. 'He was very affable and talkative,' he wrote (in Welsh) to Maggie.[13] Six months later Asquith praised a speech by Lloyd George against Balfour's Education Bill. And in July 1904 Lloyd George dined with the Asquiths in Cavendish Square. 'Very grand,' he reported. '3 or 4 Lords & Lord Rosebery there.'[14] But tension still persisted. When Rosebery petulantly resigned the leadership some years earlier, Asquith and his friends had accepted Campbell-Bannerman as stopgap leader; but as the prospect of a return to power beckoned, they hoped to replace him with Asquith as leader in the Commons under Rosebery, or possibly Earl Spencer, as Prime Minister in the Lords. When informed of this plan by Edward Grey, Lloyd George told him it was 'impossible, as it means shelving C.B. & Morley. I told him that could not be done.'[15] When the Tory government finally resigned in December 1905 he again opposed the plot to kick Campbell-Bannerman upstairs, which would have left Asquith leader in the Commons. His objection was not to Asquith personally, but to the Liberal Imperialists having too much of their own way.

Campbell-Bannerman – a shrewder politician than he seemed – called his detractors' bluff and formed a government which skilfully balanced the two wings of the party. Asquith became Chancellor of the Exchequer, Grey Foreign Secretary and Haldane Secretary of State for War; but Lloyd George, with no previous experience of office, went straight into the Cabinet as President of the Board of Trade, while John Morley – Gladstone's biographer – became Secretary for India. The new government immediately went to the country and won a landslide victory – the zenith, as it turned out, of Liberal fortunes. At the Treasury Asquith was unexpectedly innovative. In his 1907 budget he differentiated between earned and unearned incomes, raised death duties, and wanted to move to a graduated income tax – a measure later implemented by Lloyd George. The following year he announced the introduction of old age pensions, though again it was Lloyd George who carried them through and reaped most of the credit. Lloyd George meanwhile was a notably constructive President of the Board of Trade, carrying several important pieces of regulatory legislation and displaying a flair for resolving industrial disputes. When Campbell-Bannerman's health failed in April 1908, Asquith was his unchallenged successor; and Lloyd George, after only two years in government, took his place at the Treasury.

Asquith toyed with the idea of retaining the Treasury himself, as Gladstone had done in 1880; but he was persuaded that he must promote 'a man of the left' to maintain the balance of the government, and that effectively meant Lloyd George.[16] Nevertheless it was a bold appointment which illustrates Asquith's self-confidence. 'The offer which I am privileged to make,' he wrote, 'is a well-deserved tribute to your long & eminent services to our party, and to the splendid capacity which you have shown in the administration of the Board of Trade.' Yet the new Chancellor was not only an advanced radical, distrusted by many as a vulgar demagogue, but wholly ignorant of finance. Asquith knew that the challenge might either make Lloyd George or break him: 'It is at once the most thankless, & the most full of opportunities, in the whole Government.'[17] If not yet formally recognised as the second job in the government, it was the stepping-stone from which Gladstone, Disraeli and he himself had reached the premiership. Not surprisingly, Lloyd George accepted gratefully: 'I thank you for the flattering proposal contained in your letter, & even more for the generous terms in which it is conveyed to me . . . I shall be proud to serve under your Premiership & no member of the Government will render more loyal service & support to his chief.'[18]

At the same time, however, he felt obliged to deny responsibility for leaking the names of the new cabinet to the *Daily Chronicle*: he knew that his rapid rise had made him powerful enemies and that he was peculiarly dependent on Asquith's protection. 'Men whose promotion is not sustained by birth or other favouring conditions,' he wrote, 'are always liable to be assailed with unkind suspicions of this sort. I would ask it therefore as a favour that you should not entertain them without satisfying yourself that they have some basis of truth.'[19] Asquith accepted his denial 'without reserve'; but he would always remain suspicious of Lloyd George's contacts with the press.[20]

For the next six years they worked remarkably harmoniously together. This Liberal cabinet was the most brilliant of the twentieth century. In Haldane (who moved to the Woolsack in 1912), Morley (Lord President from 1910) and Augustine Birrell (Chief Secretary for Ireland) it boasted three men of real intellectual distinction; several others were of more than average ability; while Asquith made another bold appointment by promoting the thirty-three-year-old Winston Churchill to Lloyd George's old job at the Board of Trade. Churchill, then an outspoken radical, was immediately identified as Lloyd George's younger sidekick: known as the 'heavenly twins', they struck alarm and outrage in conservative breasts by their 'socialistic' policies and 'class war' rhetoric. Asquith presided over this galaxy of talent with Olympian authority, generally resolving the inevitable conflicts with unruffled urbanity. As a former Chancellor himself he regarded his successor's unorthodox approach to finance with amused tolerance. 'I am just going to have half an hour with Lloyd George over his budget – always a baffling kind of amusement,' he wrote to his platonic love Venetia Stanley in 1914.[21] 'I had a whole hour (!) with Ll.G,' he added the next day, 'and we played about with millions and tens of millions with good humour & even gaiety. No-one can hop with greater agility from one twig (or even one tree or forest) to another.'[22] By this time Lloyd George had already been at the Treasury for six years: but a little rhyme Asquith wrote in 1909 shows that he had felt the same way from the beginning:

> George moves in a mysterious way,
> His little sums to make;
> Loose logic, lax arithmetic,
> Contribute to the fake.[23]

Asquith admired Lloyd George's resourcefulness and ingenuity, but there was a streak of intellectual snobbery in his attitude to both Lloyd George and Churchill, neither of whom had been to university. 'Our two rhetoricians,' he wrote in 1915, 'have good brains of different types. But they can only think talking: just as some people can only think writing. Only the salt of the earth' – among whom he clearly counted himself – 'can think inside, and the bulk of mankind cannot think at all.'[24] He was constantly surprised that someone so uneducated as Lloyd George could be so clever. At the same time some colleagues felt he was afraid of Lloyd George. Charles Hobhouse – whom Asquith had made Financial Secretary specifically to keep the Chancellor under some control – frequently complained that Asquith gave Lloyd George too much rope and failed to stand up to him when he should have done. When Hobhouse was driven to distraction by Lloyd George's chaotic methods, Asquith told him that 'he recognised the difficulty and experienced it himself', but appealed to him 'on personal and political grounds not to resign'.[25] He knew that, with all his failings, Lloyd George gave the government a cutting edge and dynamism which he himself could never match.

Above all, he fully supported Lloyd George's 1909 budget – the famous 'People's Budget' – which substantially raised direct taxation, specifically on land and higher incomes, to meet increased defence expenditure and the cost of old age pensions without recourse to tariffs. The strategy was deliberately planned by the two of them, *not* to provoke the House of Lords – they did not believe the peers would dare reject the budget – but to avert a Lords veto by incorporating the government's social reforms in the form of a money bill. The budget aroused a huge outcry, not only among the Tories: Rosebery emerged from semi-retirement to damn it as 'inquisitorial, tyrannical and Socialistic', and a delegation of Liberal backbenchers protested to Asquith. But Asquith was 'firm as a rock' in resisting them.[26] Unusually the budget was fully discussed by the cabinet over fourteen meetings at which the Chancellor's enemies tried to moderate or emasculate it. Several of the critics, including Haldane, Reginald McKenna and Walter Runciman, were Asquith's closest friends. Nevertheless, Lloyd George told a Welsh colleague that 'the Prime Minister has backed me up through thick and thin with splendid loyalty. I have the deepest respect for him and he has real sympathy for the ordinary and the poor.'[27] To the end of his life Lloyd George never qualified his gratitude for Asquith's support at this time. Hobhouse was more cynical about his motives: 'It is difficult to say whether he is helping Ll. G. ride for a fall, or whether he is afraid of his influence with the press and of his popularity.'[28] In fact Asquith was as committed as Lloyd George to their joint objectives, and when the House of Lords provoked a constitutional crisis by rejecting the budget he grasped the nettle of enforcing the Commons' democratic will unflinchingly.

On 30 July Lloyd George made a celebrated speech at Limehouse, in east London, in which he strongly condemned the selfishness of wealthy landowners who objected to paying increased taxes to ease the old age of the working poor. Edward VII was alarmed by what he saw as naked rabble-rousing, and Asquith felt obliged to pass on the King's 'great agitation and annoyance'. But he couched his criticism in the mildest, almost avuncular, terms:

> I have, as you know, heartily & loyally backed the Budget from the first, and at every stage; and I have done, and shall continue to do, all I can to commend it to the country. But I feel very strongly that at this moment what is needed is reasoned appeal to moderate & reasonable men. There is great & growing popular enthusiasm. But this will not carry us through – if we rouse the suspicions & fears of the middle class, & particularly if we give countenance to the notion that the Budget is conceived in a spirit of vindictiveness.

'I am sure you will take what I have written in good part,' he concluded amiably. 'My sole object is to bring our ship safely into port.'[29]

The peers' action provoked the biggest constitutional showdown of the twentieth century. After a general election in January 1910 left the the government dependent on Labour and the Irish for its majority the cabinet introduced a Parliament Bill to curtail the Lords' powers. But in May Edward VII died, prompting a political truce during which the parties tried to find a compromise solution. A Constitutional Convention met over the summer but failed to break the deadlock. Behind the scenes Lloyd George floated a daring scheme of his own for a grand coalition to resolve a wide range of national problems: not just the House of Lords, but Irish Home Rule, land reform and unemployment, even floating the possibility of tariff reform and compulsory military service. Later his willingness to compromise such vital articles of the Liberal faith was held to prove that he had always been a closet Tory just waiting for an opportunity to betray the Liberal party; it was also suggested that he was scheming to displace Asquith or send him to the Lords. But there is no evidence to validate these suspicions. He was certainly more concerned with solving problems than with doctrinal purity; and he may have shown his memorandum to Churchill and Tory friends like F. E. Smith before clearing it with Asquith. But neither Asquith nor any of his senior colleagues disowned his initiative. It was not Asquith but Balfour's determination not to split the Tory party which doomed it to failure. When the constitutional convention collapsed that autumn party strife was resumed with undiminished bitterness. Following a second general election which duplicated the result of the first, the new King reluctantly agreed to create enough new Liberal peers to force the Parliament Bill through the Upper House; and after another summer of high tension the Lords eventually gave way in August 1911. During this protracted crisis Lloyd George expressed only admiration for Asquith's cool handling of the government's case.

Meanwhile Asquith strongly backed his Chancellor's introduction of National Insurance against ill health and (to a limited degree) unemployment – another historic innovation which had to be forced through against powerful opposition from the doctors and friendly societies. And it was to Lloyd George that he turned in August 1911 to resolve a damaging rail strike, after his own efforts had only stiffened the strikers' determination. When Lloyd George succeeded in getting the strike called off after 48 hours Asquith thanked him warmly for 'the indomitable purpose, the untiring energy and the matchless skill' with which he had resolved the problem. He added: 'It is the latest, but by no means the least, of the loyal and invaluable services which you have rendered since I came to the head of the Government 3½ years ago.'[30] Lloyd George responded with equal warmth, telling Asquith's fourteen-year-old daughter Elizabeth – who had also written to congratulate him – that he would treasure her father's letter to the end of his days. 'I cannot tell you how proud I am of it. What a fine fellow he is to serve under, generous and chivalrous and so far above the pettiness which spoils most of us public men.'[31]

Asquith showed his generosity most clearly during the Marconi scandal of 1912–13, when Lloyd George and two other ministers were accused of trading improperly in shares in the American wireless company at a time when the government was awarding contracts to its British sister company. In fact Lloyd George was foolish rather than corrupt – 'insider trading', as it would now be called, was not at the time illegal; but his defence was initially lacking in candour and the episode was damaging to the government. With the Tories baying for blood Asquith could easily have accepted his resignation: he told the King that his three colleagues' conduct had been 'difficult to defend'.[32] But defend it he did, declaring in the Commons that their honour was 'absolutely unstained'.[33] He may have felt obliged to defend Lloyd George because he knew that the government Chief Whip – one of the ministers involved – had also bought Marconi shares on behalf of the Liberal party. Nevertheless the affair stands as a model instance of a Prime Minister successfully defending an embattled colleague – one which John Major and Tony Blair, for instance, were rarely able to emulate; and once again Lloyd George was properly grateful. There is just one suggestion that Asquith may have welcomed his Chancellor's embarrassment. Listening to Lloyd George speaking in the House some time later he remarked *sotto voce* to Charles Masterman: 'I think the idol's wings are a bit clipped.'[34]

Lloyd George's star was dimmed, but not for long. Despite some setbacks in the next two years – a land reform campaign which never took off and a clumsy budget in 1914 – he was still universally seen as Asquith's likeliest successor. Even at the height of the Marconi scandal Austen Chamberlain – a normally shrewd observer from the other side of the House – wrote that 'No-one could stand against George. Grey might have done at one time, but not now.' Lloyd George, he thought, was 'straining on the leash because he was determined to be the Radical candidate for the succession', while Asquith was 'very tired and almost ready to go'.[35] In fact there is no evidence either that Asquith contemplated retiring – he was only sixty in 1912 – or that Lloyd George was impatient to take over. He knew very well that he had too many enemies: he still needed Asquith's protection to enable him to pursue his own objectives. Moreover he lacked the social position then felt necessary for the premiership. His time would surely come; meanwhile he saw Asquith as an almost perfect chief under whom he was happy to serve. 'He is a big man,' he told a confidant, the news-paper proprietor Lord Riddell. 'He never initiates anything, but he is a great judge. He brushes aside all small points, and goes straight to the heart of the subject. I prefer to discuss a big project with him rather than with anyone else.'[36]

In these years Asquith needed all his imperturbability to deal with an unprecedented range of challenges: not only the House of Lords crisis, but continuing industrial unrest, the suffragette campaign, Ulster's implacable resistance to Irish Home Rule and on the continent a growing threat from Germany. On most of these issues Prime Minister and Chancellor worked closely together, and they were beginning to see more of one another socially as well. In March 1914 Asquith wrote warily to Venetia Stanley: 'I am going to dine with Lloyd George (a very unusual adventure) to talk "shop" with one or two choice colleagues.'[37] The two men's atti-tudes to meals were entirely different. Asquith liked to relax with friends, drink too much wine, and play bridge; Lloyd George disliked society and used mealtimes to conduct business – he was especially fond of working breakfasts. Yet over the next few weeks they dined twice more together and Lloyd George lunched once at Number Ten. Over Whitsun Asquith was staying in Anglesey with Venetia's parents, Lord and Lady Sheffield, when Lloyd George invited himself from Criccieth for a couple of days. 'I didn't want to see him particu-larly,' Asquith wrote to Margot, 'as it rather spoils the holiday atmosphere, and all he has to say can keep till London.' But when he came they had a good game of golf – 'Ll. George drives quite well & is not bad with his iron, but is an execrable putter' – and Lloyd George was 'in very good conversational form and made himself agreeable to the Sheffields after his fashion', going some way to overcoming their 'aversion' to him.[38]

In this last summer of peace Ireland overshadowed everything else; and once again Asquith turned to Lloyd George to try to promote a settlement. First he deputed him to persuade the Nationalist leader John Redmond to concede the temporary exclu-sion of Ulster from Home Rule; then he was determined to have Lloyd George, rather than Lord Crewe, as his colleague at a round-table conference at Buckingham Palace in July, telling Crewe that Lloyd George's 'peculiar gifts of blandishment and

negotiation would be invaluable'.³⁹ The conference came down
to a wrangle over the inclusion of parts of County Tyrone in the
area to be excluded. 'L.G. & I worked hard to get rid of the
county areas altogether & proceed on Poor Law Unions wh.
afford a good basis of give & take,' Asquith told Venetia. 'But
again both Irish lots would have none of it.'⁴⁰ The conference
was a failure. But within days, as Churchill wrote, 'the parishes
of Fermanagh and Tyrone faded back into the mists and squalls
of Ireland' as war engulfed the continent and the British cabinet
had to decide whether to join in.⁴¹

Ever since his opposition to the Boer war Lloyd George had been
assumed to be on the 'pacifist' wing of the Liberal party. This did
not mean that he was in any strict sense a pacifist, merely that he
was against excessive expenditure on the army and navy. As
Chancellor he had resisted the demands of successive First Lords
of the Admiralty – McKenna in 1908, then Churchill in 1914 –
for increased naval building. But in July 1911 he had made – with
Asquith's approval – an important speech warning Germany against
meddling in Morocco; and the following month he had written
presciently to Churchill that 'the thunderclouds are gathering. I am
not at all satisfied that we are preparing, or that we are prepared.'⁴²
So he had already moved a long way towards contemplating war
before August 1914.

   When the crisis came his position was pivotal. On one side Grey
had committed Britain so far to helping France that he would have
resigned if the cabinet had not supported him. Asquith took much
the same view, but was concerned to take the country into war
with as few resignations as possible. On 1 August he wrote that
several colleagues were on 'the *Manchester Guardian* tack' – against
war in any circumstances. 'This no doubt is the view for the moment
of the bulk of the party. Ll. George – all for peace – is more sensible
& statesmanlike – for keeping the position still open.'⁴³ The next
day Lloyd George was still against 'any kind of intervention in any
event' and still inclined towards resignation, until swayed the other
way by the German ultimatum to Belgium.⁴⁴ On 3 August he wrote
to Maggie: 'I have fought hard for peace & succeeded so far in
keeping the Cabinet out of it but I am driven to the conclusion

that if the small nationality of Belgium is attacked by Germany all my traditions & even prejudices will be engaged on the side of war.'[45] In the event only two cabinet ministers resigned. Yet Asquith was depressed to find himself cheered by patriotic crowds as he walked to the House of Commons. 'I have never before been a popular character with the "man in the street",' he wrote, 'and in all this dark and dangerous business it gives me scant pleasure . . . We are on the eve of horrible things.'[46] Lloyd George too was 'filled with horror at the prospect. I am even more horrified that I should ever appear to have a share in it but I must bear my share of the ghastly burden though it scorches my flesh to do so.'[47] Neither man doubted the gravity of what lay ahead; but the outbreak of war did not divide them. Asquith was grateful that Lloyd George came down on the right side; while Lloyd George's admiration of the Prime Minister was only reinforced by his cool handling of the crisis. Asquith, he told Riddell in October, was 'a very strong man'.[48] From now on, however, he was to become steadily more critical.

From the beginning, the two men had different conceptions of how the war should be fought. The limited and distant episode of the Crimea apart – and that was sixty years ago – Britain had not fought a European war for nearly a century. Asquith accordingly viewed 1914 from the perspective of 1793–1815, when Britain had waged war on revolutionary and Napoleonic France mainly by subsidising continental allies while maintaining her traditional supremacy at sea. Not until the very end had she put a large army into the field (and even then it was half the size of the Prussian forces). In August 1914 the cabinet agreed to send a British Expeditionary Force of six divisions – around 120,000 men – to fight alongside the French; but Asquith's initial assumption, shared by most of his colleagues, was that Britain's contribution to the Allied cause would once again be primarily naval and financial. Within weeks Lord Kitchener – the country's most famous soldier, who was appointed Secretary of State for War virtually by popular demand on the outbreak of hostilities – insisted that, on the contrary, seventy divisions would be required. Asquith assented, but it was still to be a volunteer army, recruited by Kitchener's famous poster campaign: there was to be no compulsory mobilisation of the country's youth for war. Asquith's second assumption was that the war should be fought with as little disruption as possible to the life of the country and directed by the normal procedures of cabinet government, leaving military strategy largely to the professionals.

With both these assumptions Lloyd George quickly came to differ. Once committed, he believed that the war must be fought with all the resources at the nation's command. He agreed with Kitchener's assessment of the need for massive deployment of manpower, by compulsion if necessary, and the forcible redirection of industrial capacity into arming these vast new armies. He also believed that war called for a more streamlined machinery of government than the sort of leisurely discussion that sufficed in peace. On these two issues – conscription and the need for a small war cabinet – he and Asquith were increasingly at odds. Asquith steadily gave ground on the former; but the latter eventually caused a decisive breach between them. Philosophically they marked the difference between two opposed principles. Asquith and most of his close colleagues represented the classical liberal view of relations between the individual and the state which held that the state had no right to compel its citizens to fight, nor to co-opt private business to serve the war effort, and that compulsion infringed the very liberty the war was being fought to defend. 'Prussianism', they argued, could not be defeated by Prussian methods. Lloyd George, conversely, thought that Prussianism could only be defeated by Prussian methods. He believed that the nation was fighting for its life, and that such squeamishness about means would lead only to disaster and defeat. Set against Asquith's civilised but essentially nineteenth-century conception of limited war, fought by the military on behalf of civil society, his was a more ruthless twentieth-century vision of 'total' war, waged between whole societies mobilised for the struggle. The longer the war lasted, the more certain it was that Lloyd George's unflinching vision would have to prevail.

For the first few weeks Lloyd George's energy was largely absorbed by Treasury matters: his decisive action to preserve the nation's credit won high praise from City financiers who had hitherto abhorred him. By the time he turned his attention to the fighting, Belgium and north-eastern France had been overrun, the BEF had fallen back to protect the coast and the war had settled into the grim attrition which was to last for the next three and a half years. At first his criticism was directed at the military. 'Had I not been a witness of their deplorable lack of provision,' he wrote to Asquith at the turn of the year, 'I should not have thought it possible that men so responsibly placed could have displayed so little foresight.'[49] But very soon he was focusing on Asquith's limitations as a war leader. 'He lacks initiative,' he told Riddell in March 1915, 'and takes no steps to control or hold together the public departments, each of which goes its own way without criticism. This is all very well in time of peace, but during a great war the Prime Minister should direct and overlook the whole machine.'[50] This was the nub of his difference with Asquith which widened inexorably up to December 1916.

Lloyd George was – with Kitchener – one of the first to grasp that the war was going to be long and gruelling and would demand exceptional measures undreamed of in Asquith's philosophy. But he vehemently denied reports that he was plotting to replace the Prime Minister. When Asquith challenged him directly he attributed the story to his principal enemy among his colleagues, Reginald McKenna:

As for himself . . . he declared that he owed everything to me; that I had stuck to him & protected him & defended him when every man's hand was against him; and that he wd rather (1) break stones (2) dig potatoes (3) be hanged and quartered (these were metaphors used at different stages of his broken but impassioned harangue) than do an act, or say a word, or harbour a thought, that was disloyal to me . . . His eyes were wet with tears, and I am sure that with all his Celtic capacity for impulsive & momentary fervour, he was quite sincere.[51]

Lloyd George's version, as told to his secretary/mistress Frances Stevenson, was that it was 'the old boy' who was in tears.[52] The next day he reiterated his denial to Riddell:

I have never intrigued for place or office. I have intrigued to carry out my schemes, but that is a different matter. The Prime Minister has been so good to me that I would never be disloyal to him in the smallest detail. I may criticise him amongst ourselves, as I have no doubt he criticizes me, but we are absolutely loyal to each other.[53]

In fact, far from plotting to become Prime Minister, Lloyd George was preoccupied at this time with a scheme to boost the war effort by curbing excessive drinking by key workers. 'It is characteristic of LG's versatility of interest & mind,' Asquith wrote on 25 March, 'that . . . he is for the moment red-hot with a plan, or rather an idea, for nationalising the drink trade!'[54] Six days later he was rather less amused. No sooner had he settled the row between Lloyd George and McKenna, he told Venetia, 'than this versatile & volatile personage goes off at score on the question of drink, about wh. he has completely lost his head . . . He is a wonderful person in some ways, but is totally devoid of either perspective or judgment; and on the whole during these 7 years he has given me more worry than any other colleague.'[55]

Seeing that Asquith thought his ambitious scheme impracticable, however, Lloyd George quickly modified it, vowing that 'he wd. never go ahead with anything that I disapproved'.[56]* For the moment they continued to be the best of colleagues. Lloyd George would drop in from Number Eleven to Number Ten most days for what Asquith ironically called 'his favourite morning indulgence (it corresponds in him to the dram drinking of the Clyde workmen) – a 10-minute discursive discussion of things in general'.[58] In a characteristic aside in April he noted that Lloyd George 'of course is not quite *au fond* a gentleman'.[59] But the next month it was still the Chancellor whom Asquith took most into his confidence when he reluctantly accepted the need to meet mounting criticism of the conduct of the war by forming a coalition.

Even under the stress of war Asquith had no wish to broaden his government. 'To seem to welcome into the intimacy of the political household, strange, alien, hitherto hostile figures', he wrote, was 'most intolerable'.[60] The one Tory for whom he had any regard

---

*Asquith was worried that he might be expected to follow the King's example by giving up drink for the duration of the war; but Lloyd George assured him that he would be able to get a doctor's certificate vouching that alcohol was necessary to him. 'At that,' he told Miss Stevenson, 'the P.M. brightened up. "Oh well", he said strutting up and down the room, "there will be any amount of doctor's certificates!"'[57] Lloyd George himself drank very little and was always mildly censorious of Asquith's heavy consumption.

was Balfour, whom he described with a typical mix of intellectual and social snobbery as 'the only quick mind in that ill-bred crowd'.[61] He had particular contempt for Bonar Law – a Glasgow iron merchant who, like Lloyd George, had not been to university. As Leader of the Opposition, Law should naturally have had a leading position in the new government – even the deputy premiership, like Attlee in 1940. But Asquith was determined to keep all the key offices in Liberal hands. The most urgent need was to speed up the supply of munitions to the army: it was a critical lack of shells – plus the resignation of the seventy-seven-year-old First Sea Lord, Admiral 'Jacky' Fisher, after a climactic row with Churchill – which finally forced his hand. Rather than give this vital job to Law, however, Asquith as usual turned to Lloyd George and persuaded him to take it on. This left an obvious opening for Law to become Chancellor; but Lloyd George – unwilling to give up the second place in the government – agreed to move to Munitions only on condition that the Treasury was kept open for him. Asquith agreed and appointed McKenna Chancellor on a temporary basis – Lloyd George continued to live at No.11 Downing Street – while Law was palmed off with the relatively marginal job of Colonial Secretary. Altogether the Tories received only eight places (out of twenty-one) in the new cabinet; and only Balfour, who replaced Churchill at the Admiralty, got a department directly concerned with the war.

During these negotiations Lloyd George told both his wife and his mistress that the Tories wanted him to become Prime Minister, but 'he had absolutely refused the proposal, as being unfaithful to the present P.M.'[62] There is no independent record of this: he may have been exaggerating to impress his women. But there is no doubt that Asquith still trusted him. Lloyd George reported to Maggie on 21 May that he was 'still engaged as an assistant Cabinet maker to the P.M. All day at it & we meet the Tories at 11.30 tomorrow.'[63] Evidently he was also talking to Law and Balfour behind Asquith's back. But when the new cabinet was formed, Asquith wrote him another fulsome letter of appreciation:

My dear Lloyd George,
  I cannot let this troubled & tumultuous chapter in our history close without trying to let you know what an incalculable help &

support I have found in you all through. I shall never forget your devotion, your unselfishness, your powers of resource, what is (after all) the best of all things your self-forgetfulness.

These are the rare things that make the drudgery and squalor of politics, with its constant revelation of the large part played by petty & personal motives, endurable, and give to its drabness a lightning streak of nobility.

I thank you with all my heart.

Always your affect.

H. H. Asquith.[64]

'This letter,' Lloyd George wrote in his *War Memoirs,* 'from the man who had been my colleague for ten years, and to whom I had been principal parliamentary lieutenant for seven years, gave me great delight. The black squad of envy had not yet succeeded in poisoning the wells of confidence between captain and second officer.'[65] At the time he sent it to Maggie with the comment: 'He doesn't know that I refused the Premiership from the Tories.'[66]

Asquith may have leaned on Lloyd George more than usual during this crisis because he had just received a severe emotional blow: Venetia Stanley told him on 12 May that she was going to marry one of his own younger ministers, Edwin Montagu. Asquith was devastated. Venetia was almost certainly not his lover, but he had formed a deep emotional dependence on her: he wrote to her several times a day, often during cabinet – long, intimate letters full of high-level political information. They also went for drives together, holding hands under a rug: Venetia gave him the sort of calm sympathetic support that he did not get from his highly strung and furiously combative wife Margot. But at just the moment when he needed her most, this prop was removed. The contrast with Lloyd George is telling. He too had a young female companion with whom he shared his political hopes and fears. But Frances Stevenson was unambiguously his mistress. Lloyd George was a compulsive womaniser who had enjoyed numerous affairs since entering Parliament in 1890; his wife preferred to live in Wales and came to London only rarely. Frances entered his life in 1911 as tutor to his youngest daughter, and became his secretary in 1913, which gave cover for them to be together virtually every day. For the rest of his life – including his six years as Prime Minister – Lloyd George was effectively a bigamist, dividing his time between Maggie in Wales and Frances (who finally became his second wife in 1943) in London and Surrey. During these critical years Frances gave him not only sexual and secretarial, but also moral and emotional support which helped him carry the strain of directing the greatest war in history. Venetia by contrast removed herself from Asquith's life in May 1915. 'I have made up my mind to try (with whatever I have left) to push this war through,' he wrote in one of his last heartbroken letters to her.[67] But he was never the same man again.

The formation of the coalition spelled the end of the last purely Liberal government. It also highlighted the growing difference between the Liberal and Tory approaches to the war. Asquith tried honourably to hold the two sections of the government together; but he was never comfortable dealing with former opponents, and in the battles that arose – notably over conscription – he leaned naturally to the Liberal side for as long as possible. Lloyd George by contrast was a natural coalitionist who had always been impatient of party constraints. Now his mounting dissatisfaction with the conduct of the war, and his anxiety to prosecute it more vigorously, found a readier echo among the Tories than in his own party. He still protested that he had no wish to displace Asquith. But there was an ineluctable logic leading in that direction – as a good many Liberals helplessly recognised. 'The disintegration of the Liberal Party is complete,' Charles Hobhouse lamented. 'Ll.G. and his Tory friends will soon get rid of Asquith, and the one or two genuine Liberals left.'[68] Hobhouse was one of those excluded from the new cabinet; but just a month later Walter Runciman described to him its tense dynamics:

> The P.M. on the defensive, very apprehensive, and at last alive to the consequence of his slothfulness and timidity . . . Ll. G. hand in hand with B. Law . . . Ll. G. and the P.M. hostile to and watchful of each other.[69]

Conscription was the key. Broadly speaking the Tories wanted it and the Liberals did not. Asquith responded as a party rather than a national leader. The Chief Whip, he wrote in August, was being deluged with 'letters from Liberal chairmen etc. all over the country denouncing Lloyd George as a lost soul . . . predicting that conscription would bring us to the verge, or over the verge, of revolution'.[70] And in September: 'If I were to announce myself tomorrow a reluctant but whole-hearted convert to Compulsion, I should still have to face the hostility of some of the best, and in the country some of the most powerful, elements of the Liberal Party.'[71]

His solution was to let the momentum for conscription build until it became irresistible, postponing the moment of decision by means of a scheme by which young unmarried men 'attested' their willingness to serve before they were actually called up. To his critics this was mere temporising, embodied in the deadly catchphrase 'Wait and See'. Asquith had first used it in connection with the House of Lords crisis back in 1910, when it had carried an air of strength and menace; now it seemed to epitomise a government drifting from lack of leadership. By October 1915 Lloyd George's admiration for his chief was turning to contempt, as Frances recorded:

> D. says that the P.M. has followed the 'wait and see' policy so long
> that in wartime he cannot be got to understand that it is disastrous . . .
> He says it is impossible to get the P.M. to do anything . . . He just
> sits there and uses the whole of his crafty brain to squash any plan
> for action that is put forward. D. says that if he were in the pay of
> the Germans he could not be of more complete use to them.[72]

If Lloyd George really believed this, it would soon be his duty to try to remove him.

Towards the end of 1915 Asquith did exert himself to try to grasp the situation. By this time the secretive and autocratic Kitchener was widely recognised as an obstacle to clear decision-making. Lloyd George – now working furiously to speed up the supply of munitions – threatened to resign unless he was replaced. Asquith was not above playing the two against each other. On 17 October he wrote to Kitchener that Lloyd George and his Tory allies were 'using you against me' to try to oust them both.[73] But two weeks later he contrived to pack Kitchener off to the Mediterranean for two months and took over the War Office himself, telling Lloyd George that 'We avoid by this method of procedure the immediate supersession of K . . . while attaining the same result.'[74] In Kitchener's absence he did take some important decisions: he set up a smaller War Council, initially of five, replaced Sir John French with Sir Douglas Haig as commander of the British forces in France, and appointed Sir William ('Wully') Robertson CIGS, recreating a General Staff which Kitchener had done without. These appointments lumbered Lloyd George with the two stubborn generals, the architects of the Somme and Passchendaele, who were to be such a trial to him in 1917–18. But at least they were a sign of energy. Indeed it might have been better if Asquith had retained the War Office, combining it with the premiership as Churchill did in 1940. As it was, Kitchener's return left the central political command of strategy still ambiguous.

At the end of 1915 Lloyd George came close to resignation. 'P.M. & his gang trying to sneak out of their pledges,' he wrote to Maggie on 27 December. 'If they do I wash my hands of the poltroons & come out. I have made up my mind.'[75] That afternoon he wrote to Asquith threatening to resign unless all unmarried men were conscripted at once. According to Frances, he coupled his threat with a promise, conveyed via Lord Reading, that 'if the P.M. kept his promise to the compulsionists, he (D.) would stand by him through thick and thin . . . Reading told D. that the P.M. was much touched by his promise of loyalty and help, and the message had in fact the effect of deciding the P.M. to declare at once for compulsion.'[76] 'Cabinet satisfactory,' Lloyd George wrote to Maggie the next day. 'P.M. dropped on the right side.'[77] Only one Liberal dissident resigned. In the Commons Asquith unenthusiastically defended what he called 'very limited and guarded compulsion'.[78] C. P. Scott, the editor of the *Manchester Guardian*, thought he was simply manoeuvring to keep himself in power:

> It's a duel I believe between him and Lloyd George and he means to dish Lloyd George by accepting compulsion and to prevent secessions by making the dose as homoeopathic as possible. But there is

no sincerity about the whole proceeding and no serious consideration of the country's needs.[79]

Once again the half-measure was too little and too late. By April 1916 there was a new crisis, which Asquith now blamed squarely on Lloyd George. ('Of course Lloyd George is the villain of the piece, you know what I think of him'.)[80] In fact Lloyd George was still trying to be loyal. ('D . . . is most anxious to avoid a break, for he says that Asquith himself is the only man who can get compulsion through the House of Commons'.)[81] The point was proved when the latest bill, introduced by a Tory minister, Walter Long, ran into difficulties and Asquith had to step in personally to rescue it. 'He did not much like the job,' Maurice Hankey wrote, 'and was not at his best. The House was astonishingly cold. The fact was that the people who wanted compulsory service did not want Asquith, and those who wanted Asquith did not want compulsory service.'[82]* In the end only twenty-seven Liberals (and ten Labour Members) voted against the measure; in that sense Asquith's crab-like methods had skilfully defused the issue. Yet Hankey had put his finger on the central problem.

On 22 April the editor of the staunchly Asquithian *Daily News* openly accused Lloyd George of engineering the conscription crisis in order to replace Asquith as Prime Minister. In a speech in his constituency Lloyd George characteristically met the charge head-on:

> I have worked with him for ten years. I have served under him for eight years. If we had not worked harmoniously – and we have – let me tell you here at once that it would have been my fault and not his. I have never worked with anyone who could be more considerate . . . But we have had our differences. Good heavens, of what use would I have been if I had not differed from him? . . . The councillor who professes to agree with everything that falls from his leader betrays him.[83]

*Hankey was then secretary to the Committee of Imperial Defence. He became Cabinet Secretary when Lloyd George became Prime Minister.

At this point the Easter Rising occurred in Dublin. After several days' fighting it was suppressed with heavy loss of life: the summary execution of fifteen of the rebels created a new generation of Irish martyrs. The 1914 agreement to suspend Home Rule for the duration of the war was now a dead letter. Asquith's first response was to go to Ireland himself to try to devise a new settlement. His second was his invariable recourse whenever he had a problem: he tried to persuade Lloyd George to become Chief Secretary. 'It is a *unique* opportunity,' he urged him, 'and there is no-one else who could do so much to bring about a permanent solution.'[84] There was a touch of Machiavelli in this proposal. Lloyd George was 'an ambitious man', he told his latest confidante, Kathleen Scott (widow of the hero of the Antarctic). 'He'd stand or fall by the success he made.'[85] In other words Ireland would not only get Lloyd George out of the way for a time, but his probable failure would damage him. Lloyd George was sufficiently frustrated in London, however, to agree to go to Dublin temporarily instead of accompanying Kitchener on a visit to Russia. Moreover he quickly persuaded Redmond and the Ulster leader, Sir Edward Carson, to accept immediate Home Rule with Ulster excluded, pending a permanent settlement after the war. But his scheme, though supported by Bonar Law and Balfour, was scuppered by southern Unionist opposition, with bloody consequences after 1918.

It was lucky for Lloyd George that he did not accompany Kitchener, since on 5 June HMS *Hampshire* struck a German mine off Orkney and Kitchener, with some 200 others, was drowned. His death removed one problem for Asquith, but created another. Once again he initially took over the War Office himself; but then he felt obliged to offer it to Lloyd George. Had he been cleverer he might have offered the place quickly to Law; but he still underestimated the Tory leader, and by the time he offered it Law had agreed to back Lloyd George for the job. Not that Lloyd George was sure he wanted it. He thought the war was going so badly that it would be a poisoned chalice to take over the War Office now. So he played hard to get. On 16 June Asquith told Lady Scott that 'Lloyd George was behaving absurdly & suggesting tremendous powers for himself at the W.O. – much more than K. had. Also he was suggesting leaving the Cabinet altogether, saying he could be more useful outside it.'[86] The next day he politely declined the offer. In the end, however, he dropped his haggling and took the job. Margot Asquith wrote presciently in her diary: 'We are out: it can only be a question of time now when we shall have to leave Downing Street.'[87]

Moving to the War Office gave Lloyd George no greater control of the war: he could not overrule the generals and could only watch helplessly that summer as Haig and Robertson poured men into the futile slaughter of the Somme. In September Asquith suffered another heavy personal blow when his brilliant son Raymond was killed. Understandably he became still more withdrawn and missed several cabinets; yet the loss did not diminish his determination to maintain the doomed offensive, which dragged on until November with 600,000 British and Allied casualties. Meanwhile German U-boats were sinking 100,000 tons of British shipping a month: there was a real prospect that the country might be starved into submission. More than ever the government was seen to be drifting. The War Council now numbered nine regular members and was riven by mistrust: Hankey, its secretary, wrote of its 'really dreadful' meetings.[88] Both in the press and in Parliament pressure was mounting for a change of structure or personnel, or both. The government's fate was probably sealed on 8 November when Carson – who had resigned from the cabinet the previous autumn and was now the leading Tory critic of the conduct of the war – launched a powerful attack on the strangely marginal issue of the disposal of enemy property in Nigeria. Only 73 Tory members (out of about 270) supported the government. After two and a quarter years the crisis of the war in Whitehall was finally at hand.

Belatedly Asquith realised the need to assert his authority. After eight years at the top he still believed that he was the only person who could hold the government and the country together. He was willing to concede many of his critics' demands: the one thing he did not intend to do was to resign. Yet the whole of the Tory party, half the Liberal party and most of the press wanted a new Prime Minister. Lloyd George did not set out deliberately to take his place: yet that was the almost inevitable outcome – as Bonar Law, his only real rival, recognised. Since the beginning of the war Lloyd George had been patently the most dynamic, resourceful and – except on the drink question – clear-sighted member of the government; he alone had the eloquence and popular touch to rally the country in a situation nearly as desperate as that which Churchill faced in 1940. Critical as he was of Asquith's loss of grip, he did not want to split the Liberals and hated finding himself backed by the Tories against his own leader. But his overriding priority was to win the war. Back in March he had told an old Welsh colleague gloomily: 'If I were put in charge of this war, I would see the thing through; as I shall not be, it will end in a bad peace.'[89] He cannot be blamed for believing – as did practically everyone beyond Asquith's inner circle – that he possessed the qualities needed for leadership in war that Asquith, for all his peacetime virtues, conspicuously lacked. By contrast Asquith was at fault in failing to realise that his time was up.

The final tussle began on 25 November when Bonar Law wrote to the Prime Minister proposing the establishment of a small war council comprising, as Asquith put it, just four members – 'yourself, myself, Carson and Lloyd George'. Asquith rejected the proposal on several grounds; but the one which moved him most was the threat Lloyd George's inclusion posed to his own position:

> He has many qualities that would fit him for the first place, but he lacks the one thing needful – he does not inspire trust . . . There is one construction, and one only, that could be put on the new arrangement – that it has been engineered by him with the purpose . . . as soon as a fitting pretext could be found, of his displacing me . . .
>
> In short, the plan could not, in my opinion, be carried out without impairing the confidence of loyal and valued colleagues, and undermining my own authority.[90]

A few days later Lloyd George – now acting openly with Law and Carson – came back with a new proposal designed to achieve their objectives while saving Asquith's face. On 1 December he suggested an even smaller executive of three, excluding the Prime Minister: 'The War Committee should have full powers, subject to the supreme control of the Prime Minister, to direct all questions connected with the war.'[91] Asquith was probably right to believe that this would have been unworkable:

In my opinion, whatever changes are made in the composition or functions of the War Committee the Prime Minister must be its Chairman. He cannot be relegated to the position of an arbiter in the background or a referee to the Cabinet.[92]

Instead he now proposed a committee of five, to include the Prime Minister; at the same time, however, he suggested that one of the five should act as vice-chairman in the Prime Minister's absence. This potentially conceded most of Lloyd George's purpose. But Lloyd George found this compromise 'entirely unsatisfactory'. He sent a copy of Asquith's reply to Law with a dramatic covering note: 'The life of the country depends on resolute action by you now.'[93]

Meanwhile Asquith went off to Walmer Castle in Kent for the weekend. 'It was very typical of him,' Hankey wrote, 'that in the middle of this tremendous crisis he should go away for the week-end! Typical both of his qualities and of his defects; of his extraordinary composure and of his easy-going habits.' The same day Hankey added, with a civil servant's exasperation at the egotism of his masters:

The whole crisis is intolerable. There is really very little between them. Everyone agrees that the methods of the War Ctee call for reform. Everyone agrees that the P.M. possesses the best judgment. The only thing is that Ll. George and Bonar Law insist that the former and not the P.M. must be the man to win the war. The P.M. however quite properly says that if he is not fit to run the War Ctee he is not fit to be Prime Minister. The obvious compromise is for the P.M. to retain the Presidency of the War Ctee with Ll. George as chairman, and to give Ll. G. a fairly free run for his money. This is my solution.[94]

In fact Asquith was persuaded to return to Downing Street on the Sunday morning, where he met first Law and then Lloyd George. Law told him that the Tories would resign if he did not accept some form of war committee. Under this pressure he accepted the thrust of Lloyd George's proposal which he had previously rejected: the Prime Minister would not be a regular member of the committee, but it would report to him daily and he could attend it whenever he wished. This meeting was by all accounts perfectly friendly: even now the two men could still get on quite constructively when left to themselves. Edwin Montagu – one of the few who had managed to remain close to both of them – found Lloyd George that evening relieved that the crisis was past:

> I joined George at the War Office where he expressed his great satisfaction ... that he was going to work with Asquith ... and see [him] every day. He recognised my share in this happy issue and urged me to persuade Asquith to put the agreement in writing that night, in order that there might be no watering down or alterations, and in order that it might not be misconstrued. I told him that I would do my best.[95]

Asquith too believed that he had turned another tricky corner. After dining with Montagu he wrote complacently of his disrupted weekend:

> I was forced back ... to deal with a 'Crisis' – this time with a very big C. The result is that I have spent much of the afternoon in colloguing with Messrs. Ll. George & Bonar Law, & one or two other minor worthies. The 'Crisis' shows every sign of following its many predecessors to an early and unhonoured grave. But there were many wigs very nearly on the green.[96]

Unfortunately the agreement fell apart next day. Asquith was infuriated by an article in *The Times* which reported very accurately the substance of the proposed arrangement, with the implication that he was to be sidelined. He immediately blamed Lloyd George for the leak and wrote him a stiff letter demanding a retraction: 'Unless the impression is at once corrected that I am being relegated to the position of an irresponsible spectator of the War, I cannot possibly go on.'[97] In fact it was Carson, not Lloyd George, who leaked the deal, though Lloyd George may not have been so innocent as he pretended: he had certainly been talking to the proprietor of *The Times*, Lord Northcliffe. Anyway C. P. Scott found him 'angered and excited' by Asquith's volte-face:

George was obviously taken completely by surprise and very indignant . . . He remarked caustically that this was only another illustration of the indecision and vacillation on the part of the Prime Minister that had proved so ruinous in the conduct of the war.[98]

To Asquith, however, he sent a conciliatory reply. He claimed not to have seen the offending article, begged Asquith not to 'attach undue importance to these effusions', and specifically denied wanting to force him out. 'I attach great importance to your retaining your present position – effectively. I cannot restrain nor I fear influence Northcliffe.'[99]

But Asquith now dug in his heels. ('He won't fight the Germans,' Lloyd George told Frances, 'but he will fight for Office.')[100] He saw the King and received his authority to reconstruct the government. To Lloyd George he wrote firmly that he had reversed his previous agreement and was beginning again 'with a clean slate'.

After full consideration of the matter in all its aspects, I have come decidedly to the conclusion that it is not possible that such a Committee could be made workable and effective without the Prime Minister as its Chairman . . . I am satisfied that any other arrangement . . . would be in experience impracticable and incompatible with the Prime Minister's final and supreme control.[101]

He also rejected Lloyd George's demand that Carson should replace Balfour at the Admiralty: in other words he was saying that he, not Lloyd George, would make the appointments. This was his sticking point. He did not expect Lloyd George to give way, but neither was he willing to make any more concessions to retain the shadow of power while surrendering its substance. By this point, in Roy Jenkins's view, 'Any leader of self-respect would have felt that one or the other had to go.'[102] But Asquith still thought he could prevail. With the support of most of his Liberal colleagues he resigned, apparently hoping that Lloyd George would be unable to form a government: he would then return to office with his authority enhanced. But he had grossly overestimated his support. Not only Bonar Law and Carson, but all the leading Tories wanted him out; even Balfour let him down. They were willing to serve

Lloyd George, but would not remain in a government from which both he and Law had resigned.

Lloyd George replied to Asquith's *démarche* with a dignified letter regretting the parting of the ways but explaining why he felt he had no choice:

> In spite of mean and unworthy insinuations to the contrary . . . I have felt a strong personal attachment to you as my chief. As you yourself said, on Sunday, we have acted together for ten years and never had a quarrel, although we have had many grave differences on questions of policy. You have treated me with great courtesy and kindness; for all that I thank you. Nothing would have induced me to part now except an overwhelming sense that the course of action which has been pursued has put the country – and not merely the country, but throughout the world, the principles for which you and I have always stood throughout our political lives – in the greatest peril that has ever overtaken them . . . I am fully conscious of the importance of preserving national unity . . . But unity without action is nothing but futile carnage. And I cannot be responsible for that. Vigour and vision are the supreme need at this hour.[103]

Self-serving this may have been, and clearly written for publication; but there is no reason to think it did not genuinely express his position.

That evening Asquith's daughter-in-law dined at Downing Street and described in her diary his still astonishingly calm manner in the crisis of his premiership.

> He was too darling – rubicund, serene, puffing a guinea cigar . . . and talking of going to Honolulu. His conversation was as irrelevant to his life as ever . . . He was so serene and dignified. Poor Margot on the other hand looked ghastly ill – distraught . . . and was imprecating in hoarse whispers, blackguarding Lloyd George and Northcliffe.

After dinner Asquith played bridge as usual. The family view was that 'George had been a very wily, foxy cad'; but they were confident that 'any government he succeeded in forming would only be very short-lived'. 'Was it my last dinner in Downing Street?' Cynthia asked herself: 'I can't help feeling very sanguine and thinking the P.M. will be back with a firmer seat in the saddle in a fortnight.'[104] She was as deluded as her father-in-law.

On receiving Asquith's resignation the King asked Bonar Law to form a government. Law was reluctant, thinking Lloyd George better qualified, but was willing to try if Asquith would agree to serve with him. Asquith's severest critics were still anxious to keep him in the government. But Asquith refused; he would not even serve under Balfour. When Lord Robert Cecil urged him, for the sake of national unity, to serve under Lloyd George, he rejected the idea 'with indignation and even with scorn'.[105] He was still immovable when the party leaders met the King at Buckingham Palace. 'What is the proposal?' he asked. 'That I who have held first place for eight years should be asked to take a secondary position?'[106] That was exactly the proposal; but he would not consider it. 'Asquith absolutely declined to serve under Bonar Law,' Lloyd George told Riddell. 'He said that after being Premier he could not accept a subordinate position.'[107]

This was an extraordinarily arrogant attitude at a moment of national emergency. There were plenty of precedents for former Prime Ministers accepting lesser office under a successor. In the previous century Wellington had served under Peel, and Russell under Palmerston; for the past eighteen months Balfour had been happy to serve under Asquith. In the next war Neville Chamberlain was not too proud to continue in office under Churchill. Yet Asquith could not bring himself to do the same. Rather he took the view that Pitt had taken in 1804. 'The colleagues,' he wrote – meaning his Liberal colleagues – 'were unanimous in thinking . . . that it is not my duty to join this new Government in a subordinate capacity. Apart from the personal aspect of the matter, it would never work in practice.'[108] And a few days later, to another correspondent: 'When I fully realised what a position had been created, I saw that I could not go on without dishonour or impotence, or both; and nothing could have been worse for the country and the war.'[109] Others begged to differ: Cecil specifically urged that his agreeing to serve under Lloyd George 'may make all the difference between success & failure in the war', and added that all his Unionist colleagues 'warmly agreed'.[110] But Asquith preferred to listen to his friends rather than his former opponents. Wounded pride – or rather a lofty revulsion from serving with men who had in his view behaved shabbily towards him – was his real reason for staying out. He may have thought that he was thereby preserving the Liberal party; in fact his decision fatally damaged it.

In a House of Commons still evenly composed of Liberals and Unionists, with Labour and the Irish holding the balance, Asquith's refusal meant that Lloyd George was dependent on Tory support. Around 129 Liberal MPs – about half the parliamentary party, allowing for those who were away at the war – backed him, so at the lower levels of the government he did not have too much difficulty in forming a new coalition. But all eleven Liberal members of the outgoing cabinet followed their leader in refusing office under Lloyd George. ('Such patriotism!' Frances Stevenson noted scornfully.)[111] One or two like Montagu who were divided in their allegiance came under intense pressure from Margot to stay loyal. (At first Montagu yielded, but he joined the new government seven months later.) As a result Lloyd George had no choice but to form a Tory-dominated administration. The new war cabinet of five comprised himself and three Tories – Bonar Law, Curzon and Lord Milner – plus the Labour leader Arthur Henderson; in addition Balfour took the Foreign Office, Carson the Admiralty and Lord Derby the War Office. Not until July 1917, when he defied Tory hostility to bring Churchill back as Minister of Munitions, was he able to appoint another leading Liberal to a department directly concerned with fighting the war.

Immediately he brought a new urgency and drive to the conduct of the war. Among other things he forced the Admiralty to accept the convoy system to defeat the U-boat menace; appointed national controllers for food, transport and shipping; and – perhaps most symbolically – introduced a cabinet secretariat to record and co-ordinate the decisions of the war cabinet: nothing better encapsulates the change from Asquith's languid amateurism to a modern structure of government. But he still found it hard to wrest control of military strategy from the generals.

At first Asquith did not oppose the new government. In his first speech as Prime Minister Lloyd George paid generous tribute to his predecessor. 'It is one of the deepest regrets of my life that I should part from the right honourable Gentleman . . . I never had a kinder or more indulgent chief . . . But there are moments when personal and party considerations must sink into absolute insignificance.'[112] In reply Asquith professed himself 'very glad to see a man of such ability as my right hon. Friend in the place which he so worthily occupies', and promised non-partisan support. He did not intend to be 'in any sense . . . the Leader of what is called an Opposition', because in wartime there should be no such thing – though he warned that party would revive 'in good time' after the war.[113] Behind the patriotic pieties, however, Asquith's supporters could not forgive the Judas who had in their view schemed with the enemy to supplant his leader; and the parliamentary situation quickly developed a logic of its own. 'I think I shall have to get rid of this Parliament,' Lloyd George told Frances soon after the opening of the new session in February 1917. 'It is an Asquith Parliament, and I want a Parliament of my own.'[114] When Frances objected that he could never lead a Tory government he told her: 'My dear Pussy, the thing is done. The Unionists have adopted me, and after the war it will be more and more difficult for the Liberals to receive me back.'[115]

Lloyd George did his best to heal the breach while it was still possible. In May he sent Lord Reading as an intermediary to see if Asquith would be willing to become Lord Chancellor – a position for which he was eminently qualified, and one that offered a dignified means of bringing him back into the government without direct responsibility for the war. As a relatively poor man Asquith was tempted by the salary – twice that of the Prime Minister, with a generous pension; but he still felt that he must preserve his independence. Though Reading gave him to understand that he might have 'any post I chose, except that of head of the Govt', he replied that 'under no conditions' would he serve in a government of which Lloyd George was the head.

> I had learned by long & close association to mistrust him profoundly.
> I knew him to be incapable of loyalty or lasting gratitude. I had
> always acknowledged, & did still, to the full, his many brilliant &
> useful faculties, but he needed to have someone over him. In my

judgment he had incurable defects, both of intellect and character, wh. totally unfitted him to be at the head.

He repeated that his objection was not only to Lloyd George. 'To some further vaguely tentative overtures, I replied that I could not associate myself with what he called "the counsels" of any Govt unless I had supreme & ultimate authority.'[116] His belief in his own effortless superiority was undiminished.

Twice in 1917 Lloyd George sought Asquith's help from outside the government. The first time was in connection with Ireland. With C. P. Scott's mediation they met at Montagu's house, but Lloyd George found Asquith 'perfectly sterile' and the interview 'very unfruitful'.[117] Then in December Scott tried again to bring the past and present Prime Ministers together to approve a statement of Allied war aims. Lloyd George was cautious because 'he could not trust Asquith to take a disinterested and not a partizan [*sic*] view of the situation'.

> Moreover, whatever he said to Asquith would not stop there; it would all be given to the small men around him, to McKenna and the rest. Asquith after all had a kind of intellectual bigness, though his personality was small, but these had not even that.[118]

Asquith was equally unwilling to meet Lloyd George. But he was eventually persuaded that it was his duty; so in early January 1918 they met not once but twice, at Asquith's house. Grey was also present, and they approved the draft of a major speech Lloyd George was about to make setting out his vision of a post-war international order to prevent future wars – the germ of the League of Nations. Lloyd George had got what he wanted. 'This morning I breakfasted with Asquith,' he wrote to Maggie. 'Very friendly both.'[119] But the unforgiving Margot wrote to a Liberal journalist: 'Don't fail to let the political world know that Ll. G. went to my husband – Asquith did not go to 10 Downing Street . . . My husband said he was amazed at Ll. G.'s deferential manner to him!'[120]

Four months later this wary truce was blown apart. In March 1918 the Germans suddenly broke the stalemate of the past three years and in two weeks advanced to within forty miles of Paris;

for a few days the outcome of the war hung in the balance before the German advance was halted and then thrown back. Lloyd George responded decisively to this crisis; he took personal charge of the War Office and sent extra troops to stem the tide. But there were bitter recriminations over how the Allied line had been broken. In May General Frederick Maurice, until recently Director of Military Operations in the War Office, wrote a sensational letter to *The Times* accusing the Prime Minister of misleading the House about the numbers of British troops on the western front at the beginning of the year. Maurice did not consult Asquith before writing his letter; but with feelings running high Asquith felt obliged to take up the issue. His call for a parliamentary select committee – rather than Bonar Law's offer of an inquiry by two judges – was not unreasonable: there had been similar inquiries into the Dardanelles and Mesopotamia disasters. But he badly mishandled the debate. For days the press had been building it up as a serious challenge to the government; and some of his partisans, including Margot, certainly were scheming to restore him to office. Yet he made a weak, almost apologetic, speech denying any intention of moving a vote of censure. Let off the hook, Lloyd George then went on the offensive with a passionate speech refuting Maurice's figures, denouncing his insubordination in writing to the press and insisting that Asquith was indeed trying to overthrow the government:

> If this Motion is carried, he will again be responsible for the conduct of the War. Make no mistake! This is a Vote of Censure upon the Government. If this Motion were carried, we could not possibly continue in office, and the right hon. Gentleman, as the one who is responsible for the Motion, would have to be responsible for the Government.[121]

Lloyd George always believed that attack was the best form of defence. On this occasion his figures were contentious, but the force of his righteous indignation simply blew Asquith away. Runciman was expected to reply but failed to do so. Several members begged Asquith to withdraw his motion; but he would not do that either. 'He made a great mistake,' Lloyd George told Riddell. 'As he meant to go to a division he should have continued the debate. As it was, he divided without making any reply. As usual he lacked courage.'[122] Around a hundred Liberals followed their leader into the lobby; but his motion was heavily defeated by 295 to 108. Lloyd George survived; but he did not forget or forgive those who had voted against him at such a moment.

Six months later the war was over. The Germans' spring offensive had been their final throw. From the jaws of defeat Lloyd George succeeded in snatching salvation by imposing a unified command structure under the French General Foch which, with American troops at last arriving in significant numbers to reinforce the Allies, finally drove the invader back towards his own borders. In November came the Armistice. Lloyd George was now the hero of the hour: 'The Man who Won the War'. After eight years there must be an early election. How was he to fight it? Should he wind up his victorious coalition, thank his Tory colleagues for their support and go back to the Liberals who had refused to serve with him and voted against him six months earlier? He never considered it. Having won the war, he was now eager to tackle the peace. He determined to fight the election as the head of the war-winning government with the colleagues who had backed him in the nation's darkest hour. Yet he was still willing to make room for Asquith if Asquith was willing to come aboard. Six days after the Armistice he told Hankey that he had 'had an hour and a quarter's conversation with Asquith, who was very anxious to be friends, but not to take office, though he wanted to be at the peace conference'.[123] With hindsight this could have been a conciliatory gesture on Lloyd George's part; but with a limited number of places available he would not include Asquith in the British delegation except as a member of the government. He claimed that he offered him the Woolsack again; Asquith later denied this. The likelihood is that some offer was made, but in a form that Asquith could not accept. Either way, the breach remained unhealed.

Very soon it was widened and set in stone. The logic of Asquith's refusal of office was that his supporters must be treated as the opposition, while Lloyd George and Bonar Law agreed to support each other's candidates. Around 360 Tories and 159 Liberals therefore received a joint letter signed by the two leaders. All other

Liberals were opposed by a Coalition candidate. Launching his campaign in Wolverhampton on 23 November Lloyd George appeared to make the Maurice debate the test of Liberal allegiance to himself or to Asquith. Describing Asquith's decision to divide the House in May as 'a Parliamentary conspiracy to overthrow . . . a Government that was in the midst of a crisis while wrestling for victory', he declared: 'I cannot trust that sort of business . . . If the country wants that class of men the country can choose them, but, believe me, it will be impossible to get through the great task before us.'[124] In fact the test was very crudely applied: at least four Liberals who had voted for the government were denied endorsement, while eleven who had voted with Asquith received it.[125] The criterion was the whips' judgement of future intentions, not the division list in May. But Lloyd George went out of his way to be provocative. Despite or because of his alliance with the Tories, he was keen to assert that his old radicalism was undimmed, and his new partners more progressive than his old colleagues. 'Some of the worst reactionaries I ever encountered were to be found in my own party,' he declared. 'Deadheads are not the monopoly of one party.'[126]

Asquith was incensed by Lloyd George's rewriting of history. 'I wonder how many people . . . have read through the whole of Ll. G.'s Saturday speeches,' he wrote to his latest lady friend. 'I confess that they bored me to death, except the blackguardly passage in which he described the Maurice incident as a conspiracy to overthrow the Government . . . I will give him snuff for this.'[127] Three days later at Huddersfield he called it 'a grotesque and inexcusable travesty to say that the debate and division had anything in the world to do with unity of command'. He appealed for 'the return of a new Parliament of Independent Liberals, fettered by no compromising pledges, free to think, free to speak and free to act'; and – in a scornful reference to wartime ration books – dismissed the letter to government-sponsored candidates as a 'coupon'. The description has stuck to the 1918 election ever since.[128]

Asquith and his supporters never forgave Lloyd George for what they saw as wicked treachery. 'The disintegration of the Liberal party began with the Coupon election,' Asquith himself wrote after his retirement in 1926. 'It then received a blow from which it has never since recovered.'[129] In her autobiography Margot called the issuing of the coupon 'a great political crime' which 'broke the historic Liberal party to pieces at the moment when Liberalism – and especially British Liberalism – was most needed at Versailles'.[130] Liberal historians have not ceased to repeat this view. But if it was a crime it was born of negligence rather than deliberate malice. In his hour of victory Lloyd George thought it merely common sense to get as many Liberal supporters of the government as possible returned to the new House. He actually did well to ensure that as many as 150 were spared Tory opposition. He was certainly happy to see some of his most bitter enemies like McKenna and Runciman defeated; but he did not anticipate the scale of the carnage. He hoped for a majority of around 120. 'If it is over 120 I shall be content,' he wrote to Maggie. 'If it is under that I shall be disappointed.'[131] This calculation assumed that somewhere between fifty and a hundred Asquithians would be returned. He never imagined that Asquith himself would lose his East Fife seat, which he had held for more than thirty years; on the contrary he made sure that the 'coupon' was withheld from his Tory opponent; yet the former Prime Minister lost by nearly 2,000 votes. His defeat suggests that it was only the 'coupon' that saved the Liberal party from annihilation.

The government landslide gave the Tories around 350 seats and Lloyd George's 'Coalition' Liberals 133; Labour won 63 and became for the first time the official opposition; while the Asquithian 'Independent' Liberals mustered just 28. Allowing for a considerable number of miscellaneous 'others' (and excluding 73 Sinn Fein members who refused to take their seats) this gave the coalition an overall majority of well over 300. At the time it was seen as a massive endorsement for Lloyd George. But years later Frances Stevenson recalled his misgivings as the votes were counted:

> We were gathered together in my room in Downing Street, & as defeat after defeat [for the Liberals] came in to us from the Whip Room, D. became very quiet. 'I did not want this' . . . When the news of Asquith's defeat came he was genuinely upset.[132]

The Liberal party emerged from the 1918 election split into two factions, with rival leaders, rival whips, rival organisations and even rival magazines. Rather like Taiwan after the Communist takeover of China, Asquith and his depleted band of followers still claimed to be the 'true' Liberal party; but Lloyd George commanded nearly five times as many Liberal MPs. In fact the lines of allegiance were horribly confused. Despite leading a Tory-dominated government, Lloyd George was still obviously a more radical figure than Asquith; yet the Liberals who had backed him in 1916 tended to be the more right-wing, while many of those radicals who had looked to him before the war now found themselves stuck with the more conservative Asquith. Each of them was in a sense leading the wrong faction. In the constituencies and in the House there were persistent moves over the next four years to promote reunion; but these efforts remained doomed to failure so long as Lloyd George was Prime Minister and the Asquithians – or 'Wee Frees' – part of the opposition.

Rejected by his constituency, widely disparaged – even vilified – for his leadership in the first two years of the war, Asquith found himself at the age of sixty-six isolated and generally written off, while his former Chancellor bestrode the national and international stage. It was only by the King's intervention that he was belatedly awarded the same medals as Lloyd George in recognition that he too had made some contribution to victory. He consoled himself with drink, bridge and the loyalty of his family and friends; but he did not retire. His waning interest in politics was kept alive by his deep sense of grievance at the way he had been treated and lofty distaste for the policies of his successor – above all the peace settlement, which good Liberals regarded as excessively punitive, and the spiralling violence in Ireland following Sinn Fein's declaration of an Irish Republic in January 1919. He still regarded the coalition as a vulgar abomination which would disappear when 'normal' politics resumed, and was confident that the Liberal party would then regain its pre-war position. He had not ruled out a return to office. So when a by-election in Paisley at the beginning of 1920 offered an opportunity to return to Westminster he somewhat wearily accepted it.

The vacancy arose from the death of one of the handful of

Independent Liberals elected (by a tiny majority) in 1918. The local party only narrowly chose him as its candidate. But once adopted he roused himself with surprising energy to mount a minor imitation of Gladstone's Midlothian campaign. Standing as a 'free' Liberal with no 'qualifying epithet', he addressed crowded meetings all round the constituency, denouncing the Treaty of Versailles much as Gladstone had denounced the Congress of Berlin, and calling for immediate Dominion status for Ireland, voicing the same moral revulsion from Lloyd George and all his works that Gladstone had felt for 'Beaconsfieldism'.[133] Lloyd George may have been sorry to see Asquith defeated fifteen months earlier, but he was not at all keen to see him get back. 'D. rather worried about Paisley,' Frances noted. 'People are saying that Asquith ought to get in.'[134] His return, he told Riddell, would be 'unfortunate, as it will help to re-establish the "Wee Frees"', even though he thought it would make 'very little difference in the House of Commons'.[135] He was right on both counts. Asquith won handsomely, beating Labour by nearly 3,000 votes with the government candidate – 'a foul-mouthed Tory' – losing his deposit. He left Glasgow amid scenes of extraordinary enthusiasm and was met at Euston next morning by another 'tumultuous greeting'.[136] It looked like a sensational comeback. But it turned out to be a false dawn.

Lloyd George was reluctant to attend the House when Asquith took his seat, fearing that he would be humiliated if Asquith got a warm reception. He was indeed mobbed all the way from Cavendish Square to Westminster – *The Times* compared the scenes with Keir Hardie's triumphant arrival in 1892;[137] but once inside he was met with 'stony silence' from the massed Coalition ranks, whereas Lloyd George was cheered to the echo. 'D. came back very pleased,' Frances recorded.[138] Two weeks later Asquith addressed the new House for the first time.

> Today was to have been the first sparring contest between D. & Asquith . . . Everyone expected an attack from A. against the Government . . . But it was a 'damp squib'. So far from attacking, he practically apologised for making the speech & made it clear that he was in no sense criticising the Government. So harmless a speech

was it that D. could find nothing to answer in it & consequently did not speak at all, much as he wanted to.[139]

'The Coalition House of Commons . . . was the worst in which I have ever sat,' Asquith wrote after his retirement. 'The small band of Liberals . . . were made to feel their impotence, and I myself, after I came back, was treated by the Coalition rank and file with studied contempt.'[140]* He spoke quite frequently but felt 'practically no response'.[141] The trouble was that he had only come back to salve his pride: he offered no vision for the future. The 'Wee Frees' had actually been better led by Donald Maclean in his absence. 'Asquith . . . is finished,' Lloyd George told Frances, cruelly but accurately. 'You could see on Monday that he had no fight left in him.'[142] Everyone could see this except Asquith himself. C. P. Scott found him in August 1921 hopelessly stuck in the past and consumed with bitterness against Lloyd George: 'Altogether a somewhat querulous and very old man.'[143] His one idea to revive his shrunken party was to attract some liberal Conservatives like Lord Robert Cecil; but Cecil, in so far as he was interested at all, preferred Grey as leader. Since Asquith still would not consider taking second place to anyone, the idea came to nothing.

Meanwhile Labour threatened to replace the divided Liberals as the principal alternative to the Conservatives – if they had not already done so. Lloyd George – unlike Asquith – at least recognised this reality, though his first response was clumsy. In the somewhat jittery atmosphere after the Russian revolution he tried to harness the fear of 'Bolshevism' by fusing his Coalition Liberals with the bulk of the Tory party to create a new anti-socialist party in his own image – a new version of his proposed coalition back in 1910. He persuaded himself that his leadership would suffice to make this awkward hybrid a progressive force; but his Liberal followers were unconvinced and refused to surrender their identity. After this wobble he reverted to trying to restore his Liberal credentials. At home his ambitious reconstruction policies fell foul of post-war recession and

---

*Asquith's biographer Roy Jenkins suffered a curiously similar experience sixty years later when he returned to the Commons as leader of the SDP after winning a Scottish by-election, and struggled to get a hearing in a hostile House.

consequent spending cuts; but he devoted most of his energies after 1920 to trying to secure the basis for lasting peace in Europe by softening the terms of the Versailles settlement at an exhausting series of international conferences; while in 1921 he reversed the policy of repression in Ireland – carried out by the notorious 'Black and Tans' – and opened negotiations with Sinn Fein instead. In December 1921 he persuaded them – and his Tory colleagues – to sign a treaty which recognised the independence of the twenty-six southern counties as an Irish 'Free State'. This settlement, if it did not solve the Irish question, at least drained the poison out of it for forty years: an unquestionably Liberal achievement for which the Asquithians gave him little credit.

As the war receded Lloyd George realised that the Tories would not sustain him in office for much longer: the leaders – Law, Balfour and Austen Chamberlain – might stick to him, but the rank and file were restless to regain their independence. As early as 1920 C. P. Scott wrote that Lloyd George was 'feeling his way back' to the Liberals. Asquith's return had made this more difficult – he was 'like a great boulder, blocking the way'[144] – but he was still willing to butter the old boy up when they met in the House. 'There was no constraint of any kind,' Maclean wrote after a meeting in Lloyd George's room. 'They chatted freely and L.G. was not only courteous but deferential in his manner . . . I could see them slipping back, sub-consciously, to the old days when Mr A. was P.M. and L.G. his Chancellor.'[145] Lloyd George talked of resigning voluntarily on an issue of his own choosing; but Asquith, beneath the *bonhomie*, dreaded the prospect that the prodigal might seek forgiveness. In June 1922 he reported to his lady friend a rumour that Lloyd George was now 'anxious to find a pretext for an early resignation, when he will leave his Tory colleagues . . . to "carry the baby", and declare himself a Liberal of Liberals. It is quite possible, and with our short-memoried rank and file it may be a shrewd calculation.'[146] But Lloyd George, like most Prime Ministers, could never quite bring himself to go before he was pushed.

A majority of Tory MPs finally voted – against their leaders – to end the Coalition in October 1922. Bonar Law, who had retired on health grounds the year before, returned to lead the first exclusively Tory government since 1905 and won a clear overall majority at the subsequent general election. The rival Liberal parties won almost equal numbers of seats – around sixty each. This represented something of a recovery for the Asquithians, and a halving of Lloyd George's support; but both together were surpassed by Labour, which more than doubled its representation to 142 seats and was now unarguably the second party. Whether they liked it or not, there was no future for the Liberals except in reunion.

Lloyd George grasped this reality more willingly than Asquith. After seventeen unbroken years in high office, he was ready for a rest; but he was not yet sixty and was confident of regaining power before long. He would not join Labour, so rejoining his old party was his only option. 'Events will demonstrate . . . who are the real Liberals,' he wrote to Scott, 'and who are the men who are simply using Liberalism as a vendettist weapon to avenge their own personal disappointments.'

> These men, believe me, are far too obsessed with their personal wrongs and disappointments to welcome any reunion except on the express condition that I am marooned. I am confident that my friends will not agree to this.[147]

While declaring that he was 'neither a suppliant nor a penitent',[148] he was content to defer to his old chief's seniority in the short term in the knowledge that the leadership must fall into his lap before long. Asquith by contrast still shrank from reunion. Two weeks after the election he described with his usual sardonic detachment what he called 'a kind of "fraternity" meeting between the rank and file of our lot and the ex-Coalie Liberals. The latter seem to be prepared to "reunite" on almost any terms . . . I am all against forcing the pace and surrendering any of our ground.'[149] And again to the same confidante:

> Ll. G. is evidently dallying with visions of reconciliation. He took Hogge . . . into his room last night and talked to him for an hour and a half in his most mellifluous vein. Amongst other things he declared that he was quite ready to serve with and under me (!), with whom he had never had a quarrel and whom he had never ceased to admire and respect.[150]

Meanwhile the irreconcilable Margot was having none of it. 'Don't believe a word about Reunion,' she wrote furiously to Bonar Law. 'Never was a greater lie. We would rather be out for ever.'[151]*

That summer Asquith was still 'resolved never again to accept Lloyd George as a colleague'; on this he was 'fixed and irrevocable'. He was willing to confer with him about co-operation in the Commons, but would never admit him to the 'inner council' of the party. To do so would inevitably – 'by force of personality and past position' – give him the succession to the leadership. This, the Asquithians believed, 'would disintegrate the party'.[153] They appeared to believe that they could somehow keep Lloyd George at arm's length as a sort of 'associate' member. But all such subtleties were swept aside in the autumn of 1923 when Baldwin – who had succeeded Law in May – suddenly called another general election, barely a year after the last, on the ground of seeking a mandate to impose protective tariffs. If there was one issue that united every shade of Liberal it was the sanctity of free trade: so at short notice the two wings were forced into a shotgun remarriage to defend the ark of the Liberal covenant. The two ex-Prime Ministers met and agreed to fight the election on a joint platform; and then – amazingly – Lloyd George went to speak for his old chief at Paisley. Asquith described the occasion:

> At 7 o'clock Saturday evening the rites of Liberal Reunion were celebrated at an enthusiastic meeting in the Town Hall. Ll. G. arrived with his Megan, and I was accompanied by Margot and Violet. I have rarely felt less exhilaration than when we got to the platform amid wild plaudits and a flashlight film was taken, 'featuring' me and Ll. G. separated only by the Chairman – an excellent local doctor. I spoke for about a quarter of an hour, and Ll. G. then plunged into a characteristic speech – ragged and

---

*Margot had never believed in reunion. Back in 1920 she had fiercely rebuked Maclean for stating that political conflict should not be personal: 'How can it be otherwise? Two men who were for 9 years together: one mean & a fighter – the other magnanimous, not young & not a fighter – are now opposed to each other. Can you keep kid gloves on in behaving like great gentlemen & hope to win anything? NO. Every glove must be off & every weapon & every string pulled.'[152] She more than anyone else kept Asquith's sense of grievance raw.

boisterous, but with quite a good assortment of telling points. He was more than friendly and forthcoming, and the meeting was full of demonstrative fraternity. After it was over, Ll. G. and Megan, and their bodyguard of secretaries and detectives, were swept off by their host, Lord Maclay, to some baronial retreat, and we supped here in peace.[154]*

Asquith's daughter Violet Bonham Carter added to the atmosphere of somewhat forced jollity by declaring – in reply to Tory gibes about the lion lying down with the lamb – that 'I can only say, for myself, that I have never seen Mr Lloyd George look less voracious or my father more uneatable.'[156]

Baldwin had miscalculated. The Tories lost more than 80 seats, Labour gained 50 and the combined Liberals about 40. The result was a hung Parliament in which Liberals held the balance. Fortunately the two leaders were agreed about what to do. Though the Tories were still the largest party, the country had clearly voted against protection: they had no doubt that Labour must be given its chance. 'Things are interesting,' Lloyd George wrote to Maggie. 'There will be a Socialist Govt in a month's time – or another Election! Had a long talk with Asquith last night.'[157] And again a few days later: 'I came up today for a chat with Asquith. He was most friendly & helpful. The old boy & I get on well together always when mischief makers are kept out.'[158] Asquith was amused to find himself deluged by desperate appeals that he should save the country from socialism. 'It was a novel experience for me, after being seven years the favourite target for Tory and Coalition vituperation, that I should now be suddenly acclaimed in the same quarters as a potential Saviour of Society.'[159] He was 'decidedly against' trying to form a government himself.[160] 'If a Labour government is ever to be tried in this country,' he wrote, 'as it will sooner or later, it could hardly be tried under safer conditions.'[161] Lloyd George likewise believed that 'the Labour Party are entitled to fair play from the Constitution which they are expected to obey'.[162] They differed tactically, however,

---

*Asquith had no right to sneer since he himself was staying in what he called 'a typical millionaire villa' nearby.[155]

on what they hoped would happen next. Asquith frankly hoped that office would show up Labour's incompetence, so that the Liberals might after a year or two legitimately turn them out and take office themselves; Lloyd George proposed on the contrary to 'back the Labour Party whole-heartedly . . . and in concert with it to reap a full harvest of Radical reform'.[163]

In their different calculations both were disappointed. Lloyd George was frustrated by Labour's timidity in office and soon tired of supporting Ramsay MacDonald's minority government with no return. After just nine months he backed Asquith in demanding an inquiry into the bungled prosecution of the editor of the Communist *Daily Worker* for sedition. The situation was rather like the Maurice debate six years earlier. MacDonald, like Lloyd George in 1918, treated the motion as a vote of confidence; unlike Lloyd George, however, he had no Tory majority to sustain him. He resigned, and the third general election inside two years, fought in a polarised atmosphere of hysterical anti-socialism, saw the Tories returned by a landslide while the Liberals were squeezed. Asquith lost Paisley and the party was reduced from 159 MPs to 40, crushing the hope of ten months earlier that it might be on the way back. As in 1918, the Asquithians blamed Lloyd George for this débâcle – this time with some justice, since he had deliberately starved the party of funds. Money was the issue which more than anything else bedevilled relations between the two factions. The Asquithians had very little; Lloyd George had a lot – the notorious Lloyd George Fund amassed by the sale of honours when he was Prime Minister. The Asquithians strongly disapproved of this corrupt hoard, yet still expected him to hand it over to the merged party. But Lloyd George refused to give it up to an organisation still run by his enemies; he was determined to hold on to it until he had got the party under his control. Shortage of money contributed to the collapse of 1924 and continued to poison relations until Asquith retired.

At first relations between the two leaders remained reasonably cordial. But the 'mischief makers' were never far away. 'H.H.A. is not Ll. G. proof by any means,' Maclean wrote to Herbert Gladstone in December 1923. 'We must not leave L.G. alone with H.H.A. any more than we can help.'[164] A month after the 1924 election Lloyd George actually dined with the Asquiths at their new (and smaller) house in Bedford Square. 'They were all most pleasant,' he reported to Maggie, 'Mrs A., Lady Bonham [Carter] & the old boy. You can see they are economizing. None of the old sumptuous dinners. Drank Cider or Whiskey. Very good for us all.'[165] And a few weeks later: 'Interesting news. Very confidential. Asquith going to the House of Lords. I have just left him. He is much better & fitter.'[166] Asquith had considered trying to find another seat in the Commons; but that was a forlorn hope, especially since – as he pointedly told one colleague – 'I'd sooner go to hell than to Wales.'[167] He went to the Lords as the Earl of Oxford and Asquith, and the Liberal party reverted to the nineteenth-century practice of joint leaders, one in the Commons and one in the Lords.

The wrangles about money continued. In January 1925 Asquith launched an appeal to try to raise some funds independent of Lloyd George: its failure only underlined the Asquithians' humiliating dependence. Still keen to offer a radical alternative to Labour, Lloyd George developed his own policies without reference to Asquith. That autumn he launched a land campaign off his own bat; when Asquith's colleagues pressed him to object, Lloyd George simply ignored him. The party conference endorsed his policy; and Asquith had no choice but to give it his blessing. 'The trouble is,' Lloyd George complained, 'that when you have got a policy ready and Asquith launches it, it will freeze on his lips . . . He will present it accurately, but without sympathy.' He still insisted that he 'liked Asquith [and] worked cordially with him, but as a leader he was too coldly intellectual'.[168] While Margot and others were busy stoking Asquith's resentment, Frances equally poisoned any hope of reconciliation from the other side:

> They have misused what money they had & cannot raise any more, so what on earth is the use of your giving them more . . . You are far too trustful of them even now . . . The Old Man counts for nothing, & if he is decent about things it doesn't carry any weight. If you are not careful that section of the party is going to be like an old man of the sea about your neck.[169]

The final showdown came in 1926, when the two leaders took different attitudes to the General Strike. Speaking in the House of

Lords Asquith endorsed the establishment view, supported the Tory government and condemned the strike as an intolerable challenge to the constitution. But Lloyd George in the Commons took a less alarmist line, blaming unions and government equally for the impasse. He stayed away from the next meeting of the Liberal shadow cabinet, writing to the Chief Whip to explain his position:

> I . . . cannot see my way to join in declarations which condemn the General Strike while refraining from criticism of the Government, who are equally, if not more, responsible; and I certainly think that if we support the Government in an absolute refusal to negotiate until the General Strike is called off, the struggle may be a prolonged one and the damage to the nation may well be irreparable . . . I prefer the Liberal policy of trusting to conciliation rather than to force.[170]

He attached no great importance to staying away, merely saying that 'In my present mood there'd only be a row.'[171] Nor did Asquith initially make an issue of his absence, writing the next day that Lloyd George was 'in the sulks and had cast in his lot for the moment with the clericals – Archbishops and Deans and the whole company of the various churches (a hopeless lot) – in the hope of getting a foothold for himself in the Labour camp. He is already, being a creature of uncertain temperament, getting cold feet.'[172] Over the next week, however – during which the strike was called off – the irreconcilables persuaded Asquith that their enemy had delivered himself into their hands and induced him to write a stiff letter, reminiscent of the one he had written in December 1916, rebuking him for his non-attendance. 'The reasons for your absence . . . seem to me to be wholly inadequate,' he wrote. It was the duty of all colleagues to attend. 'Your refusal to do so I find impossible to reconcile with my conception of the obligations of political comradeship.'[173] 'At last I really think the break has come,' Maclean wrote delightedly to Gladstone. 'I never thought he would come right up to it, but he has.'[174]

That night Lloyd George dined with Frances. 'He was a little late,' she wrote in her diary, 'and came in very excitedly, so that I could see something had happened.'

He said to me: 'I have been expelled from the Party'. And handed me Oxford's letter to read. I read it and remarked that it was clearly a letter intended for D.'s resignation . . . Dirty work. The Asquith women are of course at the bottom of it.[175]

Before replying Lloyd George consulted C. P. Scott, who shrewdly edited his draft, which was 'written with considerable acerbity. I cut out everything provocative and left it full of mildness and dignity.'[176] It appeared in the press alongside Asquith's letter and immediately put Asquith in the wrong. To his bewilderment the Liberal press and most of the party backed Lloyd George, who on this occasion had clearly taken the more Liberal stance. Even now the latter's delight at this turn of events was tinged with sorrow for his old chief:

> Asquith has as usual been badly advised & when he listens to those poor creatures he has a weakness for gathering around him he generally makes a fool of himself. He did so in 1916 – afterwards in 1918 when he refused the chancellorship . . . & now when he overestimates my unpopularity . . . & thinks he is now strong enough to force me out. In spite of great gifts he is a silly old man drunk with hidden conceit . . . Anyhow he has committed a bad miscalculation this time . . . They are really 'beat'. Dirty dogs – & *bitches*.[177]

Asquith defended his position in a letter to the Chief Whip, published in *The Times*:

> If the leaders of the Liberal Party . . . had adopted Mr Lloyd George's view, we should have been doing our best to weaken the authority of the Government, which was for the moment the embodiment and organ of the national self-defence against the gravest domestic danger which has threatened the country in our time . . . I have sat in many Cabinets under various Prime Ministers, and I have not known one of them who would not have treated such a communication from a colleague, sent at such a time, as equivalent to a resignation . . . Mr Lloyd George was not driven out, he refused to come in.

He added that after nearly twenty years he would not continue to hold the leadership for another day 'unless I am satisfied that I retain in full measure the confidence of the party'.[178]

Next day twelve Asquithian grandees backed him in a letter to *The Times*. ('All the people I care for,' Asquith wrote characteristically, 'have been wonderfully affectionate and loyal.')[179] But the rank and file emphatically did not. Liberal Associations up and down the country expressed 'profound dismay' at any attempt to exclude Lloyd George; the parliamentary party passed what was virtually a motion of censure; and the Liberal Candidates' Association called for unity. Asquith faced defeat with his usual complacency:

> The 'Liberal split' is running its course to its goal not far off: a dissolution of partnership between Ll. G. and myself, with all my respectable and capable colleagues. It had to come, and though it is disagreeable for the moment, because of the thick-headedness of honest and devoted followers, it is as well that it should be put through now as later on.[180]

And two days later:

> The squalid controversy . . . still goes on. I have too much sympathy with our honest, hard-working, ill-informed rank and file to be hasty in dispelling their visions and aspirations after 'unity'. But unless they are prepared to give me a whole-hearted and unreserved vote of confidence, I shall in the course of the next three days tell them (with equal unreserve) God's truth about Ll. G. As you know, it would be nothing but a relief to me to wash my hands of the whole thing.[181]

But the next day, before he could deliver this sensational exposé, he suffered a mild stroke. He recovered over the summer, but decided to resign anyway:

> The alternatives are to lead a squalid faction fight against Ll. G. in which he would have all the sinews of war; or to accept his money and patch up a hollow and humiliating alliance. I am quite resolved to do neither, so I shall *faire mes paquets* for which I have ample justification on other grounds, age, etc.[182]

In a confidential memorandum he rehearsed the dismal history of the past eight years and concluded:

We have now for nearly three years been trying the experiment of 'Liberal Reunion'. There is not one of us that does not know that in practice it has turned out to be a fiction, if not a farce . . . Under such conditions, to talk of Liberal unity . . . seems to me an abuse of language.[183]

He finally announced his resignation at an emotional meeting at Greenock in October.

Thus Lloyd George finally achieved the leadership. Once in sole command he made a tremendous effort to restore the party's fortunes. He poured his money into financing imaginative policy inquiries, recruiting a galaxy of liberal economists and academics, of whom Maynard Keynes was only the most famous, to try to revive industry and tackle the growing blight of unemployment. Many of those – like Keynes – who had been most opposed to him during and after the war now recognised that he was still the most creative force in British politics. 'When Lloyd George came back to the party,' Charles Masterman admitted, 'ideas came back to the party.'[184] He also pioneered new methods of campaigning: in the days before opinion polling a string of by-election victories in 1927–29 seemed to presage a real revival. Before the 1929 election he published a far-sighted plan for national reconstruction entitled 'We Can Conquer Unemployment', which even the die-hard Asquithians felt obliged to go along with. But all this effort was not enough to spring the two-party trap in which, under the first-past-the-post voting system the third party was now caught. The Liberals won more than five million votes but only 59 seats – enough as in 1923 to hold the balance, but not to exercise any leverage over MacDonald's second Labour government.

Meanwhile Asquith had died in February 1928. He had refused a public funeral, but was buried quietly in Oxfordshire, where he had had a country home since 1912, with a memorial service in the Abbey six days later. Lloyd George had no difficulty paying tribute in the Commons. In their great days together before the war he had genuinely admired his old leader. In his closing words he compared him to the River Thames: 'He was a kindred spirit – placid, calm, moving with a stately and serene flow, never boisterous or turbulent even in the very worst of weather.'[185] He did not need to point the contrast with himself.

Lloyd George never did get back to power. His best chance came in the economic crisis of 1931 when the Labour government collapsed and MacDonald formed an all-party government to try to save the pound; but he was ill at the crucial moment and the National Government was formed without him. He retired with Frances Stevenson to his farm in Surrey, emerging occasionally to denounce the inadequacy of successive Prime Ministers – MacDonald, Baldwin and Neville Chamberlain – but never again came close to regaining office, except in 1940 when Churchill pressed him to join his war cabinet, more as a symbol of national unity than because at the age of seventy-seven he would have much to contribute. He died in 1945, just before the end of the Second World War. He too was buried simply, in his beloved Wales, with a memorial service in the Abbey. His statue was placed in the lobby of the House of Commons, where he was later joined by Churchill and Margaret Thatcher.

Neither Lloyd George nor Asquith could be said to have 'won' their duel. Both are remembered as great Prime Ministers – one in peace, the other in war. Since war is usually reckoned the supreme test, Lloyd George perhaps ranks higher. But Asquith was – with Clement Attlee and Margaret Thatcher – one of the three outstanding peacetime Prime Ministers whose domestic reforms shaped British society in the twentieth century; while Lloyd George's war leadership in 1916–18 was destined to be eclipsed by Churchill's in 1940–45. Of course Lloyd George also deserves much of the credit for Asquith's achievement before 1914: theirs was the most enduring and constructive partnership ever between a Prime Minister and Chancellor – a relationship normally fraught with tension which often ends in acrimony (Thatcher and Nigel Lawson, Tony Blair and Gordon Brown). Though widely seen as Asquith's natural heir, Lloyd George was content with Asquith's leadership and in no hurry to displace him. Between 1914 and 1916, however, it became plain to everyone outside Asquith's immediate circle that Lloyd George was better fitted for war leadership: the tragedy was that Asquith would not step aside. By refusing to join Lloyd George's government in December 1916 he struck the first blow at the historic Liberal party; by the 'coupon' election in 1918 Lloyd George struck the second; the party was fatally split, and by the time it was nominally reunited it was too late – Labour had moved decisively to fill the vacuum on the left. Probably Labour, with its mass working-class base, was bound to prevail in the post-war world. Asquith's essentially Victorian Liberalism, rooted in free trade and Home Rule, offered nothing new by 1920; while even Lloyd George's more interventionist brand could not compete with the appeal of socialism. But 'inevitability' is one thing, events another. The rapid demise of Gladstone's party, from dominance to irrelevance in ten years, was dramatically hastened – under the stress of war – by the needless quarrel of the last two Liberal Prime Ministers.

For a long time Asquith seemed to have won the history books. Right down to her death in 1969, Lady Violet Bonham Carter guarded her father's reputation more successfully than Frances Stevenson, in her long widowhood, was able to do for Lloyd George. Books by a generation of historians, culminating in Roy Jenkins's 1964 biography, constructed an almost saintly image of 'the last of the Romans', betrayed by his treacherous Welsh rival. A reaction set in from the later 1960s when A. J. P. Taylor led a radical reassessment of Lloyd George's conduct and qualities which still largely prevails. Nowadays Liberal Democrats hark back to Lloyd George far more than to Asquith. For all his great virtues, Asquith appears to modern eyes a snobbish, post-Victorian amateur; while Lloyd George – with all his faults – ranks second only to Churchill as a vivid charismatic leader touched with genius.

Aneurin Bevan
and Hugh Gaitskell

The Asquith–Lloyd George split destroyed the Liberal party as a challenger for government. After a brief interlude of three-party confusion Labour replaced the Liberals as the progressive alternative to the Conservatives in a restored two-party system and following two short-lived minority governments between the wars finally gained power in its own right in 1945. The Labour party had been founded at the beginning of the century as an alliance of working-class trade unionists and predominantly middle-class socialists: the former commanded the numbers to win elections, while the latter provided most of the brains. Tension between the two wings was inevitable, but it was usually contained. Towards the end of the 1945 government, however, it exploded in a bitter feud between two archetypal figures: Aneurin Bevan, a former Welsh miner and self-taught Marxist, aggressively proud of his working-class roots, and Hugh Gaitskell, a public-school- and Oxford-educated Keynesian economist. Both in their different ways were convinced socialists: their differences over policy were in practice minimal. Yet their political philosophies were as different as their backgrounds; and their personal antagonism – rooted in class, exacerbated by conflicting temperaments and fanned by the tribal loyalties of their respective supporters – helped to wreck the Attlee government in 1951 and kept Labour out of office for the next thirteen years. More successfully than Asquith and Lloyd George – with whom superficially they had a good deal in common – they eventually managed to resolve their differences in opposition and seemed by the late 1950s to have forged an effective, if still wary, partnership which might have formed the basis of a future Labour government, had not both died young. Even so, the echoes of their rivalry continued to divide the party right up to the 1980s.

Bevan was born in 1897 on the eastern edge of the South Wales coalfield, the sixth of ten children of a collier, and was raised in a four-room terraced cottage in the mining village of Tredegar in Monmouthshire. Like his father and uncles, all his brothers and most of the male population of Tredegar, Nye went down the pit at the age of thirteen. He only worked underground for nine years, but the experience marked him for life. Instinctively rebellious, he was from an early age a thorn in the side of the Tredegar Iron and Coal Company, which virtually owned the town, and at nineteen he was already chairman of the local union lodge – the youngest in South Wales. After two years in London attending the Central Labour College, where he refined the crude Marxism imbibed from various mentors in Tredegar into a highly individual doctrine of democratic socialism, he returned in 1921 to face a bitter period of unemployment which left him with a lifelong hatred of the Means Test. He considered emigrating; but after a successful fight to win compensation for his dying father he became a sort of local champion representing the claims of others against the company; within the union he helped create an embryo welfare state, including free medical treatment paid for by modest deductions from the miners' wages; and in the bitter strike of 1926 – the seven-month struggle which provoked the nine-day wonder of the General Strike – he was elected chairman of the local Council of Action, organising relief and touring other coalfields to maintain the men's morale. The ultimate defeat of the strike convinced him that socialism would be achieved only through political, not industrial, action. In 1922 he became a district councillor, then briefly a Monmouthshire county councillor, before in 1929 he mounted a coup against the sitting Member to seize the nomination for the parliamentary seat of Ebbw Vale, and was duly elected at the age of thirty-one – sensationally young for a miners' MP; who were more often close to retirement. He held it with huge majorities for the rest of his life.

On arriving at Westminster, Bevan soon despaired of the help-lessness of Ramsay MacDonald's minority Labour government in the face of the world recession following the Wall Street crash. Impatient for action, he was briefly drawn to Oswald Mosley – then a Labour MP – till Mosley turned to Fascism. Holding one of the safest seats in the country Bevan was one of just fifty-four Labour Members to survive the electoral massacre of 1931; over the next nine years he made a name for himself as an eloquent and angry class warrior, denouncing in often violent language the cruelty of the dole and the heartlessness of the capitalist govern-ment's neglect of the so-called 'distressed' areas. Professing to see little difference between Toryism and Fascism he opposed re-armament and with Sir Stafford Cripps was expelled from the Labour party in 1939 for advocating a Popular Front with the Communists. During the war, however, he made a new reputation as the most persistent parliamentary critic of Churchill's leadership, maintaining that Churchill represented not the true feeling of the British people but a nostalgic imperialism which would be swept away after the war. Confident that history was on the side of socialism he was one of the very few figures in any party who anticipated Labour's victory in 1945. When Clement Attlee formed his government he shrewdly recognised the constructive ability behind Bevan's sometimes overheated rhetoric by putting him straight into the cabinet as Minister of Health.

Gaitskell, nine years younger, arrived in Parliament in 1945. Though born in London in 1906, he was a typical child of the empire, the son of an Indian civil servant with a long family connection with the Indian army, and spent his early childhood in Burma. His father died when he was nine; his mother returned to England for a time, but soon remarried and returned to Burma, leaving Hugh in the care of a variety of relations, boarding-schools and nannies. From Winchester – the most highbrow of the public schools – he went on to New College, Oxford, where he read PPE – the fashionable 'modern' package of Philosophy, Politics and Economics – but did not engage in undergraduate politics, though he was already a serious young man with 'a passion for improving the human race'.[1] He was converted to socialism partly by his tutor, G. D. H. Cole, and partly by the General Strike, in which he took the side of the strikers while most of his Oxford peers were driving buses in support of the government. His was an essentially ethical socialism, forged neither in personal experience of the labour movement, like Bevan's, nor in adolescent revolt against his parents, like that of so many middle-class socialists: it arose rather from the desire of a born public servant to see the world more rationally governed. After Oxford he spent a year working as a lecturer for the Workers' Educational Association in the Nottinghamshire coalfield, which gave him his first direct experience of the working class, before becoming an economics lecturer at University College, London. He stayed at UCL for the whole of the 1930s, apart from a year in Vienna in 1934 where he witnessed at first hand the brutal crushing of the Austrian socialist party by the Fascists – another formative experience. Back in London he joined a group of young economists engaged – under the patronage of Hugh Dalton – in converting the Labour party to Keynesian ideas of economic planning and was selected – with Dalton's help – as candidate for South Leeds in 1937. Unlike Bevan, he supported rearmament, and during the war was drafted into Whitehall as a temporary civil servant, working for Dalton, first in the Ministry of Economic Warfare and later at the Board of Trade. He proved an excellent administrator; but his donnish manner hid a steely ambition and he was determined to go into politics in his own right. Despite an untimely illness which nearly forced him to withdraw, he was swept into Parliament by the Labour landslide in 1945.

For the first three years of the Labour government Bevan would barely have been aware of Gaitskell's existence. He was fully occupied with his immense workload as Minister of Health: not merely battling with the doctors to establish the National Health Service – closely modelled on the template established in the valleys twenty years before – but simultaneously struggling to meet the demand for new housing caused by the wartime bombing, which also came under his department. Belying his reputation as a left-wing rebel he proved an exceptionally skilful and resourceful minister: after his death Gaitskell recalled that his officials had the highest regard for him – significant praise from one who had been a civil servant himself. Today it is the creation of the NHS for which Bevan is primarily remembered; but at the time housing was the more urgent and contentious issue which took up most of his energy. Though the leading left-winger in the cabinet, he had little time to worry about the general direction of the government.

Gaitskell meanwhile was quickly climbing the ladder. After only ten months as a backbencher he became parliamentary secretary under Emanuel Shinwell – another former miner – at the Ministry of Fuel and Power, where he first helped to steer coal nationalisation through the Commons – thus delivering Bevan's first political objective – then won golden opinions by his cool handling of the great fuel crisis of early 1947. Later that year he replaced Shinwell as minister, though not yet in the cabinet. In this capacity he again showed exceptional ability during the sterling crisis of 1949 when Cripps, now Chancellor, was ill; with his friend Douglas Jay – a fellow-Wykehamist – and the thirty-one-year-old Harold Wilson, Gaitskell headed a trio of relatively junior ministers (all former civil servants) who persuaded the cabinet to embrace devaluation. When Cripps retired in October 1950 Gaitskell was promoted in his place, thus becoming Chancellor after the shortest parliamentary apprenticeship since the younger Pitt. It was this rapid promotion which brought him into conflict with Bevan.

During the 1945–50 Parliament Gaitskell generally admired Bevan, initially from afar, later at first hand. In a column for his local paper the new MP singled him out as one of the government's three best ministers – though he criticised Bevan's decision to let NHS doctors take on private patients.[2] When he joined the government he began to keep a diary. His first significant comment on his future adversary came in August 1947 when Dalton – then Chancellor – told him that Bevan had pressed in cabinet for the early nationalisation of steel. 'The Chancellor said that in the last week Bevan's head had swelled enormously. He believed "his hour had come", had threatened to resign over steel and then organised the "Keep Left" boys.' Gaitskell thought this 'interesting for two reasons':

First its extraordinary naivety – he grossly exaggerates his own popularity and underestimates the notorious loyalty of the Party to its leaders. Secondly its failure should weaken his position in the Government because the others – especially the Big 5 – are very angry; his bluff about resignation has been called and . . . they can afford to be less frightened of him. This weakening is important because it will strengthen the hands of those who know that we must cut building and probably housing if we are to get exports up enough.

This itself is 'interesting for two reasons': first that Gaitskell already felt that Bevan was getting above himself, and second because it anticipates the coming conflict between social spending and economic priorities. 'All the same,' he concluded, 'it would be a mistake to assume that this is more than a setback for Bevan. He still leads in the race for Labour Prime Minister in 1960!'[3]*

During 1948 the two were brought into closer contact. First Gaitskell, as minister responsible for coal, joined a miners' outing from the party conference at Scarborough in May, and he and Bevan were photographed together at Butlin's holiday camp in Filey. Later that summer he spoke from the same platform as Bevan and his disciple Michael Foot at the Northumberland Miners' Gala. More seriously Cripps, on becoming Chancellor, began to hold weekly dinners for selected colleagues and protégés, including both Bevan and Gaitskell, which gave the latter further opportunities to assess the former:

> Personality is a funny thing. Bevan, of course, has it very decidedly. He is powerful, though maddening as well. But I feel pretty sure he will be Prime Minister one day. And probably at that level will be a good deal better than now.[5]

On these occasions Bevan would talk expansively with a broad sweep of imaginative speculation and brilliant phrase-making: Gaitskell by contrast was pedantic and factual. The difference was nicely illustrated at a lunch which Cripps held

---

*Gaitskell's friend Evan Durbin likened Bevan to Lloyd George. Gaitskell agreed, but added: 'I can't help wondering whether LL.G. was really quite so unscrupulous.'[4]

in October 1948 for five visiting Americans concerned with implementing the Marshall Plan.* Gaitskell recorded wryly:

> The lunch ended with a wordy argument between Bevan and myself about the use of the word 'democracy', to which everyone else listened in silence. It looked as though it had been staged between the left and right wing of the Government, but it was in fact purely accidental, and provoked by Bevan talking about the Russian peasant's idea of democracy, about which I felt quite certain he knew as little as I did![6]

Another difference arose on a subject nearer home when Gaitskell defended the government's arm's-length model for the newly nationalised industries against Bevan, who argued for closer parliamentary control. 'Being, of course, a glutton for power,' Gaitskell noted, 'he does not like the present policy of setting up the semi-autonomous Boards. He wants to control and answer for them; in fact to have them under him like departments.'[7]

Not only did Gaitskell in his diary clearly identify Bevan and himself as standard-bearers respectively of the left and right; he also showed a keen awareness of the jockeying that was already going on to succeed Attlee. The 'big five' figures in the government – Attlee, Ernest Bevin, Dalton, Cripps and Herbert Morrison – were all over sixty and growing old together. Morrison and Cripps were the principal contenders to succeed if Attlee retired soon; but Bevan in his early fifties was a whole political generation younger, with no obvious rival of his own age: hence Gaitskell's assumption – which Bevan shared – that he would naturally be leader in due course. Nine years younger again and less than four years in Parliament, Gaitskell at this stage did not dream that he himself would emerge as Bevan's nemesis. Yet the leadership stakes were frankly in his mind when he commented on Cripps's 1949 budget, which he feared 'would weaken Stafford's position in the Party. I am not sure whether [Bevan] really minds about this. It is just possible that he regards Stafford as a very

---

*The Marshall Plan was an imaginative American scheme to assist the economic recovery of Europe after the war.

much better future Prime Minister than Morrison, and does not think of himself as competing just yet.'[8]

Crossing swords with him at Cripps's dinners, Gaitskell thought Bevan a brilliant conversationalist. 'I think he is also a more profound thinker than he is sometimes given credit for.'

> The other evening . . . we drifted into a discussion about religion and philosophy . . . Nye started attacking religion, not as one might have expected on Marxist grounds, but far more on rationalist grounds – very sympathetic to me. It was a little embarrassing because of the Chancellor's religious views [Cripps was a devout churchman], but did reveal I think that Nye had really read and thought about these matters fairly deeply. I said to him afterwards, 'The other day you called me an "arid intellectual". And I wrote you off as a hopeless nineteenth century mystic, but I am glad to welcome you back into the eighteenth century fold after your performance tonight'.

Gaitskell found it 'refreshing to find that one's colleagues can talk about these subjects in this way'.[9] He was pleased to think that he enjoyed real friendship with some of his colleagues – Jay, Frank Pakenham, 'and even to some extent Nye Bevan'. But Pakenham – the future Lord Longford – was 'rather horrified when I said that I thought Bevan would almost certainly be leader of the Party and therefore P.M. sometime'.[10]

Before long, however, Gaitskell was beginning to think Bevan more of a liability than an asset. His notorious remark that he still regarded Tories as 'lower than vermin' was widely blamed for losing Labour seats in the February 1950 election which slashed the government's majority to a precarious margin of just five. Despite their long association, Bevan was now at odds with Cripps over the cost of the NHS. The early years of the service had revealed a greater backlog of untreated illness, and hence proved far more expensive, than had been anticipated. At a time of deepening austerity after devaluation, Cripps – despite his left-wing past now the archetypal 'Iron Chancellor' – was trying to curb the soaring cost of the service, while Bevan fought to preserve the principle of free treatment. Just before the election he reluctantly accepted the principle of prescription charges, but managed to prevent them actually being imposed by threatening resignation. After the election Gaitskell was disappointed that Bevan had not been shifted to another department:

> The worst appointment of all unquestionably is the sending back of Bevan to the Ministry of Health. He certainly wanted to move and in my view it was imperative from the point of view of finance that he should be moved. Apparently under the influence of Bevin the P.M. decided he must go back to clear up the mess he created. It only means the mess will not be cleared up . . . It is a great mistake and one which may cost us very heavily.[11]

Gaitskell believed that the government must be seen to be enforcing financial discipline and regretted that Cripps had not forced Bevan to bite the bullet. Over the next few months Gaitskell increasingly took on the job of trying to control spending. As a young minister standing in for the Chancellor he found it 'a very wearing affair – always having to nag one's colleagues, especially when they are as slippery and difficult as the Minister of Health'. At least once, 'provoked by something I had said', Bevan 'slammed down his papers and started to walk out of the room', until called back by Attlee.[12] Nevertheless Gaitskell believed that their personal relations were still friendly. 'Relations with Nye have settled down again after the great row about the Health Services,' he wrote in May.

> Although Nye still looks on himself as a sort of leader of the Left wing, his actual attitude on the essential points of policy is not nearly so far removed from Herbert [Morrison]'s as it used to be . . . He seems to have accepted his present position in the party . . . Perhaps somebody really has told him that he nearly lost us the Election . . . The thing I like about him is that one can have a terrific row with him in Cabinet Committee and yet remain on quite cordial terms with a good deal of friendly back-chat.[13]

Gaitskell still saw Bevan as unavoidably a major figure since, with all his faults, he was 'so much the best debater, so much the most effective speaker on the Front Bench, indeed in the House'.[14]

Bevan, by contrast, saw Gaitskell as a mere functionary: an economist – a dirty word in his book – not a real politician, still less
a potential leader. John Strachey, another old left-winger, now
Minister of Food, recalled that at Cripps's dinners Bevan would
'lash Hugh with the fury of his tongue'.

> Hugh would sit rather silent under it, occasionally replying with
> a dry, factual contradiction. When this had happened several times
> I walked away from one of the dinners with Bevan and asked him
> why he was doing it. 'Why', I said, 'are you going out of your
> way to make a rift between yourself and one of the really consider-
> able men of the Government?' *'Considerable!'* Aneurin replied.
> 'But he's nothing, nothing, nothing!'[15]

Bevan underestimated Gaitskell because he seemed to have risen
from nowhere: instead of working his way up through the party,
he had made his reputation entirely in Whitehall, behind closed
doors. Yet some observers already saw them as predestined antagonists. At the 1950 party conference at Margate the *Daily
Telegraph* political correspondent perceptively noted that the
turbulent Minister of Health and Cripps's unassuming deputy
were engaged in a 'duel for the future . . . leadership of the party'.[16]

Then in October, just after the conference, Cripps's health forced
him to resign. Without much hesitation Attlee appointed Gaitskell
in his place. There was really no one else. Morrison had the
seniority but not the expertise, and did not want the job. Gaitskell
lacked seniority but had the necessary expertise: he had already
been doing much of the work of the Treasury for several months.
It is unlikely that Attlee ever seriously considered Bevan, whom
he was rather thinking of moving sideways to the Ministry of
Labour. But Bevan felt slighted at being overlooked. He had
expected Cripps to recommend him and thought it 'disgraceful,
monstrous' when told that he had not.[17] When Gaitskell's appointment was announced he 'launched a torrent of abuse against the
Prime Minister in the hearing of the policemen, the officials of
the House and Tory MPs, until Douglas Jay pushed him into the
Chancellor's room and closed the door'.[18] He fired off an angry
letter to Attlee expressing his 'consternation and astonishment . . .

I think the appointment of Gaitskell a great mistake. I should have thought it was essential to find out whether the holder of this great office would commend himself to the main elements and currents of opinion in the Party.'[19] He told Dalton that he had had 'a tremendous row with Clem', arguing that 'these key positions should go to people who had some standing in the Movement'.[20] Neither gave him much sympathy. Dalton was Gaitskell's mentor and champion, and Attlee replied curtly that 'I do not think that your views are shared by many people.'[21] This was true: most Labour MPs thought Gaitskell the obvious appointment, while Bevan was the last person they would have seen as a credible keeper of the nation's purse strings. In fact it is doubtful whether Bevan really wanted the job himself: he just resented a jumped-up public-school boy getting it – as Gaitskell recognised. 'I suspect that Nye is not so much jealous but humiliated at my being put over him.'[22]

For the moment he nursed his grievance in silence. By the New Year Gaitskell was writing that 'outwardly Nye Bevan is quite friendly again'. But he knew that this quiescence was deceptive: 'The real struggle will come when we try and settle expenditure policy and get nearer to the Budget.'[23] He was relieved when Bevan agreed to move to the Ministry of Labour in January 1951.

> That might make a lot of difference to my financial policy. It is too early to speak but it may be the removal of the obstacle in the way of general economy on public expenditure not only in the Ministry of Health but in other fields as well.[24]

Restraining the level of government expenditure was already a problem in 1949–50. It became still more urgent in 1950–51 with the outbreak of the Korean war. Gaitskell was predictably a strong believer in the need to combat Communist aggression wherever it arose; but Bevan was initially no less hawkish. Though never happy to play second fiddle to the Americans he was a surprisingly strong Cold Warrior: in 1948, before the Allies hit on the less confrontational device of an airlift to raise the Soviet blockade of Berlin, he had favoured sending in tanks; and he supported the decision to make a British atom bomb. Though he had criticised the 'gorged and swollen defence estimates' in the past,[25] he now accepted the need for a substantial temporary diversion of manpower and resources into rearmament; and with his move to the Ministry of Labour he became responsible for carrying it out. On 15 February he delivered a brilliant speech in the Commons defending the government's commitment to spend another £4,700 million on defence. It is true that most of his speech was a warning against trying to rearm too fast and an assertion of his faith that Communism would be beaten by ideas – by the superiority of democratic socialism – not by force of arms. But his conclusion unequivocally endorsed the government's commitment, so it appeared an entirely loyal speech: the young Tony Benn – not then on the left – thought it 'immeasurably strengthened his claim to the leadership . . . and to the next premiership'.[26] Gaitskell was equally admiring – though with growing reservations:

> Nye gave one of the most brilliant performances I have ever heard him give . . . glittering with striking phraseology . . . What a tragedy that a man with such a wonderful talent as an orator and such an interesting mind and fertile imagination should be such a difficult team worker, and some would say even worse – a thoroughly unreliable and disloyal colleague. Will he grow out of this? Will he take on the true qualities that are necessary for leadership? . . . Time alone will show.[27]

But then Bevan suffered a second blow to his pride. Another of the government's 'Big Five', Ernest Bevin, resigned through ill health, creating a vacancy at the Foreign Office. If Bevan's particular gifts were not best suited to the Treasury, he certainly fancied himself as Foreign Secretary: his speech in the defence debate might have been expressly designed to show off his grasp of broad geopolitical horizons. Instead Attlee appointed Herbert Morrison, who had no interest in foreign affairs but wanted the job to bolster his credentials for the premiership. Years later Attlee wrote that Bevan had put himself 'out of the running' because he had made 'too many stupid remarks about the Americans'.[28] He should have been bolder, as when he made Bevan Minister of Health in 1945. Morrison turned out to be one of the worst Foreign Secretaries ever; Bevan might have been a great one. Moreover, promoting him would have bound him more firmly to the government: failing to do so left him more than ever restless and aggrieved. From now on he was a time bomb waiting to explode.

Several factors contributed to Bevan's discontent. After six exceptionally difficult years the Labour government had lost its sense of direction. The senior generation of leaders was tired, ill and, one by one, retiring. At fifty-three Bevan was unquestionably the leader of the next generation. Having got the NHS successfully up and running he was ready for a new challenge, yet he was repeatedly passed over. He felt that the government was losing its socialist conviction, settling under Morrison's influence for a cautious programme of 'consolidation' when he believed they should be pressing on with the irreversible transition to socialism: if he was not clear precisely what this should involve, he knew that it was vital to maintain momentum. He sensed that the labour movement was being taken over by a cadre of public-school-educated academics who merely wanted to manage capitalism; and felt that this insidious process was personified by the rise of Gaitskell at the Treasury. Earlier he thought that he had seen off the threat of charges in the NHS before he agreed to move from the Ministry of Health. But now under cover of the expanded rearmament programme Gaitskell was renewing the attack. Bevan saw this as a personal challenge which he was determined to resist, at the same time elevating the issue of free medicine into the touchstone of the government's commitment to socialism. In those days arguments within the cabinet usually stayed private; but on 3 April he broke cover by telling a heckler in Bermondsey that he would not remain in 'a Government which imposes charges on the patient'.[29]

Gaitskell was equally determined – first on his economic objective of enforcing financial discipline on the Health Service, but equally on the political importance of the cabinet being seen to overrule a minister who was defying his colleagues. As a new and untried Chancellor facing an exceptionally difficult budgetary situation, he also had a personal need to assert his authority. Furious at Bevan's attempt to bounce the cabinet by going public, he told Dalton that his 'influence was very much exaggerated . . .

We could not always be blackmailed and give way. If we didn't stand up to him, Nye would do to our party what L.G. had done to the Liberals.'[30] He was persuaded not to persist with prescription charges, on the ground that they penalised patients who were genuinely ill; but he was adamant that he must include in his budget the introduction of charges for NHS false teeth and spectacles.

Unluckily Attlee was ill in hospital during the crucial days before the budget. In his prime the Prime Minister's clipped authority might possibly have imposed a compromise; but in his absence Morrison, who loathed Bevan, clearly backed Gaitskell. At two long meetings on 9 April Bevan found himself isolated, with only Harold Wilson, the youngest member of the cabinet, giving him any support at all. He felt that Morrison and Gaitskell were deliberately driving him into a corner where he must either be humiliated or resign. 'Aren't I worth 23 millions?' he demanded melodramatically.[31] But personalising the issue in this way only antagonised the rest of the cabinet, most of whom had been required to make painful cuts in their own budgets. Between the two meetings Bevan's anger boiled over. 'Who are they?' he raved to Dalton in the Commons Smoking Room. 'I didn't choose them. The P.M. chooses them. They are either old men or rootless men, like Gaitskell and Gordon Walker.' They were 'dismantling the Welfare State . . . slaughtering the Health Service'. At the second cabinet of the day – which happened to be Gaitskell's forty-fifth birthday – Dalton noted that 'Nye's hatred of him glared out all the time'. Gaitskell by contrast was firm but modest, insisting that if the cabinet did not back him he would have to resign, but promising to go quietly and not make any trouble. Dalton thought this 'a high moral attitude compared with Nye'.[32] In fact Gaitskell could afford to be stubborn, since the government could hardly have survived the Chancellor's resignation on the eve of his budget.

But Bevan's resignation would be scarcely less damaging. Much as they disliked his emotional blackmail, therefore, several colleagues did try to persuade Gaitskell to make some last-minute concession that would allow him to stay: announcing a ceiling on NHS spending, for instance, and asserting the possibility of charges without actually announcing their introduction. Douglas

Jay was one of those who urged his friend to compromise. But Gaitskell told him that 'you could hardly run a democratic Cabinet on the principle that, if there was a division of 18–2, the view of the 18 should prevail when X was one of the 18, but the view of the 2 should prevail when X was one of the 2'. Jay found this 'a difficult argument to refute'.[33] In the end he agreed to leave out the date on which the charges would come into effect. But this was too little, too late. Half an hour before Gaitskell got up in the Commons Jim Callaghan, on behalf of a group of anxious junior ministers, went to see Bevan to beg him not to resign. Callaghan did not feel that Nye was looking for an excuse to resign; on the contrary, he felt he was 'tormented as to whether he was taking the right course'. But at one point Bevan burst out: 'Hugh is a Tory. Why do they put me up against it? They have known my position for weeks.'[34] He still felt that he was being deliberately driven out.

Gaitskell's budget speech won almost universal praise. 'He rose a comparative tyro,' according to the *Glasgow Herald,* 'and sat down an acknowledged star'; the London *Evening Standard* hailed 'a new force in politics'; while in the House Churchill mischievously complimented him on his 'evident lack of hatred and malice'.[35] Significantly he placed his budget firmly in the context of the Cold War – 'the clash and conflict . . . between Soviet imperialism on the one side and parliamentary democracy on the other'.[36] But he also stressed the fair sharing of the burden of increased defence expenditure between different sections of society. He was careful to meet most of the cost by higher taxation of the better-off, not by cutting social services: he protected pensions and actually increased NHS spending overall. In this context the charges for teeth and spectacles – just £13 million in 1951–52 , or £23 million in a full year – were small beer: their effect more symbolic than serious. But it was precisely the symbolism that Bevan objected to. He listened to the speech not from the front bench but standing by the Speaker's chair, 'red in the face and breathing like an angry bull', according to the Tory diarist 'Chips' Channon who was standing next to him.[37] When Gaitskell reached the passage announcing the charges Jennie

Lee – Bevan's wife – cried 'Shame'; but there was no other audible dissent.* Bevan turned on his heel and stormed out.

But he did not immediately resign. At the party meeting after the budget it was clear that Labour MPs almost unanimously approved the budget. ('We had all expected far worse things,' wrote Tony Benn, 'and the most noticeable reaction was sheer relief.')[38] Bevan made a conciliatory intervention; he pleaded that it was 'not too late for modifications to be made', but was loudly applauded when he said that 'he had decided not to take a certain course'.[39] The crisis seemed to be over. Next day, however, the cabinet refused to postpone the charges. Bevan growled at Gaitskell, 'Why should I have to put up with these bloody absurdities?'[40] For another ten days he hesitated, torn between colleagues and friends on the one hand who begged him to stay, and his closest associates – principally Jennie Lee and Michael Foot – who urged him to kick over the traces. There were further attempts to appease him by promoting some sort of fudge. Gaitskell was persuaded to state that the charges 'need not necessarily' be permanent; but Bevan dismissed this as 'a bromide'. Then a vicious editorial in the left-wing weekly *Tribune* – edited by Foot – comparing Gaitskell to the turncoat Philip Snowden – Labour's first Chancellor who had followed Ramsay MacDonald into the Tory-dominated National Government in 1931 – alienated his last sympathisers. Finally Attlee concluded characteristically: 'Well, we cannot go on like this. He must behave properly if he is to remain a member of the Government', and from his hospital bed sent him an ultimatum that he must abide by cabinet decisions.[41] Bevan resigned the next day, 21 April, followed by Wilson and a junior minister, John Freeman. But this was just the beginning.

In his resignation statement in the Commons Bevan widened the issue beyond the narrow question of NHS charges to condemn the rearmament programme which he had previously

---

*Jennie Lee and Bevan were colleagues in the 1929 Parliament, She was a feisty Scottish left-winger much more prominent at the time than him; but she lost her seat in 1931, after which she subordinated her career to his. They married in 1934, but had no children. She was re-elected in 1945, and after Bevan's death was a notable Minister for the Arts in Harold Wilson's government.

supported but which he now argued could not be delivered. Here he had a good case, if only he had made it earlier. In fact he had raised doubts about the feasibility of the programme, but then he had let himself be diverted by hatred of Gaitskell into staking everything on the untouchable integrity of the NHS. Half a century later his speech reads quite well; but its tone was bitter, arrogant and gratuitously offensive. First he echoed *Tribune* by charging that 'the Budget was hailed with pleasure in the City'.

> It united the City, satisfied the Opposition and disunited the Labour Party – all this because we have allowed ourselves to be dragged too far behind the wheels of American diplomacy.

He went on to make the loftiest claims for the government's socialist objectives which he believed the budget had betrayed:

> Ever since 1945 we have been engaged upon the most remarkable piece of social reconstruction the world has ever seen. By the end of 1950 we had . . . assumed the moral leadership of the world . . . There is only one hope for mankind, and that hope still remains in this little island. It is from here that we tell the world where to go and how to go there, but we must not follow behind the anarchy of American competitive capitalism.

He then personalised the issue again with his own prescription for socialist finance and a direct attack on Gaitskell:

> Take economic planning away from the Treasury. They know nothing about it . . . It has been perfectly obvious on several occasions that there are too many economists advising the Treasury, and now we have the added misfortune of having an economist in the Chancellor of the Exchequer himself.

This brought him back to the specific issue on which he had resigned. If the Chancellor had found it necessary this year 'to mutilate . . . the Health Services for £13 million out of £4000 million', he demanded, 'what will he do next year?'

After all, the National Health Service was something of which we were all very proud, and even the Opposition were beginning to be proud of it. It had only to last a few more years to become part of our traditions ... Why should we throw it away? In the Chancellor's speech there was not one word of commendation for the Health Service – not one word.

Gaitskell's figures, he jeered, were 'the arithmetic of Bedlam'.

He cannot say that his arithmetic is so precise that he must have the £13 million, when last year the Treasury were £247 million out. Why? . . . Why has it been done?'[42]

The implication was that it had been done deliberately to provoke him to resign.

Like most others on the Labour benches, Benn was appalled by Bevan's intemperate performance:

He abused the Government, he threw in a few anti-American remarks for good measure . . . The fact is that though there was substance in what he said Nye overplayed his hand. His jokes were in bad taste. I felt slightly sick.[43]

'His style', Benn added the next day, 'was that of a ranting demagogue'; and he concluded: 'Nye will never be in another Government until and if he forms his own.'[44] Dalton was delighted by Bevan's own goal:

Nye flopped in the House today . . . No cheer when he entered . . . nor when he rose . . . hardly any cheers while he was speaking, nor when he sat down . . . A most vicious speech, most quotable by the Tories.[45]

At the party meeting the next day Gaitskell drove home his advantage by making a powerful defence of his budget. 'It was a stirring speech,' Benn wrote, 'put over with force and conviction. These twin qualities of intellectual ability and political forcefulness make up Hugh Gaitskell's greatness.' It was 'rather ironical', he thought, 'that Nye should have been largely responsible for making

Gaitskell into the major political figure that he now is'. But then Bevan shot himself in the foot again.

> When Nye rose he shook with rage and screamed, shaking and pointing and pivoting his body back and forth on his heels. His hair came down, his eyes blazed and I thought at times that he would either hit someone or collapse with a fit . . . He screamed, 'I have been martyred by the platform', a tragic insight into his persecution-ridden mind that shocked us all . . . The megalomania and neurosis and hatred and jealousy and instability he displayed astounded us all.[46]

Once again Gaitskell was quietly satisfied by his rival's self-destruction:

> Bevan made things even worse for himself by . . . a shocking outburst of bad temper which was evidently a revelation to many people in the Party. He almost screamed at the platform. At one point he said, 'I won't have it, I won't have it'. And this of course was greeted with derision. 'You won't have it?' called other members of the Party. Of course in the Cabinet we have had this on a number of times but they had not seen it before.[47]

Older members were unpleasantly reminded of Mosley. In the end it was less his resignation itself that damaged Bevan, than the manner of it. At his best he commanded enormous admiration, affection and respect; but Bevan at his worst was an ugly sight, and these two dreadful performances after his resignation convinced many in the party that he should never be leader.

Yet there were the rights and wrongs on both sides. First, Bevan was proved right about the rearmament programme: six months later the incoming Tory government recognised that it was impracticable and scaled it down. Second, he was entitled to feel that the NHS he had created was one of Labour's greatest achievements which should not be compromised: in standing up for the principle of an entirely free service he had a powerful idealistic case which appealed strongly to Labour party members. Unfortunately, however, he had already breached the principle himself by accepting the possibility of prescription charges in 1949, so that his righteous inflexibility in 1951 appeared to be driven less by principle than by wounded pride. He argued his case appallingly badly because he was so eaten up with his own grievances, his contempt for most of his colleagues and above all his loathing of Gaitskell, whom he refused to rate seriously as a rival. ('The Party,' he assured Callaghan, 'will sweep him away!')[48] On the other hand he had some reason for suspecting that Gaitskell, abetted by Morrison, was targeting the NHS deliberately to provoke him. In an earlier age he might, like Castlereagh in 1812, have called his colleague out; and by the standards of that earlier age he might have been justified.

On the other hand Gaitskell was not Philip Snowden reborn: he was not, as Bevan alleged, a closet Tory, and he did not frame his budget to appease the City. But he did believe in responsible finance; he believed that a Labour government must prove its competence to govern prudently, and he did think – as did others – that Bevan had been allowed to get away with unchecked extravagance in the NHS, which could not be a bottomless pit. He also believed strongly in the Atlantic alliance and the overriding importance of standing with the US against Communism, even at the cost of some temporary sacrifice of Labour's domestic programme: guns before butter. In these circumstances, once he had identified charges for teeth and spectacles as one way – among others – to make the necessary economies, and won the backing of the cabinet for including this option, he could not afford to be pushed off them by the opposition of a single difficult colleague. He thought that Attlee and Cripps had indulged Bevan for too long; and as a young Chancellor he saw the chance to assert his own authority. But he also saw the issue as a critical showdown between competing visions of the party – protest and easy rhetoric on the one hand versus responsible government and hard economic choices on the other. 'It is really a fight for the soul of the Labour Party,' he told Dalton. 'But who will win it? . . . I am afraid that if Bevan does we shall be out of power for years and years.'[49]

The irony was that Gaitskell did win it, but the party was still out of power for years and years. There was a genuine gulf of political philosophy, and a greater one of temperament, between the two rivals. But Bevan – most of the time – was a much more serious and constructive politician than Gaitskell gave him credit for; just as Gaitskell was in his own way a truer socialist than Bevan acknowledged. Over the whole range of practical policy, from nationalisation to defence, their differences were really very small, and should have been bridgeable by sensitive leadership. Unfortunately this was lacking because Attlee was ill. Previously 'the little man' had proved immensely skilful in resolving potentially destructive tensions between the big beasts of his government – Morrison and Bevin, Dalton and Cripps; but at the crucial moment in 1951 he was sidelined, leaving a vacuum of leadership in which the enmity of Bevan and Gaitskell was allowed to fester to the point where there was no way that either could back down. The result was that the great Labour government of 1945, instead of renewing itself around a new generation of leaders, was divided and demoralised and six months later went down to defeat at an unnecessarily early general election. Then the feud which had opened up between two middle-ranking colleagues flared into a full-scale civil war for control of the party.

Bevan's resignation changed the dynamics of the Labour party for a generation. Hitherto the various strands of the party's 1945 majority had remained remarkably disciplined. The 'Keep Left' group – a loose collection of around fifty independent-minded backbenchers including Michael Foot, Richard Crossman, Barbara Castle and the slightly sinister Ian Mikardo – had offered some mild dissent, particularly on foreign affairs, but always from a position of broad loyalty. Now suddenly, with Bevan's angry departure from the government, this awkward squad had a leader and a cause. The 'Bevanites', as they now became, held group meetings at the Commons to concert tactics; they organised 'brains trusts' in the constituencies, at which panels of entertaining mavericks openly defied the leadership; while *Tribune*, still inspired though no longer edited by Foot, did all it could to widen the rift, stridently championing Bevan while casting his enemies – specifically Morrison and Gaitskell – as Tories and traitors. The right reacted with alarm and fury, fearing that this upsurge of vocal leftism must inevitably harm the party at the next election, and sought to crush it. 'Herbert and I,' Gaitskell noted in August, 'think that the PM has taken a very weak line about Bevan.'[50] Battle lines were drawn which would divide the party for twenty years.

Bevan himself was always torn between rebellion and loyalty. All his life he insisted that the Labour party was the only possible vehicle to deliver Britain to socialism. As a young man he had never been tempted to join the Communist party when many of his more impatient contemporaries were doing so; and after the 1931 débâcle he was contemptuous when Jennie Lee – not yet his wife, but a young Scottish member of James Maxton's Independent Labour Party (ILP) – followed Maxton in disaffiliating from the Labour party. 'You will not influence the course of British politics by as much as a hair's breadth,' he told her. 'Why don't you get into a nunnery and be done with it? . . . I tell you, it is the Labour party or nothing.'[51] Labour's strength was that it was rooted in the trade unions. The conservatism of the union leaders often drove him to despair; but he knew that the unions represented the working class which in those days comprised the great majority of the electorate. At the heart of his quarrel with Gaitskell was the conviction that he, sprung from the working class, naturally embodied the aspirations of the labour movement in a way that a public-school-educated economist never could. Yet the big union bosses whose block votes dominated the party conference were at that time staunchly right-wing; and in the early 1950s, as Bevin died and Morrison aged, they adopted Gaitskell as their new champion. So Bevan, fighting for a left-wing vision of the party's aims and ethos, with his handful of mainly middle-class supporters, found himself confronted by the whole weight of the organised working-class movement ranged behind the very man who had forced his resignation in 1951. This almost incomprehensible paradox never ceased to enrage him, provoking further angry explosions which twice over the next few years nearly got him expelled from the party. Yet he always wanted to be loyal. He welcomed the support of his Bevanite cronies in the Smoking Room, but he did not approve of factions within the party and did not want to lead one. Ian Mikardo, who more than anyone else tried to form the Bevanites into a cohesive force, despaired of Bevan as any sort of leader:

> He loved to let his mind wander round wide horizons and he did that with a breadth of imagination, an originality of analysis and a fertility of prescription far beyond the capacity of anyone else I've ever known. But he had no patience for the nitty-gritty of who should do what when . . . To anyone who knew him and worked with him the idea of Bevan as a power-hungry conspirator was a belly-laugh.[52]

At the party conference that preceded the election which Attlee rather wearily called in October 1951, Bevan pleaded for unity to prevent the return of a Tory government. 'We must never allow the British Labour Movement to become schismatic.'[53] But the right saw this as pure hypocrisy and Bevan himself as the principal source of schism. Each side blamed the other for the loss of the election: the left condemned the sell-out of the party's convictions in a timid strategy of 'consolidation', while the right blamed the Bevanites for the squabbling which had given so much ammunition to the Tory press. Though Labour actually polled more votes, the Tories won a narrow majority of seats, giving Churchill the satisfaction of reversing his rejection in 1945 and ushering in what would turn out to be thirteen years of Tory rule. At the time neither faction believed that this setback was more than a brief interruption of Labour's inevitable forward march: neither Gaitskell nor Bevan imagined for a moment that they would never hold office again. Defeat only intensified the struggle for control of the next Labour government.

For the moment Attlee continued as leader. At the age of sixty-eight, after sixteen years – eleven of them as Prime Minister or deputy Prime Minister – he should have retired, but the obvious successor was Herbert Morrison, whom he was determined to block. There was really no alternative, since Bevan by his resignation had ruled himself out of contention, at least for the moment, while Gaitskell was still too little known: he saw himself as a challenger the next time round, in five or ten years' time, but for now he was happy to see Morrison take his turn while he concentrated on building up his following in the party and working to counter the malign influence of the Bevanites by offering 'responsible' opposition to the new government. So Attlee stayed on, purely to deny Morrison, until 1955. The lack of leadership which had proved so disastrous in 1951 thus dragged on for another four years, while the champions of left and right fought a shadow contest for the eventual succession.

After the 1951 election Bevan declined to stand against Morrison for the deputy leadership, knowing that he would have lost. He also declined to stand for the shadow cabinet, preferring to retain his independence to speak out over the whole range of issues. But as soon as he came back to the Commons he dominated it again with a series of scintillating speeches lambasting the Tories with a wit and force that no one else could match, while retrospectively vindicating his resignation. On the one hand he ironically welcomed the government's reduced rearmament programme; on the other he condemned Rab Butler's immediate extension of NHS charges, which showed that Gaitskell's initial breach had been the thin end of the wedge as he predicted. (In November the *Economist* encapsulated the continuity between Gaitskell and Butler at the Treasury by inventing the composite figure of 'Mr Butskell', which neatly made the Bevanites' point for them.) Bevan also warned against allowing the Americans to convert the Korean war into a global crusade against Communism. These speeches went a long way towards restoring his standing among Labour MPs. 'When he speaks in the House,' Dalton noted, 'he exercises a hypnotic influence over many of our people. It's pathetic and dangerous to watch their eyes fixed on him.'[54] Gaitskell started organising younger friends like Tony Crosland and Roy Jenkins to try to counter his influence.

The first serious row in the new Parliament occurred in February 1952 when fifty-six Labour members followed Bevan in voting against the government's defence estimates in defiance of the shadow cabinet's decision to abstain. There was immediately a clamour for the rebels to be disciplined which Gaitskell – behind the scenes – strongly supported. Dalton found him 'very strung up against the Bevanites' and pressing for 'a showdown';[55] while Gaitskell himself wrote scornfully of the fainthearts who were 'frightened at the prospect of Bevan and some of the others having to go out of the Party altogether. I was naturally quite prepared for this to happen, and indeed there would have been some advantage for it would have left us much freer to attack him'.[56] At the party meeting to resolve the question, Bevan made another angry speech refusing to bind himself to toe the party line; but the centrist 'Keep Calm' group, who did not want to see him driven out, succeeded in carrying a conciliatory motion against the platform, and a showdown was averted – for the moment.

Over the summer, tension between the two camps continued to mount. In April Bevan published a much-hyped – but actually very woolly – personal manifesto entitled *In Place of Fear*, setting out his vision of democratic socialism, and drew enthusiastic audiences wherever he spoke; while the *Tribune* 'brains trusts' went from strength to strength. This was an age before most people had television. Loyalist MPs felt that they were being undermined in their own constituencies, much as their successors thirty years later felt they were being undermined by Militant. Increasingly they complained that the Bevanites were constituting themselves 'a party within a party'. Dalton, trying to play the peacemaker, warned Gaitskell that he was 'in danger of having an obsession about the Bevanites'; but Gaitskell was adamant. 'He said one must realise that there was a bitter struggle for leadership going on. It might last several years. The Bevanites might win. Then he'd have to consider whether he could go on in public life . . . He was very tense and unsmiling.'[57] At the same time Crossman was embarrassed by Bevan's equally entrenched hostility to Gaitskell, who he suggested should be reduced to the rank of 'junior clerk in the next Labour Government'.[58] There was an awkward incident in the House at the end of July when Bevan – from a back bench – intervened after Gaitskell had effectively put Churchill on the spot: instead of reinforcing the attack on Churchill he launched 'a personal attack on Gaitskell', which was heard 'with enormous relief by the Tories and with icy silence' on the Labour benches.[59]

The party conference at Morecambe that autumn was the most bilious ever. Dalton thought it 'the worst . . . for bad temper and general hatred, since 1926'; even Foot called it 'rowdy, convulsive, vulgar, splenetic'.[60] Normal fraternal courtesies were ignored as right-wing speakers were booed and heckled, and a series of sharply left-wing motions was carried from the floor. Most dramatically of all the Bevanites swept six of the seven places on the National Executive elected by the rank and file, defeating both Morrison and Dalton.* This – especially the humiliation of Morrison – was a challenge which the right could not ignore. Two days later Gaitskell picked up the gauntlet in a speech at Stalybridge in which he alleged that 'about one-sixth of the Constituency Party delegates appeared to be Communists or Communist-inspired', and claimed that 'the stream of grossly misleading propaganda with poisonous innuendos and malicious attacks on Attlee, Morrison and the rest of us' poured out weekly by *Tribune* made unity impossible. The right had suffered these attacks in silence for too long. 'It is time to end the attempt at mob rule by a group of frustrated journalists and restore the authority and leadership of the solid sound sensible majority of the Movement.' Otherwise, he warned, the party would not deserve to be returned to government.[61]

This speech clearly established Gaitskell as a future leader. Hitherto he had been widely seen as a slightly prissy technocrat, more civil servant than politician: now he had shown that he was willing to get his hands dirty. His allegation of Communist influence and his characterisation of the leading Bevanites – not inaccurately – as 'frustrated journalists' made him a hero of the loyalists (and the Tory press), while making him more than ever a hate figure for the left. But it had the desired effect. A number of senior party figures supported him; and finally even Attlee came off the fence. In a speech at the Royal Festival Hall he declared that 'the existence of a party within a party with separate leadership, separate meetings, supported by its own Press' was 'quite intolerable', and – in a typically head-masterish image – called for unity and teamwork: 'The most brilliant player on the left wing is no use if he plays a selfish game. He certainly would not help if he put the ball through his own goal.'[62] Ten days later he demanded and won – by 188 votes to 51 – a vote

---

*Bevan topped the poll, followed by Barbara Castle, Tom Driberg, Mikardo, Wilson and Crossman; of the old guard only Jim Griffiths survived, in sixth place.

of the parliamentary party to disband all unofficial groups. Foot and some of the other Bevanites wanted to defy the ban, insisting on their right to freedom of speech and association. But now Bevan's gut loyalty came into play. 'To continue the Group now,' he told Crossman, would be 'to perpetuate schism. If you were to continue the Group in these conditions and I were the Leader, I would have you expelled. The Group is intolerable.'[63] So the Bevanites were formally wound up, though they did not disappear.

Bevan then stood for deputy leader, winning 82 votes against Morrison's 194 – considerably more than the core Bevanite vote. He also stood for the shadow cabinet, though here he only just secured twelfth and last place with 108 votes. (Gaitskell was third with 179, behind Jim Griffiths and another veteran, Chuter Ede.) For a time it seemed that Attlee's belatedly knocking heads together had done the trick. Within weeks Crossman was writing that 'mysteriously, and with quite astonishing rapidity, the mood of the Parliamentary Party has changed. The Bevanite and anti Bevanite feeling has melted away and . . . everyone is rather shamefacedly aware that both sides are on the same side after all.'[64] By returning to the front bench Bevan was back where he belonged.

But this was premature. During 1953 there was a lull in hostilities; but it was a temporary truce. Tension still simmered and occasionally boiled over: Bevan could always be provoked by Gaitskell's role as Shadow Chancellor. Once when Gaitskell spoke of the danger of indiscipline, Bevan fixed him with 'a glare of concentrated hatred' and told him scornfully, 'You're too young in the Movement to know what you're talking about.' When Jim Callaghan suggested that he was looking for an excuse to resign, he indignantly denied it; but a little later he walked out in a huff saying, 'Whatever you agree to in your present mood, I am against it.'[65] Bevan still felt isolated, prickly and resentful.

Gaitskell admittedly was not an easy colleague. Though charming and passionate in private, he was fundamentally shy and conducted himself politically with a cool reserve which all but his closest friends found difficult to penetrate. Tony Benn worked with him on broadcasting during the 1951 election.

I could see very clearly how the character of Gaitskell and his mannerisms would have driven Nye Bevan to fury . . . In a way it is his attractive, public-school character that made him both pleasant and detestable. I thoroughly enjoyed it even though it made me more sympathetic to Nye Bevan than I had been at the start.[66]

Of course Benn was very conscious of being a public-school boy himself. Two years later his reservations had increased. 'He is intellectually arrogant, obstinate and patronising. I respect – but cannot quite admire – him.'[67] Many others voiced similar feelings. By his very reasonableness Gaitskell had a knack of rubbing people up the wrong way. Nothing was more calculated to enrage Bevan than being patronised.

In March 1954 Bevan's restraint suddenly cracked, though his anger was initially directed at Attlee rather than Gaitskell. Attlee was in the middle of replying, quite cautiously, to the Foreign Secretary, Anthony Eden, about an American proposal to create a South-East Asian equivalent of NATO to resist Communism in Indo-China when Bevan – without consulting any of his supporters – pushed his way along the front bench, 'stood literally on Attlee's toes and denounced the whole idea lock stock and barrel in a way that made him seem to be repudiating Attlee's leadership'.[68] The next day, rather than apologise, he flounced out of the shadow cabinet saying that he had been humiliated and – as in 1951 – immediately tried to widen the issue, telling his followers that their tactic now should be 'to attack the Right wing of the Party all along the line' and to 'destroy the bogus reputation of Clement Attlee'.[69] This outburst, however, stretched their loyalty too far. Harold Wilson, who been runner-up in the elections the previous autumn, wasted no time in filling the vacant place in the shadow cabinet. Bevan was furious, but the only result of his latest tantrum was that he was left more isolated than ever.

Yet he promptly opened a new front by announcing his intention of contesting the party treasurership which fell vacant that summer. The job was unimportant in itself, but carried a seat on the National Executive; it therefore offered a good opportunity for Gaitskell to consolidate his growing stature in the party. Since the office was effectively in the gift of the big unions, his victory was a foregone conclusion. Nevertheless Bevan threw up his own seat on the executive in order to oppose him. 'But you will be defeated,' someone said. 'Of course,' said Nye, 'but in defeating me they will split every trade union and expose Deakin and Tom Williamson by making them prefer an intellectual like Gaitskell to a miner like me.'[70]* He took it for granted that at least his own union would back him; but even there he was rejected. 'How can you support a public school boy from Winchester against a man born in the back streets of Tredegar?' he demanded furiously of the miners' leader Sam Watson.[71] Gaitskell duly won the block vote by more than two to one – by 4.3 million votes to two million. Bevan took the result as final proof of the takeover of the party by soulless bureaucrats. Freed now of any collective restraints he poured out his frustration at the annual *Tribune* meeting at the party conference:

> I know now that the right kind of leader for the Labour Party is a desiccated calculating machine who must not in any way permit himself to be swayed by indignation. If he sees suffering, privation or injustice he must not allow it to move him, for that would be evidence of lack of proper education or of absence of self-control.[72]

It was generally assumed that the 'desiccated calculating machine' he had in mind was Gaitskell. In fact it was probably Attlee, who had warned the previous day against 'emotionalism'. Privately Bevan denied that he had meant Gaitskell since the former Chancellor was 'highly emotional and couldn't count'! – a mocking reference back to 1951.[73] But the phrase stuck to Gaitskell, while Bevan's intemperate language simply confirmed his reputation as a bad loser.

The biggest row of all erupted six months later when Bevan again appeared to go out of his way to pick a quarrel with Attlee on the floor of the House. This time it was about the use of nuclear weapons. Unlike many on the left, Bevan had never opposed Britain's possession of the atom bomb. But now the

*Arthur Deakin and Tom Williamson were the leaders of two of the biggest unions, the Transport & General Workers' Union and the National Union of General and Municipal Workers respectively.

stakes had been raised by the development of the still more powerful hydrogen bomb; and on this he had not yet reached a settled view. When Attlee followed the normal practice of both front benches by refusing to spell out the circumstances in which Britain might use nuclear weapons, Bevan – having given no hint of disagreement at the party meeting a few days earlier – aggressively interrogated him before abstaining with sixty-two others in defiance of the whip. Once again the loyal majority demanded sanctions against the rebels – withdrawal of the whip, leading to possible expulsion from the party. Thus the country was treated to the extraordinary spectacle of the main opposition party, in what was likely to be an election year, solemnly debating the expulsion of its most charismatic member.

Gaitskell's first instinct was that 'sooner or later he [Bevan] would have to go, but I was not sure whether this was the right moment'.[74] But soon he could not resist stirring the pot. Bevan's conduct, he told an audience in Doncaster, constituted 'a direct challenge to the elected Leader of our Party', adding that 'effective leadership and good team work becomes impossible if all the time we have to face disruption from within'.[75] At a party meeting a few days later Bevan denied having challenged Attlee and accused Gaitskell of spreading a deliberate lie. On the contrary, he charged, indicating the shadow cabinet, 'These are the men who are working against the leadership, those hatchet-faced men sitting on the platform.'[76] The hatchet-faced men asked Attlee to make it clear that they would all resign if the whip was not withdrawn from Bevan. But Attlee – even though or because he had been the one directly challenged – summed up weakly; and the meeting voted narrowly – 141–112 – to withdraw the whip. This Dalton thought 'a very poor result . . . It will now be more difficult for the N.E.C. to expel Bevan.'[77]

Once committed, however, Gaitskell felt he must support his union backers and took the lead in pressing for expulsion. He revealed the depth of the right's paranoia about Bevan in conversation with Crossman. 'Bevanism,' he insisted, 'is and only is a conspiracy to seize the leadership for Aneurin Bevan.'

'It is a conspiracy because it has three essentials of conspiracy, a leader in Bevan, an organisation run by Mikardo and a newspaper run by Foot.' I laughed and said, 'You really believe in this talk about the Bevanite organisation of Mikardo?' Gaitskell said, 'Certainly. It's widespread in the constituencies' . . .

I tried to suggest that Bevanism was also a protest against the totally inadequate leadership of Morrison and himself. I said that in my view Nye was only half wanting to be Leader and that certainly there had been no serious conspiracy to replace Attlee with Nye. Gaitskell then repeated his whole speech at length and said, 'It's got to be cleaned up. There are extraordinary parallels between Nye and Adolf Hitler. They are demagogues of exactly the same sort . . . There are minor differences but what is striking is the resemblance'.[78]

Bevan was called to appear before a NEC sub-committee, where he said he would refuse to be 'cornered by Gaitskell'.[79] In fact Gaitskell intervened only once to ask if he agreed that attacking the leader was a bad thing and would refrain from doing it in future. Bevan replied truculently: 'I refuse to answer that question. It is a trap.'[80] But he did apologise to Attlee, who then succeeded – by a single vote – in carrying the executive against expulsion. By now Gaitskell regretted having supported the attempt. But his summing up of the episode was couched in frankly military terms:

> The whole thing may be regarded as a stalemate. The attack was mounted, but no breakthrough was achieved because the Commander in Chief [i.e. Attlee] really did not like the plan from the start. The enemy counterattack was only partially successful. We might be said to have gained some ground after heavy casualties. If Bevan misbehaves again in the near future, his position will certainly be more precarious as a result of all this. On the other hand, the right wing is rather dispirited, and . . . my own position is no doubt weaker.[81]

Though Bevan was the one always accused of scheming for the leadership, Gaitskell never took his eye off his own prospects.

A few days later Churchill finally retired and Eden, on becoming Prime Minister, immediately called a general election. There was never much doubt that the Tories would win comfortably. Against the relatively youthful team of Eden (58), Harold Macmillan (61) and Rab Butler (53), the Labour shadow cabinet – Gaitskell excepted – looked elderly and tired. Moreover the Tories had benefited from the ending of austerity and the first shoots of affluence. 'For the first time in living memory,' Bevan wrote in *Tribune*, 'a Tory Government managed to exist for more than three years without inflicting mass unemployment on the country.' Labour, he argued, was 'the victim of its own success'.[82] But it was clearly not helped by the poisonous divisions of the past four years. The 1955 election was the first since 1931 at which Labour's vote had not increased. Each faction promptly blamed the other for the setback. 'Can anyone honestly say that if the Labour Party had chosen a policy which reflected more or less the line of the Communist Party we should have achieved a larger vote?' Gaitskell demanded.[83] Bevan was emphatically not a Communist; but essentially this was what he did believe.

> What is the common factor which Labour people share and which sharply distinguishes us from the Tories? It is Socialism. If it is not that, then there is nothing, at least nothing worth bothering about. The more we play it down, the less we differ from our opponents and the less reason there is for people to vote for us . . . The fight for Socialism unites and excites the party. To mute the fight is to disunite and deflate it.[84]

Here in classic form is the argument that has tormented opposition parties ever since – notably Labour in the 1980s and the Tories after 1997. Are elections won by enthusing your core support, as Bevan maintained, or in the middle ground, as Gaitskell (and more recently Tony Blair) more pragmatically believed? History overwhelmingly supports Gaitskell.

After 1955, however, both sides made an effort to keep the argument on a comradely basis. Bevan stood for shadow cabinet again and came seventh, with many of the old guard standing down. He did not oppose Morrison for deputy, but did contest the treasurership again, losing even more heavily than in 1954. At Margate in October Gaitskell made an effort to shed his 'desiccated' image by making a passionate, unscripted avowal of his own socialist faith – stressing equality and social justice but also including nationalisation as a 'vital means' to that end. Bevan 'red-faced and furious' at the back of the hall, called it 'sheer demagogy'; but the conference was impressed by this glimpse of a different Gaitskell.[85] Back at Westminster he won further praise for his furious denunciation of Rab Butler's cynical withdrawal, immediately after the election, of all the goodies he had given away in his pre-election budget in the spring. By the time Attlee finally decided to retire in December it was obvious to most of the party that Gaitskell was the only possible successor.

Morrison still thought the leadership should be his by right of seniority: he was warned that he risked humiliation if he insisted on standing, but refused to listen. Gaitskell was reluctant to oppose him, but was eventually persuaded that he must stand to be sure of stopping Bevan. 'Of course, my boy,' Morrison told him complacently, 'you go ahead if you want to, you'll be out on the first ballot.'[86] Bevan was bound to stand as the champion of the left; he knew he could not win, but still raged at the idea of Gaitskell winning. 'You can't force the Party to accept Gaitskell,' he told Crossman, 'and I must warn you that, if he is Leader, I might not be able to collaborate.' 'You've got to understand that many of us know all the drawbacks of Gaitskell,' Crossman told him, 'but accept him as inevitable because you've ruled yourself out.'[87] In a doomed attempt to prevent the inevitable, however, Bevan proposed that he and Gaitskell should both stand down to give Morrison a free run. This was not only cynical but also made no sense. Morrison was patently no longer up to the job, while the party desperately needed to settle the issue of the leadership, not postpone it again. The episode dismayed his own supporters and made Gaitskell even more unstoppable. In the event Gaitskell was comfortably elected with 157 votes against 70 for Bevan and just 40 for Morrison. (At this period only MPs voted for the leader.) This was the widest margin by which any Labour leader was elected until Neil Kinnock in 1983, under a different system.

Gaitskell's was also the quickest rise to the leadership of any major party in modern times until the recent cult of inexperience:

just ten years from entering Parliament, beating Kinnock's thirteen years and Tony Blair's eleven.* He had worked hard for it, but he knew that he had been lucky and also whom to thank: 'The leadership came to me so early', he told a friend, 'because Bevan threw it at me by his behaviour.'[88] 'Nye had the leadership on a plate,' Attlee agreed. 'I always wanted him to have it. But you know, he wants to be two things simultaneously, a rebel and an official leader, and you can't be both.'[89] If Attlee had really wanted to groom Bevan for the leadership he should have promoted him in 1950–51; but it was true that Bevan's own behaviour since then had largely ruled him out. Henry Fairlie wrote that Bevan lost 'primarily because he treated the parliamentary Labour party with barely concealed contempt'.[90] In the end Bevan really had only himself to blame. By comparison Gaitskell was exceptionally untried by the standards of the time, having sat just twelve months in cabinet; moreover he too was a divisive figure, not a healer. Yet he looked and conducted himself like a potential Prime Minister, as Bevan did not; and most of the party, including most of the leading Bevanites, were desperate to leave behind the quarrels of the past four years. Harold Wilson – ironically, as it turned out – wrote to Gaitskell that 'in my view, the issue of the leadership is settled for twenty years'.[91] And Gaitskell did his best to make a fresh beginning. At the party meeting following his election he held out an olive branch: 'Nye, we haven't got on in the past, but if you will accept this vote, as I would have had to accept it if it had gone the other way, I promise you I will not be outdone in generosity.' Bevan replied graciously, offering congratulations and support and wishing Gaitskell 'higher office'.[92]

Contrary to his image up to 1955 – and again after 1959 – Gaitskell was a remarkably consensual leader in his first four years. He made a real effort to reconcile differences and unite the party, to the extent that arguably he did not give a sufficiently clear lead. He expected to win the next election, so spent the years of opposition

---

*Since 1997 the Tories have lowered the bar even further, with William Hague (eight years), Iain Duncan-Smith (nine) and David Cameron (four) – the two latter (like Kinnock and Blair) having no government experience at all.

conscientiously preparing for government. Harold Macmillan, who replaced Eden as Prime Minister at the beginning of 1957, mocked his seriousness, saying that by being so responsible he missed all the fun of opposition.[93] Many Labour people, too, would have liked a more aggressive approach; the fact that Labour actually lost in 1959 more heavily than in 1955 gave retrospective credence to this criticism. But Gaitskell believed that his priority must be to restore Labour's credibility as an alternative government. Bevan grumbled, and tension persisted beneath the surface loyalty; he was still torn between the irreconcilables among his supporters – principally Foot and Jennie Lee – who were always needling him to reject what Jennie called 'the mush of unity',[94] and the more power-hungry – Wilson, Crossman and Castle – who urged him to co-operate. He never fully accepted Gaitskell's leadership; but he too was sick of the battles of the past few years. He was just as keen as Gaitskell to regain power and he knew that they must forge and maintain a common front. In fact, given their previous relations, they managed it astonishingly well.

At first Bevan was still inclined to be difficult. Having come second in the leadership election he thought he should be deputy leader. 'There ought to be no *election* to the deputy leadership,' he told the Chief Whip. 'Gaitskell should *appoint* me as Deputy Leader. I am the leader of the Party in the country.'[95] Instead he had to stand for the job, and lost to the emollient Jim Griffiths – another South Wales miner, but one with no enemies – by 30 votes (141–111). Once again he took defeat with an ill grace. At Manchester two days later he complained that he was 'fed up' with being told to 'play with the team' when he had only contempt for the game the rest of the team was playing.

> Play inside the team, indeed! When you join a team in the expectation that you are going to play Rugger, you can't be expected to be enthusiastic if you are asked to play tiddlywinks.

Then – without naming him – he repeated his view that the new leader was a middle-class parvenu who had hijacked the Labour party:

You would have thought that some of these people had only just arrived in the socialist movement. You would have thought that the history of the socialist movement began when they came into it. The history of the socialist movement looks as though it is beginning to end when they came into it.[96]

'During the course of the weekend,' Gaitskell wrote in his diary, 'Mr B made a vitriolic speech attacking me and everybody else. And of course the papers were all speculating as to what we should do about it.'[97] In fact he decided to ignore it. He had already decided not to give Bevan one of 'the big jobs' in the shadow cabinet, but Griffiths's elevation left a vacancy shadowing the Colonial Office, so after some hesitation he decided to offer it to Bevan.

> He came in, evidently expecting that we were going to put him on the mat about his weekend speech – swaggering in a sort of defensive way. So I said very sweetly, 'Come along, Nye, come and sit down' and went on, 'Allocation of jobs'. He was quite startled, and quite obviously surprised at this development. Then I said, 'We would like you to take the Colonies'. He then proceeded to talk in a more sensible and rational manner than I have heard him for a long time. He said, 'I would have liked Foreign Affairs'. I ignored that, and then he went on, 'The only difficulty about the Colonies is that I really know so little about them'. This is a very rare admission from Mr B! I said, 'Well, you'll have to learn a lot – it's a job with a lot of work attached to it. But it's something to get your teeth into . . .' Finally he said, 'All right, I'll take it'.

'We are giving him every possible chance,' Gaitskell concluded.

> If, despite this, he refuses to work in the team, and goes on behaving as he has been doing recently, sooner or later he will simply get himself out of the Party. But whether he will do that, or whether after all he will settle down, we cannot yet say . . . his pride will always make it very difficult indeed for him to work in a team under my leadership, or indeed under anybody else's who is now on the scene.[98]

(*Left*) Pitt by James Gillray, 1789

(*Below*) Fox by Karl Anton Hickel, 1794

'Britannia Between Death and the Doctor' by Gillray, 1804. Pitt tramples on Fox and kicks Addington out of the door, while Napoleon threatens Britannia

Canning painted by
Sir Thomas Lawrence, c.1809

Castlereagh by Henry Hoppner Meyer, 1814

Pistols at Dawn: the Canning–Castlereagh duel as seen by Isaac Robert Cruickshank, 1809

Gladstone photographed in 1858, Disraeli in 1861

'Rival Stars' by
r John Tenniel,
1868

Asquith painted by André Cluysenaar, 1919

Lloyd George in 1916

Asquith and Lloyd George as seen by David Low in the 1920s

(*Left*) Bevan speaking at the
Labour party conference, 1957

(*Right*) Gaitskell with his 1951 budget

Gaitskell arrives at the 1959 conference in front of Bevan and leaves behind,
as drawn by Vicky

Macmillan and Butler, 1959

"WELL, SO LONG, RAB! I'M OFF TO SEE THE FAMILY, BUT I KNOW
THAT YOU'RE THE BEST BABY SITTER WE HAVE!"

(*Left*) Vicky's view of the long-suffering
Butler (1958), (*below*) ultimately stabbed
in the back by 'Mac the Knife' (1964)

ON THE SIDEWALK SUNDAY MORNING
LIES A BODY OOZING LIFE.
SOMEONE'S SNEAKING 'ROUND THE CORNER,
IS THE SOMEONE MAC THE KNIFE?

—The Threepenny Opera

All smiles: Thatcher and Heath at the Conservative party conference, 1970

" A woman leader! Hee, hee, hee, is she serious?"

Thatcher as Boadicea by Franklin, 1974

The future leader carries off her predecessor, 1973

Joined at the hip:
Brown and Blair at the Labour
party conference, 2005

Blair and Brown as seen
by (*above*) Dave Brown (2001)
and (*right*) Steve Bell (2003)

During much of 1956 Bevan kept his head down, missing more shadow cabinet and party meetings than he attended. 'It certainly makes things very much easier when he stays away,' Gaitskell noted.[99] In March he failed to appear for the group photograph. 'One doesn't know whether he just forgot about it, or whether he decided that he could not be seen in this particular company by posterity.'[100] But then in July he started attending more often. 'One can usually be sure that . . . he will be somewhat obstreperous, always arguing, always talking too much and generally, though not always, arguing the wrong way.'[101] That summer he stood again for the treasurership. This time the right's candidate was George Brown. Ostensibly Gaitskell played no part, but he pushed hard for Brown behind the scenes, and was disappointed when Bevan narrowly won. Yet this was an important stage in Bevan's accommodation with his leadership. Tony Benn wrote that by winning at last Bevan 'took his place in the hierarchy – secure, accepted and still very much loved, for all his mischief as much as despite it'.[102] Accepting the job he joked that he now considered himself a calculating machine, though he hoped not yet desiccated.[103]

His reconciliation was further assisted by the Suez crisis – the greatest British foreign policy blunder between Munich in 1938 and the invasion of Iraq in 2003. Gaitskell and Bevan were united in condemnation of Eden's calamitous military response to the Egyptian dictator's unilateral nationalisation of the Canal, carried out in secret collusion with Israel in defiance of the Americans, and swiftly and humiliatingly aborted. Gaitskell was strongly criticised by the Tories for appearing to change his mind on the issue. His first speech in the Commons was broadly supportive of the government; but that was because he accepted Eden's assurances that he had no intention of using force to recapture the Canal. When he found that he had been deceived he felt personally betrayed, and denounced the operation with all the moral outrage at his command, in the high-minded tradition of Gladstone denouncing Disraeli. Bevan's initial response was also surprisingly hawkish: he disappointed the left – who thought the Egyptians perfectly entitled to nationalise the canal – by condemning Colonel Nasser as strongly as the British government. ('If the sending of one's police and soldiers into the darkness of the night to seize someone else's property is nationalisation,' he argued the following year, 'then Ali Baba used the wrong terminology.')[104] 'He did not of course say that he agreed with me,' Gaitskell noted after a meeting of the shadow cabinet, 'but . . . he was in no doubt about Nasser being a thug and . . . the need for international control.'[105] But then both of them were equally appalled by Eden's clumsy resort to military intervention in defiance of international law. Gaitskell's passionate legalism ('An act of disastrous folly whose tragic consequences we shall regret for years') and Bevan's scornful rhetoric ('If Sir Anthony is sincere in what he says – and he may be – then he is too *stupid* to be Prime Minister') complemented each other perfectly.[106] For months afterwards the Tories tried to make mischief between them, accusing Gaitskell of opportunism – if not treason – for failing to support British troops in action, while praising Bevan as somehow more patriotic. In the Commons Butler wittily parodied a popular song of the moment:

> Anything Hugh can do, Nye can do better,
> Nye can do anything better than Hugh.[107]

At the end of the year Crossman noted an 'extraordinary press campaign . . . suggesting . . . that Bevan is the only man fit to lead the Labour Party . . . It actually, of course, compels Nye to be loyal to Hugh.' The result was that what he called 'the Gaitskell–Bevan axis' was 'now pretty firm'.[108]

His performance over Suez led Gaitskell to offer Bevan the foreign affairs portfolio, in place of Alf Robens whom he had effortlessly overshadowed during the crisis. Gaitskell was still doubtful about promoting Bevan – 'If it were not for Alf's failure I wouldn't think of it'[109] – but Bevan accepted gratefully with 'a graceful little speech' at the party meeting. 'The Party cheered itself silly,' Benn optimistically recorded, 'in delighted relief at the formal recognition of the final end of all our splits.'[110]

The reality was not quite so simple. In April 1957, as part of his new brief, Bevan made a four-week tour of Asia, from where he wrote a rare letter home to Jennie:

The more I reflect on Gaitskell the more gloomy I become and the more I dread the ordeal before me if ever he becomes Prime Minister . . . Even the thought of the effort needed to influence him to the right courses makes my spirits sink.[111]

Yet he did very much want to be Foreign Secretary, and for that prize he was ready to swallow his doubts. He could easily have made difficulties over a new statement of policy that summer which attempted to resolve the thorniest and most symbolic issue dividing the two wings of the party: nationalisation. On one side the 'revisionists' around Gaitskell – notably Tony Crosland, whose influential book *The Future of Socialism* was published the previous year – wanted to devise more flexible and selective forms of public ownership in place of the party's traditional commitment, embodied in Clause Four of the party constitution, to wholesale nationalisation of the 'commanding heights of the economy', which they believed had been an electoral handicap since 1950. On the other side *Tribune* and the unreconstructed left still regarded nationalisation as the very essence of socialism and looked to Bevan to defend the true faith. The resulting document, *Industry and Society,* was a fudge which included no list of future candidates for takeover but proposed to achieve the same result by taking a controlling stake in major companies. In *Tribune* Jennie scorned it as 'Too Pink, Too Blue, too Yellow', and vowed defiantly 'We'll Keep The Red Flag Flying Here!'[112] Privately, Bevan agreed; but he had made up his mind that unity must take priority. It was, he told Foot, 'a lousy document, but one can't spend all one's time fighting'.[113] He was anxious not to be seen to have surrendered his principles; but at the same time he wanted credit for not rocking the boat. He gave the document his blessing, and conference approved it by a margin of four to one.

Nationalisation was the dog that did not bark at the 1957 conference. The real drama erupted the next day over the other deeply contentious issue facing the party: nuclear weapons. Here Bevan did not merely keep his head down: he actively confronted the left and dismayed his own supporters by the ferocity with which he followed Gaitskell's line. Ever since 1951 he had flirted with unilateral nuclear disarmament. This was the issue on which he had almost got himself expelled in 1955. Emotionally he was on the side of the disarmers: he still hated seeing Britain as the junior partner in the Atlantic alliance. Yet he also believed that Britain's bomb gave an opportunity for moral leadership in the world: he prided himself on his contacts with non-aligned world leaders like Nehru in India, Tito in Yugoslavia, Pierre Mendes-France in France and Pietro Nenni in Italy – democratic socialists like himself who wanted to find a third way independent of both the Americans and the Soviet Union. Bevan believed – in Mikardo's words – 'that if he ever got to be Prime Minister or Foreign Secretary of Great Britain he could put together an anti-Cold War axis strong enough to divert the two superpowers from their collision course';[114] but he knew that he could not hope to achieve this unless Britain retained its own nuclear capability as a bargaining counter. Accordingly he stood up at Brighton and begged the conference not to send the next Labour Foreign Secretary – himself – 'naked into the conference chamber'. Heckled from the floor, he responded angrily by rubbing the unilateralists' noses in their own impotence.

'Do it now', you say . . . Do it now as a Labour Party Conference? You cannot do it now. It is not in your hands to do it. All you can do is pass a resolution . . . And you call that statesmanship. I call it an emotional spasm.[115]

'At noon today,' wrote James Cameron, 'the star of Aneurin Bevan skipped in its course . . . and at least one aspect of politics can never be the same again.'[116] Following his acquiescence in *Industry and Society* the day before, this was the moment when Bevan publicly turned his back on his old allies and bound himself irrevocably to work with his once bitter rival. 'The Bevan–Gaitskell axis,' Crossman wrote, 'is now securely and publicly established.'

Nye has burnt so many boats and bridges that he will find it very difficult to get back to Bevanism and the *Tribune* . . . Gaitskell and Bevan have strengthened their position with the electorate at large by curbing the Party extremists and asserting their authority over them in defiance of their dogma.

As a former Bevanite who had already gone over to Gaitskell some time earlier, Crossman saw the outcome starkly as a matter of personalities:

> It has, of course, been a complete victory for Hugh . . . Every member of the Executive has watched this test of strength between him and Nye and knows from inside the qualities each man showed – Hugh firm, obstinate, not very adroit, but keeping his eye fixed on his long-term objectives; Nye immensely more powerful personally, tactically far more skilful but completely failing to achieve his long-term objectives because of the pendulum swing of his emotions.[117]

For the next two years, up to the 1959 election, Bevan was impeccably loyal, at least in public. Crossman – the closest chronicler of their relationship after Gaitskell abandoned his diary in 1956 – got quite carried away by his enthusiasm for their new accord. Two weeks after Brighton he recorded that they had each invited the other to lunch – 'really decisive events in the life of these two men, who have never had a drink with each other, much less a meal in their whole lives'.[118] In fact they had dined weekly with Cripps in 1948–50, and had lunched together at least once in 1956. But it was a measure of a reasonable *modus vivendi*. Both realised that they must work together in order to win the election, and they did. Yet it was not easy. In his heart Bevan still despised Gaitskell. 'He simply isn't a Leader,' he complained in December 1958. 'Baldwin, Chamberlain, Attlee were not leaders like Churchill, but at least they had an instinct and at least they knew when to stop talking. This man is hopeless from the start.'

Nevertheless there was no alternative. 'I think we shall win the Election and the trouble will come very soon afterwards.' He now conceded that Gaitskell was 'an honest man, a man of integrity', but he was not an intellectual: he was 'an intelligent man who hates ideas' and surrounded himself with 'dreary' advisers like Roy Jenkins and Patrick Gordon Walker.

> He isn't a man you can advise. He's too brittle for that. If he disagrees with you, that's that, and you can't influence him . . .

Gaitskell's piddling all the time for fear of losing the Election . . .
and every single principle is sacrificed.[119]

Ex-miner though he was, Bevan liked to see himself as a natural aristocrat, whereas Gaitskell was irredeemably 'bourgeois'.[120] 'His idea
of reconciliation,' Jenkins wrote, 'was to try to patronize Gaitskell
as though he were Charles James Fox dealing with Lord North.'[121]

Gaitskell meanwhile, though still wary, was grateful for Bevan's
quiescence, believing that 'there was no danger of Nye's ratting
on him before the next Election'.[122] Jenkins felt that he handled
his difficult colleague pretty well. 'Not the least of his achievements,' he wrote after Gaitskell's death, 'was that, for a time, he
acquired the knack of working closely with Bevan's rumbustious
but magnetic personality . . . harnessing its force without hiding
himself beneath its shadow.'[123] Over the summer of 1959 Bevan
again stood firm against a renewed drive to commit Labour to
unilateral nuclear disarmament, now led by the new left-wing
leader of the TGWU, Frank Cousins. During interminable wrangles on the NEC Crossman was struck by Nye's 'great buoyancy
and good humour and the way he was standing by Gaitskell, even
on points where he could well have extorted a concession from
his Leader'.[124] Had he come out against resuming tests, Crossman
believed that 'Nye could quite easily have overthrown Hugh'.[125]
As a result he thought that 'Hugh is getting really fond of Aneurin,
whose loyalty and basic integrity he stresses, in sharp contrast to
Harold' – that is Wilson, now Shadow Chancellor, whom both
of them regarded as an unprincipled careerist.[126]

That summer Bevan accompanied Gaitskell and his wife Dora on
a visit to Russia intended to match Macmillan's successful visit earlier
in the year. But the trip was not a great success, either politically
or personally. After Bevan's death Gaitskell recalled that 'Nye was
on tremendous form throughout those ten days . . . Ebullient, gay,
full of enthusiasm.'[127] In fact enforced proximity for so long exacerbated the strain on their relations. Having been to Russia several
times before in his own right, Bevan was bored and irritated at
having to undergo the same round of formal hospitality as Gaitskell's
deputy; and he came back with increased reservations about his
leader ('sincere enough in his own beliefs, but no Socialist') and

foreboding about their ability to co-operate in government. 'Gaitskell is constantly interfering. He will never leave you alone to carry on the job . . . I don't know how long I will be able to stand it.'[128]

The visit was cut short when Macmillan called the general election. Since taking over a demoralised government in the aftermath of Suez, Macmillan had turned the Tory party's fortunes around. His famous boast – actually more of a warning – that most of the electorate had 'never had it so good' expressed no more than the truth: the economy was growing, ordinary people had money in their pockets and access to cars, washing machines and television sets as never before, and the Tories took the credit, while Labour was firmly saddled with the memory of rationing and austerity. With hindsight it seems obvious that Labour was never going to win. Yet the opinion polls were still close, and Gaitskell remained confident: he had his cabinet list already written out before polling day. He fought, by general consent, an excellent campaign, making Labour's case with an impressive mixture of forensic detail and moral passion, completely eclipsing Bevan – already a sick man and gloomy about the outcome even if Labour were to win – who confined himself largely to foreign affairs. 'He has suddenly become a television star,' Crossman recorded, 'a political personality in his own right – confident, relaxed, a Leader – with Nye as a rather faded elder statesman behind him.'[129] But he made one major blunder when he unwisely promised not to increase income tax. 'He's thrown it away,' was Bevan's immediate reaction when he heard the news. 'He's lost the election.'[130] Bevan was furious that Gaitskell had tied the hands of the incoming government in advance, detecting echoes of 1951. 'Indeed, this convinced Nye that there was a real conspiracy going on to strangle the last traces of Socialism.'[131] If Gaitskell's pledge did damage Labour it was more because it seemed a cheap electioneering stunt and therefore out of character. Either way it provided a convenient explanation of Labour's heavy defeat. The party's vote fell for the third election running, and the government stretched its majority to three figures. Gaitskell faced defeat with great dignity; but Bevan – who scorned the modern paraphernalia of polls and swings – thought him wrong to concede before all the results were in.

The post-mortem began at once. The fact that Labour had lost again so heavily despite having fought a good campaign raised fundamental questions about the party's policies and image, and reignited all the old antagonism between left and right that had been successfully banked down since 1955. Some of Gaitskell's friends were quick – too quick, in the left's view – to propose scrapping the party's commitment to nationalisation and even suggested changing the party's name. At first Gaitskell was more cautious: he knew the importance of keeping Nye on side. On the Tuesday after the election he lunched 'bibulously' with Nye and Jennie at Asheridge – the Chilterns farm where Bevan (like Fox) liked to play the country gentleman – to float his ideas for reform of the party constitution, though not at this stage Clause Four.[132] That evening he told Crossman that 'Nye had made it clear that he would like to succeed Jim Griffiths as deputy leader and he had shown no signs whatsoever of wanting to lead a Left attack on moderate policies'. Crossman warned him that Bevan should have a veto on any change of policy on nationalisation. 'Hugh looked a bit surprised but, on reflection, saw this was sensible.'[133]

By the time the party conference – delayed by the election – met at Blackpool in November Gaitskell had determined to tackle Clause Four head on. Once again Bevan was torn between his emotional hankering for full-blooded socialism and his more real-istic pragmatism. When Gaitskell showed him his speech in advance, he made no objection, reportedly saying that he 'could not fault it in any way'.[134] This was perfectly consistent with the line he had taken back in 1952, in his book *In Place of Fear*, where he had explicitly supported a mixed economy:

> I have no patience with those Socialists, so-called, who in practice would socialise nothing, whilst in theory they threaten the whole of private property. They are purists, and therefore barren.[135]

That was essentially all that Gaitskell said at Blackpool. He specif-ically did not rule out further nationalisation. But he insisted that public ownership was 'not itself the ultimate objective; it is only the means to achieving the objective'. To pretend, as Clause Four did, that Labour's ultimate goal was complete state ownership of the economy – 'the whole of light industry, the whole of agriculture, all the shops, every little pub and garage' – only exposed the party to 'continual misrepresentation'.[136]

Yet the left erupted with furious charges of betrayal; and momentarily Bevan shared their outrage. It seemed that he had 'misunderstood or misheard' what he had been told the night before; he was now said to be 'absolutely livid'. That evening 'he was still wondering whether to blow the whole thing wide open . . . and he was not in much of a mood to be talked out of it'.[137] Yet the next day he had reversed himself again. He was too tired to make a fight of it. He wound up the debate with a brilliantly conciliatory speech in which he contrived to agree with both Barbara Castle and Gaitskell, squaring the circle by citing Euclid's dictum that 'if two things are equal to a third thing, they are equal to each other'.

> Yesterday Barbara quoted from a speech I made some years ago . . . that Socialism in the context of a modern economy meant the conquest of the commanding heights of the economy. Hugh Gaitskell quoted the same thing. So Barbara and Hugh quoted me. If Euclid's deduction is correct they are both equal to me and therefore must be equal to each other.

What mattered, he argued, was not nationalisation but economic planning. He still took it for granted that the challenge of the second half of the century would come from the socialised economies of the Soviet bloc.[138]

Bevan's speech – his last, as it turned out – was generally reckoned to have saved Gaitskell's bacon. 'Nye's speech this afternoon,' Benn wrote, 'was witty, scintillating, positive, conciliatory – the model of what a Leader should do. He didn't knock Hugh out but he gently elbowed him aside.'[139] The great cartoonist Vicky drew the two of them riding into Blackpool on a tandem bicycle with Gaitskell in front and Bevan behind, then riding out again with the positions reversed.[140] Over the next few weeks there was a lot of wild talk that Bevan was now ready to move against Gaitskell and seize the leadership. Years later Ian Mikardo still believed he could have done it: 'The contrast between Gaitskell's inept performances over the previous three months and Nye's cool, confident mastery of the situation was too glaring to be missed even by the right-wing majority' in the parliamentary party.[141] In fact it is unlikely that Bevan would have challenged Gaitskell even had his health allowed. He had never been primarily interested in the leadership for its own sake, only in promoting and protecting his views within the party; now, as deputy to a weakened leader, he was in a strong position to do that. Gaitskell could no longer afford to quarrel with Bevan, but would need him to protect his left flank – not only over modernisation and Clause Four but in the battle over nuclear weapons which was about to erupt again. As the keeper of the party's conscience, Bevan – far more than John Prescott in relation to Tony Blair thirty-five years later – was finally in a position to wield real influence.

But it was not to be. Bevan was diagnosed with abdominal cancer soon after Christmas, and died six months later in July 1960. His death – aged sixty-three – left an enormous sense of loss. Not seeking to disguise their differences over the past ten years, Gaitskell's tribute in the Commons was generous:

> His death is as if a fire had gone out, a fire which we sometimes found too hot, by which we were sometimes scorched, a fire which flamed and flickered unpredictably. But a fire which warmed us and cheered us and stimulated us . . . Now that it has gone out I think we are peculiarly conscious of the change, of a certain coldness and greyness that has come . . .
>
> He made enemies as well as friends, but even his enemies never failed to recognize his outstanding qualities and the power of his presence. Even those who were his victims came to have not only respect but a deep and abiding affection for him.[142]

That was pushing it a bit; but it was true that Gaitskell always had a greater regard for Bevan's qualities than Bevan had for his. Bevan would have been hard put to compose a similarly gracious encomium had it been Gaitskell who died first.

Gaitskell's battle with the unilateralists was resumed with redoubled fury in 1960–61. At the 1960 conference, three months after Bevan's death, he lost the vote but famously vowed to 'fight and fight and fight again to save the party we love';[143] the following year he successfully reversed the result, restoring his authority within the party and greatly enhancing his reputation in the country. As the Macmillan government ran out of steam in 1962 he was increasingly seen as the Prime Minister in waiting: this time Labour would surely end its long travail in the wilderness and Gaitskell would secure the prize at last. But in January 1963 he too suddenly died – of a rare virus – aged only fifty-six. The shock was comparable to that of John Smith's death in 1994 when apparently on the threshold of Downing Street. Like Bevan, Gaitskell inspired extraordinary devotion in his closest followers; many, like Roy Jenkins, felt that all the joy and hope, decency and integrity in politics were extinguished by his death. From the shabby pragmatism of the Wilson years they looked back to a shining hero who had embodied all the political virtues. Yet he also inspired extraordinary loathing – not just on the left, where former Bevanites like Barbara Castle never forgave his stubbornness in the 'teeth-and-spectacles' row of 1951, but also in the centre where many like Tony Benn thought him a divisive leader who could never have united the party. Those who were not members of his inner circle greeted his death as a welcome deliverance and embraced with enthusiasm a successor – Wilson – who had long ago left Bevanism far behind and now seemed perfectly qualified to transcend the old antagonism.

It did not happen. The fault lines went too deep. Bevan's legacy – in terms of policy – meant little to him, but Wilson's personal loyalties were all to the left. Though bound to include leading Gaitskellites like Jenkins and Crosland in his government, he remained deeply suspicious of them, and they of him, while his intimates were all former Bevanites. Labour's civil war was not resolved in Wilson's time; its echoes reverberated well into the 1980s and 1990s. Neil Kinnock's political ancestry was Bevanite – he grew up in Ebbw Vale and for years claimed to be writing a book about Bevan; but his fight to defeat Militant and rid the party of outdated policies which made it unelectable was ironically – though he hated the comparison – pure Gaitskellism. John Smith, conversely, had cut his teeth in the early 1960s as a Gaitskellite and was proud to be part of that tradition. Tony Blair was the first leader without loyalties to either faction; but almost his first act was to take up Gaitskell's unfinished business in relation to Clause Four. Jenkins and other old Gaitskellites who had defected from the party in 1981 warmly endorsed him, and several returned to the New Labour fold. Old-style socialists, bitter that a rootless public-school boy had hijacked the party from its true course, felt exactly as Bevan had felt about Gaitskell in the 1950s.

So who won the Bevan–Gaitskell duel? In their lifetime, obviously Gaitskell. Bevan, an MP since 1929 and a cabinet minister from 1945, had a huge head start. Gaitskell only entered Parliament in 1945 and the cabinet in 1950. Yet he was immediately promoted over Bevan's head and provoked – at least half deliberately – a crisis which pushed Bevan off the track and set himself on course for the leadership, which he achieved just four years later. Bevan was compelled to play second fiddle to a man he believed scarcely belonged in the Labour party at all. Gaitskell failed at his first attempt in 1959, but would surely have become Prime Minister, had he lived, in 1963 or 1964. Game, set and match, therefore, to Gaitskell. Yet in the longer perspective the score is much more even. Both were cheated by their early deaths, but half a century on Bevan is by far the more resonant figure. Gaitskell might have made a great Prime Minister: but he held senior office for just one year and left no lasting monument – only the fading memory of promise unfulfilled. Bevan likewise might have been an outstanding Foreign Secretary: he might even – had he not died first – have made it to Number Ten on Gaitskell's death. But that is fantasy. What Bevan had incontestably to his credit – achieved while Gaitskell was still beavering invisibly in the Ministry of Fuel and Power – was the foundation of the National Health Service: the one creation of the 1945 Labour government which the British people really took to their heart and cherished as their own. Since his death the principle of a free NHS – the principle for which he resigned in 1951 – has been battered almost out of all recognition, by successive governments of both parties. Yet it remains a potent ideal which ensures that Bevan's name lives on while Gaitskell's is largely forgotten.

But Bevan failed in his wider aim. If anyone could have converted Britain to democratic socialism it was him; instead by the end of his life he could already see that the public was rejecting the social transformation which he, all his life, had confidently predicted. His Marxist understanding of the march of history turned out to be wrong: capitalism had a greater capacity to reinvent itself than he supposed. Gaitskell, though no Marxist, would be equally dismayed by the fading of the socialist ethic. But he better anticipated the way the Labour party must change in order to survive. Bevan's ideal of an entirely free health service was unrealistic; but it was Gaitskell who first breached the principle. Likewise he recognised as early as 1959 the need for Labour to shed some of its fundamentalist baggage and its cloth-cap image: he was Labour's first 'moderniser', thirty-seven years before Tony Blair finally persuaded the party to drop Clause Four. He would have hated New Labour as much as Bevan: yet he was its godfather.

Their successors still represent different strands in the party. Blair and Brown – like Wilson and Callaghan before them – have broadly followed Gaitskell's resolute Atlanticism; but Bevanism survived in the left's opposition to the Vietnam war in the 1960s, and its echoes were clearly audible in 2003 in the opponents of the Iraq invasion, who loathe – as Bevan did at the time of Korea – the unquestioning subordination of British foreign policy to American military leadership. Bevan's attempt to see beyond the rigid confrontation of the Cold War still offers – in a world of globalisation, religious fanaticism and climate change – a more appealing vision, even if it appears – at least up to the global 'credit crunch' of 2008 – as chimerical as ever. The fact is, however, that both Bevan and Gaitskell speak to us from a vanished world – a world of aspiration, confidence and optimism, a world in which Britain was still assumed to exercise moral leadership and episodes like Suez were seen as shameful aberrations. Most of their assumptions, both nationally and internationally, have been sadly belied. As a result, though they both died less than fifty years ago, they seem already dated and strangely irrelevant figures. Their quarrel – so bitter, so earnest, so apparently important at the time that it almost tore the Labour party apart – was left behind, like socialism itself, by the triumph of Thatcherism and global capitalism. Neither won. Both lost. The rivalry of the bolshie miner and the prissy Wykehamist stands only as a glaring example of Britain's deep – and still enduring – class divide.

Harold Macmillan
and R. A. Butler

At the same time that Bevan and Gaitskell were battling openly for the soul of the Labour party, a much more discreet and gentlemanly contest was being waged on the other side of the political divide. By now it was generally recognised that a politician's real enemies are not those ranged on the benches opposite him in the House of Commons, but those to be found among his honourable and right honourable 'friends' behind and beside him. It is true that both Fox and Pitt in the eighteenth century, and Disraeli and Gladstone in the nineteenth, started out as rivals in the same parties; but they fought their great parliamentary duels as declared opponents across the floor of the chamber. Asquith and Lloyd George too started and finished in the same party; but the years of their antagonism found them on opposite sides of the House. By the middle of the twentieth century, however, as the power of the whips reduced debate to little more than formal point-scoring, Parliament lost its central importance as the cockpit of political struggle. The great duels of the last half-century have been fought not between party leaders but between colleagues in the same party. Like their contemporaries Bevan and Gaitskell, Harold Macmillan and R. A. Butler co-existed in one party throughout their careers and competed more or less openly for the leadership of that party while serving – like Canning and Castlereagh, but without actually coming to pistol shots – in the same cabinet.

Macmillan and Butler differed over policy even less than Bevan and Gaitskell contending over different forms of socialism. Until the 1970s the Tories did not go in for ideological disputes: their opposition was almost entirely one of style and personal history. There was no great social gulf between them, though they sprang from different sections of the professional middle class. They rose to the top of the Conservative party by very different routes, and made a different appeal to different tribes of followers. The young Macmillan was a rebel, at odds with the party leadership on both domestic and foreign policy, a late starter whose career up to 1940 seemed to be going nowhere; Butler by contrast was an insider who rose rapidly with the help of a succession of influential patrons and seemed to be bound inevitably for the top. By the time they came into direct rivalry in the 1950s Macmillan cut a more dashing and radical figure than the more cautious and pedestrian Butler. Yet both were exceptionally ambiguous personalities, so the contrast is less clear-cut than at first appears. Judged on the conventional political spectrum it is impossible to say which was more to the left or right. Both played crucial, complementary parts in the recovery of the Tory party after 1945 and its thirteen years of electoral success in the 1950s. Both were well qualified to be Prime Minister. What is unusual in their duel is that it was the older man who prevailed, with a calculated ruthlessness unmatched since Pitt's trouncing of Fox.

Harold Macmillan was born in London in 1894 and educated at Eton and Oxford. Yet his origins were less conventional than that sounds. His great-grandfather was a crofter on the Scottish island of Arran; his grandfather came south to seek his fortune and founded, with his brother, the publishing firm of Macmillan. By the time of Harold's birth his father was a partner in the now solidly established company, with a proud stable of distinguished authors including Kipling and Hardy; but his mother was American – pushy and artistic while his father was bookish and shy. These conflicting influences marked him for life: part businessman, part scholar, part showman, ambitious yet diffident, he was always hard to classify – still more so when he added another layer of complexity by marrying into the aristocracy. As a boy at Eton he was unhappy and often ill: he was coached at home by the celebrated

Anglo-Catholic Ronald Knox and fell heavily under his spell, though
he did not in the end follow Knox in going over to Rome but
remained all his life a devout Anglican. He won a classical scholarship to Balliol where he found his feet as a member of the doomed
'golden generation' before 1914. He took a first in 'Mods', but
when the war came joined up immediately without taking 'Greats';
he was treasurer and librarian of the Union and would almost
certainly have been president the following term had he stayed on.
He served with the Grenadier Guards in France, was badly wounded
but survived – the only one of six Balliol scholars in his year to
do so: another experience which marked him for life. Ever conscious
of those who had died, he never concealed 'a certain contempt' for
those like Butler, Gaitskell and Harold Wilson who (often through
no fault of their own) did not serve in either war.[1] After the war
he did not go back to Oxford but spent a year in Canada on the
staff of the Governor-General, the Duke of Devonshire, and successfully wooed his daughter, Lady Dorothy Cavendish. Their wedding
in 1920 was a grand society event, but her relations looked down
on Macmillan as a mere publisher – he joined the family firm the
same year – and she was soon unfaithful, inflicting another painful
wound to his already fragile self-confidence.

In 1923 Captain Macmillan stood unsuccessfully for the
northern industrial seat of Stockton-on-Tees; but the following
year the collapse of the Liberal vote allowed him to win it, and
thereafter he held it – with a two-year interruption in 1929–31
– until 1945. Stockton defined the first half of his career. The
poverty caused by the decline of its major industries – shipbuilding
and heavy engineering – made a deep impression on him, and he
joined a number of other younger Tories impatient with the
Baldwin government's inertia in the face of mounting unemployment. In 1927 four of them, including Macmillan and the much
more flamboyant Robert Boothby, published a short book urging
government action on the lines that were simultaneously being
advocated by Lloyd George and Keynes. (Keynes was published
by Macmillan.) But such unorthodoxy was not the way to get on
in Baldwin's Tory party. Macmillan gained no quick promotion,
and in 1929 he lost his seat to Labour – the same year that 'Rab'
Butler was elected.

Butler, born in 1902, was nearly nine years younger. He was christened Richard Austen, but was always known by his initials and universally nicknamed 'Rab'. Like Gaitskell he was a child of the empire, born and raised until the age of ten in India, where his father, Sir Montague Butler, rose to be Governor of the Central Provinces. The Butlers were a distinguished academic dynasty comprising Cambridge dons, college heads and headmasters going back over many generations. These two influences, India and Cambridge, formed Rab's character. Had he not gone into politics he could have been a civil servant or a don: at the end of his life he claimed that the one job he really regretted missing was Viceroy of India. At the age of six he broke his right arm in a fall from his pony: the injury never properly healed and the arm hung limply all his life, precluding him from sports – or military service. He was actually too young to fight in the First War – he was only fifteen when it ended – and too old in the second; but his useless limb unfairly contributed to the subtle scorn with which those who had fought tended to disparage him. (Macmillan liked to characterise himself as a 'swordsman' whereas Rab was a mere 'gownsman': alternatively Rab was a 'cardinal . . . creeping about the Vatican', while he was a 'warrior'.)[2] From Marlborough – which he chose because too many of his family had been to Harrow – Rab won a scholarship to Pembroke College, Cambridge, where he effortlessly gained a double first in languages and history and was also president of the Union. He wrote his thesis, significantly, on Peel's downfall at the hands of Disraeli; and briefly took up a fellowship at Corpus Christi.

He was saved from the need to earn a living, however, by his marriage the following year to the daughter of the textiles magnate Samuel Courtauld, who settled a handsome income on him for life. Sydney Courtauld was a strong-minded young woman who, until her early death, provided much of the drive behind Rab's early career. The Courtaulds' money also parachuted him into the safe Tory seat of Saffron Walden in rural Essex; he was duly elected in 1929, aged twenty-six. This smooth – almost eighteenth-century – passage into Parliament was probably a handicap in the long run: promotion came to him too easily, and roused jealousy among his peers.

By contrast, 1929 was a bad time for Macmillan. Not only did he lose his seat, but this was the year when his wife started a long relationship with his fellow Tory maverick Bob Boothby. It never got into the papers, and the marriage was outwardly preserved; but everyone in society knew the truth. The humiliation of being so openly cuckolded by a colleague hardened Macmillan's heart and sharpened his ambition over the next three decades; loneliness is a great spur to ambition.* In the short run it led him to flirt with political extremes. Out of Parliament as the world spiralled into depression following the Wall Street crash, Macmillan despaired of the established party system and dreamed of a radical realignment to be led by the younger men of all parties; like Nye Bevan, he was briefly drawn to Oswald Mosley, who spectacularly resigned from Ramsay MacDonald's feeble Labour government to form his own New Party before rapidly falling into Fascism. This occasioned Macmillan's first recorded brush with Butler. In May 1930 Macmillan wrote to *The Times* ironically congratulating Mosley on the novel idea that parties should try to implement the programme on which they were elected, incautiously suggesting that unless the rules of the political game were altered, 'a good many of us will feel that it is hardly worth bothering to play at all'.[4] Rab was thought to have been behind a crushing response which appeared the next day, signed by four young Baldwin loyalists, expressing 'interest and some surprise' at Macmillan's letter:

> When a player starts complaining 'that it is hardly worth while bothering to play' the game at all it is usually the player, and not the game, who is at fault. It is then usually advisable for the player to seek a new field for his recreation and a pastime more suited for his talents.[5]

In his memoirs Rab recalled that this riposte 'caused chuckling in the Opposition Whips' Office'.[6] But Macmillan never forgot the slight.

---

*Without mentioning anyone by name, Butler told his PPS in 1938 that 'when a man becomes "*cocu*" his political future ends. Something in the man seems to snap, self-confidence goes and with it motive power.'[3] If he was thinking of Macmillan he was wrong: cuckoldry affected Macmillan quite the other way.

Macmillan regained Stockton in the National Government landslide of October 1931. But he remained an isolated figure on the far left of the Tory party. Baldwin once told Butler that his job as leader was to steer a middle path 'between Harold Macmillan and John Gretton' (a prominent figure on the far right).[7] In fact Macmillan was pursuing a middle path of his own between the extremes of capitalism and socialism, developing his Keynesian ideas of economic planning in a series of far-sighted publications with various collaborators which culminated in a personal manifesto entitled *The Middle Way* in 1938. But he gained few adherents. Earnest, toothy, bespectacled and gauche, he was seen at this time as the most boring man in the House – quite unlike the stylish persona he developed after 1945. As the shadow of war once again fell across Europe, however, he began to develop a second theme. Macmillan was one of the first Tories to echo Churchill's warnings against the threat of Nazism and the folly of appeasing Hitler. But he was not yet one of Churchill's inner circle, and for the moment this second front of rebellion gained him no more allies than the first. When he resigned the whip in protest at the ending of sanctions against Italy imposed after Mussolini's invasion of Abyssinia, Henry ('Chips') Channon – a government loyalist – was withering:

> Harold Macmillan, the unprepossessing, bookish, eccentric member for Stockton-on-Tees (and incidentally the Duke of Devonshire's son-in-law), having voted against the Government on the Foreign Office vote of censure, has now repudiated the Government Whip, and has received a frigid note from Mr Baldwin.[8]

Among the younger generation of anti-appeasers the unchallenged star was Anthony Eden. Three years younger than Macmillan, Eden had also fought with distinction in 1914–18, winning the Military Cross. A glamorous figure with matinée idol looks but a fragile temperament, he had entered Parliament in 1923, became Under-Secretary in the Foreign Office in 1931 and was appointed Foreign Secretary by Baldwin in 1935 at the age of thirty-eight, but then won huge acclaim by resigning in 1938 over Chamberlain's weakness towards Mussolini.* In the last year before the war Churchill and Eden – the old lion and the young pretender – headed two distinct groups critical of the government. But Macmillan was not fully a member of either: he was still a maverick more interested in forging cross-party links with Labour figures like Hugh Dalton. No one at that date dreamed that he was a future Tory leader.

While Macmillan languished on the back benches throughout the 1930s, Butler was climbing the ladder almost as rapidly as Eden. Even before entering Parliament he had acted as secretary to Sir Samuel Hoare; when the Tories returned to government in 1931 he naturally followed his patron to the India Office as his PPS, before being made Under-Secretary the following year. Though the youngest member of the government – only twenty-nine when appointed – he won universal admiration for the way he steered Hoare's massive and controversial 1935 Government of India Bill through the Commons, skilfully defusing the violent opposition of the die-hard imperialists led by Churchill. Nobody thought him brilliant, but he was an exceptionally safe pair of hands. 'Mr R. A. Butler is not handicapped by genius, originality or emotion,' one commentator wrote; but he was 'an ideally efficient minister, industrious, full of accurate information which he is too cautious to divulge, and immune from warmth. He has drifted steadily forward with uninterrupted success.' He seemed 'a young man predestined to leadership'.[10] 'Chips' Channon, who became his PPS in 1938, thought him at first 'a scholarly dry-stick, but an extremely able, cautious, canny man of great ambition'.[11] The more he saw of him, however, the more he was impressed:

> Rab is a curious chap, my charming chief; with the brains and ability of a super clever civil servant, but completely unprejudiced. He seems to have no bias on any subject and looks upon the whole human race as mental![12]

*Butler encapsulated Eden in a characteristically waspish *aperçu*. Noting that his father was a somewhat 'strange' baronet and his mother 'an outstandingly beautiful woman', he commented: 'And that is Anthony – part mad baronet, part beautiful woman.'[9]

He is shrewd and his mind, while never flashy, is alert and far-sighted. He sometimes looks, acts and appears as most ingenuous, even naif, but only a fool would be deceived. If he had more outward gifts, he might be PM.[13]

This fatal reservation would recur again and again over the next twenty-five years.

On succeeding Baldwin in 1937 Neville Chamberlain gave Butler a brief domestic stint at the Ministry of Labour before switching him to the Foreign Office: he was still only Under-Secretary, but with the Foreign Secretary, Lord Halifax, in the Upper House he quickly became the principal apologist for appeasement in the Commons, coolly defending the Prime Minister's betrayal of Czechoslovakia at Munich against the passionate denunciation of Churchill, Eden and the thirty-odd Tories (including Macmillan) who refused to support the government. This was the crucial divide in the Tory party which threw its shadow over the next two decades. Right up to the outbreak of war and beyond, Butler was an enthusiastic appeaser, insisting that peace could still be preserved and war would solve nothing. Channon called him 'the PM's blue-eyed boy';[14] while years later Macmillan still remembered him as 'the most cringing of the Munichites'.[15] When Chamberlain was finally brought down in May 1940 Butler was horrified at the idea of Churchill becoming Prime Minister. With other disappointed loyalists – John Colville (Chamberlain's private secretary) and Alec Dunglass (his PPS), he gathered in the Foreign Office to drink a toast to 'the king over the water' – that is Chamberlain – in champagne supplied by Channon.

Rab said he thought the good clean tradition of English politics, that of Pitt as opposed to Fox, had been sold to the greatest adventurer of modern political history. He had tried earnestly and long to persuade Halifax to take the Premiership, but he had failed. He believed this sudden coup of Winston and his rabble was a serious disaster and an unnecessary one: the 'pass had been sold' . . . to a half-breed American whose main support was that of inefficient but talkative people of a similar type.[16]

Of course they all became devoted to the 'half-breed American' once he emerged as the great war leader.* Churchill quickly got rid of most of the leading appeasers, including Rab's patrons Halifax and Hoare; but he recognised Rab's ability and left him at the Foreign Office, even though Rab continued for some time to voice his preference for a negotiated peace – once, indiscreetly, to the Swedish minister in London, which most Prime Ministers engaged in a life-and-death struggle would have treated as a sacking offence; in 1941 he moved him to quieter pastures at the Board of Education. In the short run Butler's smooth ascent was not harmed by his association with appeasement: so long as Churchill led the Tory party his support for Munich was forgiven. In the longer run, however, it was a fatal liability, unfairly compounding his lack of military experience in 1914–18. To the rising generation of young Tories who fought in 1939–45, to have clung to Chamberlain in the crisis of 1940 when all right-thinking patriots had rallied to Churchill was like not having been at Agincourt:

> And gentlemen in England now abed
> Shall think themselves accurs'd they were not here,
> And hold their manhoods cheap whiles any speaks
> That fought with us upon Saint Crispin's Day.[17]

And no one applied this test more harshly than Macmillan.

Churchill's accession brought Macmillan office at last, as Parliamentary Secretary at the Ministry of Supply: it was not an exciting job, but after sixteen years he was grateful for anything. Channon unkindly recorded 'some amusement over Harold Macmillan's so very obvious enjoyment of his new position'.[18] In 1942 he was promoted to Under-Secretary for the Colonies; but he was restless and dissatisfied when he was suddenly plucked from this backwater and sent to be minister resident in Algiers,

---

*Colville stayed in Number 10 to serve Churchill as ardently as he had previously served Chamberlain, later becoming one of the principal keepers of his flame. Dunglass – who became the fourteenth Earl of Home in 1951 – was somehow never tarred with the stain of Munich as Rab was.

liaising with the Americans and the Free French – that is Generals Eisenhower and de Gaulle – and reporting directly to Churchill in London. This fortunate appointment transformed his career. With an ill-defined brief and considerable autonomy, he was able to play an important part in the latter stages of the war in the Mediterranean, sorting out tricky diplomatic problems thrown up by the defeat of Italy and civil war in Greece. His success gave him a new self-confidence, particularly in foreign affairs. Butler meanwhile was doing equally important but much less glamorous work on the home front, skilfully carrying through the 1944 Education Act which opened the grammar schools to clever boys and girls from all backgrounds, selected by the 'Eleven Plus' exam – thus earning the gratitude of a generation of working-class achievers (but also the resentment of those who failed to make the cut). He also chaired the government's reconstruction committee, looking at post-war social reform generally. Both men finished the war with their standing greatly enhanced. Both were included in Churchill's 'caretaker' cabinet which held office between Labour's withdrawal from the coalition in May 1945 and the general election in July – Butler as Minister of Labour, Macmillan as Secretary of State for Air. But Macmillan's advance was much the greater. He was now part of Churchill's coterie; he had had a conspicuously 'good war', forging valuable international contacts which would serve him well in the years ahead, while Rab had been merely a 'Whitehall warrior' – 'wiping children's bottoms', as Churchill disparagingly called it.[19] Moreover Macmillan had not only been on the right side over appeasement: the Keynesian revolution that he had vainly championed between the wars was now widely accepted as the new economic orthodoxy. After Labour's unexpected landslide swept the Conservatives from office Harold Nicolson noted that the younger Tory backbenchers wanted a fresh start. 'They feel that Winston is too old and Anthony [Eden] too weak. They want Harold Macmillan to lead them.'[20]

Both Butler and Macmillan were among the few to foresee the Tory débâcle. It is perhaps not surprising that Rab, whose job included framing the Tory response to the Beveridge Report, could read the mood of public opinion; more remarkable that Macmillan, away in the Mediterranean for most of the last two years of the war, should have done so. But as early as October 1942 he was predicting 'extreme socialism' after the war;[21] while in September 1944 Channon was complacently ridiculing 'the foolish prophecy of that nice ass Harold Macmillan who goes about saying that the Conservatives will be lucky to retain a hundred seats after the election'.[22] In fact they did better than that, but won only 213 seats to Labour's 393. Macmillan lost heavily in Stockton, and even Rab's comfortable majority in Saffron Walden was cut to a bare 1,100. But Macmillan was now such a prominent figure that a safe seat was quickly found for him in Bromley, and he was back in Parliament within weeks. He came back a changed man. Almost overnight the gawky rebel who had sat for industrial Teesside gave way to a new Macmillan – a suave patrician from suburban Kent. Cause or effect? Did his new constituency colour his politics, or reflect a shift that had already occurred? Either way, there has been no more startling personal reinvention in British politics.*

The transformation of the Tory party in the years after 1945 was almost as striking. The scale of the party's defeat not only cleared out a lot of dead wood but convinced the party grandees that it could not oppose but must come to terms with Labour's social revolution. Churchill himself, though remote from the detail of domestic policy, rediscovered the sentimental paternalism of his Liberal youth: far from retiring, he was determined to do whatever was necessary to reverse the verdict of 1945. He had already put Butler in charge of reconstruction in the last years of the war: now he appointed him chairman of the Conservative Research Department, charged with overhauling the party's image and policies – specifically to expunge the association with inter-war unemployment which was the biggest reason for its recent rejection. David Cameron faced a comparable task in trying to modernise the party after its third consecutive defeat in 2005. Rab, with the equally conciliatory Lord Woolton as party

---

*The closest comparison is Harold Wilson, who likewise transformed himself from a boring young statistician into a lovable Yorkshire comic. He did so in conscious emulation of Macmillan.

chairman, succeeded so well that the Tories not only regained power in 1951 but held it with increasing majorities in 1955 and 1959. Though Rab was quintessentially a man of government, continuously in office for all but six years between 1932 and 1964, these six years in opposition paradoxically represented his greatest achievement. He redefined the meaning of Conservatism, and brought on the brightest of the next generation of Tory leaders: Reginald Maudling, Iain Macleod and Enoch Powell all cut their teeth in Rab's Conservative Research Department.

Butler's achievement, ironically, was to bring the Tory party to embrace the sort of policies that Macmillan had been derided for espousing before the war. Hitherto Rab, largely occupied with foreign affairs and education, had not shown much interest in economic policy. But full employment was now the holy grail, and Keynesian demand management combined with universal welfare in the context of a mixed economy was the way to ensure it. Years later in his memoirs Macmillan recognised that Rab was 'largely responsible for the development of the new policy', and had promoted it 'with extraordinary skill'. But he also boasted that 'the policy and character of the party were now almost miraculously developing on the lines I had preached during those sterile years between the wars'.[23] Rab in turn did not dispute that 'a great deal of the intellectual background of the Industrial Charter' – the most famous embodiment of the new policy, published in 1947 – 'was due to him'.[24] Macmillan was a member of the small committee, chaired by Rab, which produced the Charter, and took a prominent role – more prominent than Rab – in propagating it. 'Crossbencher' in the *Sunday Express* dubbed the Industrial Charter, not inaccurately, the 'second edition' of *The Middle Way*.[25] Yet at this very moment Macmillan began to distance himself from his own past. Many of the party faithful – including the young Margaret Roberts (soon to be Thatcher), who attended her first conference in 1948 – despised what they called 'milk and water socialism' and still hankered for more traditional Tory policies. Opportunistically Macmillan began to stress the importance of not stifling private enterprise. While Butler got the credit for making the party electable again by moving its policies to the left, Macmillan – with a safe seat now under his belt – tacked subtly to the right to raise his credit with the rank and file. While Rab was operating largely out of the public eye, Macmillan took a much more visible role in opposing the tiring Labour government in the House of Commons. After a slow start, his ambition to make up ground was almost tangible.

When the Tories narrowly regained power in October 1951 – helped by Bevan's acrimonious resignation from the Labour cabinet six months earlier – Churchill made Butler, to general surprise, Chancellor of the Exchequer. This was a signal mark of confidence, making him effectively the third man in the government. Eden – already Churchill's heir apparent for the past ten years – returned to the Foreign Office. Macmillan, by contrast, was dismayed to be offered only the Ministry of Housing. This, he wrote in his diary, was 'not my cup of tea at all . . . I really haven't a clue how to set about the job'.[26] He suspected that he had been deliberately handed a poisoned chalice so that he should be seen to fail: 'I suppose Eden and Butler are those indicated.'[27] But he could not refuse; and he soon realised that the Prime Minister had actually given him a great opportunity. In opposition the Tories had criticised Bevan's record on housing, claiming that he had failed to meet the need for new homes because of his doctrinaire preference for council housing over private builders. At the 1950 party conference the platform had yielded to pressure from the floor and committed the next Tory government to build 300,000 new homes a year (against the current rate of about 200,000). Rab – in charge of policy, though not at this point expecting to be Chancellor – should have opposed this rash promise, but failed to do so. Macmillan was now put in charge of honouring it. Though a relatively junior member of the cabinet, he held the party's reputation in his hands. House-building in those days was all a matter of securing scarce materials – timber, steel and cement. Meanwhile Butler's job at the Treasury was all about controlling imports and allocating materials to boost exports. Thus Macmillan was soon fighting a running battle with Butler to squeeze out of a reluctant Treasury the materials he needed to reach his target. Economic priorities dictated fewer resources for house-building; but politics argued the other way, and Churchill could usually be relied on to back Macmillan – so

Macmillan usually got his way. By the end of 1953, with a flourish of trumpets, the 300,000 target was achieved. Macmillan had scored a clear political success – at Butler's expense.

Rab was generally reckoned a cautious but successful Chancellor for most of the four years he held the job. After a tricky start, facing a balance of payments crisis caused by Labour's inflated defence programme (inherited from Gaitskell), he was gradually able to relax wartime controls, cut taxes and end rationing, fulfilling Churchill's election promise to 'set the people free'. Helped by improving terms of trade after the ending of the Korean war he presided benignly over a welcome period of expansion, laying the foundations for the 'affluence' for which Macmillan later took the credit. He was no showman and eschewed gimmicks; but he was calm, capable and well-mannered and his budgets were much admired. In 1954 he looked forward – accurately, as it turned out – to the doubling of living standards over the next twenty-five years. But his reputation in the Tory party was compromised – like Gaitskell's in the Labour party – by the *Economist*'s coining of the term 'Butskellism', suggesting that there was no essential difference in economic management between the Tory Chancellor and his predecessor. It was not really true. Behind the superficial similarities – they were both polite, reasonable and donnish, with similar Indian backgrounds and similar devotion to the public service – they were very different in temperament and political philosophy. Butler believed in going with the grain of public opinion, but he was no socialist: he had no wish to extend nationalisation, for instance. Yet once again the more carnivorous Tories muttered about 'milk and water socialism'.

At the same time Macmillan in his diary was constantly critical. 'I do not feel that Rab has really grasped the nettle . . . He seemed not to have a real grip of the situation.'[28] 'The Protean Chancellor,' he wrote in July 1952, 'is impossible to pin down to any precise statement. He twists and turns, like the Old Man of the Sea. He seems never to abandon his brief, which he cons like a breviary.'[29] Fighting for his 300,000 houses, Macmillan believed that he was 'fighting for my own political life and that of the party'. He added disingenuously:

I cannot help feeling that there is a certain piquancy in the struggle, because Butler dislikes and fears me . . . I like both Butler and Eden. They both have great charm. But it has been cruelly said that in politics there are no friends at the top. I fear it is so.[30]

There is no evidence that Butler at this stage particularly disliked Macmillan, or saw him as a rival. It is Macmillan who can be seen in his diary candidly eyeing up his colleagues and calculating his chances. Churchill, he wrote in September, was seventy-eight and ageing fast. The universal assumption was that Eden would soon take over unopposed. But Eden, Macmillan shrewdly judged, though 'admirable technically, cannot really act as Prime Minister. Time will show whether, if he gets the opportunity, he will rise to it.' Rab, meanwhile, 'has time on his side and can afford to wait'.[31] Macmillan, older than both, was very conscious that he did not have time on his side. But he drew comfort from the precedent of 1911, when Arthur Balfour was harried into giving up the leadership: the two leading contenders, Austen Chamberlain and Walter Long, were evenly matched, allowing the unfancied Bonar Law to slip in between them. Macmillan hoped to do the same.*

The undeclared contest was complicated in June 1953 (just after the coronation of the young Queen Elizabeth) when Churchill suffered a serious stroke – at a time when Eden was also ill in America and (just to add to the catalogue of medical misfortune) Macmillan too was about to go into hospital for a gall bladder operation. This was the first occasion when Butler might and probably should have become Prime Minister. In fact Churchill's family and loyal secretaries managed to conceal the truth of the old man's condition, helped by the fact that Parliament was in recess and the obliging willingness of the Fleet Street proprietors to participate in a cover-up. The nation was merely told that the Prime Minister had been advised to rest, while Butler quietly took over the running of the government, with Lord Salisbury (Lord

---

*He was encouraged in this fantasy by Lord Beaverbrook, who (as plain Max Aitken) had managed Law's campaign in 1911. 'Yes,' Macmillan replied, 'but who is to be my Max Aitken?'[32]

President of the Council) acting as Foreign Secretary. Effectively Rab was keeping the place warm for Eden: it was felt to be too cruel that 'dear Anthony', after waiting so long, should be denied his inheritance by an accident of timing. Rab accepted this gentlemanly arrangement uncomplainingly. Between 29 June and 18 August he chaired sixteen cabinet meetings, but made no attempt to seize the premiership. It would have been out of character. 'How differently,' Roy Jenkins reflected, 'Lloyd George, Harold Macmillan, and Mrs Thatcher, to take only a few examples, would have behaved.'[33] Macmillan considered postponing his own operation, but realised that the moment was not ripe for him.

> The situation is really fascinating. Butler is, of course, playing a winning game. He has on his side his comparative youth, his oriental subtlety, his power of quiet but effective intrigue – and the absence of any real competition so well equipped . . . Churchill cannot really last very long . . . But can Eden last?

If Butler were to become Prime Minister, he wondered, whom would he appoint as Chancellor? Rab, he believed, would not want a strong Chancellor who might dominate him, as Neville Chamberlain had dominated Baldwin: this, he reckoned, ruled Macmillan himself out of contention.[34] Though still very much the outsider, Macmillan plainly thought himself the strongest personality of the three contenders. A few days later he had a talk with Walter Monckton, Minister of Labour, who said that he would be willing to serve under Eden, but not Butler, whom he called 'a slab of cold fish'. This, Macmillan wrote, was 'too hard on Butler – who is able and sincere, but wildly and almost pathologically ambitious'.[35] Here indeed was the pot calling the kettle black! Macmillan constantly labelled Butler 'devious', 'intriguing' and 'Jesuitical'. In fact all these adjectives applied far more to himself: he was the one who was 'wildly ambitious'. After his operation he received 'a charming letter from Butler, wh made me rather ashamed of my suspicions of last week'.[36] But he still thought him essentially weak.

Churchill made a remarkable recovery, but still refused to step down, obsessed with the belief that he – and only he – could reach an accommodation with the Soviet Union following the death of Stalin. Both Macmillan, directly, and Butler, more subtly, were among those senior cabinet ministers who tried to persuade him to go; but whenever he seemed to agree he always found another reason for hanging on. In October 1954 he moved Macmillan to the Ministry of Defence – a reward of sorts for his success at Housing, but in practice not much of a job so long as Churchill treated defence as his personal domain and Eden remained Foreign Secretary. Macmillan really wanted to be Foreign Secretary himself. He got his wish when Churchill finally retired in April 1955 and Eden came into his long-delayed inheritance. He relished the promotion and reflected on the 'extraordinary ups and downs' of politics, recalling Churchill saying of his own bumpy career: 'It's not a flat race, it's a steeplechase.'[37] But he soon found that occupying the Foreign Office under Eden – who had never served anywhere else – was another unrewarding task.

By this time things had started to go wrong for Butler. At the end of 1954 his wife died of cancer, aged fifty-two. Her death hit Rab hard, and undoubtedly affected his political judgement over the next couple of years when he made a series of blunders, both economic and political. He did not fully regain his touch until he remarried in 1959. First rising inflation and renewed balance of payments difficulties forced him in February 1955 to raise the bank rate and impose credit restrictions, which took some of the gilt off his economic success. Then when Eden tried to move Rab from the Treasury, he resisted. As he later admitted, he would have been wiser to agree: he had served four years and was ready for a move. Instead he stayed at the Treasury and produced a frankly electioneering budget – taking sixpence off income tax – to help Eden increase the Tory majority at an immediate general election. Rab's apologists insist that this was due to faulty Treasury statistics rather than cynicism; but it further damaged his reputation when a run on the pound obliged him to come back to the House with an emergency autumn budget which took back much of what he had given away in the spring. Gaitskell – keen to exorcise the ghost of Butskellism – accused him of duplicity and a fraud on the electorate. Macmillan took a malicious delight in his colleague's discomfiture. 'Rab has always rather paraded his virtue (sometimes to the disgust of his colleagues),' he wrote in his diary, 'so this sort of attack he will find very wounding.'[38] When Labour attacked Rab's 'honour' he noted cynically: 'His colleagues (who are often rather bored with Rab's appeal to what is "honourable" in Cabinet) will not be able to avoid a certain amusement. But I'm sure everyone will rally round.'[39]

Butler was battered further by constant speculation that he was about to be moved. Eden had already sounded out Macmillan about moving to the Treasury in September – as much because he regretted giving Macmillan the Foreign Office as because he wanted a new Chancellor. But just as he had failed to overrule Rab's resistance in April, so he was too weak to impose his authority now. Macmillan smelt his weakness, and ruthlessly exploited it. He was just beginning to enjoy the Foreign Office (which was why Eden wanted him out of it) and thought the Treasury another poisoned chalice. ('Butler has let things drift, and the reserves are steadily falling. If and when they are all expended, we have total collapse, under Harold Macmillan!')[40] If he was going to take it, it must be on his own terms. First he stipulated that he must be free to make 'considerable changes . . . For there is no point in my leaving the F.O. to be an orthodox Chancellor of the Exchequer. I must be, if not a revolutionary, something of a reformer.' Then he insisted that he must have not only Eden's firm support, but 'a position in the Govt not inferior to that held by the present Chancellor'.

> As Chancellor, I must be undisputed head of the home front, under you. If Rab becomes Leader of the House and Ld Privy Seal, that will be fine. But I could not agree that he should be Deputy Prime Minister . . . You will realise that the presence of a much respected ex-Chancellor of the Ex . . . must somewhat add to my difficulties, however loyal he will try to be. If he were also Deputy P.M. my task would be impossible.[41]

This was an outrageous demand. In his memoirs Macmillan denied that he was 'actuated by some degree of personal rivalry with Butler', claiming that he had no reason to anticipate Eden's early departure, and no ambition beyond the Foreign Office. He only wished to ensure that if he moved to the Treasury he would have the same 'scope and authority . . . within my own sphere' that he had at the Foreign Office. 'When the time came for Eden to retire, Butler, who was five years younger than Eden and eight years younger than me, would be the natural successor.'[42] In fact it is clear that Macmillan did not think that Eden was likely to last long, and was deliberately manoeuvring to outflank Butler. He explicitly told Lord Woolton that he 'saw no reason why if he was going to take over all the troubles of the Treasury, he should be ruled out of the succession for the Premiership in order to ease in Butler'.[43] A stronger Prime Minister would have told him to get lost. But Eden still dithered, unwilling to upset Rab but unable to face down Macmillan either. The *New Statesman* in November had a shrewd idea of what was going on: 'Now that Mr Butler has become a political liability, and Sir Anthony has demonstrated beyond doubt his pathological reluctance to take decisions, Macmillan's stock is inevitably rising.'[44] Eden first offered what Macmillan called a 'satisfactory' division of responsibilities, except that Rab would chair cabinet meetings and deputise for the Prime Minister in his absence – as he had done after Churchill's stroke in 1953 – 'which begs . . . the whole question'.[45] Macmillan suggested that Salisbury should deputise instead. Eden rejected this, so Macmillan gave way. 'I have given in about Butler "presiding" at Cabinet,' he wrote, 'but have won my point about the position of Deputy Prime Minister . . . On all other points, P.M has really met me.'[46]

Rarely can a politician be seen striving so blatantly for advancement at the expense of a rival than in this episode: Lloyd George in 1916, Canning in 1809, come to mind; but they at least had the excuse of a war going badly to lend a gloss of patriotism to their conduct. Macmillan's was pure ambition to leapfrog Butler in the succession stakes. In another age Butler, when he learned that Macmillan had been bargaining for his job with the Prime Minister behind his back – very much as Canning had bargained with Lord Liverpool – might have challenged Macmillan to a duel. Instead he allowed himself to be shoved aside without complaint. Not only did he give up the Treasury, but he failed to demand another job of comparable status. If Macmillan could bully a weak Prime Minister, Rab too should have stood up for himself. He would have liked the Home Office, and could have insisted on it. Instead he let himself be fobbed off with the high-sounding but non-executive office of Lord Privy Seal and Leader of the House, responsible for co-ordinating government business but with no department of his own. Harry Crookshank, whom he replaced – who was incidentally one of Macmillan's oldest friends – warned him that he was committing 'sheer political suicide'.[47] In his memoirs Rab acknowledged the truth of this and identified December 1955 as the moment when his hitherto unstoppable career stalled.

> Though later I was to sit on dizzy heights as Chairman of the party, Leader of the House and Principal Secretary of State . . . and to be Foreign Secretary, it was never again said of me, or for that matter of the British economy either, that we had *'la puissance d'une idée en marche'*.[48]

There is a tide in the affairs of men, and Rab had missed it.

Eden's brief premiership was already in trouble before the fiasco of Suez brought it to a humiliating end. Despite winning his own mandate in the summer of 1955, Eden was in several respects unfit to be Prime Minister. He was insecure, hypersensitive and prone to bursts of temper; his health – both psychological and physical (following a botched bile duct operation) – was poor; and he had no experience of home affairs or knowledge of Whitehall beyond the Foreign Office. Neither Butler nor Macmillan had much faith in him; the difference was that while Butler, bruised by his removal from the Treasury and still depressed by the loss of his wife, retreated into his shell and went through the motions of his non-job with a visible lack of enthusiasm, Macmillan coolly took advantage of the Prime Minister's weakness to position himself for the vacancy which he correctly anticipated might come sooner rather than later. It would be 'interesting to see how long Anthony can stay in the saddle', he told Eden's press secretary, William Clark, as early as January 1956.[49] That month there was flurry of rumours that Eden was about to retire and be succeeded, it was assumed, by Rab: an unprecedented official denial only fuelled the speculation. In an interview with the *Manchester Guardian*, Rab's professions of loyalty were ambiguous and decidedly lukewarm. First he declared his 'determination to support the Prime Minister in all his difficulties'; then, when asked if Eden was 'the best Prime Minister we have', he assented, allowing the paper to imply that the damning phrase was his own.[50] To the end of his life he protested that he never said it; but he certainly did not offer a ringing endorsement.

Macmillan meanwhile presented himself as the new broom at the Treasury clearing up the mess which Butler had left behind, and played on Eden's ignorance of economics by threatening resignation when necessary to get his way. The cabinet was 'impressed by the gravity of the situation', he wrote in his diary on 12 January. 'Rab had really let things slide for over a year, and never told his colleagues into what a mess they were slowly but steadily subsiding.'[51] 'He is certainly a strange fellow,' he added some days later. 'He seems to have little idea of the state of affairs or of the financial or economic dangers which threaten us. But he promised me support in the Cabinet.'[52] The next day he recorded that 'Butler (except for a natural tendency to minimize the gravity of the situation) backed me up quite loyally.'[53] But he was immediately alert when Rab chaired the cabinet when Eden was away in Washington. 'He is trying (in spite of the agreement) to set himself up as a "Deputy Prime Minister". But at present his position in the party is weak and his reputation in the country low.'[54] 'I feel sorry for him – for he sees his successor "taking a stand" and all that – which he did not do.'[55] Sympathy went out the window, however, when Macmillan came to prepare his budget: he proposed to reverse the sixpence cut in income tax which Rab had made the year before. After 'a frank talk' with Rab on 28 March, his diary was once again transparently disingenuous:

He was in rather a queer mood, I thought – almost pathological. He thinks too much about himself – his failures or successes. He feels that his work as a Chancellor will be written down as a failure (wh is absurd. He had 4 years hard labour and did jolly well). He thinks that the Treasury let him down. He feels that a reversal of his (much criticised) decision to take off 6d last year wd be a direct slur on him. He wd have to resign. He might come back later: but he wd have to resign now. 'Yet' he added rather naively, 'I want you to succeed'. I told him that I thought he exaggerated all this . . . I calmed him a bit – but not (I fear) convinced him. He is in a mood of self-pity. It is the reaction after his wife's death. She was a woman of tremendous character and he depended on her vitality and strength. Now he is alone.[56]

In the end Macmillan decided not to raise income tax after all, settling for spending cuts instead. But he had made his point.

Maybe Butler was not quite so passive as Macmillan's diary makes him out. Eden's press secretary William Clark wrote of this tense period that 'All these three, Eden, Macmillan and Butler, watched each other like hostile lynxes.'[57] Nevertheless Rab does seem to have drifted with the tide that summer, while Macmillan made the running. Above all, Rab was ill in July when Nasser seized the Suez Canal; he missed the first cabinet to discuss Britain's response and was not included on the committee which Eden established to handle the crisis (though he sometimes attended). Thereafter he was little more than a spectator of a disaster he felt powerless to prevent. He voiced his doubts and urged caution, but not very hard; he was inhibited by loyalty and by the shadow of Munich. When Eden and Macmillan were loudly equating Nasser with Hitler and Mussolini, Rab felt he could not afford to be branded once again as an appeaser. Macmillan, by contrast, played a leading part in pushing Eden towards military action, threatening – again – to resign if force were not employed.* 'If Nasser "gets away with it",' he wrote in his diary, 'we are done for. The whole Arab world will despise us . . . So, in the last resort, we must use force and defy opinion, here and overseas.'[58] He was well aware that the risks were great,

---

*Many years later when Mrs Thatcher consulted Macmillan during the Falklands crisis, he advised her not to include the Chancellor, Geoffrey Howe, in her war cabinet. Events might have turned out differently if Eden had excluded Macmillan from the Egypt Committee in 1956.

but believed – in a last spasm of imperial delusion – that it was a matter of national survival. 'Without oil and the profits of oil,' he reported Eden telling the Egypt committee on 24 August, 'we cd not exist ... We must secure the defeat of Nasser, by one method or another. If not, we shd rot away.' Macmillan, supported by Salisbury and Alec Home (now Commonwealth Secretary) 'strongly' agreed. Only Rab was unconvinced; but he failed to press his objection.

> I was left with the impression that Butler was uncertain, altho' he agreed that we must achieve our purpose somehow. He wanted more time, so as to shew [sic] that every possible method had been tried, before the final decision to use force.[59]

By September the government was coming under pressure – from the Americans, the Labour opposition, the Liberals and the Churches – to refer the dispute to the United Nations. Like Mrs Thatcher over the Falklands, Eden – egged on by Macmillan – was determined not to do so. Macmillan explicitly saw the crisis as a re-run of the 1930s, with the same sort of people taking the same sorts of stance. 'This puts us in a difficult position,' he wrote on 13 September, 'esp as a good many Tories, mostly young and mostly sons of "Munichites" – like Richard Wood [son of Lord Halifax] – began to rat too.' Even Eden 'began to waver'; but Macmillan stiffened him. 'Butler was for giving the pledge – "no force, without recourse to the U.N.". I was for standing firm ... If the P.M. were to "climb down" under Socialist pressure, it wd be fatal to his reputation and position.'[60] Thus Macmillan lured Eden on to his downfall.

Macmillan burned his diary for the climax of the Suez crisis and its aftermath – supposedly at Eden's request. This was an extraordinary act for a compulsive diarist, so determined to record his version of events. Clearly it was to protect his own reputation more than Eden's, after the operation had gone horribly wrong. 'It was a very bad episode in my life,' he admitted to his biographer years later.[61] He never fully acknowledged the secret collusion with Israel whereby the Israelis were encouraged to attack Egypt so as to give Britain and France a pretext to intervene to 'separate the combatants' and secure the Canal – though his diary earlier in the summer is quite candid about the need to contrive a *casus belli* and he must have been a party to it. He did accept responsibility for the critical failure to anticipate the Americans' strong opposition to military action, which caused a run on the pound that in turn forced the abandonment of the invasion after just a few days. First he placed too much faith in his wartime relationship with President Eisenhower, which led him to underestimate the Americans' ingrained hostility to what they saw as British colonialism; then when Eisenhower condemned the use of force it was he, as Chancellor, who had to tell Eden that he must order an immediate ceasefire in order to save sterling. Thus he who was the keenest on military action was the first to run up the white flag; in Harold Wilson's stinging phrase, he was 'first in, first out'. Yet from this humiliation, for which he more than anyone else was to blame, he managed to emerge as Prime Minister.

Butler meanwhile had shown the better judgement, but lacked the courage of his convictions. He did not conceal his doubts about his colleagues' policy: on the contrary he aired them freely in private, while publicly and in cabinet going along with it. The result was that in trying to be loyal he was actually perceived as disloyal. 'God how power corrupts,' wrote William Clark, who himself resigned in protest at Eden's folly. 'The way RAB has turned and trimmed.'[62] 'I should have resigned, shouldn't I?' Rab lamented later.[63] Two junior ministers did resign, but they did not matter. As deputy Prime Minister in all but name, and Eden's anticipated heir, Butler by resigning, or just by threatening to resign, could have prevented the invasion. But Rab was not the resigning type: his instinct was to stay and try to limit the damage from within. When Eden's health collapsed and he retreated to Jamaica to recover, it was Rab who had to clear up the mess. He did it, in his quiet way, superbly, drawing on his own good relations with the US Treasury Secretary George Humphrey. 'I got the troops out, I restored the pound and . . . I re-established the Alliance,' he boasted to his biographer.[64] Macmillan, he wrote generously in his memoirs, 'stood shoulder to shoulder with me in those difficult days'.[65] But Rab got little credit for his salvage work, while Macmillan, defiantly unapologetic, managed to give the impression that the invasion had not only been right but had achieved its purpose by getting the UN involved. The fact was that Suez divided the country. It has gone down to history as a disastrous folly, but in 1956 teaching uppity natives a lesson was still popular: the government's poll rating actually increased, while most of the Tory party took the view, in John Ramsden's words, that 'it was better to have tried and failed than never to have tried at all'.[66] Macmillan had at least tried. Or as one young MP more graphically put it:

> Rab Butler, it was generally felt, had had his head well down beneath the parapet . . . when the shot and shell were at their fiercest . . . Harold Macmillan, it was felt, had like the Grand Old Duke of York marched his men to the top of the hill and then very smartly turned about and marched them down again. But it was also felt that he had at least been in action.[67]

From the other side of the House, Tony Benn noted that 'Butler is intensely suspect now.'[68]

On 22 November Rab addressed a meeting of Tory backbenchers. Unwisely he took Macmillan with him. Rab spoke first, quite briefly, characteristically trying to lower the temperature. Then Macmillan spoke for around thirty-five minutes and completely upstaged him with an emotional, uplifting appeal to the future, described by one witness as 'a real leadership speech'.[69] Enoch Powell – a keen Butler supporter – thought it 'one of the most horrible things that I remember in politics . . . seeing the way in which Harold Macmillan, with all the skill of the old actor-manager, succeeded in false-footing Rab. The sheer devilry of it verged upon the disgusting.'[70] Macmillan claimed that he had merely been trying to hold the party together over the weekend.[71] But it was obviously a calculated bid for the succession.

Eden returned from Jamaica shortly before Christmas. He still hoped to carry on; but it was immediately made clear to him that he had lost too much support, and his doctors told him firmly that his health would not stand it. He reluctantly resigned on 9 January. The almost universal assumption was that Butler would succeed. 'If Sir Anthony were to lay down the Premiership tomorrow,' the

Economist declared authoritatively in December, 'there really is no doubt that the Queen would be constitutionally bound to send for Mr Butler.'[72] That was nonsense; but on paper there should have been no contest. Rab had a much longer record of senior office, and had deputised successfully as Prime Minister under both Churchill and Eden; while over the last two years Macmillan had held no job long enough to make a mark in it: Defence for six months, the Foreign Office for eight, Chancellor for just a year. His meteoric progress through the great offices of state was rather like John Major's sudden emergence in 1989–90 – and culminated in the same result. Rab confidently expected to be chosen: he even asked his sister what he should say in his first broadcast to the nation.[73] But he underestimated both the degree of opposition he aroused in some sections of the party, and the way Macmillan had been sowing doubts about him – to the extent of hinting that he would not serve under Rab.[74] *The Times* reflected this carefully planted story, reporting on 10 January that Rab was still the favourite: 'But recent events have suggested that he might not be acceptable as leader to the strong right-wing element of Conservative MPs and Mr Macmillan might prove a more acceptable choice.' Nevertheless the editorial still on balance favoured Rab:

> MR MACMILLAN's gifts are obvious. He has shown a wise and firm hand at the Exchequer. He commands much support within the Conservative Party. MR BUTLER, on the other hand, has for long been the hope and leader of the younger Conservatives. It is with the younger Conservatives and what they stand for that the future of the party must rest . . . Provided MR BUTLER has fully recovered his health, vigour, and grasp, he would seem the more likely successfully to lead the nation in its present straits and the party at the next General Election.[75]

In fact the succession was sewn up before Rab even realised there was a contest. Two senior peers, Lord Kilmuir (the Lord Chancellor) and Lord Salisbury (Lord President of the Council) took it upon themselves to sound opinion. They spoke to each member of the cabinet individually, immediately after Eden announced his resignation. 'Well, which is it to be,' Salisbury asked them, 'Wab or Hawold?'[76] No more than three colleagues are believed to have backed Rab. They also asked the party chairman, the chairman of the backbenchers' committee and the Chief Whip (Ted Heath), who all preferred Macmillan.* Of all the senior figures in the party the outgoing Prime Minister was almost alone in backing Butler: though Eden did not formally advise the Queen on the choice of his successor, he made it clear how well he thought Rab had managed in his absence.[77] Churchill, with Munich doubtless in mind, backed Macmillan. 'Look, old cock,' he told Rab later, 'we went for the older man.'[78] 'This whole operation,' Dick Crossman wrote in his diary, 'has been conducted from the top by a very few people with great speed and skill, so that Butler was outflanked and compelled to surrender almost as quickly as the Egyptians at Sinai.'[79]

Macmillan was summoned to the Palace at two o'clock the next day. 'What do *they* want?' Lady Dorothy asked her husband, wondering why he was wearing his tailcoat for lunch.[80] Meanwhile Heath was deputed to break the bad news to Rab. He found him sitting alone in the Privy Council Chamber. 'As I entered, his face lit up with its familiar charming smile . . . "I am sorry, Rab", I said. "It's Harold". He looked utterly dumbfounded.'[81] Rab wrote in his memoirs that he was 'not surprised'.

> I had been overwhelmed with duties as head of the government, and had made no dispositions for the emergency which occurred. Horace Evans [Eden's doctor] had told me that Anthony Eden would get better, and I had relied on him going on.[82]

In truth he was devastated. Heath thought it was 'a shock from which he never fully recovered'.[83] Outwardly he took his disappointment stoically. Patrick Buchan-Hepburn (one of his few supporters in the cabinet) found him that afternoon 'very calm and sensible . . . He said he would carry on, and make a success of the "middle thing".'[84] But privately he blamed what he called

---

*The whips carried out their own canvass. Boothby, for instance, was rung up in Strasbourg to be asked his view. Predictably, he was for Macmillan. It is not clear that they were equally assiduous in canvassing those who were likely to support Butler.

'the "ambience" and connections of the present incumbent of the post at Number 10'. To friends who telephoned to commiserate he spoke bitterly of 'our beloved Monarch' for having lent herself to a plot to exclude him.[85] Allegedly he said 'savage' things to the *Daily Express* correspondent, Derek Marks, who honourably did not print them – a restraint unimaginable today.[86] Years later he told Macmillan's biographer: 'I couldn't understand, when I had done the most wonderful job – picking up the pieces after Suez – that they then chose Harold.'[87] Yet in public he managed to play the gracious loser: at the party meeting to acclaim the new leader he seconded his rival's formal nomination with just the barest hint of his own feelings. Nigel Nicolson – one of his supporters, who was deselected by his constituency for opposing Suez – thought he did it with an endearing melancholy:

> It wasn't the melancholy of personal disappointment, but the melancholy that right had not triumphed and that he was being obliged to contribute to a grotesque legend . . . Today he played his part well. He proposed his supplanter gracefully.[88]

It was manifestly unjust, yet politics is seldom fair. In the bleak circumstances of January 1957, in the ruins of a policy which the bulk of the party could not admit to have been a failure, Macmillan was the right choice, despite his responsibility for the disaster. The situation called for flair, nerve and a measure of hypocrisy which Macmillan possessed and Butler plainly did not; and most of the party recognised this. The very stoicism with which he accepted the result confirmed that it was the right decision. Rab's rejection was 'sad for the left wing of the Tory party', Nicolson conceded, 'but I daresay that in the circumstances it was right'.[89] Back in 1940 the anonymous writer who had thought Butler 'predestined to leadership' had added the shrewd reservation that he embodied none of the qualities the Tories looked for in their leaders: 'the passionate patriot, the philosophic aristocrat or the honest simpleton'.[90] (He presumably had in mind Churchill, Balfour and Baldwin respectively.) Seventeen years on, this turned out to be uncannily prescient: Rab was none of these things, whereas the reinvented Macmillan could play each role as required.

Rab's mastery of the business of government was undisputed; but he lacked inspiration. Above all his reputation for appeasement in one form or another – from Munich through his remaking of post-war party policy to Butskellism and his ambivalence over Suez – had repeatedly offended the more red-blooded instincts of the Tory party, as Brendan Bracken wrote to a friend in the United States:

> It was of course quite inevitable that Macmillan should succeed Anthony Eden. Butler had been too long on the halls as an inevitable successor and so the audience is tired of him. He is credited with highly contradictory characteristics such as being naïve and sly. A large number of Tories regard him as a Fabian whose only policy is to steal the Opposition's clothes. This is not an unfair estimate of Butler's devious leftish approach to politics. He is not, of course, by nature, a man of the left, but he holds the simple view that in a democracy the only method of keeping and maintaining power is to bribe the mob.[91]

Macmillan did not in practice think very differently. Bizarrely, however, in view of his pre-war record as an extreme left-winger, Macmillan was now seen as the right-wing candidate. His victory worried *The Times*, which held that the spirit of the age was liberal. 'The degree to which the Macmillan Government succeeds,' it warned the day after his appointment, 'will depend on the degree to which it is Butlerite.'[92] This too was accurate. Macmillan only pretended to be right-wing in order to win the leadership. As Prime Minister he continued to touch the sort of chords – particularly in foreign policy – that reassured the right; but commentators soon realised that he used his patrician style and mock-Edwardian manner as a smokescreen behind which he actually led the party away from most of the policies which those who backed him in 1957 had expected. Macmillan's government for the next six years was indeed Butlerite.

On top of everything else there was the simple fact that Macmillan – upright, silver-haired and stylish – *looked* like a Prime Minister, while Butler – rumpled, stooped and balding – did not. With the arguable exception of Churchill in 1940, Macmillan was the first party leader chosen on grounds of image, rather than experience and trust. For the past half-century – most obviously in Labour's choice of Tony Blair over Gordon Brown in 1994 – it has been increasingly accepted that image, or perceived vote-winning ability, should be the primary consideration. The choice of Macmillan over Butler in 1957 was the triumph of politics over government.

In his diary – which he resumed (or rather did not burn) as soon as he had secured the premiership – Macmillan gave a typically dishonest account of what happened next.

> I made up my mind that Butler (whose feelings of disappointment I could imagine only too well) was the key figure. I saw him at once, and offered him whatever office he might wish. (I only tried to steer him off the F.O. to wh he had some leanings, but from wh I think he really shrank in today's circumstances. I was determined to keep Selwyn Lloyd, because I felt one head on a charger should be enough) . . .
>
> Rab was very nice and reciprocated at once the attitude I took. We had preserved the Govt by our loyalty and comradeship before Christmas – during Eden's absence in Jamaica. We must do the same now, or we shd certainly founder . . . I hoped he wd continue to lead the House, but perh he wd like an office as well. He accepted this idea, and returned about noon the next day with his decision. He wd take the Home Office. I at once agreed.[93]

In fact Rab very much wanted the Foreign Office. 'The Foreign Secretaryship, for which I asked in 1957,' he stated in his memoirs, 'was withheld from me by Macmillan throughout his Premiership . . . His memory plays him false in averring that I "chose the post of Home Secretary". But he was clearly relieved when I chose to accept it.'[94] Ted Heath, whom (as Chief Whip) Macmillan consulted closely in forming his government, corroborated Butler's version.

> He [Macmillan] knew that Butler would ask for the Foreign Office, but he was determined not to let him have it. I thought this was rather unfair. Rab would have been a useful Foreign Secretary at that point. Although his inscrutability would have contrasted with

the directness of the Americans, his quiet charm could have won them over, and we desperately needed that after the bitterness of Suez. I did not see how keeping Selwyn Lloyd in the post could restore the 'special relationship'.[95]

Many agreed. But Macmillan, like so many Prime Ministers – and having suffered himself as Foreign Secretary under Eden – was determined to be his own Foreign Secretary and (like Eden) preferred a pliable stooge like Lloyd to be his bag carrier. It actually made sense to keep Rab fully occupied on the home front while he as Prime Minister roamed the world stage; nevertheless, Rab was entitled to feel aggrieved to be denied not only the premiership but the other job he most fancied as well. He could have insisted, since Macmillan could not have formed a government without him. But once again Rab was not the resigning type. 'There is a big difference between public life and private life,' he told a journalist. 'In public life one has to do one's duty. I certainly would not desert the ship at a time like this.'[96] So he took the Home Office, while continuing as Leader of the House.

Butler was a good modernising Home Secretary. He was the first really senior figure to hold the post for some time and held it for five years, so he had both the time and the muscle to put through a series of major reforms over a wide field, shaking up the criminal justice system and loosening the law on licensing, charities, gambling and prostitution. Generally speaking he was as liberal as the political climate of the 1950s allowed, paving the way for Roy Jenkins to go several steps further in the mid-1960s. Macmillan left him 'a completely free hand', in a 'spirit of indulgent scepticism', recognising that most of his measures were overdue but happy for Rab to take the flak from the hangers and floggers in the Tory party who furiously opposed them. ('We already have the Toby Belch vote,' he remarked characteristically in the run-up to the 1959 election. 'We must not antagonize the Malvolio vote.')[97]* Every year at conference Butler had to face

*Toby Belch, the fat knight in *Twelfth Night*, taunts the strait-laced steward Malvolio: 'Dost thou think, because thou art virtuous, there shall be no more cakes and ale?'[98]

down those he called 'Colonel Blimps of both sexes' – adding that 'the female of the species was more deadly . . . than the male'.[99] One of these female Blimps was Margaret Thatcher, who entered Parliament in 1959 and quickly drew attention to herself by calling for the return of corporal punishment. Butler invariably routed his critics, but only at the cost of confirming his reputation with the right of the party as dripping wet.

Rab was also a successful Leader of the House, with an unrivalled ability to charm opponents while deflecting difficult questions without answering them. Macmillan found him invaluable both for sorting out every sort of problem across Whitehall and for standing in for him when necessary, as he complacently recorded in his diary. In November 1957, for instance, he had a heavy cold: 'Cabinet at 11am – but I felt too ill to go, so asked Butler to take my place. (I rather like doing this occasionally. It pleases him).'[100] Or in 1958: 'Butler came in after the House rose, for a general talk. He is *much* better in health and spirits and a great help to me in every way.'[101] In February 1959, however, it was Rab's turn to be laid up with flu: 'This rather a bore, as there is a lot to be done before I go to Moscow in clearing up matters at home.'[102]

Rab naturally deputised whenever Macmillan went abroad, as he did frequently. With long-haul aviation now fully established, he travelled more than any previous Prime Minister (with the exception of Lloyd George's endless round of European conferences between 1919 and 1922). A two-month tour of the Commonwealth in 1958 and six weeks in Africa in 1960 were just the longest of his excursions. He was content to leave Rab 'holding the baby' – Rab's phrase[103] – because he was confident both that Rab would manage affairs efficiently and that he posed no threat to him in his absence.* Rab still imagined that by deputising loyally as he had under Churchill and Eden he was establishing a claim to the succession which could not be denied

---

*Roy Jenkins describes Rab fantasising wistfully in 1959, that if Macmillan were to be arrested in the park it would come to him as Home Secretary, though unfortunately 'I couldn't do anything about it. I would have to leave it to the law.'[104] Jenkins was then a young Labour MP. Rab was wonderfully indiscreet.

him again. He was delighted when Peter Thorneycroft, whom Macmillan had appointed Chancellor the year before, removed himself from contention by resigning on the eve of the Prime Minister's departure in January 1958: 'Nobody seems to have spotted that this is a great Butler victory,' he gloated to the journalist Bob McKenzie. 'It has been a wonderful week.'[105] Macmillan nonchalantly dismissed his Chancellor's resignation as 'a little local difficulty' and left Butler to sort it out. But some observers clearly sensed that Rab's moment had passed. 'Mr Butler is a spent political force,' Tony Benn wrote in his local Bristol paper, 'who has not one chance in a hundred of succeeding to the premiership.'[106]

From the depths of Suez in 1956, Macmillan led the Tory party to a stunning general election victory less than three years later, almost doubling the government's majority to exactly 100. Macmillan – ironically dubbed 'Supermac' by the cartoonist Vicky – happily took the credit for a booming economy and rising living standards ('Let us be frank about it, most of our people have never had it so good.')[107] Yet the foundations of the new affluence owed much to Butler's stewardship of the Treasury at the beginning of the decade, for which he got little credit. Still the government's comfortable return increased Rab's hopes of taking over in due course: he was still only fifty-seven, nine years younger than Macmillan. His remarriage, two weeks after the election, also seemed to put a new spring in his step.

But then Macmillan started to mess him about. First he asked Rab to add the chairmanship of the party to his two government jobs. This was an uncongenial assignment, involving a lot of travelling round the country visiting constituencies, and with the next election four or five years away an unrewarding one, which also conflicted uncomfortably with his role as Leader of the House. Characteristically Macmillan's real motive was to punish Lord Hailsham, who had been a highly successful chairman up to the election but was now taking too much credit for the result for Macmillan's liking. ('H is in a very over-excited condition,' he wrote in his diary, 'and keeps giving ridiculous "Press Conferences".')[108] Accordingly, he demoted Hailsham to Minister of Science and, seeking a less self-promoting chairman, turned as always to the faithful Rab. 'The appointment of Butler,' he persuaded himself, 'is *very* good symbolically. It shews the world that, after our great victory, we intend to remain progressive and not slide back into reaction.'[109] In his memoirs he claimed that his purpose was to 'add to, rather than diminish [Rab's] position and strength within the Party', and that the appointment underlined the government's progressive commitment.[110] But this was humbug. Rab should have refused the additional burden. But as usual he did not.

Then, the following summer, Macmillan switched Selwyn Lloyd to the Treasury and promoted Alec Home to the Foreign Office in his place. This was a triple hit at Butler. First, he persuaded Lloyd that leaving the Foreign Office would better position him to challenge Rab. 'He must realise that to go to the home side makes him a possible rival to Butler in considering the succession. Altho' he is not ambitious in any wrong sense, he is conscious of Rab's weakness and oddness (wh seems to grow not lessen).'[111] Second, Macmillan knew perfectly well that Rab still wanted – and deserved – the Foreign Office, but was still determined that he should not have it. When they discussed the matter, Rab noted that Macmillan 'said it would be like Herbert Morrison' – fantastically insulting, considering that Morrison was widely regarded as the worst Foreign Secretary in living memory. 'I did not agree with this diagnosis,' Rab tamely recorded, 'but accepted it.'[112] His acquiescence allowed Macmillan to claim that he had offered Rab the job but he had refused it – rather as Lloyd George claimed to have offered Asquith the Woolsack in 1918. Third, having appointed Home instead, he pressed Rab to take Home's old place at the Commonwealth Office – another insult, since Home had been a mere PPS in 1938 when Rab was already Under-Secretary under Halifax. This he did have enough pride to refuse. 'Rab does not want anything but his present position,' Macmillan wrote blithely, 'so that is settled.'[113]

Next, in October 1961, with the government now trailing Labour in the polls, Macmillan decided that he needed a younger and more inspiring party chairman after all and determined on Iain Macleod. Rab was happy to give up the chairmanship; but Macleod would not take it on without the leadership of the House as well, which Rab was reluctant to relinquish. In order to persuade him, Macmillan conceded that he should be named – unofficially – as deputy Prime Minister – while still insisting, as he had in 1955, that there was no such post. Rab could not be formally appointed, he wrote in his diary, for three reasons:

1) The Queen has in the past rightly pointed out that there is *no* such official post . . .
2) I must not let the Press say that I am failing in mind and health!
3) I must not be accused of trying to appoint my successor.

Nevertheless he hoped to 'find a form of words for the purpose of covering Rab's abandonment of two important posts', believing that 'these moves will be of great value to the Party and our hope of reviving our fortunes before the next Election'.[114]

Rab was not happy to be told that he lacked fire and was 'too old'; still less to be asked if he had 'ever thought of a peerage'.[115] 'I am in a spot,' he told Harold Evans. 'It is a turning point. Giving up two plumes is a big thing.' He was anxious about how the reshuffle would be presented – 'One doesn't wish to appear to have been pushed out by the P.M.'[116] – and particularly did not relish facing the Blimps at the party conference with his status so pointedly diminished. But as usual he gave way. 'I could have dug my heels in and refused to give up the Commons,' he wrote to Alec Home. 'But I have accepted all without saying anything, as it is Harold's wish.'[117] In the event he made one of the best speeches of his career at Brighton and scored an unexpected triumph. Macmillan's pleasure at his colleague's success was typically barbed and condescending:

> Butler defeated his 'flogging' critics with . . . ease. This is certainly a reward for firm leadership. Rab has always 'hedged' on crime, as on everything else. He has brought much of his trouble on himself by his appearance of vacillation. This is not really fair to him. Like Arthur Balfour, he has a fine academic mind, wh I personally admire but he is out of tune with a modern style . . . I am particularly happy about *Butler*. He was rather depressed and this will cheer him up.[118]

Now Macmillan had to find more work to keep Rab busy. For some time, needing a new direction for foreign policy after Suez, he had been moving towards applying to join the European Common Market. At the same time as moving Home to the Foreign Office he had also appointed Ted Heath as his deputy to lead the negotiations. But he also had to watch his back. He knew that Rab was doubtful about Europe: he sat for a rural constituency, and was a natural champion of the farming interest. Macmillan feared that Rab might come out and lead the strong element in the party that was opposed to entry. In his diary he speculated that Rab might play the role of a latter-day Disraeli and destroy him, as Disraeli had destroyed Peel, in defence of British agriculture. In fact his historical imagination was running away with him: he should have known that from his student days Rab's hero had been Peel. Nevertheless Macmillan tried to make sure by putting him in overall charge of the negotiations. True to form, Rab went with the flow. In August 1962 he invited the Prime Minister to dinner at his club and told him his decision.

> He told me that in spite of a) the farmers b) the Commonwealth c) the probable break-up of the Conservative Party he had decided to support our joining the Common Market. It was too late to turn back now. It was too big a chance to miss, for Britain's wealth and strength. But we must face the fact that we might share the fate of Sir Robert Peel and his supporters.[119]

Meanwhile Macmillan had given Rab another task. Frustrated by the friction between the Colonial Office and the Commonwealth Office over the future of the Central African Federation he asked Rab to sort it out. This was a curious job for the Home Secretary, but Rab was 'wise and wily – both useful qualities in this tangled problem'; while 'his appointment to this African work [would] not excite the jealousy of the other ministers concerned'.[120] Rab protested: 'It'll kill me.' 'Nonsense,' Macmillan replied: 'Look what North Africa did for me. It'll make you, Rab.'[121] Rab wrote that he accepted, 'out of a sense of duty and also, I think, out of a sense of adventure'.[122] His unspoken mission was to liquidate the ill-starred federation. As usual he discharged it with subtlety and skill, presiding over the independence of Malawi (formerly Nyasaland) and Zambia (formerly Northern Rhodesia) – though leaving the future of Southern Rhodesia (Zimbabwe) unresolved to plague future Labour and Tory governments for another sixteen years. Yet this was another housekeeping job which gained him little credit with those in the Tory party who still kicked against the reality of imperial retreat.

Finally, while heaping all these additional burdens on him, Macmillan deprived Rab of his last proper job. This was part of a sweeping reshuffle known as 'the night of the long knives' when the Prime Minister reacted to continuing poor opinion polls and by-election losses by sacking a third of his cabinet, starting with Selwyn Lloyd. He seems to have felt threatened by Rab, whom he suspected of leaking his intentions to the *Daily Mail,* and determined to assert his authority. Yet his drastic action only demonstrated that the supposedly 'unflappable' Prime Minister had lost his touch. While most of those he sacked were substantially younger than himself, those he promoted (including Enoch Powell and Keith Joseph) were younger still: the government as a whole probably benefited from a more youthful image, but Macmillan himself – now sixty-eight – was left looking increasingly elderly and out of touch, vulnerable to the mockery of *Beyond the Fringe, That Was The Week That Was* and *Private Eye,* which all began around this time. Rab – still under sixty – was unsackable (though he admitted: 'I feel my neck all the time to see if it is still there').[123] Still, Macmillan now removed him from the Home Office, leaving him with only his African responsibility but compensating him with the hollow titles of First Secretary of State and – finally – deputy Prime Minister. When Macmillan proposed these changes Rab protested with pained dignity:

> The last time that arrangements were made with the Press to show that I was helping you very little came of it. I lost the Leadership of the House and chairmanship of the party – and the general impression was 'Butler Down' . . .
> I will to the public mind have no duties except Africa . . . Without a classical office such as Lord President, I shall be out on a raft, as I was after Anthony Eden's decision in 1955 . . . I shall be out

on an African limb, as there has never yet been any clearly defined position for an undefined deputy.[124]

He was of course quite right – as the subsequent experience of Geoffrey Howe and John Prescott has fully confirmed. Willie Whitelaw played an important (though generally compliant) role under Mrs Thatcher; but the only deputy who has really made much of the job was Michael Heseltine, who was a strong character under an unusually mild Prime Minister. The title of deputy Prime Minister, Rab reflected in his memoirs, is one 'which can constitutionally imply no right to the succession and should (I advise, with the benefit of hindsight) be neither conferred nor accepted'.[125] Yet once again, almost masochistically, he acceded to the Prime Minister's wish.

During 1963 Macmillan's authority continued to decline. The cancellation first of the British 'Blue Streak' delivery system, then of the American Skybolt missile which Macmillan had agreed to buy instead, exposed the dependence of Britain's nuclear deterrent on American goodwill. Then General de Gaulle abruptly vetoed British membership of the EEC, leaving the government's whole geopolitical strategy in ruins, while at home the economy was stalled, with both inflation and unemployment rising. Finally a series of embarrassing security scandals culminated in an unprecedented media circus surrounding the affair between a cabinet minister, John Profumo, and a call girl: suddenly Macmillan's pose of lofty Edwardian detachment appeared merely anachronistic – a mood skilfully exploited by the chirpy new Labour leader, Harold Wilson, who had succeeded Gaitskell in January. That summer, faced with newspaper headlines predicting his imminent departure, Macmillan was forced to think seriously about stepping down.

Butler was still the obvious successor: but Macmillan was more than ever determined to deny him. His ostensible reason was the need for a younger leader to connect with the spirit of the new age:

'Macmillan must go' is the cry. Faced with *Wilson* (47 or so) we must have a young man (Heath or Maudling). This line of approach leaves out poor Butler as well as me. Of course, there's something in it. We have had a run of bad luck. Once this starts everything seems to go wrong.[126]

For some time he had been promoting the leaders of the next generation to give them the chance to make their mark – putting Heath in charge of the Common Market negotiations, making Macleod Leader of the House, then appointing Maudling Chancellor. But none of them had quite seized their opportunity. For a time Maudling seemed to have established himself as front runner, but his star faded as quickly as it rose. In this situation Macmillan began to cast the net wider. By an accident of timing Tony Benn's long battle to be allowed to disclaim his father's peerage was just culminating in legislation which would – for a brief period – permit existing peers to disclaim their titles. This opened the prospect of two more candidates throwing their coronets into the ring: Lord Hailsham and (more improbably) Lord Home. Home was roughly the same age as Butler; Hailsham four years younger. Both, as it happened, had been on the 'wrong' side over Munich – Home as Chamberlain's PPS, Hailsham (Quintin Hogg as he then was) the government candidate at a famous by-election in October 1938; but somehow they were less tarred by the association than was Butler. They could not have been more contrasting characters – Hailsham a brilliant, impulsive populist, Home a quiet, self-effacing aristocrat – but Macmillan convinced himself that either would be better than Rab. That summer he told Hailsham that he wanted him to succeed, and gave him a chance to show his paces by sending him (instead of Home) to Moscow to conduct the negotiations for a nuclear test ban treaty. When Hailsham asked 'What about Rab?' Macmillan replied dismissively: 'Rab simply doesn't have it in him to be Prime Minister.'[127]

Rab himself was half reconciled to the possibility that he had missed the boat. He made little attempt to take advantage of Macmillan's difficulties. In a television interview on 8 July he conceded: 'I think I am pretty well aware that people want us to give a fresh impression of vigour and decision before the next election.' This was scarcely a ringing statement that he was the man to provide it.[128] In his diary he wrote fatalistically: 'It is no good thinking there is no life left if one is not elected Pope. One can always be a respected Cardinal.'[129] And in a later interview he told Kenneth Harris: 'I reached the conclusion in June of that year . . . that it was almost inevitable that the Conservative party would choose a younger man.'[130] Nevertheless he still believed that if there was any justice the job would yet fall to him. He did not take very seriously the idea that Hailsham or Home might renounce their peerages. 'Of course,' he told Benn, Hailsham 'would like to be Prime Minister, but he feels his job in the Lords is just as important. Alec Home won't because his is a very old title.' He went on plaintively:

> Everybody always writes about me as a possible successor to Macmillan. When the Prime Minister's popularity slumps, which it often does, my name always pops up. Nobody ever writes about what I do. It's getting me down. And we're told that because of Wilson we need a younger man too. But the PM will carry on. He's in good shape. And we may win the Election.

This was the same mistake he had made in 1955, when he believed that Eden would carry on and consequently failed to make his own dispositions. Benn wrote that he enjoyed talking to Rab because he was 'wildly indiscreet . . . I felt rather sorry for him this time as he obviously sees the premiership slipping away for ever. I'm sure he's right. That sort of chance never comes twice.'[131]

By mid-July *The Times* took it for granted that Macmillan would go soon, and thought the succession a two-horse race between Maudling and Butler, with most of the cabinet favouring Rab, 'though the sudden emergence of a third compromise candidate should not be entirely discounted'.[132] From Macmillan's diary it seems that Rab had made some effort to promote himself (though whatever he said was too gnomic to be widely reported):

> The position in the race to succeed me is quite amusing. Macleod is (for the moment) hardly a starter. There wd be long odds against Ted Heath. Rab (Butler) is coming up and gaining on the favourite, Maudling. But his speech was thought to be in bad taste and has done him harm. (His hat had been put firmly in the ring by his

supporters.) There was no need to throw it in again himself, and in rather an ungracious way towards me . . . With all eyes now on Moscow, people are wondering whether [Maudling] has enough experience over the whole field to be P.M.[133]

Over the early autumn Macmillan swithered between resigning immediately, resigning in the New Year or staying on to fight the election. On 11 September he saw Rab and was 'rather careful *not* to give him any idea about wh of the several alternatives I wd choose'. After 'long talks . . . before and after dinner' he recorded his (possibly self-deceiving) view of Rab's position:

He wd naturally (if I resign) accept the Premiership if there was a general consensus of opinion for him. But he doesn't want another unsuccessful bid. He wd not go in for a ballot of the Party or back-benchers. But he wd serve in this Parlt and the next, in office or in opposition. He is 60. He likes politics. He doesn't want to go into business, for he has enough money. It is clear that in his heart he does *not* expect any real demand for him. He wd prefer to be Warwick, (wh. he cd be) and not try to be King (wh. he can't be).* On the whole, he is for Hailsham. I have never seen him so well . . . or so relaxed.[134]

At this stage Macmillan was willing to go quickly only if he could create a consensus for Hailsham. On 30 September he had lunch with the senior Conservative grandee Lord Swinton:

He is – on the whole – in favour of . . . my resignation in January; but *only* if we can get *Hailsham*. Altho' an old and devoted friend of *Butler*, S. thinks he wd lose the election disastrously. Maudling wd be worse, electorally. S. thinks that Butler wd be prepared to stand down for Hailsham, but he is not sure. If H. cannot be got by agreement, I ought to stay on, at whatever inconvenience to myself.[135]

Prime Ministers can usually find reasons for not resigning. Macmillan now decided that he could not guarantee Hailsham's succession, so

---

* 'Warwick the Kingmaker' was the fifteenth-century Earl of Warwick who changed sides twice during the Wars of the Roses, first helping the Yorkist Edward IV to seize the throne and then helping to restore the Lancastrian Henry VI.

he resolved to announce at the party conference that he intended
to carry on, and persuaded himself that this was Rab's preference
too: 'In the course of the morning, I saw Butler – who wd clearly
prefer me to go on, for – in his heart – he does not expect the
succession *and* fears it.'[136]

But then, on the eve of the conference, Macmillan was struck
down with prostate trouble. Convinced that he was more seriously
ill than he really was, he decided that he must resign immediately
and sent Home to Blackpool with a message announcing his
decision. As soon as it was known that Macmillan would not be
attending, Rab acted with unaccustomed decisiveness: first he and
his wife occupied the suite reserved for the Prime Minister in the
conference hotel; then he insisted – against some opposition –
that he would deliver the leader's closing speech on the last day
of the conference. This suggested that he realised he must exert
himself to claim the prize. Yet when it came to it he failed to rise
to the occasion. The *Times* political correspondent wrote that
'Mr Butler needs to make the speech of his life here tomorrow
afternoon if he is to strengthen his hopes of winning the leadership.'[137] Rab was sufficiently proud of his speech to reprint two
pages of it in his memoirs, describing it as 'a deliberate attempt
to bring the philosophy of the Charters [of the 1940s] up to date
and to project Conservative social policy into the next decade'.[138]
But this worthy stuff was not what the faithful wanted to hear
in the heated atmosphere of a conference which now resembled
an American convention. Attempting to seize the moment,
Hailsham had impulsively chosen to announce at a fringe meeting
that he was disclaiming his peerage immediately, offering himself
to the party as plain Quintin Hogg: the resulting scenes of wild
enthusiasm reminded many observers of a Nuremberg rally. Rab's
speech by contrast was a deliberate attempt to cool the atmosphere, so that the decision about the leadership could be taken
calmly in London the next week. But he miscalculated badly, just
as he had when addressing the 1922 committee after Suez. His
speech, in Ted Heath's recollection, was 'monotonous and ineffective and did him no good whatever'.[139]

All three leading contenders blew their chances in Blackpool.
Not only did Rab fail to set the conference alight, but Maudling

delivered an equally lacklustre effort in the economic debate, while Hailsham's egotistical performance confirmed the doubts many senior Tories already felt about his judgement, halting his bandwagon in its tracks. In these circumstances Macmillan – directing operations from his hospital bed in London – switched his support overnight to Home, who made the best speech of the week in the foreign affairs debate. Rab was still the bookies' favourite and the public favourite; a *Daily Express* poll gave him 39 per cent against 21 per cent for Hailsham, 11 per cent for Maudling and just 9 per cent for Home.[140] It was significant that Home was even listed as a runner. Few politicians or journalists took his candidature seriously: a hereditary Scottish aristocrat, the fourteenth Earl of Home was the epitome of the grouse-moor image which had done so much to damage Macmillan – the very antithesis of Harold Wilson, who just two weeks earlier had fired the Labour conference with his vision of a new Britain 'forged in the white heat of . . . the scientific revolution'.[141] He was not even a member of the House of Commons. But in his quiet way he was not unambitious, and he played to perfection the part of the reluctant candidate willing to be drafted for the sake of party unity. His greatest asset was that he had no enemies, whereas both Rab and Hailsham, for different reasons, did.

Macmillan in his diary was as usual disingenuous, pretending that he had nothing to do with encouraging the gathering bandwagon for Home. 'The "draft Home" movement,' he wrote on 14 October, 'was in reality a "Keep out Butler" movement.' He claimed to be 'struck by the fact' that both the Lord Chancellor (Lord Dilhorne) and the Chief Whip (Martin Redmayne) had switched from Hogg to Home. 'Both are agst the Butler succession on the ground that the party in the country will find it depressing.' But he had to admit that no element of the party at this stage wanted Home: 'The party in the Country wants Hogg; the Parly Party wants Maudling or Butler; the Cabinet wants Butler. The last 10 days have not altered this fundamental fact.'[142] Three days later, however, he recorded a very different conclusion:

The remarkable and to me unexpected result of all these 4 groups of people asked to give their views was . . . a *preponderant first* choice for Ld Home (except in the constituencies, who hardly knew he was a serious candidate but agreed that he wd be universally acceptable if *drafted*) and an almost universal *second* choice. There were *strong* pro-Butlerites; but equally violent *anti*. There were strong – very strong – pro Hailsham – but very violent anti. On Maudling the feelings were not so strong in either direction.[143]

In those days, when Tory leaders mysteriously 'emerged', with neither MPs nor the membership having a vote, the group that really should have mattered was the cabinet. Neither Home nor anyone else could form a government without the support of senior colleagues. After canvassing the cabinet Dilhorne reported to Macmillan that ten were for Home against only five for Butler, four for Maudling and three for Hogg. But Dilhorne's figures were later widely disputed: in particular he put Macleod in Home's column, which was nonsense. There was much more support for Rab than he allowed – particularly once Hogg and Maudling had abandoned their own ambitions and rallied their supporters behind him to try to stop Home. Above all, Rab himself had an effective veto. 'We all understood that Alec could not form a government unless Rab agreed to serve,' the Queen's secretary, Sir Martin Charteris, told a royal biographer many years later, 'and, if not, the Queen would have had to send for Rab.'[144] When they realised what was afoot, Macleod and Powell took the lead – following a late-night meeting at Powell's house – in trying to convince Rab that if he only stood firm the premiership was his. Powell later spoke graphically of having put a loaded revolver in his hands, but Rab refused to press the trigger.[145] Hogg also telephoned him late at night; Rab told him that he was 'just dozing off'. 'This is no time to sleep!' Hogg urged him. 'Don your armour, dear Rab! You must fight, dear Rab! There is still time.' Rab replied: 'I take note of your remarks, but now I really must doze off.'[146] By the next morning it was too late.

Macmillan professed to find the attempt to block Home improper:

The idea was an organised revolt by all the *unsuccessful* candidates – Butler, Hailsham, Maudling and Macleod – against Home. Considering their intense rivalry with each other during recent weeks, there was something rather 18th century about this (Fox–North Coalition perhaps) and somewhat distasteful.

This was humbug. The only impropriety was Macmillan trying to impose his own candidate against the will of more than half the cabinet. Home himself was uncomfortable with the proceeding:

> Home rang up and felt somewhat aggrieved. He had only been asked to come forward as a compromise candidate, for unity. He felt like withdrawing. I urged him not to do so. If we give in to this intrigue, there wd be chaos. Butler wd fail to form a Govt; even if given another chance (for the Queen might then send for Wilson) no one else wd succeed. We shd have a Wilson Govt; a dissolution; and our Party without even a nominal leader . . . This was a most critical moment, but I decided to go on. My letter of resignation was sent and delivered to the Palace at 9.30 a.m.[147]

At 11 a.m. the Queen paid an unprecedented visit to Macmillan in hospital, where he read her a memorandum containing the result of his rigged soundings. To preserve the fiction of the royal prerogative he stopped short of formally advising her to send for Home: having resigned, he no longer had the constitutional right to give advice. No previous Prime Minister had attempted to influence the choice of his successor in this way. But she accepted his view of the party's choice. At 12.30 Home was summoned to the Palace – not to be asked definitely to form a government, but to be invited to try.

Rab could still have refused to serve; but it was not in his character to do so. He still thought he would have been a better Prime Minister than Home, whom he described just a few months later as 'an amiable enough creature', but totally lacking in knowledge of economics or home affairs.[148] But Home was an old friend and an honourable man whom it was impossible to dislike, whatever he thought of Macmillan's machinations. Above all he would not split the party. Back at Cambridge forty years before he had written his thesis on the Corn Law crisis of 1846, when Peel had split the Tory party for a generation; this, he later told Elizabeth Longford, was 'the supremely unforgettable political lesson of history . . . I could never do the same thing in the twentieth century, under any circumstances whatever.'[149] Most of the ablest younger members of the cabinet – Hogg, Maudling, Macleod, Powell and Edward Boyle – would have stayed out if he had given the lead; but once Home had been to the Palace it would have been a very messy business to have forced him to go back and admit failure. The first person Home saw was naturally Rab. He offered him the Foreign Office – the very job Macmillan had always denied him – and Rab inevitably accepted. After that Maudling agreed to stay at the Treasury and Hogg to continue as Lord President: only Macleod and Powell refused to serve, in protest at the way Home had been foisted on the party. But they were both mavericks whose intensity the party distrusted.* Home duly kissed hands, renounced his peerage and was returned to the Commons at a by-election three weeks later as Sir Alec Douglas-Home, with a maximum of twelve months as Prime Minister before he would have to face the electorate.

This time – unlike in 1957 – there is no doubt that Rab should have won the prize. He was still only sixty-one but immensely experienced, and supported by most of the cabinet. He was denied by the deliberate resolve of his old nemesis, who had beaten him to the job in 1957 and even as he reluctantly let go the reins six years later was still determined not to pass them on to him. Rab was clearly the man best equipped to lead a government. The only argument against him was that he was not very inspiring: he looked older than he was, and Macmillan was not alone in doubting if he was the man to beat Wilson at the next election. On simple electioneering grounds there might have been a case either for Hailsham, until he imploded, or for skipping a generation and going for a younger man: *The Times* favoured Ted Heath, but failing him still preferred Butler to any other candidate.[150] But on this argument it made no sense at all to choose Home, whose slightly goofy upper-class image and ignorance of economics – encapsulated by his confession that he used matchsticks to work

---

*Macleod became editor of the *Spectator* and wrote a bitter article alleging that the choice had been manipulated by Macmillan working through a narrow 'magic circle' of Old Etonians. He was particularly angry that as chairman of the party he had been excluded from the 'loop'.

out financial problems – were a gift to the satirists. In fact Home did surprisingly well in October 1964, holding Labour to a majority of just four seats, which suggested that the electorate was not yet so impressed by youth and novelty over experience and character. But then surely Rab would have done better still, and might even have won the Tories a fourth consecutive term (with incalculable consequences for the Labour party). Wilson certainly believed so; ironically both Home and Macmillan came to think that it would have been better for Butler to have been chosen in 1963, even if he had gone on to lose in 1964.[151] The pre-eminent Tory historian Robert Blake wrote in 1980 that by blocking Butler, Macmillan 'did a lasting disservice to his party'.[152]

Macmillan always denied that he had acted improperly to deny his old rival. 'It is quite untrue that I was determined to "down" Rab,' he wrote after Home's appointment. 'It *is* true that of the three I would have preferred Hailsham, as a better election figure.' But immediately he contradicted himself.

> All this pretence about Rab's 'progressive' views is rather shallow. His real trouble is his vacillation in any difficult situation. He has no strength of character or purpose and for this reason shd *not* be P.M.[153]

It can be argued that Butler's failure to fight his corner in the days after Blackpool proved Macmillan's point. 'If you had seen him yesterday morning,' one of his supporters lamented, 'dithering about in a gutless sort of way, you would not want him to be Prime Minister of this country. I was quite appalled; quite disgusted.'[154] Macmillan certainly felt vindicated:

> The more I reflect on the events of the last week the more astonished I am at the failure of Rab . . . to *do* anything about the crisis. I had made it clear that I cd not go on and he shd have at least tried to get some method of testing opinion organised.[155]

Rab himself recognised the truth of this analysis. For the rest of life he nursed his regrets, harping almost obsessively on his disappointment. Years later he asked John Boyd-Carpenter: 'Do you think that if I had stood firm in 1963 I would have been

Prime Minister?' 'Yes,' Boyd-Carpenter replied. '"I think so too", he said with a sigh.'[156] Another time he told his private secretary: 'If I had been less of a gentleman I could have been Prime Minister.'[157] But at the same time he did not think that, in the absence of any policy difference, he could decently have refused to serve Home simply to advance himself. 'The Chief Whip said to me later that it would have been possible to alter the whole decision in my favour,' he wrote in his memoirs, 'but that he thought I would never have been happy again if I had done so. With this diagnosis I agree . . . My temperament is that of a reformer, not of a rebel, and each of us must act according to his character.'[158]

Rab served dutifully but without distinction as Foreign Secretary up to the 1964 election. 'He was often a little patronising about the Prime Minister, but never disloyal,' Nicholas Henderson recalled.[159] Home was not conspicuously loyal in return. Had he won the election, he intended to replace Rab with Christopher Soames; as it was, he offered him an earldom (which Rab refused), and eased him out of the Research Department which had been his fief for twenty years. At this Rab realised that his political career was over: he accepted a life peerage from Wilson, and the Mastership of Trinity College, Cambridge – an eminently suitable return to his family's academic roots. He died in 1982.

Macmillan declined a peerage for another twenty years. He had no sooner resigned than he regretted it, and right up to the mid-1980s continued to believe that he might return to lead an emergency coalition to tackle the recurrent economic crises of the Wilson, Heath and early Thatcher years. Between 1966 and 1973 he churned out six volumes of stodgy, self-justificatory but un-revealing memoirs, which were elegantly trumped by Rab's single slim volume, *The Art of the Possible,* in 1971. ('I have eschewed the current autobiographical fondness for multi-volume histories,' he wrote, in favour of 'a single book which is not too heavy for anyone to hold up and doze over in bed'.)[160] Neither of them cared much for Mrs Thatcher's harsh brand of Conservatism, which turned its back on so much that they had both stood for; but whereas Rab merely muttered waspishly in private, Macmillan came out openly on television and – when he finally accepted an earldom – in the House of Lords to condemn her for quarrelling with the miners and 'selling the family silver'. By now he had become a revered but slightly pathetic figure, more than ever a caricature of an Edwardian elder statesman. He attended Rab's memorial service, still denying that he had deliberately done him down, and finally died himself in 1986, aged ninety-two.

Who won their rivalry? Macmillan, unquestionably, at every turn. Twice when Rab seemed to have the premiership on a plate Macmillan denied him – first vaulting into the place himself, then manoeuvring shamelessly to install a far less qualified candidate. In addition, during his six years in Number Ten, he treated him almost contemptuously as his uncomplaining deputy, or 'willing camel', taking advantage of his good nature to pile burdens on him – 'the honours of Pooh Bah,' Rab called them – and then remove them almost at will, while denying him the one great office he had never filled and really wanted.[161] A late developer who languished on the back benches while Rab forged ahead in the 1930s, Macmillan seized his opportunity when it came with flair and ruthlessness, and for five years or so filled the highest office with compelling style, linking his name indelibly with the brief flowering of 'affluence' in the late 1950s – even if in the long run doubts have been raised about his lasting achievement. Of course Butler shared responsibility for the failures of the Macmillan years, just as he deserves some of the credit for the successes. He was not a visionary, so it is hard to argue that he would have managed the decline of Britain's world role in these years – from Suez through the retreat from empire to the bungled approach to Europe – more skilfully than Macmillan did. Yet his legacy – much of it achieved before he first failed to become Prime Minister – was perhaps more lasting: the 1944 Education Act; the reshaping of the Tory party in the late 1940s; and, under Macmillan, the modernisation of much outdated Victorian legislation at the Home Office. Prime Ministers are doomed to be judged more harshly than those whose promise is unfulfilled. While Macmillan is seen, half a century on, as a rather seedy conjuror whose tricks never quite came off – remembered for Premium Bonds, Dr Beeching's short-sighted pruning of the railway network, Selwyn Lloyd's Pay

Pause, Maudling's unsustainable boom and the Profumo scandal – Rab Butler will always head the list of those – like Hugh Gaitskell, Denis Healey and Roy Jenkins – routinely dubbed 'the greatest Prime Minister we never had'. 'Rab's failure,' wrote Edward Pearce in a book devoted to three such 'nearly men' in 1997, 'was more brilliant than most politicians' success.'[162]

Reflecting as he did constantly on the reasons for his 'failure', Rab reflected ruefully on the difference between his safe career path and Macmillan's more adventurous route to the top:

> I trod a different path, serving the establishment with patient if unglamorous tenacity. This is not a sure recipe for success in achieving the highest political rewards. As I invariably inform young men who now come and ask me about politics, the lives of leaders the world over have frequently been advanced by colourful rebellion or resignation. [He cited the examples of Churchill, Eden and Wilson, as well as Macmillan.] My own career, by contrast, exemplifies the advantages of the long haul, namely the steady influence one may exert by being at all times on the inside.[163]

The reward of Rab's 'long haul' was twenty-six and a half years in office over a period of thirty-four years – a record exceeded in the twentieth century only by Churchill. Not a bad consolation prize for a loser.

Edward Heath and
Margaret Thatcher

On 25 November 1974 Margaret Thatcher went to see Edward Heath in his room at the House of Commons to tell him of her intention to challenge him for the leadership of the Conservative party. He was fifty-eight, had been leader for nine years and Prime Minister for three and a half, until narrowly defeated at a general election earlier that year. She was forty-nine and had been Education Secretary in his government. Heath received her coldly, did not ask her to sit down but merely told her gruffly: 'You'll lose.'[1] Few commentators thought any differently. Despite losing two elections inside a year, Heath still had the overwhelming backing of his senior colleagues, the Tory party in the country and most of the press. But he had antagonised a large number of his backbench MPs: and these, under the new system for choosing the leader put in place by Alec Douglas-Home after the farce of his own controversial 'emergence' in 1963, were now the people who mattered. Ten weeks later, on 4 February 1975, Heath and his closest colleagues gathered again in his room at the Commons to hear the result of the ballot: Mrs Thatcher had beaten him by eleven votes. 'So,' he told his stunned supporters, 'we got it all wrong.'[2] He stood down, and a week later Mrs Thatcher was elected the first female leader of a major party in the western democratic world. Four years later she became Prime Minister.

This 'Peasants' Revolt' was an upset unparalleled in modern British politics. Heath was the first party leader since Austen

Chamberlain in 1922 to be ousted against his will with no pretence of age or ill health to provide a cover – and even Chamberlain was not actually defeated in a leadership contest: he was merely compelled to resign when the party voted against his advice to withdraw from the Lloyd George coalition.* His half-brother Neville was forced to resign the premiership in May 1940, but he remained Tory leader until his death five months later. Anthony Eden's authority was destroyed by Suez, but he was genuinely ill when he resigned in January 1957. Alec Douglas-Home stepped down more or less voluntarily nine months after the Tories' defeat in 1964. The closest parallel is Arthur Balfour's resignation in 1911. Like Heath, Balfour had been leader for around a decade but had been Prime Minister for less than four years and had lost two general elections inside a year. But at least Balfour resigned: he did not suffer the humiliation of being defeated in open combat by one of his junior colleagues. Labour has generally been kinder to its leaders: except for Ramsay MacDonald, who was expelled from the party after forming a National Government with the Tories in 1931, only George Lansbury in 1935 has been pushed out. But he too knew when it was time to go. Even the rapid turnover of Tory leaders since 1997 has been bloodless: John Major, William Hague, Iain Duncan-Smith and Michael Howard all fell on their own swords when they knew they had lost the party's confidence to carry on. Heath's fate remains unique. To make it worse, he had never considered his assassin as a rival: Mrs Thatcher was a middle-ranking cabinet minister of no great distinction whom practically no one had seen as a potential leader. Above all she was a woman – a class of politician for whom he had minimal respect. It is no wonder that he found his defeat exceptionally hard to stomach.

Though their paths had first crossed a quarter of a century earlier, Heath and Mrs Thatcher were not perceived – by themselves or anyone else – as rivals until the moment when she resolved that if no one better qualified would stand against him, she would. She was nine years and a whole political generation younger than

---

*The '1922 Committee' of Conservative backbenchers still takes its name from this historic revolt.

him: if anything she was seen as a loyal protégée, not as his potential nemesis. Their provincial origins and family background, their career paths and even their political personalities were in fact remarkably similar. But from the moment she took her courage in her hands and overthrew him they were bitter opponents: rivals until 1979 for the loyalty of a still divided party, thereafter the embodiment of starkly opposed visions of Conservatism who throughout the 1980s defined themselves explicitly against each other. Heath naturally was the more bitter in his loathing of everything that Mrs Thatcher stood for; but she was equally determined that her government would be in every respect the opposite of his. Yet as the perspective of history lengthens, they can be seen to be more alike than either could have recognised at the time. His premiership is remembered as an ignominious failure, hers as a triumphant success. Yet the Thatcher 'revolution' was built on the foundations of what Heath had attempted – prematurely – a decade earlier. Her success was built on the ruins of his failure: she needed him to fail before she could succeed. They were bitter rivals, yet their fortunes were umbilically linked.

Edward Heath was born in July 1916 in Broadstairs on the very south-eastern tip of England. His father was a carpenter who had achieved his own business as a small builder; his mother a former lady's maid with a powerful ambition for her elder son. 'Teddy', as he was known, was a studious boy with a talent for music. He won a scholarship to a fee-paying grammar school up the road at Ramsgate, but twice failed to win a scholarship to Oxford. He did secure a place, however, and with the help of a loan from Kent County Council and his mother's savings he went up to Balliol in 1935 to read Philosophy, Politics and Economics. Once there he won an organ scholarship, which eased the burden on his parents. Like Asquith in the 1870s, he thrived in the relatively egalitarian atmosphere of Balliol. Contemporaries from similar grammar school backgrounds included Denis Healey and Roy Jenkins; like them, Heath threw himself into undergraduate politics, winning the presidency of the Union in his final year. Unlike them, however, he was a staunch Conservative – reflecting equally his father's small business outlook and his mother's social aspirations. Yet he made his name as an opponent of appease-ment – a brave stand in those days for a young man with no family or means behind him – and played a prominent part in the famous Oxford by-election of October 1938 (at which the young Quintin Hogg saw off the anti-Chamberlain challenge of the Master of Balliol, A. D. Lindsay). His clear-sighted anti-Fascism was informed by a series of journeys around Europe in his summer vacations – to Germany in 1937 (where he attended a Nuremberg rally and met Himmler); to Spain at the height of the civil war in 1938 (where he came under fire in Barcelona); and in August 1939 to Germany and Poland, where he was nearly caught by the outbreak of war. These experiences were the foun-dation of his lifelong dedication to the cause of European union.

Heath had a good war – another formative influence – rising to the rank of Colonel in the Royal Artillery while fighting his way across Europe from Normandy to Hanover in 1944–45. He always retained a certain military style of command. On coming out of the army, however, he sat the civil service entrance exam-ination and passed equal top. He joined the Ministry of Civil Aviation and gained useful inside knowledge of Whitehall; but he was always set on a political career and had to leave the civil service after only twelve months when he was adopted – at his fourth attempt – as candidate for the marginal Labour seat of Bexley, in south-east London. While nursing the constituency he worked briefly as news editor of the *Church Times* and then as a trainee with a merchant bank before he was narrowly elected at the general election of February 1950. During this time he might have married a local Broadstairs girl whom he had known since schooldays; but she tired of waiting for him and married someone else. Thereafter he had no time in his life for women. He pursued his political ambition single-mindedly, with music his only relaxation until in his fifties he took up sailing.

Margaret Thatcher's early life was similarly single-minded. She was born in the Lincolnshire market town of Grantham in 1925, the second daughter of a small grocer, Alfred Roberts, who was also a pillar of the local Methodist church and a prominent town councillor, chairman of the finance committee, later alderman and mayor. If Heath was his mother's blue-eyed boy, Margaret Roberts was her father's favourite: he treated her as the son he never had, supervised her reading, took her with him to committee meetings and generally encouraged her interest in politics, instilling his own dedication to hard work, plain living, stern morality and public service. Though nominally an independent, Alfred was in reality a Conservative, and Margaret never considered being anything else: her first political experience, aged nine, was running errands for the Tories in the 1935 election. She won a scholarship to the local girls' grammar school and from there gained a place at Somerville College, Oxford, to study chemistry – a sensible vocational subject which suited the practical cast of her mind. Most of her contemporaries joined the Wrens or the WRAC on leaving school in 1943; but, war or no war, she determined to go to university immediately. Women were still debarred from membership of the Union; but she applied herself assiduously to politics and – like Heath before her – became president of the university Conservative Association (only the second woman to hold the post), making a lot of useful contacts among rising Tory MPs, some of whom – like Quintin Hogg and Peter Thorneycroft – later served under her. Like Heath, she gained a second-class degree; but she made very little impression on her contemporaries, who recalled her as humourless and dull. She had as little time for boys as Heath had for girls.

On leaving Oxford she had to earn her living. She got a job as a research chemist in Essex and joined the Colchester branch of the Young Conservatives where she quickly made a reputation as a forceful right-winger, instinctively opposed to the consensual policies then being promoted by Rab Butler. In 1948 she attended the party conference at Llandudno, where she met the chairman of the Dartford constituency association which was looking for a candidate; he encouraged her to apply and she was adopted, beating four male candidates, in February 1949. She had no hope of winning – Dartford was a rock-solid Labour seat with a majority in 1945 of over 20,000; but she was twenty-three years old, the youngest female candidate in the country, and she attracted a lot of wide-eyed media attention. ('She is easy to look at,' wrote the *Daily Mail*, 'soft-voiced, feminine, charming and clearheaded . . . and very fashion conscious.')[3] From now on she skilfully exploited her femininity, discovering a gift for photo-opportunities and a hitherto unsuspected love of the limelight which blossomed twenty-five years later.

Thus 'Teddy' Heath and Margaret Roberts found themselves Tory candidates in adjoining Kentish seats at the 1950 general election. Bexley and Dartford were grouped with two other neighbouring seats, all at the time Labour-held, so they were thrown quite a lot together and spoke at one another's meetings. 'When we met,' Lady Thatcher wrote in her memoirs, 'I was struck by his crisp and logical approach – he always seemed to have a list of four aims, or five methods of attack.' He was also of course much older and more experienced than her. 'Though friendly with his constituency workers, he was always very much the man in charge . . . and this made him seem, even when at his most affable, somewhat aloof and alone.'[4]

Despite the similarity of their backgrounds, the age difference was crucial to their political personalities: they came of different generations, which fundamentally shaped their political philosophies. Heath was a child of the 1930s: he had grown up under the shadow of mass unemployment at home, Fascism abroad and the looming threat of war. As an idealistic young Conservative coming out of the army in 1945 he was imbued with an essentially bipartisan commitment to full employment as the first obligation of economic policy, universal welfare and international co-operation. This inheritance still dictated his response to problems at home and abroad in the 1970s. Margaret Roberts, by contrast, came to adulthood after the war, under a Labour government, just as Churchill's 'Iron Curtain' was falling across Europe. As a young activist in Colchester and Dartford she reflected grass-roots Tory antipathy to 'socialism' in all its forms, embodied in the domestic context by rationing and vexatious wartime controls and internationally by the Soviet occupation of Eastern Europe and the onset of the Cold War. Above all, their experience of 1939–45 had been quite different: while Heath and his male contemporaries had seen the reality of war in Europe, North Africa and the Far East, Miss Roberts – through no fault of her own, of course – knew it only as a schoolgirl doing her homework under the kitchen table (Grantham was heavily bombed) and later as an Oxford undergraduate rejoicing vicariously at the liberation of

Paris and the fall of Berlin. Moreover from 1942 Lincolnshire was full of American airbases and young American airmen, flying out daily to bomb Germany: this gave the young Margaret a lifelong sense of the United States as Britain's one true ally in the defence of freedom, while the continental Europeans were either enemies to be defeated or feeble collaborators needing to be saved by Anglo-American resolve. While Heath made his life's mission the unification of Europe, Mrs Thatcher as Prime Minister in the 1980s still viewed Britain's European partners with ill-disguised contempt.

They both fought the 1950 election on Churchill's anti-socialist slogan 'Set the People Free', but with significant differences of emphasis, particularly on the question of nationalisation. While Heath routinely condemned public ownership and promised that the Tories would reverse Labour's nationalisation where possible, he clearly – like the party leadership – did not believe it would be possible in many cases; Miss Roberts – fighting on the defiantly combative slogan 'Vote Right to Keep What's Left' – took a much harder line. The tone was set at a rally at Dartford in August 1949 attended by Anthony Eden and all the North Kent candidates. Heath was present on the platform, but it was the young Miss Roberts who was invited to propose the vote of thanks. She capped Eden's cautious promise of no further nationalisation with a ringing defence of free enterprise couched in terms that would have been instantly recognisable thirty years later. Nationalisation, she declared, stifled initiative: 'You cannot have the dream of building up your own fortune, by your own hopes, your own hands and your own British guts.'[5] Even as an obscure young candidate in a hopeless seat the future Mrs Thatcher was already an embryonic Thatcherite.

On polling day she sent Heath a good luck telegram: 'I hope you Gallup to the top of the poll' – one of her few recorded jokes.[6] It can be safely assumed that he did not send her one.* Heath

---

*Mrs Thatcher was always good at gestures of this sort. The next year, when Heath's mother died just before the 1951 election, she sent him what even he in his memoirs called a 'most generous' handwritten letter: 'I am so glad your mother saw your initial success and the way in which you followed it up with a steady ascent to great things.'[7]

scraped in at Bexley with a majority of 133 (helped by a Communist who took nearly 500 votes). Miss Roberts did well to cut Labour's majority by about a third (to 13,638). But by fighting such a vigorous campaign she had forced Labour to keep in Dartford workers who might otherwise have gone to help in Bexley; so Central Office treated her as part of a winning team who should be quickly found a better seat. She attended a victory ball for the candidates who had won their seats, where a famous photograph was taken showing Heath grinning awkwardly between Patricia Hornsby-Smith, who had captured Chislehurst, on one side – one of only six successful Tory women – and the loser of Dartford on the other. Miss Roberts was also invited to the lavish eve-of-session parties thrown by the chairman of the Kent Conservatives, Sir Alfred Bossom, at his house in Carlton Gardens, just as if she had been elected. Her chances of finding a winnable seat, however, were handicapped by the likelihood of another election very soon. The 1950 result had left the Labour government hanging on by a thread: in this situation no sitting Member was going to announce his retirement, so she was obliged to commit to fighting Dartford again. Meanwhile she had met a member of the local party, a wealthy paint manufacturer ten years older than herself named Denis Thatcher. They got engaged just before the 1951 election and were married a few weeks later. This, as she coolly told an interviewer years later, was 'the biggest thing in one's life sorted out'.[8] In the long run marriage gave her the security and financial independence to devote her life to politics. But in the short run motherhood set back her career just when it was taking off.

Meanwhile Heath rose rapidly. He joined One Nation, a group of the brightest younger Tories – including Iain Macleod and Enoch Powell – and made a notable maiden speech urging British participation in the European Coal and Steel Community (the precursor of the Common Market) before he was appointed an opposition whip in February 1951. Within six months of Churchill's return to office that autumn he was promoted to deputy Chief Whip; and in Eden's reshuffle of December 1955 – the same one in which Macmillan replaced Butler as Chancellor – he became Chief Whip. Though in later years the myth grew up that he was a rigid disciplinarian, in fact he was an unusually sensitive Chief Whip, famed for his broad smile and easy manner – one newspaper profile praised his 'skill in human relations'.[9] He won universal admiration for the way he handled both wings of the party during the trauma of Suez, then worked closely with Macmillan to restore party morale; he got his reward in 1959 when he was appointed Minister of Labour (briefly) and then Lord Privy Seal to lead Britain's first application to join the Common Market. Though the application was eventually vetoed by General de Gaulle in January 1963, Heath's conduct of the negotiations won high praise. He was now widely seen as a potential leader.*

The idea that a woman could ever lead the Tory party was beyond the realm of fantasy in 1952. Yet that year – to mark the accession of the young Queen Elizabeth – the new Mrs Thatcher, still seen as a rising star after her exposure at Dartford, wrote a remarkable article in a Sunday newspaper urging more women to go into politics and unequivocally setting out her stall.

> Should a woman arise equal to the task, I say let her have an equal chance with the men for the leading Cabinet posts. Why not a woman Chancellor – or a woman Foreign Secretary?[10]

While still at Oxford she had regretted reading chemistry, realising that law would have been a better training for politics. Now, freed from the need to earn a living, she determined to make up for lost time and set about reading for the Bar. (Denis had to put his foot down to stop her studying accountancy as well.) Soon, however, she was pregnant: undaunted, she gave birth to twins in August 1953, immediately hired a nanny to look after them – a bold thing to do at the time – and sailed through her final exams in December. She specialised in tax law and after a period of pupillage joined chambers in Lincoln's Inn. But the itch to get into Parliament did not lessen. When her twins were barely a year old she tried for Orpington, another suburban Kentish constituency:

---

*His mastery of the detail of food prices led *Private Eye* to nickname him 'The Grocer'. The name stuck and gained ironic piquancy a decade later when he was overthrown by a younger colleague who really was a grocer's daughter.

she was shortlisted but lost to the local Association chairman, thus failing to find a seat in time for the 1955 election. She spoke for neighbouring Tory candidates in Kent and Essex, including Heath in Bexley. But she hated being a supporting player. 'Once you have been a candidate,' she wrote in her memoirs, 'everything else palls.'[11]

From 1957 she set about seriously trying to secure a winnable seat for the next Parliament. As a young mother normally up against older public-school men with good war records, it is not surprising that she failed three times – at Beckenham, Hemel Hempstead and Maidstone: it is a measure of her extraordinary energy and star quality that she succeeded at only her fourth attempt. In 1958 she was selected for the North London seat of Finchley, which she won comfortably the following year and held for the next thirty-three years. Prosperous, suburban and heavily Jewish, Finchley shaped her political outlook as surely as Stockton influenced Macmillan. Once in Parliament she made an immediate mark and was one of the first of the 1959 intake to be given office: after just two years as a backbencher, Macmillan appointed her joint Parliamentary Secretary at the Ministry of Pensions and National Insurance. The work was unglamorous, but she soon displayed an awesome command of detail and a feisty personality in the House. She was disappointed not to be promoted, but stayed at Pensions until the 1964 election. During this time she strongly supported Britain's application to join the Common Market, with no sign of her later reservations about the loss of sovereignty; but she became disillusioned with Macmillan's cloudy ambiguities and was not sorry when he resigned. She seems to have given no thought to Heath or Maudling, but welcomed the succession of Alec Home, whom she recognised, beneath his diffident manner, as a steely Cold Warrior after her own heart – 'an Iron Man in resolve' who had the virtue, 'unfortunately rare among politicians', of saying exactly what he meant without wasting words.[12]

Heath by contrast had been close to Macmillan (though somewhat less so after the failure of the Common Market negotiations). There is no indication that he seriously considered throwing his own hat in the ring in October 1963, despite the backing of

The Times. One poll during the party conference placed him fourth behind Butler, Hogg and Maudling, and the cartoonists regularly included him among those scrabbling for the crown. But the *Economist* judged that 'despite the enthusiasm with which he is undoubtedly regarded by many of the younger members of the party', he was 'thought of more as the next Tory leader but one rather than being in line for the immediate succession'.[13] That was indeed how it turned out. Home's controversial 'emergence' following the shambles of Blackpool delivered the leadership to Heath within two years by ruling all his better-placed rivals, for one reason or another, out of contention. Butler had missed his last chance. Hailsham had blown it by his over-eagerness. Macleod and Powell were damaged by their refusal to serve under Home. Maudling, though still ostensibly the front runner, was diminished by having failed to grasp the prize at the first attempt. As a leader of the new generation of 'classless' modern Tories, Heath should have been as outraged as Macleod and Powell by the elevation of a little-known hereditary aristocrat. In fact he had worked with Home in the Foreign Office and had a good deal of respect for him: he also cannot have failed to calculate that Home's leadership might well prove short-lived and would give him the opportunity to emerge as a more convincing leader to oppose Harold Wilson.

Home made Heath President of the Board of Trade, which gave him the chance to show his modernising paces before the 1964 election by abolishing the outdated system of fixed prices known as retail price maintenance, while Maudling, as Chancellor, further damaged his reputation by presiding over an uncontrolled pre-election boom. When the Tories went into opposition after the election Heath replaced him as Shadow Chancellor and again used the position to lead a powerful parliamentary assault on Labour's first Finance Bill. He denied that he actively caballed to drive Home out; but well before Home decided to step down in July 1965 Heath already had a highly professional campaign team, headed by Peter Walker, set up and ready to spring into action in the event of a vacancy. Mrs Thatcher by contrast wrote that she was 'stunned and upset' when Home resigned. ('I never ventured into the Smoking Room, so I was unaware of these

mysterious cabals until it was too late.')[14] After Blackpool, Home
had introduced a more transparent procedure whereby future
leadership contests would be decided by a direct vote of Tory
MPs. At this first trial of the new system there were only two
serious contenders (though Enoch Powell also stood on a quixotic
free market platform of privatisation and sweeping tax cuts, then
considered so far off the map of practical politics as to be barely
sane). Between Maudling and Heath there was little to choose on
policy, except that Maudling was more sceptical on Europe; both
were roughly the same age, both 'modern' Tories, though Maudling
was a public-school boy from a more comfortable middle-class
background. The contest was therefore all about personality and
image – Maudling relaxed and easygoing, with substantial interests in the City; Heath thrusting, impatient and single-mindedly
focused on politics. Of the two, one might have expected Mrs
Thatcher to be clearly for Heath. (She does not seem to have
considered Powell, though his way-out programme anticipated
what eventually became known as Thatcherism.) In fact her first
inclination was to back Maudling, who was MP for Barnet (part
of the same borough as Finchley), on the ground that 'I liked his
combination of laid-back charm and acute intellect'. She had
known Heath much longer, but their acquaintance, as she later
put it, 'had never risked developing into friendship'.[15] Others,
however, thought Maudling *too* laid-back, to the point of lazi-
ness. It was Keith Joseph, ironically, who persuaded her to switch
to Heath. 'Ted,' he told her, 'has a passion to get Britain right.'[16]
She was convinced, and immediately set about persuading others.
'He will be a hard taskmaster,' she told the *Finchley Press*, 'but
will only drive others as hard as he drives himself.'[17]

Maudling was the favourite and up to the last minute – like
Butler in 1955 – confidently expected to win; but Tory leadership contests – going back to Bonar Law in 1911 and Baldwin
in 1923 – rarely deliver the predicted winner. Heath won narrowly
but decisively by 150 votes to 133 (with just fifteen for Powell).
For a brief honeymoon period he was hailed as the British
Kennedy, a leader of energy and vision fit to take on Harold
Wilson. Very soon, however, when he turned out to be wooden
on television and no match for Wilson at the dispatch box, the

party began to think it had made the wrong choice. Within a year Wilson went back to the country and managed to turn his hair's-breadth majority of 1964 into a comfortable majority of nearly 100. Heath fought a vigorous campaign; but after eighteen months' probation the country was ready to give Labour a proper mandate. Before he was fully established in the job, therefore, defeat cast Heath unfairly as a loser. Though they had elected him precisely because he was a new kind of Tory leader – not another Old Etonian, but the grammar-school-educated son of a carpenter – many Tories were soon sneering at his tortured accent and harking back wistfully to the days of Macmillan and Home. Heath suffered a lot of cruel snobbery at this time. In this respect, as in others, he prepared the way for Mrs Thatcher, taking a lot of social vitriol which she, a decade later, was largely spared. Under this constant criticism, he retreated into his shell: the popular Chief Whip was replaced by a more prickly and defensive character. But he never lost confidence in himself: doggedly he prepared for government, more thoroughly than any previous opposition; and in June 1970 he got his reward. Deceived by the opinion polls, Wilson went to the country confident of re-election. Senior Tories were already sharpening their knives for another leadership contest. But then to general astonishment Heath gained an overall majority of thirty – still the only time since 1945 that a clear majority for one party has been turned into a clear majority for the other on a single night.

During the years of opposition Heath gave Mrs Thatcher a succession of shadow posts, all of which she discharged with exemplary diligence. Once he had eased out the relics of the Macmillan era and appointed his own supporters in their place, Heath kept most of his colleagues in the same shadow post for several years: this was part of his philosophy of preparing for government. The exception was Mrs Thatcher, whom he treated as a useful maid of all work who could be fitted in anywhere: she was switched to a new portfolio every session – first Housing, then a stint in Iain Macleod's shadow Treasury team – Macleod was one of the very few who spotted her potential – then Power, Transport and finally Education: not because he was grooming her – though actually it was very good training – but because he had to put her somewhere. He thought of putting her in the shadow cabinet after the 1966 election, but Willie Whitelaw, then Chief Whip, presciently advised against it. 'Willie agreed she's much the most able,' Heath told his PPS, Jim Prior, 'but he says once she's there we'll never be able to get rid of her. So we both think it's got to be Mervyn Pike.'[18]* With Barbara Castle prominent in Wilson's cabinet he needed one woman in his team, but he had no wish to have two. When Miss Pike stepped down in 1967, however, he had little choice but to promote Mrs Thatcher. Surprisingly, he did not slot her straight into the more conventionally feminine social services vacancy, but gave her the very masculine brief of Power – coal, oil, nuclear and North Sea gas – followed in 1968 by Transport. Then when Edward Boyle retired from politics in 1969 he switched her again to Education, which was the portfolio she was shadowing when the election came.

Heath never had much time for women politicians; but Mrs Thatcher, with her hats and pearls, her cut-glass accent and immaculate hair, was the type he liked least of all. (If anything, he preferred rather mannish women.) She irritated not just Heath but the whole shadow cabinet by talking too much. 'How she talked!' Peter Rawlinson remembered. 'She certainly irked the Leader. Instinctively he seemed to bridle at her over-emphasis. I believe that she honestly did not realise how irritating she was.'[19] Other colleagues complained that she never stopped arguing.[20] In her memoirs Lady Thatcher wrote that she felt marginalised. 'For Ted and perhaps others I was principally there as a "statutory woman" whose main task was to explain what "women" . . . were likely to think and want on troublesome issues.'[21] Perhaps that was why she felt she had to talk so much. But she was not at this time seen as particularly right-wing: in the interest of getting on she had toned down her views since Dartford. Heath later claimed to remember her 'talking a good deal about the interests of the middle class' at a famous shadow cabinet weekend at Selsdon Park in January 1970.[22] But when he moved her to

---

*Mervyn Pike had held a couple of junior positions under Macmillan and Home, but was never a high-flyer. Like most Tory women before Mrs Thatcher she was unmarried.

Education several commentators congratulated him for not choosing a known opponent of comprehensive schools, but 'an uncommitted member of the "shadow" Cabinet who has won a high reputation for her grasp of complex issues'.[23] 'Not so dumb blonde,' the *Sunday Times* captioned a picture of her in 1967. 'Exceptionally able . . . particularly on questions of cash.'[24] The *Sun* now tipped her as a possible future Chancellor;[25] but still no one imagined that a woman, however able, could ever be Prime Minister. The *Sunday Times* priced her at 1,000–1, far behind men like Peter Walker at 10–1 and Prior at 33–1.[26] She herself batted away the question with a typically tart reply: 'No, there will never be a woman Prime Minister in my lifetime – the male population is too prejudiced.'[27]

When Heath formed his real cabinet he confirmed Mrs Thatcher as Education Secretary 'because she had shadowed it so effectively'.[28] In a book entitled *Heath and the Heathmen*, which highlighted the unprecedented number of ministers from lower-middle- or working-class backgrounds, the journalist Andrew Roth included 'the coldly efficient grocer's daughter, Margaret Thatcher' among their number.[29]* Despite her gender, she was seen as an archetypal 'Heathman': a dependable technocrat in her leader's image. In fact she ruffled a few feathers in her first few days in office. As Heath recalled it, 'Instead of explaining her views . . . to her senior officials, she simply marched in with a list of demands which she expected Pile [her Permanent Secretary] to carry out without question. I had to resort to a meeting at Chequers with Margaret, William Pile and the head of the Home Civil Service, Sir William Armstrong, to sort out the problem.'[30] 'The bold and beautiful Minister for Education,' as the Sunday *People* called her,[31] upset the education world by instantly withdrawing her Labour predecessor's circular requiring local authorities to prepare schemes for comprehensive schools; but the effect was mainly declaratory. The tide of comprehensivisation was at its height, and over the next three and a half years – to her subsequent shame – Mrs Thatcher approved more comprehensive schemes

*The others were Anthony Barber (who became Chancellor on the sudden death of Iain Macleod), Peter Walker and Geoffrey Rippon.

than any other Education Secretary before or since. Her most controversial action at the time was to withdraw free milk from primary-school children. Few drank it, and Labour had already withdrawn it from secondary schools; nevertheless, this entirely sensible economy made her the most unpopular minister in the government, pursued wherever she went by chants of 'Thatcher, Thatcher, Milk Snatcher'. In this baptism of fire, Heath stoutly backed her. When the press bayed for him to sack her he invited her again to Chequers to discuss her future plans and praised her warmly in the Commons. 'I like to think that it showed Ted's character at its admirable best,' she wrote in her memoirs, adding characteristically: 'However unreliable his adherence to particular policies, he always stood by people who did their best for him and his Government.'[32]

It is often said that Heath disliked her. He certainly placed her down the far end of the cabinet table on the same side as himself, so that he could not see her and it was hard for her to catch his eye; but she was one of the most junior members of the cabinet, and someone has to sit there. Her penetrating voice and insistent manner unquestionably irritated him: he accorded little weight to her views and – since Education was a pretty marginal department with little input into the major areas of government policy – he did not encourage her to air them. She was therefore – as she had been in the shadow cabinet – pretty isolated. But Rawlinson's recollection that they were 'enemies, naked and unashamed' owes more to hindsight than to truth. 'There was such obvious antagonism between Ted and Margaret,' he claimed in 1989, 'that anyone could have foretold that if ever opportunity presented itself, the political dagger would be cheerfully slipped out of the stocking top and into the substantial frame of her Leader.'[33] But no other member of the government detected such antagonism at the time. She simply was not seen as being that important.*

---

*A telling indication of the way Heath disregarded her was that in his conference speeches, when he generally singled out individual ministers by name to highlight their achievements, he never mentioned her once in four years.

In November 1972 Heath considered switching her to Consumer Affairs – that is, prices – under Peter Walker in the Department of Trade. This would have been a sideways move rather than a demotion, since the new job was still in the cabinet. He probably thought it a suitable job for a woman; but it was a strange time to think of moving her, when she was just about to publish the major education White Paper which she had been working on for the past two years. He still saw her as an uncomplaining dogsbody who could be switched around at will. Had she moved she would have become responsible for the government's ill-fated prices and incomes policy; in fact Walker, given the choice, preferred Geoffrey Howe, who drew the short straw instead. Meanwhile Mrs Thatcher's White Paper projected a 50 per cent rise in education spending over ten years, including a 40 per cent increase in the number of teachers, an ambitious target for free nursery education and continued expansion of higher education. By contrast with her later attitude to public spending, she was an exceptionally effective departmental minister, adept at squeezing money from the Treasury. After her shaky start, she finished up as a widely praised Education Secretary: *The Times* wrote of her 'remarkable political rebirth'.[34] 'I generally left her to get on with her job,' Heath wrote many years later. 'Margaret needed little encouragement in defending her corner and enjoyed the freedom that this gave her, proving very proficient at spending taxpayers' money.' When the oil crisis in late 1973 dictated drastic cuts, 'Margaret Thatcher put up a particularly stubborn fight to protect her greatly expanded Education budget in full.'[35]

But the government itself ended in tears. Heath came into office with ambitious talk of a 'quiet revolution' which aimed to make the British economy leaner, more competitive and more efficient: in opposition he specifically ruled out subsidising 'lame duck' industries or the statutory control of prices. But the attempt to tackle the 'British disease' of unofficial strikes by creating a new legal framework of industrial relations provoked bitter opposition from the unions (which had already defeated a very similar attempt by Wilson and Barbara Castle in 1968). Early in 1972 rising unemployment hit the symbolically resonant figure of one million; and the next month the government was forced to back down in the face of a determined miners' strike which exposed the public to crippling power cuts. Confronted by this triple challenge Heath changed tack. He had honestly tried to inject a more market-driven ethos into the economy: but he was at heart still a product of the post-war settlement. He – and senior colleagues of the same generation like Willie Whitelaw, Robert Carr and Peter Carrington – could not tolerate the return of pre-war levels of unemployment.* Reversing their previous 'hands-off' approach, he and Barber tried to stimulate industry by pouring money into it, then dealt with the resulting inflation – further fuelled by soaring world commodity prices – by introducing the most complex statutory control of prices, incomes and dividends. These two dramatic U-turns – made in response to almost universal pressure from the press – were supported by all but a maverick handful of Tory MPs. Very soon Mrs Thatcher would claim to have been deeply unhappy at the change of policy. But their colleagues were adamant that neither she nor Keith Joseph made any objection at the time. 'Should I have resigned?' she later asked herself.

> Perhaps so. But those of us who disliked what was happening had not yet either fully analysed the situation or worked out an alternative approach. Nor, realistically speaking, would my resignation have made a great deal of difference.[36]

So she kept quiet and got on with her job, gratefully spending the extra millions that were available for education.

Mrs Thatcher was to all appearances a loyal member of Heath's exceptionally united cabinet (which over three and a half years suffered no resignations over policy and few leaks). Not only did

---

*Heath's government was unusually denuded of senior figures with previous cabinet experience. Of his three leading contemporaries, Macleod died four weeks after taking office as Chancellor; Maudling served two years as Home Secretary before being forced to resign by a financial scandal; while Enoch Powell had been sacked from the shadow cabinet in 1968 following his lurid warnings about coloured immigration. Only Alec Home and Quintin Hogg – both back in the Lords with life peerages – survived from the Macmillan years, the former back at the Foreign Office, the latter on the Woolsack.

she offer no opposition to the economic U-turns, but she strongly supported the government's one enduring achievement: British entry into the EEC. This was the high point of Heath's career, the culmination of a ten-year mission to overcome French opposition to British membership. He personally persuaded President Pompidou to lift de Gaulle's veto in May 1971, then – with the help of 69 Labour pro-marketeers led by Roy Jenkins, outweighing 39 Tory dissenters – carried the historic Commons vote for membership by 366 votes to 244. In years to come Lady Thatcher would become stridently anti-European, belatedly echoing the warnings of Powell and others about loss of sovereignty; but in 1972, as she admits, she was 'wholeheartedly in favour of British entry'.[37]

When the government's incomes policy (which had worked pretty well for more than a year) broke on the rock of a second miners' strike in January 1974 – taking advantage of the quadrupling of oil prices following the 1973 Arab–Israeli war – Mrs Thatcher was one of those ministers who favoured an early appeal to the country, believing that the government 'had to pick up the gauntlet, and that the only way to do that was by calling and winning a general election'. She thought the government would have won an election fought 'unashamedly' on the issue of union power. But Heath, now committed to a policy of 'partnership' with industry and the unions, tried desperately to avoid a divisive election and delayed too long. She was frustrated by Heath's 'strange lack of urgency . . . He seemed out of touch with reality . . . more interested in the future of Stage 3 [of the incomes policy] and the oil crisis than he was in . . . the survival of the Government.'[38] By the time he did reluctantly call an election in February 1974 he had missed the moment when he might have won. Still more afraid of winning by an unmanageable landslide than of losing, he fought a strangely half-hearted campaign, and the electorate returned an ambiguous answer. The Tories won 230,000 more votes than Labour; but Labour won four more seats. After trying unsuccessfully to cut a deal with the Liberals (who won nearly 20 per cent of the vote, for a meagre return of fourteen seats), Heath was obliged to resign and Harold Wilson unexpectedly returned to office at the head of a minority Labour government.

At the bleak last meeting of the outgoing cabinet, only one minister felt that she could not let the moment pass without a word of valediction. It was Margaret Thatcher who insisted on speaking 'in emotional terms of the wonderful experience of team loyalty that she felt she had shared since 1970'.[39] Was this hypocrisy, or just her idea of good manners? Probably the latter. In her memoirs she was notably forgiving towards Heath's mistakes in government, as she then saw them. 'With the benefit of two decades' hindsight,' she wrote, 'I can see more clearly how Ted Heath, an honest man whose strength of character made him always formidable . . . took the course he did . . . It is easy to comprehend the pressures upon him.'[40] She could not have guessed that ten years later she would face similar pressures herself. But when she did, she was determined to draw the right lessons from his experience.

1974 was the pivotal year which turned Heath and Margaret Thatcher into rivals. At the beginning of the year he was still Prime Minister, while she was just a loyal but middle-ranking member of his cabinet. By its end she was challenging him for the leadership of the Tory party. Their reactions to the loss of office were diametrically opposed. Heath, bruised by defeat, retreated into defiant refusal to admit any mistakes over the previous three years, insisting that his policies had been right and would have worked if allowed more time. His senior colleagues – Whitelaw, Carrington, Carr, Prior and Walker – all agreed with him. There was bound to be another election very soon: Labour, unprepared for office, was badly split between right and left, pro-Europeans and anti-Europeans. They believed that if they simply held their nerve they would be returned to power. Just one ex-minister initially took a different view. Sir Keith Joseph had been Health Secretary and – with Mrs Thatcher – the other big spender in the late government. A well-meaning but hypersensitive Jewish intellectual with a family background in business, Joseph underwent something like a conversion experience on leaving office when economist friends convinced him that everything the Heath government had done to try to reduce unemployment and inflation had been wrong. First, he was persuaded that only the free market could create employment, while subsidies intended to

preserve jobs actually destroyed them; second, he discovered monetarism, the doctrine developed by the Chicago economist Milton
Friedman which held that inflation was simply caused by having
too much money in circulation. Armed with these two insights
he decided that he had not been a true Conservative up to now
but a 'statist', and set out to convert the Tory party back to
Conservatism. Only one colleague responded eagerly to his new
gospel: Mrs Thatcher. She was cautious at first, characteristically
concentrating on her new job shadowing Environment. She did
not take a leading part in the intellectual ferment which captured
those members of the party who had been disillusioned by Heath's
government. But when Joseph secured Heath's approval to set up
a new think-tank, the Centre for Policy Studies, to study free
market solutions to the country's problems, she 'jumped at the
chance to become Keith's Vice-Chairman'.[41] For his part Heath
was equally slow to grasp that she had shifted position: he probably thought she was too sensible to fall for what he dismissed
as economic mumbo-jumbo. When Joseph was about to blow
party unity apart by making an explosive speech at Preston, Jim
Prior asked Mrs Thatcher to use her influence to try to stop him.
She declined; yet she still did not commit herself publicly to Joseph's
views.

When Wilson called the second general election of the year in
October, Mrs Thatcher was in the forefront of the Tory campaign.
Heath's one new idea to try to reverse the verdict of February
was to appeal to home-owners with a package of blatant electoral bribes, all of which fell into her sphere. Two were policies
she would later make her own: the sale of council houses and
abolition of the rates – though at this stage she was doubtful
about both. But the most controversial was a plan to hold the
cost of mortgages below 10 per cent. This directly contradicted
the free market principles she was just embracing: yet she was
always keen to help middle-class home-owners – those she would
later call 'our people'. So she allowed herself to be bullied by
Heath into promising to peg mortgages at 9.5 per cent. 'I had to
hold a private meeting with Mrs Thatcher and William Whitelaw
to talk her round to supporting these ideas,' Heath admitted.[42]
Her version was that 'I felt bruised and resentful to be bounced

again into policies which had not been properly thought out.' But she had not yet committed herself to Joseph's rebellion: Heath was still the leader and she was still willing to conform to protect her career. 'I thought that if I combined caution on the details with as much presentational bravura as I could muster I could make our rates and housing policies into vote-winners for the party.'[43]

Having once committed herself, however, she was not prepared to modify them. Heath's other pitch for the October election was to advocate a government of national unity. Though Labour still portrayed him as the embodiment of 'confrontation', whose abrasive premiership had provoked industrial conflict culminating in a three-day week, he tried to present himself as a national leader above politics. This was unconvincing, and a hopeless rallying cry for a party fighting an election. Neither Joseph nor Mrs Thatcher wanted anything to do with it. But a week before polling day, when she was due to appear on *Any Questions?*, she was summoned again to see the leader to be told the coalitionist line he wanted her to take. 'I was extremely angry,' she recalled. 'I was not going to retreat from the policies which at his insistence I had been advocating. I went away highly disgruntled.'[44] Instead she went on air and insisted that her housing promises were 'non-negotiable, happen what may'.[45]

The second general election of 1974 was scarcely more decisive than the first: in the circumstances Heath did well to restrict Labour to an overall majority of just three. But he had now lost three elections out of four. He still had the support of most of the shadow cabinet and, perhaps surprisingly, the party in the country; but his remoteness and personal rudeness had alienated a large number of Tory MPs. His best chance of surviving as leader would have been to submit himself to an early vote of confidence, which he might well have won: at this point the dissidents had no convincing challenger to run against him. Alternatively, had he resigned immediately he could have been succeeded by another leader of his own stripe: Willie Whitelaw or Jim Prior. Instead he refused to do either, but stubbornly insisted on carrying on, giving no ground to his critics. The result was that he gave time for the dissatisfaction with his leadership to coalesce around a new figure whom few had hitherto considered as a potential leader: Margaret Thatcher. It was Heath himself who created the conditions in which a rank outsider could emerge to snatch his crown.

Her possible candidacy was discussed in the press, even before the October election. 'Mrs Thatcher, because of sheer ability, is a real contender,' the political editor of the *Sunday Times* suggested, 'despite the apparent handicap that she is a woman.'[46] The *Times* star columnist Bernard Levin thought her 'a gifted and practical politician, whose strength of character belies that Dresden appearance'. But he did not think the party or the country was ready for a woman leader: and he was not sure that she would be an improvement on Heath.

> Besides there is the too-cool exterior (if only she would burst into tears occasionally); if the voters would not warm to Mr Heath they are unlikely to warm to Mrs Thatcher, and there is no point the party jumping out of the igloo and onto a glacier.[47]

More bluntly Enoch Powell expressed a common anti-feminist view: 'They would never put up with those hats or that accent.'[48]*

Mrs Thatcher herself still insisted that the time would not be ripe for a woman Prime Minister – 'unless there really clearly is no alternative man available' – for at least the next ten years. 'Now let's not think beyond that.'[49] But she was now certain that Heath must be replaced at once, and as soon as the election was over she threw her weight behind Joseph. 'By the weekend,' she wrote in her memoirs, 'I had virtually become Keith's informal campaign manager.'[50] Joseph felt obliged to say that he would stand as soon as Heath could be forced to submit himself for re-election; but he was a tortured soul who plainly lacked the nerve for leadership. Almost immediately he made a disastrous speech in which he seemed to suggest that working-class mothers should

---

*Powell had stood down as a Tory MP in February 1974 over opposition to Europe, but returned in October as an Ulster Unionist. Since he was no longer a member of the Tory party, however, he could not be a candidate for the leadership in 1975.

be prevented from having too many children. Vilified as a monster of eugenics, he tried to retract; but his anguished attempts at explanation only exposed him to further ridicule, and soon afterwards he told his principal backer that he could not stand the heat and would not after all be a candidate. Mrs Thatcher, according to her own account, did not hesitate. 'I heard myself saying "Look, Keith, if you're not going to stand, I will, because someone who represents our viewpoint *has* to stand."'[51] With hindsight, it can be seen that her denials that she could or would ever want to be leader were always carefully phrased to leave her a let-out clause. When she told Denis her intention he thought she was mad. But ever since her article in the *Sunday Graphic* in 1952 she had backed her own ability, if ever the opportunity should arise. Now it had arisen, and she seized it.

She still did not expect to win. Like most of the commentators she saw herself as a stalking horse whose purpose in standing would be to flush out other more serious candidates. It undoubtedly took courage to put herself forward; but it was not a gamble that would have ended her career had she failed. By standing she would raise her profile as a candidate for the future – just as Harold Wilson, for instance, put down a marker by standing against Gaitskell in 1960. The *Economist* thought it would simply be good for the party to have an election to let the party choose between Heath and Whitelaw.

> If Mr Edward Heath is capable, under whatever election procedure is devised . . . of being beaten . . . by Mrs Margaret Thatcher, then he is well out of a job . . . Mrs Thatcher is precisely the sort of candidate . . . who ought to be able to stand, and lose, harmlessly.[52]

Heath still saw no need of a contest at all. 'I am the leader of the Conservative Party,' he declared a few days after the October election, 'and my job now is to organise the Opposition. I am getting on with that job and that is what the party has got to get on with.'[53] But his hand was forced by the executive of the backbench 1922 Committee. Since the rules under which he had been elected in 1965 applied only in the event of a vacancy – no one had then imagined the possibility of an incumbent leader being challenged – he was obliged to ask Lord Home to draw up a new procedure. What Home came up with actually made it harder for an incumbent to be re-elected by adding a subtle requirement that the winner needed a 15 per cent margin, not merely of votes but of all those entitled to vote – thus giving crucial importance to abstentions. The new rules, unveiled the week before Christmas, were promptly dubbed 'Alec's Revenge'.

Meanwhile Mrs Thatcher had told Heath of her intention to stand. Punctiliously she went to see him in his room at the Commons. The story that he neither stood up nor invited her to sit, but merely told her 'You'll lose', can only have derived from her. Her published version, years later, was not materially different. 'I need not have worried about hurting his feelings,' she wrote acidly:

> I went in and said: 'I must tell you that I have decided to stand for the leadership'. He looked at me coldly, turned his back, shrugged his shoulders and said 'If you must'. I slipped out of the room.[54]

Heath in his memoirs wrote simply 'I thanked her', while wondering why she bothered to tell him since the weekend papers had already foreshadowed her announcement.[55] There is no suggestion that he was much worried by her challenge, or thought it disloyal of her to stand. He may have thought she would be the first of several hopefuls to throw their hats in the ring: alternatively, like the *Economist,* he probably thought that if she was the best his opponents could come up with he had little to fear.

Even at this stage she would still have withdrawn in favour of someone she regarded as better qualified, and specifically for Edward du Cann, chairman of the 1922 Committee. Du Cann had no cabinet experience, but he was a plausibly self-important businessman who had quarrelled with Heath when serving with him at the Board of Trade in 1963–64; his exclusion from office in 1970–74 meant that he was uncompromised by the failures of the government, and as chairman of the 1922 Committee he was well placed to foment discontent with Heath. He decided, however

– wisely, as it turned out – that his business affairs would not bear the close scrutiny of a leadership campaign: so he too told Mrs Thatcher that he would not be standing. Other imposing names were canvassed: Christopher Soames (Churchill's son-in-law, who had left politics in 1966 to become ambassador in Paris); Julian Amery; Hugh Fraser. Much of the party was still desperate for a throwback to the patrician style of Macmillan and Home; they did not want another Heath. Mrs Thatcher was seen as too strident, too suburban and too lightweight: 'Heath in a skirt,' as one wit called her, or more crudely 'Heath with tits'.* But since none of Heath's other colleagues would break ranks to stand against him, the dissidents had no one else. Du Cann's withdrawal brought into her camp another old enemy of Heath: Airey Neave, a senior backbencher famous for having escaped from Colditz during the war. Neave first tried to persuade Whitelaw to stand, then Du Cann; failing them, he offered his services *faute de mieux* to Mrs Thatcher. He immediately set about organising her campaign and quickly transformed her from a stalking horse into a serious challenger.

Heath unwittingly gave her a perfect opportunity to show her paces by making her deputy Treasury spokesman under Robert Carr. He hoped that her appointment would stiffen the emollient Carr and 'disarm the right'.[56] He should have remembered that it was precisely the position of Shadow Chancellor that he himself had exploited to overtake Maudling in 1964–65. Mrs Thatcher likewise seized her chance by twice taking on and demolishing the Chancellor, Denis Healey, an intellectual bully who tried to patronise her while portraying her as a champion of privilege for opposing Labour's new Capital Transfer Tax. Instead of denying Healey's slur she positively gloried in it, reminding the House of her distinctly unprivileged origins while affirming the middle-class values of property and inheritance which Healey was hypocritically attacking. Demoralised Tory MPs had not heard such fighting talk for years. 'Here was a senior figure,' Nicholas Ridley recalled,

*Later this sort of sexist put-down had to be revised: in reality, the party realised, she was 'Heath with balls'.

'who didn't seem beaten at all: she exuded confidence and certainty. She made a lot of converts.'[57] 'As a result of this two minute speech,' *The Times* wrote the next day, 'far fewer members . . . are speaking dismissively of a woman's candidature . . . than they did a fortnight ago when she announced her challenge.'[58]

When nominations closed on 29 January 1975 there was a third contender: Hugh Fraser, younger son of the sixteenth Lord Lovat, sometime Secretary of State for Air, quixotically put his name forward. As an old-fashioned right-winger more directly critical of Heath than Mrs Thatcher could be, he might have taken votes from her; he also offered an alternative for those who could not bring themselves to vote for a woman. The only effect of his intervention, therefore, was to make it harder still for Heath to win on the first ballot. Over the next week the *Daily Telegraph* gave all three candidates plus some of those who might come forward on a second ballot – Whitelaw, Joseph, Prior and Carr – a platform to set out their vision of 'My Kind of Tory Party'. Once again Mrs Thatcher did not pull her punches, starting from a premise which Heath could not admit:

> To deny that we failed people is futile, as well as arrogant. Successful Governments win elections. So do parties with broadly acceptable policies. We lost . . . One of the reasons for our electoral failure is that people believe that too many Conservatives have become socialists already.[59]

In a speech in her constituency the next day she repeated that line and spelled out still more firmly what she meant:

> If a Tory does not believe that private property is one of the main bulwarks of individual freedom, then he had better become a socialist and have done with it . . . Why should anyone support a party that seems to have the courage of no convictions? . . . I am trying to represent the deep feelings of those many thousands of rank-and-file Tories in the country . . . who feel let down by our party and find themselves unrepresented in a political vacuum.[60]

By contrast Heath's article in the *Telegraph* the day before the ballot was a self-parody of woolly centrism, composed entirely of vague appeals to moderation, harmony ('a fundamental Conservative word') and national unity, while his conclusion was fatuously complacent: 'Let us continue the intellectual renaissance we have started in the new chapter of British politics which lies ahead. Government will then come to us again; and Government will have been deservedly achieved.'[61] With hindsight Mrs Thatcher's more positive appeal seems obvious. As Francis Pym – one of Heath's closest allies – later admitted: 'Amid the shambles and doubts of that time, here was one person who could articulate a point of view with conviction.'[62] Yet it was not obvious at the time. Right up to the ballot neither the press nor the polls – nor even the bookies – took her challenge seriously. The *Telegraph* reflected on the party's problems from a distinctly Thatcherite standpoint, but merely hoped that Heath when re-elected would take more notice of his critics.[63] *The Times* wanted Heath to make way for Whitelaw, but barely mentioned Mrs Thatcher at all.[64] Not one paper either tipped or backed her. A *Daily Express* poll found that 70 per cent of Tory voters still preferred Heath to Whitelaw or any other alternative: while *The Times* reported that 'Constituency Associations in all parts of the country are making known to their MPs that Mr Heath is their preferred leader.'[65] Against this background Airey Neave waged a cunning campaign: instead of talking up his candidate he deliberately played down the possibility of her winning, so that MPs who wanted to get rid of Heath felt they could safely support her as a way of letting Whitelaw enter the contest, with no risk of ending up with her as leader. Few of them knew her very well, so he arranged for her to meet them singly or in small meetings at which she skilfully projected the softer side of her personality, wooing them by listening to their concerns – by contrast with Heath's arrogant remoteness – and careful not to appear too right-wing. If she won she promised to include Heath in her shadow cabinet, but not to bring back Enoch Powell.

In short Mrs Thatcher, under Neave's direction, fought a highly professional and well-organised campaign, rather like Heath's against Maudling in 1965; whereas Heath's this time was complacent and inept – ironically like hers in 1990 when challenged by Michael Heseltine. Heath's team, headed by his two PPSs (Timothy

Kitson and Kenneth Baker), thought they had 130–140 'pledges' – though that was only half the parliamentary party, pretty damning for an incumbent leader. Neave had 120 – but admitted to only about 70, telling waverers that 'Margaret is doing very well, but not quite well enough.'[66] Privately he advised the Labour MP Tam Dalyell: 'Put your money on the filly, Tam, if I were you.'[67] By this tactic a good many left-of-centre MPs who later came to regret it were persuaded not to abstain, as they initially intended, but to back 'the filly' in order to ensure a second ballot. The result when it came was a shock not only to Heath and his senior colleagues but to most of the party. Heath mustered only 119 votes to Mrs Thatcher's 130. (Fraser took 16, with six abstentions and five spoiled ballots.) Not only he but his whole team – not least Willie Whitelaw who was supposed to have a special feel for the mood of the party – had got it all wrong. He resigned at once, appointing Robert Carr as caretaker leader while the final outcome was decided.

Mrs Thatcher had not won outright; but by knocking out the incumbent she had established a clear moral title to the crown. (By contrast Michael Heseltine in 1990 did well enough to force Mrs Thatcher to resign, but not well enough to stop John Major coming forward as a compromise candidate to deny him.) By most reckoning she had won already: it would have been churlish to deny her now, and there was still a strong streak of gallantry among Tory MPs. They admired her courage in standing, and the way she had conducted herself under fire: they were suddenly excited by the novelty of becoming the first major party in the democratic world to elect a woman leader. Whitelaw, having held back when the leadership was his for the asking, now felt obliged to put his name forward; but his heart was not in it and his platform was even more platitudinous than Heath's. Three other candidates – Jim Prior, Geoffrey Howe and John Peyton – also threw their hats in: but there was something cowardly about these male fainthearts emerging from the shadows to try to steal the prize which she had won in open combat. If they had been serious about stopping her they should all have rallied behind Whitelaw. As it was, Mrs Thatcher had too much momentum to be caught. On the second ballot she only picked up another sixteen votes, but she not only had a wide margin over Whitelaw but a narrow overall plurality and that, under the rules, was enough.*

Much of the party was horrified by what it had done. 'There is no reason in logic, history, philosophy or expediency,' Ian Gilmour warned, 'why the Tory Party should join the Labour Party in moving towards the extremes.'[68] But it was not a deliberate turning to the right. Tory MPs had voted for Mrs Thatcher's clarity and freshness, not for her – or Joseph's – ideas, which she had kept studiously vague, talking in terms of values rather than specific policies. They voted for her primarily because she was not Ted Heath. Even supporters like Norman Tebbit who had helped in her campaign were not sure what they had voted for – 'There was little point changing the leader if we were going to be stuck with the same policies';[69] while the *Sun* had no idea what to expect: 'No doubt Mrs Thatcher and her colleagues will quickly work out . . . what Tories really stand for. What is important is that they should once again be clearly seen to be standing for SOMETHING.'[70] In the first dazed moment of her victory she stressed continuity with the recent past. 'To me it is like a dream that the next name in the lists after Harold Macmillan, Sir Alec Douglas-Home [and] Edward Heath is Margaret Thatcher.'[71] But even as she settled into the job, and over the next four years as Leader of the Opposition, she still had to play her cards close to her chest. She was the beneficiary of an unprecedented backbenchers' revolt: the whole of Heath's shadow cabinet had voted against her, yet she had no choice but to keep most of them in place. At the same time the party's instinct was to close ranks behind the new leader: she was helped by the determination of senior figures like Whitelaw, Carrington and Hailsham, who could have made her position impossible had they wished, to lend no encouragement to any hint of factionalism. She was also greatly helped by the graceless behaviour of her predecessor.

Heath took his defeat badly. Less than a year after being rejected

---

*The full result was Thatcher 146, Whitelaw 79, Howe 19, Prior 19 and Peyton 11, with two abstentions.

by the electorate this was his second humiliation in eleven months. 'They are absolutely mad to get rid of me, absolutely mad,' he told the chairman of the parliamentary Labour party, Cledwyn Hughes. He confidently expected to be reinstated before long. Meanwhile he was holding himself 'in reserve'.[72] He sent his formal congratulations and wished Mrs Thatcher 'every success in her new job', making plain his intention to return to the back benches 'for the time being'.[73] She wrongfooted him, however, by calling in person at his house in Wilton Street the day after her election so as to be seen to honour her commitment to offer him a place in her shadow cabinet. The meeting was brief and chilly, and their two camps leaked contradictory accounts of it. Rather like Lloyd George's contested offer of the Woolsack to Asquith in 1918, Mrs Thatcher let it be known that she had offered Heath a place, but that he had refused – supposedly in childish monosyllables, 'Shan't' and 'Won't' – though this is unlikely: she had then invited him to lead the Tory campaign in the upcoming European referendum.[74] He angrily denied both the offer and any discourtesy, insisting that she merely asked his advice about handling the press: 'At no time during the meeting did she invite me to become a member of the Shadow Cabinet or to play any part on her front bench.'[75] Doubtless – like Lloyd George – she did not press him very hard: probably she said something like 'I understand that you do not wish to join the front bench' and got the answer she was looking for. Nevertheless by going to see him – being photographed going in and coming out – she appeared to have extended an olive branch and put the onus on him for having rejected it. She always had a ruthless instinct for a photo-opportunity.

Thereafter, his refusal to acknowledge her victory only damaged himself and embarrassed his friends. He was formally loyal in so far as he did not attempt to lead any sort of faction against her: he merely withdrew into a huff of wounded dignity and tried to ignore her. He would have done better to play the elder statesman and patronise her by ostentatiously offering the benefit of his long experience. He might not have been a great success as leader, but he still had a powerful position in the party: the press, his former colleagues in the shadow cabinet and much of the party in the country still saw him as the one real heavyweight the Tories possessed to put up against the formidable team of Wilson, Callaghan, Healey, Jenkins, Tony Crosland and Barbara Castle on the government side. There were good precedents for a former leader serving under his successor: both Balfour and more recently Alec Douglas-Home had served as Foreign Secretary after being Prime Minister. Had he only been prepared to offer a degree of subtly qualified support, Heath could still have retained serious influence over the next four years and made it impossible for Mrs Thatcher to exclude him from her government in 1979; but through pride, egotism and his stubborn refusal to admit any mistakes he threw it away.

Ironically the first challenge that confronted Mrs Thatcher was the referendum on whether Britain should stay in or withdraw from the EEC, just four months into her leadership in June 1975. The referendum was designed purely to allow Wilson to perform a cynical somersault. Having opportunistically opposed entry in 1971 on the grounds that Heath's terms represented a bad deal, Wilson and Callaghan conducted a cosmetic 'renegotiation' over the summer of 1974 before recommending that the country should stay in after all, while about a third of the cabinet – led by Tony Benn, Michael Foot and Barbara Castle – were allowed to campaign and vote the other way. Europe was a difficult issue for Mrs Thatcher. She was already rather less enthusiastic than she had been in 1962 and 1971; but she could not reverse such a central plank of party policy even had she wanted to, and in fact she still supported British membership. But Europe was quintessentially Heath's issue: taking Britain into the community was the one unquestioned achievement of his government. For a new leader anxious to set her own agenda it was a no-win situation: she had no choice but to campaign for a 'Yes' vote, yet she was bound to be in her predecessor's shadow. Her response was to keep as low a profile as she could get away with and leave it to Ted: she was fortunate that Wilson also took a back seat, which lent some symmetry to the campaign.

Even so, she seemed almost to abase herself when she spoke at the dinner to launch the 'Yes' campaign, with Heath in the chair. 'You have done more than anyone else to ensure Britain's place in Europe,' she told him. 'It is naturally with some temerity that the pupil speaks before the master, because you know more about it than the rest of us.'[76] Twenty-three years later he quoted these words with some relish in his memoirs.[77] During the campaign he duly eclipsed her: he appeared on television twenty-three times to her eleven, drew large and enthusiastic audiences wherever he spoke and was generally credited – with Roy Jenkins – with securing the overwhelming victory of the pro-European cause. 'The quality . . . of Mr Heath's contribution to the referendum debate', wrote *The Times*, 'showed him to be his country's leading statesman, more clearly now than in the height of his power.'[78] In the Commons Mrs Thatcher also paid tribute: 'All of us on this side of the House, and many on the other, would wish to hand the campaign honours to my right hon. Friend the Member for Sidcup.'[79]* But Heath, 'head in hand, stony-faced . . . made no acknowledgement'.[80] His refusal to accept even her praise angered many Tories.

The next month, however, he outpointed her again when the Labour government imposed a flat limit of £6 a week on pay increases. Whatever her personal convictions, Mrs Thatcher was not yet in a position to condemn incomes policy, which was still the only method of fighting inflation that most of her party, or the public, understood. She made a poor speech deriding Labour for being so slow to act, and the opposition weakly abstained. Barbara Castle, a sympathetic observer of her performances from the other side of the House, noted that she had 'flopped', not for the first time, whereas Heath's speech in support of incomes policy later in the same debate was 'by common agreement the best he has ever made. Apparently it made Margaret look like a tinny amateur and speculation began to circulate as to whether she could survive.'[81] She enjoyed only the briefest honeymoon in the polls. But what damages a party most is the appearance of disunity; so Heath's refusal to endorse her drew as much criticism as her failure to stamp her authority. By September Bernard Levin was writing that 'Mr Heath's prolonged fit of the sulks' was doing great damage to the party.[82]

*As a result of boundary changes Heath's Bexley constituency was renamed Sidcup in 1974. In 1983 it changed again to Old Bexley and Sidcup.

Representatives at the annual conference were desperate for some sign of reconciliation. When Heath took his place on the platform he received a standing ovation of astonishing warmth in which Mrs Thatcher was obliged to join. Then as they both rose to leave the platform, 'Mrs Thatcher extended her hand to Mr Heath, rather tentatively, as some observers thought, and Mr Heath unhesitatingly clasped it. There was almost a sigh of relief in the hall that they had got it over.'[83] The next day's papers carried pictures of the two of them smiling fixedly for the cameras, Heath looking like the father of the bride. But still he failed to give the unequivocal endorsement the party was looking for. She in turn, in her triumphant closing speech – she was always better at conference than in the House – paid him another generous tribute; but at the same time subtly consigned him – with Churchill, Eden, Macmillan and Home – to the Tory past.

For the next three years there prevailed a sort of guarded truce – though Mrs Thatcher gave a good deal more ground to accommodate Heath than he did in return. While he continued unapologetically to defend his own record, she – though she continued to develop a ringing rhetoric of enterprise, self-reliance and rolling back the state – was notably cautious in respect of specific policies. The only one of her predecessor's policies she explicitly repudiated was his commitment to Scottish devolution. Stuck as she was with a shadow cabinet still dominated by Heath's largely unrepentant former colleagues her priority was to keep her party united, at least up to the election. She therefore made no promises of tax cuts, barely mentioned the money supply, said nothing at all about privatisation and still did not rule out an incomes policy. 'Thatcherism', if it was more than a twinkle in her eye, was kept very firmly under wraps. The two broad statements of economic policy published in these years – *The Right Approach* in 1976, followed by *The Right Approach to the Economy* in 1977 – were, as *The Times* noted, 'markedly closer to Mr Heath than to Sir Keith Joseph':[84] so carefully fudged that Heath was able to welcome the former as 'essentially a continuation of the mainstream policies of the Conservative Party over many years'. Through gritted teeth he even brought himself for the first time to express 'complete confidence' in 'Margaret Thatcher and her colleagues on the platform' – the emphasis perhaps on the latter rather than the former – and was rewarded with another rousing reception from party members desperate for him not to rock the boat. 'Mrs Thatcher was the first to rise on the platform to applaud him and the whole hall stood in a sustained round of cheers and welcoming back.'[85]

But an open split finally broke out over incomes policy at the 1978 conference. Labour's conference the previous week had rejected the government's 5 per cent norm for pay increases, fore-shadowing a winter of industrial trouble; while Callaghan's postponement of the expected autumn election tore the sticking plaster from the Tory divisions. (Callaghan had replaced Wilson as Prime Minister in April 1976.) Supported by Joseph and Geoffrey Howe, Mrs Thatcher now felt strong enough to repudiate the whole paraphernalia of pay restraint, and in a television interview unambiguously promised the unions a return to free collective bargaining. In a 'stuffy and charmless speech . . . devoid of all the courtesies and graces which the occasion required',[86] Heath heavily rebuked her for saying that Labour's guidelines had already broken down. If that were so, he warned, 'there is nothing for gloating, nothing for joy. We should grieve for our country.' On television himself that evening he openly supported the govern-ment's 5 per cent limit, insisting that 'free collective bargaining produces massive inflation . . . We cannot have another free for all.' Asked if the opposition should learn from his enforced U-turn in 1972 he replied: 'Yes. Why should I go on making the same mistake?' The implication was that Mrs Thatcher was sadly inexperienced, but would quickly bump up against reality if she were to find herself in government.[87]

Not only was Heath explicitly contradicting his leader and her shadow Chancellor; he was giving comfort to Labour by endorsing the central plank of the government's policy. He defended himself by quoting from *The Right Approach to the Economy* to show that it was he who was sticking to the party line, she who was departing from it. Moreover the polls showed that Heath's approach enjoyed greater public support: 71 per cent said they were impressed by his speech to the conference, only 56 per cent by hers. Still more dramatically, the Tories' narrow lead of 3 per cent over Labour soared to 14 per cent if Heath were still leader; when asked which would make the better Prime Minister, 55 per cent said Heath, only 33 per cent Mrs Thatcher.[88] There was no possibility that Mrs Thatcher could be challenged before the election, and Heath denied that he had any such intention; but her position that autumn was perilously weak.

She was saved by the 'Winter of Discontent', when Callaghan's pay policy collapsed in a welter of public sector strikes which finally discredited the whole basis on which Heath had staked his reputation. His position was destroyed, ironically, not by his own failure in 1972–74, but by Callaghan's. With Labour humiliated by the unions just as he had been, the way was now clear for Mrs Thatcher to try a different approach. Callaghan rightly sensed a 'sea-change' in the political climate.[89] Now that the unions were suddenly the overriding issue, Mrs Thatcher was widely seen as the leader most determined to tackle them; the 'softly-softly' approach that Jim Prior had been peddling for the past four years was quickly replaced by tougher language. The Tories' lead in the polls stretched to 20 per cent, and Mrs Thatcher's victory in 1979 seemed to be sewn up.

Heath later claimed that he knew that she would not include him in her government when he read a newspaper interview in February in which she declared that 'As Prime Minister, I couldn't waste time having internal arguments . . . It must be a conviction Government.'[90] Nevertheless he played a prominent and loyal part in the election, drawing large audiences up and down the country, barely mentioning Mrs Thatcher by name but saying nothing controversial: having decided that she was going to win, he seemed to be belatedly staking his claim to the Foreign Office. 'Whenever I have been asked to serve my country,' he declared pompously in a speech at Stirling, 'I have done so.'[91] 'If anyone was going to issue a rebuff,' he wrote in his memoirs, 'it was not going to be me.'[92] For her part Mrs Thatcher firmly refused to name her cabinet in advance. Towards polling day, however, the Tory lead fell steadily, down to about 3 per cent. Again one survey showed it more than tripling if Heath were Tory leader. When another poll gave Labour a narrow lead the party chairman, Peter Thorneycroft, proposed asking Heath to share her final press conference. This was a red rag to Mrs Thatcher. Her speechwriter Ronnie Millar was there. 'Margaret exploded in a mixture of fury and supreme contempt. "Scared rabbits! They're running scared, that's what's the matter with them! The very idea! How *dare* they?"'[93] Thorneycroft's suggestion, she wrote in *The Path to Power,* 'was about as clear a demonstration of lack of confidence in me as could be imagined'.

> If Peter Thorneycroft and Central Office had not yet understood that what we were fighting for was a reversal not just of the Wilson–Callaghan approach but of the Heath Government's approach they had understood nothing. I told Janet Young [party vice-chairman] that if she and Peter thought that then I might as well pack up.[94]

The next day she absolutely refused to share a platform with Heath. 'After all the flak she had taken from him since she replaced him as Leader, she wasn't going to have him come in at the last minute, kiss and make up and claim he'd won the election for her.'[95]

Despite this wobble Mrs Thatcher won quite comfortably with an overall majority of 43. While she was waiting in Conservative Central Office for the call to see the Queen the telephone rang: it was not the Palace, but Ted Heath ringing to congratulate her. She did not take the call, but quietly asked an aide to thank him.[96] Heath also wrote her a note, then went to Wiltshire for the weekend to stay with friends. While he was there, she sent a dispatch rider with a short handwritten letter (coolly signed 'Margaret Thatcher') telling him that after thinking 'long and deeply about the post of Foreign Secretary', she had appointed Lord Carrington 'who – as I am sure you will agree – will do the job superbly'.[97] Heath was not surprised, and let it be known that he intended to stay in the Commons. But ten days later she wrote again inviting him to become ambassador to Washington. There is a long history of Prime Ministers using the Washington embassy as a dumping ground for rivals whom it is inconvenient to have at home: Austen Chamberlain was insulted when offered it by Baldwin in 1923; Lloyd George likewise rejected it from Churchill in 1940; but Halifax in 1941

did not feel able to refuse. To offer it publicly to Heath was a calculated snub. He replied icily that he had already declared his
intention of remaining in the House. 'I am sure you will be able
to find somebody to do the job well.'[98] Some years later he told
an interviewer scornfully that he was 'not cut out to be a postman'.[99]
After the delicate diplomatic dance of the last four years this was
the moment when their relations shifted into open hostility.

From the moment she became Prime Minister Mrs Thatcher
defined herself by *not* being Ted Heath. Free now to cast off her
disguise, she packed the economic departments with the few
colleagues she characterised as 'true believers': Howe at the Treasury
(with John Biffen as Chief Secretary and Nigel Lawson as Financial
Secretary), Joseph at Industry, and John Nott at Trade. Most of
these, it should be said, had been convinced monetarists a good
deal longer than she had. The cabinet was still dominated by Heath's
friends, soon dubbed scornfully the 'wets': Whitelaw (Home Office),
Carrington (Foreign Office), Prior (Employment), Francis Pym
(Defence) and Peter Walker (Agriculture). But Prior was the only
'wet' with any input into economic policy, which Mrs Thatcher
kept firmly in 'dry' hands; it was never discussed in full cabinet at
all. As she and Howe pursued their monetarist experiment – cutting
taxes, cutting expenditure, abolishing exchange controls and
attempting to control inflation by cutting the money supply – against
a background of world recession, manufacturing was devastated
while both unemployment and inflation soared. Very soon there
were squeals of pain not only from the unions but from industry
and business too, supported by most of the press and much of the
Tory party, all calling for a change of direction. It was widely
assumed that – like Heath in 1972 – Mrs Thatcher would be forced
to abandon her radical intentions and perform some sort of U-turn.
She was intensely conscious of the parallel, but was determined not
to follow his example. At the party conference at Brighton in October
1980 she gave her defiant answer (supplied by Millar):

> To those waiting with bated breath for that favourite media catch-
> phrase, the U-turn, I have only one thing to say. 'You turn if you
> want to; the lady's not for turning.'[100]

For the first year or so Heath held his peace, diverting his energy into the Brandt Commission – an international inquiry into the widening 'North–South divide' between the rich developed world and the poor developing and undeveloped world, chaired by the former West German Chancellor, Willy Brandt. Its report, published in June 1980, urged increased aid from the rich countries to the poor and made a considerable public impact – it sold 68,000 copies in Britain alone – but Heath's passionate advocacy was enough to ensure that Mrs Thatcher totally ignored it. By now Tory alarm at the effect of the government's policies was beginning to mount as a succession of senior figures, headed by the eighty-six-year-old Harold Macmillan, called for a change of tack. Still Heath kept silent until, three weeks after Mrs Thatcher's conference speech, he suddenly cracked: he was sitting in a television studio at three o'clock in the morning commenting on the American presidential election when Milton Friedman came on the line from Chicago. Thus provoked, he exploded: Friedman's 'ruinous monetarism', he charged, had bankrupted British industry and pushed unemployment up to nearly three million, compared with just 600,000 in 1973. 'People realise now what the merits of the last government, the last Conservative government, were, compared with the catastrophic things they see happening to themselves today.'[101] In the Commons next day, however, Mrs Thatcher hit back effectively by quoting Heath's own words in his foreword to the 1970 Tory manifesto:

> Once a decision is made, once a policy is established, the Prime Minister and . . . colleagues should have the courage to stick to it. Nothing has done Britain more harm in the world than the endless backing and filling which we have seen in recent years.

She was sure that Heath would now agree that the government should have the courage to stick to its policy. In his front row seat below the gangway, *The Times* reported, 'Mr Heath looked decidedly uneasy.'[102]

But he had only voiced what a lot of Tory MPs were thinking. Three weeks later, he intervened on the last day of the debate on the Queen's Speech to launch a more sustained indictment. 'Our generation,' he asserted simply, 'came into politics to prevent unemployment.' Yet now unemployment was rising again to the levels of the 1930s. Strict monetarism was defeating its own ends. 'The cost of unemployment produced by the present interest rates' – then standing at 16 per cent – 'is greater than the interest rate benefit itself.'[103] Now it was the Tory benches who heard him in uncomfortable silence. But the next day Mrs Thatcher used a radio interview to repeat that it was the reckless spending and borrowing of previous governments which had created the problem in the first place; there was 'no alternative' to sound money, however painful it was to achieve it.[104] She reiterated that 'There Is No Alternative' so often that the press nicknamed her 'Tina'.

In the summer of 1981 riots in London, Liverpool, Bristol and a dozen other cities seemed to bear out the critics' warnings of the social consequence of unemployment. While Mrs Thatcher insisted that 'Nothing, but nothing, justifies what happened', Heath had no hesitation in blaming the government's 'incomprehensible policies'.[105] He still called explicitly for a U-turn, and reacted angrily when he was attacked for being disloyal or 'wet'.

> I object to the whole level of political discussion at the moment, that there must never be a U-Turn, that people are 'wet' or 'dry' and so on. This is childish . . . If a Government finds that circumstances change . . . is it not stupid to say we must not change anything we have been doing or which we planned four years ago?[106]

In July Mrs Thatcher faced a cabinet revolt: even two of her 'true believers', Nott and Biffen, abandoned her. Her response was a comprehensive reshuffle in which she sacked three of the less prominent 'wets' and exiled Prior to Northern Ireland, promoting in their place three younger men whom she could rely on to support her – Nigel Lawson, Cecil Parkinson and Norman Tebbit. This was the clearest possible assertion that she did not intend to change course. But Heath only stepped up his critique. Just before the party conference he launched 'his fiercest attack so far' on the folly of monetarism. 'If more than three million unemployed are needed to get inflation down to a level higher than it was 2½ years ago,' he demanded, 'how many more millions

of unemployed will be required to bring it down to . . . to what
level? – to a level that has never been revealed?'

> Many of us have remained almost silent for a long time . . . perhaps
> for far too long, in order that the dire consequences of the present
> dogmatic policies could be widely recognised . . . The time has come
> to speak out . . . It is imperative in our present circumstances . . .
> that we should make a completely fresh assessment of Conservative
> economic policy.

He proposed a package of policies, including a programme of
capital investment and a 'massive' retraining programme. 'The only
alternative is to drag on down the dreary path of ever-deepening
recession.' To the charge that such expenditure would fuel inflation
he retorted – still defending his own record – 'How dare those
who run the biggest budget deficit in history reproach others with
the heinous crime of printing money?'[107]

This 'devastating speech', *The Times* judged, showed that Heath
was still the government's 'most weighty' critic. 'This time the
Conservative reflex which brands him as disloyal will be struggling with a growing suspicion . . . that he is saying exactly what
needs to be said.'[108] But this time Mrs Thatcher got her retali-
ation in first. Heath's advance text, advocating 'a return to consensus
politics', reached her on a visit to Australia. From the other side
of the world she pre-empted him with a 'blistering retort':

> Consensus seems to me to be the process of abandoning all beliefs,
> principles, values and policies . . . It is something in which no-one
> believes and to which no-one objects . . . It is the process of avoiding
> the very issues that have to be solved . . . What great causes have
> ever been fought and won under the banner of 'I stand for
> consensus'?[109]

At Blackpool Heath repeated his argument more moderately
and was heard respectfully. But the conference still backed Mrs
Thatcher – though it was actually Howe who answered him most
effectively; she was relatively conciliatory, while still insisting: 'I
will not change just to court popularity.'[110] In fact she did tack
significantly. Recognising that the strict monetary targets they had

been aiming at were unrealistic, Howe quietly adjusted the targets and introduced a much less draconian budget in 1982 than in 1981, with some modest inducements to industry. This allowed Heath jubilantly to announce 'the death of monetarism':

> His action is pragmatic . . . and I congratulate him on it . . . We have won the intellectual battle against monetarism and dogma . . . The alien doctrines of Friedman and Hayek remain only to be buried.[111]

His purpose was plainly to proclaim that the Lady had performed her U-turn. But strict monetarism turned out to be just the top dressing of Thatcherism, not its essence. Its abandonment did not imply any weakening of Mrs Thatcher's determination to achieve her broader purpose. Economists still argue over whether the government's harsh measures in 1979–81 promoted recovery or postponed it; either way, the economy did start to recover from the third quarter of 1981, and with it – slowly – the government's popularity. From a nadir at the end of the year, when Mrs Thatcher was the most unpopular Prime Minister since polling began, facing the prospect of almost certain defeat at the next election if she was not removed by her colleagues first, she was just beginning to look as if she might have turned the corner when the whole political situation was transformed by the Falklands war. This crisis, largely of her own making, could easily have ended her premiership in humiliation and disgrace, as Eden's was by Suez; instead she turned it to her advantage by a bravura display of nerve and supercharged patriotism which – with the professionalism of the forces and a good slice of luck – lifted her to a level of popularity and personal dominance which she was able to sustain for the next seven years. She resisted the temptation to hold a 'khaki' election immediately the war ended; but the 'Falklands Factor' swept her back to office with a landslide majority twelve months later in June 1983.

The Tories actually won fewer votes, and a slightly smaller share of the electorate, than in 1979; but this reflected the intervention of the Social Democratic Party, founded in 1981, which took more than three million votes, mainly but not entirely from Labour.

It was the almost equal division of the opposition between Labour and the SDP/Liberal Alliance which accounted for Mrs Thatcher's inflated majority of 144. There was some speculation that Heath might join the SDP; but there was never any chance of that. His purpose was to convert the Tory party back to what he regarded as true Conservatism – not to concede the field to Mrs Thatcher. The 1983 election, however, ended whatever hope Heath had of overturning the verdict of 1975 and staging any sort of comeback. Hitherto his form of slightly soggy 'One Nation' Conservatism had enjoyed a legitimacy within the party at least equal to her more radical blend of free market liberalism and 'Victorian values'. After 1983, however, for the remainder of the decade, Thatcherism swept all before it, as the triumphant 'Iron Lady' and her sycophantic acolytes jubilantly consigned not only Heath and the former 'wets' but the whole legacy of recent Tory governments – Macmillan and Butler as well as Heath – to the scrapheap of history: they were all virtual socialists who had merely alternated indistinguishably with Labour governments in feather-bedding industry, appeasing the unions and stoking up inflation and unemployment, until Mrs Thatcher had arrived in the nick of time to stop the rot, reverse the inexorable decline and lead Britain to recovery by banishing socialism at home as resolutely as she had driven the invader from the Falklands. That was the heroic myth, and it contained enough truth to leave Heath discredited and almost totally isolated. The last of the old 'wets' were purged from the government – though Willie Whitelaw soldiered on loyally till 1988; while the rising generation of younger Heathites – Douglas Hurd, Kenneth Baker and John MacGregor (who had all served as his private secretary); William Waldegrave (who had served in his 'think tank'); Chris Patten (who had been chairman of the Research Department) – hastened to reinvent themselves as good Thatcherites, accepting the new orthodoxy. Heath himself was virtually written out of the party's history, like Trotsky in the Soviet Union: either an embarrassment never to be mentioned, or a pantomime villain. Once he had accepted the role in which he was now irrevocably cast Heath rather relished his isolation: he did not abandon the House of Commons but sat massively immobile on the front bench below the gangway, impervious to the mockery of the loyalists behind him, intervening occasionally to call down his solitary anathemas on the government – attacking almost everything Mrs Thatcher did. He was applauded only by the Labour benches, which forgot that they had once demonised him as the most right-wing Tory since Genghis Khan and now recognised him as a more powerful embodiment of anti-Thatcherism than the blustering and lightweight Neil Kinnock could ever be.

Heath's unmitigated opposition actually played into Mrs Thatcher's hands. He was so untouchable within the Tory party that his scathing criticism – of privatisation, trade union reform and her handling of the miners' strike; of rate-capping and the abolition of the Greater London Council; of the continuing high level of unemployment (until it eventually turned down in 1986), Nigel Lawson's tax cuts and Baker's educational reforms – ensured that whenever a possible revolt threatened no ambitious back-bencher would wish to be seen in the same lobby with him. His criticism, however cogent, could always be ascribed to jealousy deriving from his inability to accept his defeat in 1975, now widely described as the 'longest sulk in history'. Of course there was a large element of sour grapes in his attitude: but on many issues he articulated a powerful case against the centralisation, middle-class bias and social divisiveness of the government's policies, as well as the Prime Minister's increasingly autocratic style. The trouble was that his own performance in office left him vulnerable to withering retorts. When in May 1988 he called Mrs Thatcher 'divisive, authoritarian and intolerant', *The Times* recognised some truth in the charge but chided that 'in the light of his own record as Prime Minister he is the last Conservative politician' entitled to make it.[112] The cruel truth was that, by every critical test, Mrs Thatcher had succeeded where he had failed. She had held her nerve in 1981 and not been seen to perform a U-turn; helped by unemployment and a change in public sentiment after the 'Winter of Discontent' she had finally taken on and broken the power of the unions; most symbolically she had avenged Heath's humiliating defeats at the hands of the miners in 1972 and 1974. And she was an electoral winner – after 1987 a triple winner – whereas under his leadership the Tories had lost three elections out of four.

On one issue above all others Heath attacked with real conviction. For most of her first two terms he actually made little complaint about Mrs Thatcher's approach to Europe. He thought she was 'quite right' to try to renegotiate Britain's contribution to the Community budget, which had been set too high in 1972, though he criticised her intransigent methods. He thought the settlement which she finally achieved in 1985 'fair and just', and in his memoirs positively congratulated her on it.[113] He also welcomed her support – in her most pro-European phase – for the Single European Act which, he later pointed out, was whipped through Parliament in just twelve days in 1986 compared with the forty-nine days' debate on the original Accession treaty in 1972.[114] In this respect alone he could claim that she was building on his achievement. But when – from about 1988 – she turned against the Community with increasingly lurid warnings that the French President of the Commission, Jacques Delors, was trying to transform it into a 'European superstate' with a central bank, a single currency and 'some identikit European personality',[115] Heath felt compelled to respond. 'In the eyes of the public, I was the man most associated with Europe and I could not stand back and watch history, and my own record, being grossly misrepresented.'[116] In May 1989, in defiance of the convention that political opponents should not criticise the government when abroad, he deliberately went to Brussels (where she was attending a NATO summit) to answer her. 'I have come here today,' he declared, 'to wipe away the stain . . . left behind . . . last September by what is now known as the Bruges Speech by the British Prime Minister.' He went on to ridicule her ignorance and distortion of history, trusting that the British people would 'reject such false populism and such distortions of the truth for the patronising, self-serving hypocrisy that they are'.[117] The outcry was terrific. The *Daily Telegraph* denounced his speech as 'disgraceful' and 'an ill-bred performance'.

> In other circumstances, his crushing loneliness and political disappointment would command sympathy. As it is, his behaviour yearly diminishes the dignity of the place he can expect in the history of the Conservative party, and of post-war British politics. The best service Mr Heath can now offer to the state is his silence.[118]

But Heath had the last laugh. Three weeks later, following a crassly negative campaign ('Stay at home on 15 June and you'll live on a diet of Brussels'), the Tories suffered a heavy defeat in the European elections. Though the elections themselves were unimportant this was Mrs Thatcher's first defeat since becoming leader in 1975, a portent which signalled the beginning of the end of her long hegemony. Several other factors contributed to her government's slow disintegration, not least the ill-fated poll tax. This derived, ironically, from Mrs Thatcher's pledge, at Heath's insistence, to abolish the rates back in 1974. But her promise then, as Heath did not fail to point out, was to replace them with 'taxes more broadly based and related to people's ability to pay'. The flat rate poll tax by contrast was 'a reactionary regressive proposal' which, he accurately predicted, 'will always be held against us'.[119] This was one issue on which Heath's clear-sighted opposition attracted a substantial backbench revolt; but it was still not enough to deflect the Prime Minister from her folly. The poll tax may have been more damaging in the country; but at Westminster, and particularly within the cabinet, it was her furious hostility to Europe which alienated her colleagues: first Nigel Lawson in November 1989, then Geoffrey Howe a year later, resigned over disagreements originating in her determined obstruction of any form of further European integration. The knife was wielded by Michael Heseltine, who had also resigned over a Europe-related issue back in 1986. Heath played no part in the final drama of her downfall – he had the good sense for once to hold his tongue – but he was naturally delighted by the outcome, and especially by the fact that the immediate cause of her defeat was Europe: *his* issue, which made it in some sense his vindication.* When the news of her resignation came through he telephoned his office with a gleeful instruction to 'Rejoice! Rejoice!' – a reference to her famous celebration of the recapture of South Georgia during the Falklands war – and bought his staff champagne.[120]

---

*Mrs Thatcher beat Heseltine comfortably by 204 to 152; but she was four votes short of the margin required under Home's revised 1975 rules to win on the first ballot. Thus 'Alec's Revenge' did for her too in the end.

Heath voted for Douglas Hurd on the second ballot. Mrs Thatcher threw her weight behind John Major as her favoured heir; but it was soon clear that Major was no Thatcherite, and she became swiftly disillusioned with him – particularly for failing, as she thought, to hold a sufficiently firm line on Europe. Heath by contrast welcomed Major's emergence as a return to the sort of consensual pro-European Conservatism he had always stood for, which he portrayed as a return to the mainstream after the 'aberration' of Thatcherism: 'At last we are beginning to shed the albatrosses that have weighed us down over the last few years . . . To hear John Major say that he wants Britain to be at the heart of Europe,' he enthused, 'was truly welcome.'[121] But while Major tried desperately to hold his party together on the European issue which eventually broke his premiership too, his two predecessors placed themselves more outspokenly than ever at the head of the opposing factions. When Mrs Thatcher used a speech in New York to mount her strongest assault yet on the whole concept of European union – proposing instead a much looser Atlantic free trade area – Heath responded furiously in an interview for Channel Four News. 'At times,' the *Daily Mail* reported, 'his rage was so intense that he was almost spluttering. Several times he refused to allow presenter Jon Snow to interrupt him as he blasted the woman who ousted him from the Tory leadership.'[122]

> Mrs Thatcher is entirely out of touch with events in this country. She does not realise the situation John Major is having to deal with; she does not realise she was the cause of it; and she doesn't realise that in Europe she is regarded as not just irresponsible but entirely not to be considered at all in any way . . . She goes on talking about the results of freedom in this country; she shows no appreciation of the ghastly legacy she has left her successor.[123]

This was 'the most extraordinary attack ever by one former Prime Minister on another'.[124] The papers likened them variously to Punch and Judy or Darby and Joan – 'dinosaurs wrestling in mud' or 'ferrets in a sack'.[125] But the predominant view was that Mrs Thatcher had invited Heath's rebuke by the disloyalty of her undermining of Major, which was more damaging than anything he had ever said about her. He drove home his advantage in an article in the *Mail* a few days later:

> Mrs Thatcher's utterances have come as no surprise to me, for I have come to expect them, but I have been incensed by the way she has chosen to run away to America, where sympathetic and ill-informed audiences will flatter her vanity, rather than face up to the reality in Britain . . . I will offer her a challenge. I propose a television debate between us . . . in which the question of Europe could be fully aired.[126]

Mrs Thatcher, however, let it be known that she was treating Heath's challenge 'with the contempt it deserves'.[127]

That autumn Heath made a point of attending the whole of Major's first party conference as leader, sitting prominently on the platform every day – except the morning that Mrs Thatcher made a regal appearance, and received a rapturous reception, when he stayed away. Major tried to present himself as the heir equally of 'the builder's son from Broadstairs' and 'the grocer's daughter from Grantham', and praised them both – which must have been gall to Mrs Thatcher – for forging Britain's place in Europe.[128] When Parliament reassembled the two titans clashed directly for the first and only time in the Commons after Mrs Thatcher made a storming speech denouncing the forthcoming Maastricht treaty as a 'conveyor belt to federalism' and demanding a referendum before it was approved.[129] The next day Heath magisterially rebuked her, quoting her own words against the 1975 referendum. The House held its breath as Mrs Thatcher, sitting two rows behind on the other side of the aisle, rose to intervene. 'I know that I inherited that position from him,' she conceded, 'and I loyally upheld it' – emphasising the word 'loyally'. But now, she asked him, if all three parties supported the single currency, how were the people to make their views known? 'This occurs constantly in parliamentary history,' he replied loftily; the voters could make their views known 'in a variety of ways'. Mrs Thatcher did not press her question, and the moment passed.[130] But the next day she returned to the attack on television, calling Major 'arrogant and wrong' for refusing a referendum. The spectacle of Mrs Thatcher calling her diffident successor arrogant caused great amusement. Major, *The Times* reported, was 'said to be furious at the stream of disparaging remarks from his predecessor . . . He shares the view of senior Tory figures that Edward Heath's criticism of her leadership pales into insignificance when compared with the damage she is causing to the party's re-election prospects.'[131]

In fact she was happier with Maastricht than Heath was: he was as disappointed as she was pleased by the concessions Major succeeded in negotiating which allowed Britain to opt out of the single currency and the so-called 'social chapter'. Nevertheless he insisted on treating these concessions as purely tactical: at the general election in May he campaigned not just – as he had done in 1983 and 1987 – for the return of a Conservative government, but expressly for Major, whom he placed in a pantheon of Tory leaders from Churchill to the present, with just one name missing. He even spoke in Major's Huntingdon constituency. Mrs Thatcher was outwardly loyal, and appeared with Major at a rally for Tory candidates, but otherwise played a low-key role; she herself was leaving the Commons for the Lords, and spent the last week of the campaign in America. Within days of Major's unexpected victory, however, an interview appeared in the American magazine *Newsweek* in which – clearly anticipating his defeat – she damned him with the faintest praise and scornfully declared that there was 'no such thing as Majorism'.[132] For the next five years of Major's unhappy premiership Lady Thatcher, as she now was, never let up in her coded disparagement of the Prime Minister and sometimes overt support for those of his colleagues and the hard core of Eurosceptic backbenchers who made his life impossible. She even dropped hints of support for Labour's new leader, Tony Blair, suggesting that if elected he would 'not let Britain down'.[133] (If her criterion was that Blair would not reverse her key policies and would cleave to America even more closely than she had done, she was proved right.) After Major's defeat in 1997 she continued to breathe unhelpfully down the neck of his successors, William Hague and Iain Duncan Smith, until advancing age and a series of minor strokes in 2002 eventually reduced her to silence.

Heath meanwhile refused to retire. He accepted the Garter in 1992, but stayed in the Commons until 2001 – by which time he was nearly eighty-five – doing his best to support Major and his still broadly pro-European senior colleagues (Heseltine, Hurd and

Kenneth Clarke) but increasingly angry at the Tory party's inexorable slide into Europhobia, which on the issue which had furnished
his one historic achievement threatened to give his old nemesis the
victory after all. The two former Prime Ministers met occasionally
at state dinners and the party conference – once they were made
to sit uncomfortably together in armchairs at the side of the platform – when they sometimes managed to make polite conversation
for the cameras but were more often caught determinedly avoiding
eye contact. There were no more direct clashes. In her memoirs –
published in 1993 and 1995 – Lady Thatcher was surprisingly
generous to Heath, recognising that he had promoted and backed
her between 1970 and 1974 and unwittingly given her the opportunity which she had seized in 1974–75; in his – finally published
in 1998 – he was much less so to her. He never admitted that she
had been anything but a disaster for Britain; had she died first he
would have struggled to pay any sort of tribute. As it was, when
he died in July 2005, her office put out a brief but subtly self-
serving statement calling him 'a political giant'.

> He was also, in every sense, the first modern Conservative leader
> – by his humble background, his grammar school education and
> by the fact of his democratic election.

In all these ways, of course, he paved the way for her; just as the
failure of his premiership had paved the way for her success.

> As Prime Minister, he was confronted by the enormous problems of
> post-war Britain. If those problems eventually defeated him, he had
> shown in his 1970 manifesto how they, in turn, would eventually be
> defeated. For that, and much else besides, we are all in his debt.[134]

* * *

Mrs Thatcher emphatically 'won' her duel with Heath. She not
only challenged him successfully for the Tory leadership in 1975,
but went on to win three general elections and serve eleven and a
half years as Prime Minister, recasting not only the party but the
whole political landscape according to her own ideas. She had set
out to banish 'socialism' – in which she contemptuously included

Heath's form of centrist Conservatism – and succeeded beyond her wildest expectations. After eighteen years of Tory rule the Labour opposition – re-branded 'New Labour' – could make itself electable only by scrapping practically all its old beliefs and values; once elected in 1997, Tony Blair governed unapologetically within the free market, business-friendly orthodoxy established in the 1980s. Heath's world of subsidies and incomes policies, strikes and power cuts, in which government appeared to be possible only by permission of the unions, was a distant nightmare from which the country had been mercifully released. Of course Mrs Thatcher did not single-handedly bring about this transformation; but she led it, articulated it and gave her name to it, as surely as Heath – along with Wilson and Callaghan – embodied the dark days that had gone before. In the heroic mythology of Thatcherism his misguided corporatism was the dragon she had slain to save the country. Yet it was not quite so simple as that. As her back-handed tribute to him implied, the first stirrings of what became Thatcherism had been visible in the late 1960s, as the post-war settlement within which all governments – Labour and Conservative – from Attlee to Wilson had operated more or less unthinkingly began to fall apart. Heath in his 1970 manifesto had tried to trim his sails to this breeze, adopting some of the language of markets and competition; but as soon as unemployment rose and the unions dug their heels in, he turned tail. Not only were he and his senior colleagues creatures of the post-war settlement, but public opinion was not yet ready for a new approach. The unions – above all the miners – were still both powerful and popular. Heath was driven ingloriously from office after the humiliation of the Three-Day Week. It took another five years of strikes, economic failure and threat of social breakdown before the 'Winter of Discontent' gave Mrs Thatcher her chance. Even then public opinion was not ready: in 1980–81 she was the most unpopular Prime Minister ever, with riots in the cities and half her party on the brink of open revolt, before the Falklands war and the beginnings of economic recovery saved her. Only after 1983 was she able fully to impose her hegemony.

The point is that she was lucky, as successful politicians have to be: her ideas – or rather the instincts which she had revealed at Dartford way back in 1950 – came into their own just at the moment when an unlikely combination of circumstances gave her the opportunity to embody them. She did not invent 'Thatcherism': she was merely the British embodiment of a revolt against collectivism which swept the world in the last quarter of the twentieth century from China to Peru. But she rode her good fortune, and by her courage, clarity and showmanship deservedly triumphed. Heath, by contrast, was an unlucky politician. Serious-minded, well-intentioned and formidably equipped, ten years earlier or ten years later he might have been, with all his faults, a great Prime Minister; but he achieved office just at the moment when the political weather was changing and – sailor though he was – he could not change his sails fast enough to catch the new wind. The economic tempest of the early 1970s sank him, as it sank most other democratic leaders in that decade. In personal terms he made it worse for himself by his inability to accept what was happening. By stubbornly clinging to office after his defeat he created the opportunity for Mrs Thatcher to challenge him; over the next fifteen years, by his refusal to give her any credit he allowed her to marginalise and demonise him. But her success was founded on his failure; the country had to go through his attempts first to sort out the unions, then to deal with inflation and unemployment by the old tripartite methods one more time, before it would accept that the post-war system was irretrievably broken. Heath and Thatcher were rivals, enemies even, who came to embody opposite approaches to the nation's problems. One 'failed'; the other – at considerable social cost – 'succeeded'. But they represented different stages of the same process. Margaret Thatcher was a continuation of Ted Heath by other means. And in the longer run of history, his taking Britain into Europe in 1973 will probably turn out as important as her transformation of the economy in 1979–90. So he may yet have the last laugh.

Gordon Brown and
Tony Blair

Gordon Brown and Tony Blair are different from every other pair in this book because they were friends before they became rivals. This gave a sharp personal edge to their rivalry lacking in most of the others. Though their backgrounds are very different and they came into politics by different routes, they are near-contemporaries and entered Parliament in the same year. Of all the other pairs discussed, only Castlereagh and Canning were closer in age: most of the others were separated by the best part of ten years and became rivals, through the accidents of politics, more or less unexpectedly. In every case but one – Macmillan over Butler – the younger prevailed over the elder. In fact it is remarkable how rarely over the past two hundred years contemporaries from the same parliamentary cohort have competed directly with each other for the top job. Brown and Blair are the exception.

Yet in an important sense they are not of the same generation at all. Though born only two years earlier, Brown left school four years before Blair: he went to Edinburgh University at the age of sixteen in 1967, while Blair went to Oxford only in 1971: in those four years the youth revolution of the late 1960s transformed society in general, and student life in particular, almost out of recognition. Even as a student Brown always seemed old for his years, while Blair remained extraordinarily youthful even in middle age. From his teens onwards Brown steeped himself single-mindedly in Labour politics, so that by the time he finally secured a winnable parliamentary seat at the age of thirty-two he was an experienced and battle-hardened politician. Blair by contrast was a late developer who drifted into politics with no very clear convictions before he was fortunate to land a safe seat at the age of thirty.

For their first ten years in the Commons Brown was almost universally seen as a future Labour leader, Blair as a promising junior partner to his far more experienced friend. But this relationship was reversed almost overnight by the sudden death of John Smith in 1994, less than two years into his leadership. With a hitherto unsuspected ruthlessness, Blair leapfrogged his friend to snatch the inheritance which Brown had expected would be his. Brown never forgave what he saw as an act of betrayal, and his abiding sense of grievance poisoned their friendship. Though Brown had to cede first place, however, Blair was obliged to concede Brown an unprecedented degree of shared power when Labour regained office in 1997. For ten years they formed, on paper, the most enduring and successful partnership of Prime Minister and Chancellor in modern politics, surpassing the seven years of Asquith and Lloyd George. Despite the unresolved tensions they managed for some time to work effectively together. But the double-headed government became increasingly strained, as Blair repeatedly defaulted on what Brown understood to be a promise to hand over to him some time in the second term. As a result they constantly obstructed each other, and in the end achieved less together than they should have done. Eventually Blair was forced to step down earlier than he had wanted, but later than Brown had hoped. By a last bitter irony, when Brown finally gained his life's ambition at the age of fifty-six he found it a poisoned cup.

Gordon Brown was born in February 1951 in Glasgow, though his parents moved to Kirkcaldy in Fife – on the other side of Scotland – when he was five. His father was a Church of Scotland minister whose house was always open to the poor and unlucky, and young Gordon – the second of three brothers – was raised in a strong family ethic of Christian socialism. He was a clever, serious-minded boy, and keen on sport as well; he was fast-tracked through grammar school by a local authority scheme which sent him to university at sixteen. But in his first year he suffered a rugby injury which cost him the sight of one eye and nearly left him completely blind: to save his second eye he had to lie in a darkened room for six months – a frightening experience from which he emerged with an exceptional sense of driven purpose. When he recovered, he threw himself into student journalism, becoming editor of the university newspaper in his second year, and student politics, at the high tide of campus militancy, while still working hard enough to take a First in politics and modern history. He stayed on to start a doctorate on Scottish Labour politics between the wars, then as a postgraduate was elected Rector of the university. The holder of this hitherto largely honorific post, unique to the Scottish universities, was elected by the students: putting up their own candidate, instead of the usual absentee celebrity, was a stunning coup since it gave a student the right to chair the university court. When the Vice-Chancellor and the university authorities tried to change the statutes to prevent this, Brown took them to court and won. At twenty-two he was already engaged in serious politics.

Tony Blair's background was very different. Where Brown was thoroughly rooted in the Scottish Church, Scottish politics and the Scottish education system, Blair's heritage and early life were Anglo-Scots-Irish and curiously rootless. His father Leo was the illegitimate child of English music hall artistes who gave him up for adoption by a Glasgow docker and his wife (named Blair). Leo was an active Young Communist in the 1930s whose life was transformed by the Second World War: on coming out of the army he worked initially as a tax officer while studying law at night, became a law lecturer and then a barrister, having married a Protestant Irish girl from Donegal. Tony, their second son, was born in May 1953 in Edinburgh, but spent his early childhood in Australia, where Leo held a lectureship for three years, before the family returned to Britain and settled in Durham. Leo practised at the Newcastle Bar and became chairman of the local Conservative Association: he was seeking a parliamentary seat when he suffered a stroke at the age of forty-one which effectively ended his career (though he lived until 2001). Tony was eleven at the time: his father's stroke affected him as profoundly as Brown's brush with blindness did him, though Blair's ambition took longer to show itself. After six years at the Durham Cathedral choir school he was sent to Fettes College in Edinburgh (sometimes described as Scotland's Eton), where he shone as an actor and developed a mildly rebellious streak, but did well enough to win a place at St John's College, Oxford, to read law. Unlike Brown he took no part in student politics, but played in a pop group, discovered an intensely personal Christianity and began to develop an idealistic but unfocused interest in 'community'.

Thus for four years the two future friends and rivals were both in Edinburgh, physically just a mile or two apart but inhabiting quite separate worlds: Brown, at the university, was already an ambitious politician while Blair was still a callow schoolboy. Though for a time he adopted the shoulder-length hair of the period, Brown was rarely seen without a jacket and tie, the legacy of his Presbyterian upbringing to which he still adheres: he was a serious young socialist with no time for the playground posturing of the far left – though he did find time for a string of glamorous girlfriends. Spiritually he belonged to the early Sixties (which in Scotland were still pretty grey), if not the Fifties. By contrast Blair – not only four years behind, but a far more laid-back personality – was typical of the late-Sixties flower power generation, long-haired, casually dressed, vaguely leftish but with little interest in history and no clear political agenda. Between Fettes and Oxford he spent a gap year bumming around London trying to be a rock promoter. While Brown was serving as Rector of Edinburgh in 1972–75, Blair did nothing in particular in his time at Oxford. Yet a contemporary remembers that 'He had an aura about him even then; people noticed him . . . He was already developing the sorts of assets – trendiness and charm – which have been in evidence ever since.'[1]

While finishing his Ph.D. Brown lectured in politics at Glasgow College of Technology but devoted most of his energy to making his way in the Scottish Labour party. In 1975 he edited an uncompromisingly socialist collection of essays entitled *The Red Paper on Scotland*. Labour in Scotland was much less riven by the sort of Trotskyist militancy which almost tore it apart in England over the next decade; but it was still solidly left-wing, and Brown's prescription called for more nationalisation, a planned economy and 'a massive and irreversible shift of power to working people'.[2] He also took an active part in the campaign for devolution, working closely with John Smith (the minister responsible for the Callaghan government's doomed attempt to legislate a Scottish Parliament) and Donald Dewar, and against Robin Cook, a leading opponent of devolution, who became a lifelong enemy. He was elected to the executive of the Scottish party in 1978, and the next year – still only twenty-eight – chaired the campaign for a 'yes' vote in the devolution referendum. Since 1976 he had been candidate for the safe Tory seat of Edinburgh South. In 1978, however, he had the chance of going for the Labour seat of Hamilton. He turned it down for a mixture of reasons – a sense of obligation to Edinburgh South, but also a reluctance to force a fight: the first of several occasions when Brown, for all his ambition, showed a significant lack of ruthlessness. Had he secured Hamilton he would have got into Parliament in 1979, four years ahead of Blair. As it was, he had to kick his heels for another Parliament, working as a producer for Scottish Television while turning his doctorate into a biography of the idealistic Clydeside left-winger James Maxton – a sort of Scottish Nye Bevan – which was eventually published in 1986. In 1983, with the backing of the Transport and General Workers' Union, he finally secured the safe Labour seat of Dunfermline East, just a few miles from his childhood home in Kirkcaldy, which has been his stronghold ever since.

Blair meanwhile got his law degree from Oxford and moved to London, where he passed his Bar exams, joined the chambers of Derry Irvine (a rising young Scottish barrister whom he later appointed Lord Chancellor) and began to build a practice in employment law. Seeking an outlet for his social conscience he had already joined the Labour party, first in Chelsea, then in Wandsworth; but it was through Irvine that he began to make useful contacts in the party, and also met a brilliant fellow-pupil in his chambers, Cherie Booth, who sharpened his hitherto un-focused ambition. They married in 1980 and moved to Hackney, where they were active in the local party while both looked for constituencies to fight. In 1982 Blair secured the candidacy at a by-election in true-blue Beaconsfield, held in the middle of the Falklands war. He came third behind the newly formed Social Democratic Party, and lost his deposit; but he still gained useful national exposure and an encomium from the party leader, Michael Foot. In many ways Blair was natural SDP material himself; but the combination of Cherie's deeper roots in the party and his own ambition kept him loyal to Labour. Then Cherie was selected for Thanet North, while Tony looked as if he would have no seat to fight at the general election. At the very last moment – after Mrs Thatcher had already called the election – a vacancy suddenly appeared in a newly created but cast-iron Labour seat at Sedgefield. A public-school-educated London barrister was an unlikely candidate for a mining constituency, but it was only ten miles from Durham so he could plausibly present himself as a local candidate, and by a mixture of good timing and exactly the sort of opportunism Brown had failed to show at Hamilton, he won the nomination; he was duly elected less than three weeks later. Without this stroke of luck he would have had to wait until 1987: as it was, he now found himself the youngest Labour MP.

It was the worst and best of times to become a Labour MP. On the one hand, 1983 was the lowest point in the party's destructive civil war, when Labour under Michael Foot fought on a left-wing manifesto famously dubbed 'the longest suicide note in history', promising wholesale nationalisation, massive public spending, the restoration of trade union privileges, unilateral nuclear disarmament and withdrawal from Europe – any one of which might have rendered the party unelectable – against a Tory government riding high in the afterglow of the Falklands war, and won just 28 per cent of the vote, the party's lowest share since 1918 and barely ahead of the SDP–Liberal Alliance with 26 per cent. What was left of the parliamentary party comprised a mere 209 demoralised MPs, against 397 rampant Tories (and a meagre 23 for the Alliance). Foot immediately resigned, and the new electoral college – created to take the choice of leader away from the MPs and give more power to the unions and the constituencies – elevated the forty-one-year-old, popular but quite untried Welsh left-winger Neil Kinnock in his place, with the more right-wing and experienced Roy Hattersley as his deputy. It would plainly be a long road back. On the other hand it is always better, from a career point of view, to enter Parliament at the nadir of your party's fortunes, as part of a very small new intake, when a lot of old wood has been swept away, than as part of a triumphant landslide. Reaching Westminster in the wake of a disastrous defeat offered Brown and Blair a wonderful opportunity to be in at the beginning of the recovery.

Brown, coming from Scotland where Labour was less out of step with public opinion and still won more than half the seats, was shocked by the scale of the débâcle in England, but quickly grasped the need to drop much of party's ideological baggage in order to achieve its social objectives. Blair, though he had stood on Foot's manifesto, was much less disturbed by the rejection of a lot of left-wing dogma he had never believed in anyway. The difference was clear in the maiden speeches which both made within weeks of their election. Brown's was a powerful analysis of the impact of unemployment in Dunfermline, angry and eloquent, characteristically packed with statistics but also spiked with scornful wit. A Tory 'wet' who spoke later in the debate – one of several MPs who recognised an important début – called it 'a magnificent speech . . . because he was speaking with an absolute mastery of his subject . . . So much of what he said was undeniably true.'[3] Blair's – three weeks earlier – was equally 'articulate and confident', but much more broad-brush: he too described the unemployment in his constituency and demanded government investment in the region.* 'After all,' he declared, 'that is the essence of Socialism' – one of the few times he ever used the word. 'I am a Socialist,' he explained, 'not through reading a textbook that has caught my intellectual fancy, nor through unthinking tradition, but because I believe that, at its best, Socialism . . . is both rational and moral. It stands for cooperation, not confrontation; for fellowship, not fear.'[4] Brown, with his track record in the party, had no need to mention socialism; Blair, as a virtual unknown, evidently felt that he had to parade his credentials – but his definition of socialism

---

*Both Brown and Blair represented traditional mining areas: both made a point of mentioning that there were no pits still open in their constituencies – and this was before the 1984–85 miners' strike.

was so broad as to be almost meaningless. His impatience with theory and 'unthinking tradition', however, would become ever clearer in years to come. Unlike Brown, Blair never pretended any interest in Labour history: he regarded the party's record over the past century – just twenty-eight years in power, and no Labour government ever winning two full terms – as nothing to be proud of. Yet from their different starting-points both Brown and Blair understood that Labour had to change radically to make itself electable again, and were determined to play a leading part in driving that process. Within weeks they had become firm friends and arranged to share an office – a tiny windowless cupboard off the main committee corridor, always piled with Brown's books and papers. They were quickly identified both by the new leadership and by the press as the brightest of the new Labour intake.

They were very close in those early days – often described as blood brothers, or even twins, 'joined at the hip'. 'Tony and Gordon were an extraordinary duo,' one aide who worked with them told Blair's biographer, Anthony Seldon. 'It was thrilling listening to them. It was exceptional, the regard they had for each other, the love, the human warmth.'[5] But they were not equals. Blair recognised Brown's much greater experience and knowledge. Brown taught the politically naïve Blair all about Labour politics, parliamentary procedure and how to handle the press; in the words of their mutual friend Charles Falconer, Blair was 'mammothly dazzled by Brown's power'.[6] Soon the duo became a trio, when Kinnock appointed the thirty-two-year-old Peter Mandelson as Labour's Director of Communications. Mandelson, previously a television producer, coached the other two in broadcasting techniques, created opportunities for them to project themselves and generally acted as their manager. Though Mandelson was officially working for the whole party, the three were constantly together. 'Their relationship ran deeper than any I have ever seen,' another friend recalled of this period. 'It was rare to find three men locked in just one mission – and that was to save the Labour Party.'[7] In fact Mandelson was slightly closer to Brown – partly because Blair had a wife and (by 1988) three children to go home to, while Brown and Mandelson were both unmarried; partly because both had Labour in their blood – Mandelson's grandfather was Herbert Morrison, deputy leader under Attlee – as Blair had not. 'While Mandelson admired Blair, he idolised Brown.'[8] Right up to 1994 he saw Brown as 'unquestionably the senior and the more capable of the two'[9] – as did practically everyone around them, including Alastair Campbell, a young *Daily Mirror* journalist then close to Kinnock, who saw Brown as the obvious future leader and Blair as 'a very likely Chancellor'.[10] There was no rivalry at this stage: Brown was pleased to have a keen disciple, Blair grateful to have a mentor. 'Gordon was in charge . . . and Tony was happy with that. It's how he learned everything.'[11]

Blair was actually the first to reach the front bench – but only because Brown turned down the first offer made to him. In November 1984 Brown was invited to join Donald Dewar's team shadowing the Scottish Office, but declined because he did not want to be confined in the small pond of Scottish politics – a decision which underlined both his ambition and his self-confidence. Blair had no such hesitation when invited to join Hattersley's shadow Treasury team: though no economist, he learned quickly and used his barrister's skills to make an immediate impression. 'He comes across as fluent, intelligent and sincere – not at all the normal party politician,' his Durham neighbour Giles Radice noted in his diary. 'I am sure he has big leadership potential.'[12] Blair's easy manner also made him the first to be invited on to *Question Time* on BBC Television, three years before Brown. But Brown got his chance in 1985 when he was appointed to speak on regional policy under his friend John Smith, and he was the first to be elected to the shadow cabinet after the 1987 election (at which Labour again lost heavily), in eleventh position with 83 votes. (Blair only just failed to make the cut with 71 votes.) Smith now became Shadow Chancellor, with Brown his deputy as Shadow Chief Secretary, while Blair became City spokesman (under Bryan Gould). In 1988 both seized their opportunities to shine. First Blair mounted a lethal indictment of the government's handling of the collapse of the Barlow Clowes investment group, in which a lot of pensioners lost their life savings: this, in Gould's view, was 'the issue that made Blair's name'.[13] Then Brown stood in when Smith suffered a heart attack and performed brilliantly, tormenting the hitherto complacent Nigel Lawson just as his vaunted boom was beginning go bust (very much as Mrs Thatcher, thirteen years before, had shown her leadership mettle by demolishing Denis Healey). Both were rewarded in that autumn's Shadow cabinet poll; Brown came top, overtaking even Smith, while Blair was elected for the first time in ninth place. He was now appointed Shadow Energy Secretary – replacing John Prescott – to oppose the nationalisation of electricity. 'There is no doubt,' Radice wrote, 'that Blair and Brown are the coming men in the Labour Party, the party's future.'[14]

That summer they made the first of several trips together to the United States, where they attended the Democratic Convention which nominated Michael Dukakis as the party's candidate for the presidency. In November Dukakis lost heavily to Ronald Reagan's Vice-President, George Bush, which reinforced their conviction – even before Bill Clinton showed how to do it four years later – that left-of-centre parties must build an appeal beyond their core supporters to have a chance of winning. They visited America again in 1991, and again after Clinton's victory in 1992, studying his successful vote-winning strategies and establishing close links with their Democratic counterparts. Smith also sent them to Australia in 1990 to study a successful Labour government in action. Already they were preparing the groundwork for what would become New Labour.

In 1989 Brown was given his own brief shadowing Trade and Industry (replacing Gould), while Blair climbed to fourth place in the annual beauty contest – behind only Brown, Smith and Robin Cook. Switched to Employment, with a mandate to loosen Labour's traditional links with the unions, he proceeded coolly and single-handedly to abandon the party's support for the closed shop, which had been a millstone round its neck for years. This 'almost brilliant coup', as Hattersley described it, demonstrated the unsuspected steel behind his eager manner, and alerted several commentators – and colleagues – to the idea that Blair was not just Brown's sidekick but a potential leader himself.[15] Brown was 'certainly leadership material', Radice judged shrewdly, 'if he doesn't burn himself out too soon. With the glowering looks of a Heathcliff, he is very much a "driven" politician.'[16] Blair, by contrast, was 'young, glamorous, responsible – possibly Kennedyesque'.[17] For the moment, however, they were inked in for senior positions in the government which Kinnock hoped to form in 1992.

They were both hit hard by Labour's failure to win the election that year. With Mrs Thatcher's messy removal seventeen months earlier the long Tory hegemony seemed to be coming to an end. But John Major's unassuming decency proved a more difficult target than Labour had expected, while Kinnock failed to convince as a credible Prime Minister. Labour did better than in 1987, but increased its share of the vote by only three percentage points (from 32 to 35 per cent), mainly at the expense of the Liberal Democrats (as the Alliance had become), and Major crept back with an overall majority of 21. Obviously Labour had still some way to go. Kinnock and Hattersley resigned: John Smith was the clear favourite to succeed. But this presented the first real test of the Brown–Blair alliance. The shadow budget which Smith had unveiled a month before the election, gratefully seized on by the Tories as 'Labour's Tax Bombshell', was widely blamed for losing the election. Both Blair and Brown feared that Smith – though only fifty-four – was too wedded to traditional Labour 'tax-and-spend' policies to press on with the radical overhaul the party still required. The day after the election the two young bucks met in Sedgefield. Blair urged Brown to seize the moment and stand against Smith for the leadership, while he would stand for deputy. But Brown, cautious as always, would not do it. First, he had promised Smith that he would not stand against him and felt bound by that undertaking. Second, he could not be sure that he would win, and believed it would be damaging to his career to stand and lose. Blair, impatient to skip a generation, thought he was being over-cautious, and told friends that Brown had 'bottled out'.[18] He considered standing himself but realised that he was not yet ready. He then pressed Brown to stand for deputy leader; but Smith vetoed that, on the sensible grounds that two Scots would not make a balanced ticket. Blair, as an English MP, was not open to the same objection. 'Tony is definitely interested,' Radice recorded, 'but has to consult with his friend, Gordon Brown.'[19] But Brown was strongly against Blair going for deputy, and Blair did not yet feel able to go against his advice. This later became a bone of recrimination, with the Blairites wishing that their man had gone for it in 1992, while the Brownites denied that Gordon had blocked him to prevent Tony stealing a march on him: 'We talked Tony out of running for the deputy leadership not because we were jealous of him, but to protect him. He couldn't win. We had Tony's best interests at heart.' Looking back, they wished they had let Blair stand and – as they believed – be humiliated for his presumption.[20] So neither stood for either post. Smith overwhelmingly beat off the token challenge of Bryan Gould, while Margaret Beckett comfortably beat Prescott and Gould for the deputy's job.

In practice only one Labour deputy since Attlee – Michael Foot – has ever gone on to win the leadership and it did not bring Foot much joy: the post might easily have proved the kiss of death for Blair, as it did for Nye Bevan, George Brown, Roy Jenkins and Denis Healey. Nevertheless their inconclusive jostling in 1992 changed the dynamic between the two friends. It was now that Blair – stiffened by Cherie, who always resented Brown's assumption of seniority – resolved that next time there was a vacancy he would not let Brown stand in his way again. The press quickly picked up on this new rivalry. The day after Smith's elevation in July the *Sunday Times* ran a profile of Blair under the headline 'Labour's Leader in Waiting'; and the London *Evening Standard* two days later trailed 'The Coming War Between Brown and Blair'.[21] But all this was academic, since no one expected a vacancy to arise for many years.

The two were still close colleagues, with a shared mission to modernise the party and a shared frustration with Smith, whom they thought 'complacent, conservative and lazy' for assuming that 'one more heave' would see Labour elected next time.[22] But they no longer shared an office, so they saw less of each other day by day; while Smith's shadow cabinet dispositions dealt them crucially different hands. Succeeding Smith as Shadow Chancellor, Brown was determined to banish Labour's reputation for profligacy by enforcing strict control of spending commitments. It was now that he acquired the image of responsibility and 'prudence' which he exploited so successfully in government; but it won him no friends among his colleagues in opposition. He also strongly backed Britain's membership of the European Exchange Rate Mechanism (ERM), which the government had joined right at the end of Mrs Thatcher's time: haunted by the past, Brown was determined that Labour should not be tagged again, as in 1947 and 1967, as the party of devaluation. But this left him wrong-footed and unable to exploit the government's humiliation when it was forced to leave the ERM on 'Black Wednesday' five months after the election. The Tories' reputation for economic competence never recovered from this débâcle. But Brown's reputation was also damaged by his identification with their failed policy. In the 1993 shadow cabinet poll he slipped from first place to fourth, behind Cook, Prescott and Frank Dobson.

Blair by contrast had been given the home affairs brief with the job of reversing the perception that Labour was soft on crime. The need to show that Labour understood public anger about 'law and order' without betraying the party's liberal traditions suited his ambiguous mixture of idealism and moralism perfectly. Ironically, the soundbite which encapsulated his twin-track approach – 'tough on crime, tough on the causes of crime' – was coined for him by Brown. Blair also eloquently articulated the nation's horror at the killing of a toddler, Jamie Bulger, by two boys on Merseyside; and he consistently scored well against the saturnine Home Secretary, Michael Howard, in the House. Steadily the idea gained ground that Blair was overtaking Brown in the succession stakes. Even Smith, though he sometimes thought Blair too pushy and warned him after his Bulger speech to 'stop hogging the limelight',[23] was said to have concluded during 1993 that when he stepped down 'Tony is probably the one'.[24] At the end of the year the *Sunday Telegraph* declared categorically: 'The succession is decided . . . Step forward Tony Blair. Give way Gordon Brown.'[25]

But there was still no expectation of an early vacancy. Smith had every intention of leading Labour back into government in 1996 or 1997, and meanwhile he played off his two Young Turks against each other. He was sceptical of their enthusiasm for the way Clinton had transformed the Democrats, and objected to their unconcealed project to 'Clintonise' the Labour party. At the 1993 conference he pushed through – with John Prescott's support – a contentious reform of the party's internal procedures, establishing the principle of one man, one vote (OMOV) for party elections. He thought he had boldly risked his leadership by pushing the party so far; Brown and Blair thought he had still been too cautious in compromising with the dinosaurs. But Brown was ready to play a long game, while Blair was becoming restless. By the spring of 1994 he was so frustrated with Smith's leadership that he talked of leaving politics. 'I will not go on doing this job for ever,' he told friends. 'I don't want still to be stuck as an opposition MP while friends at the Bar are getting on with their careers.'[26] But then unexpectedly the situation was transformed.

On 12 May 1994 John Smith died suddenly of a massive heart attack. The events of the next three weeks have spawned a mountain of analysis, interpretation, spin and counter-spin, which has created a widely held myth that Tony Blair moved ruthlessly and perhaps unscrupulously to steal the Labour leadership from under the nose of Gordon Brown. In reality the momentum had already swung decisively towards Blair before Smith died. In 10 Downing Street, for instance, the immediate reaction of John Major's office was 'Oh, my God, it'll let in Tony Blair.'[27] William Hague – then a junior minister – wrote that within minutes of the news breaking Blair was the overwhelming favourite to succeed;[28] and the majority of Labour MPs thought the same. 'Tony is the only candidate with the strength of character to be party leader,' Radice wrote. 'Gordon is too brittle, Robin [Cook] too warped and Prescott too unpredictable. Tony could also put over our message in a new and interesting way.'[29] Gerald Kaufman recalled: 'When John Smith died it was clear to *everyone* that Tony was the obvious leader. Politics is about timing. Gordon's moment didn't coincide with the chance for leadership: Tony's did.'[30]

Brown was unlucky that Smith's death caught him at the low point of his popularity, when he had been playing the hard-faced Shadow Chancellor for two years while Blair was winning golden opinions as Shadow Home Secretary. Two or three years later their reputations might have been reversed again. Brown took it for granted that despite these temporary ups and downs he was still the senior partner. He and Blair had agreed that whatever happened they would not split the modernising vote by standing against each other: in 1994 Brown assumed that this agreement still held – just as he had felt debarred from standing against Smith in 1992. 'This deal was his protection, his insurance, for making himself so unpopular.'[31] Blair acknowledged the existence of this understanding. Even after he had won the leadership he told Alastair Campbell that 'he still believed GB was in many ways a superior politician'.[32] But the overriding fact of British politics by the 1990s was that knowledge and experience counted far less than a fresh image, likeability and the ability to connect with voters. Blair possessed the latter in abundance – he also had a photogenic family – while Brown, for all his intellectual power, was increasingly seen as a dour technician; his lack of a wife and family – giving rise to unfounded whispers that he was gay – was a major handicap. Finally, after two Celtic leaders – Kinnock and Smith – who had struggled to overcome their respective national stereotypes Labour needed a leader who spoke for Middle England. It was unfair, as politics often is, but irresistible. A party that had been in opposition for fifteen years wants above all a winner. Within hours of Smith's death Blair came under overwhelming pressure to stand, and quickly convinced himself that Brown's hesitation in 1992 had released him from his word: 'Gordon had had his chance in 1992, but he ducked it.'[33]

Blair was visiting Aberdeen when he heard that Smith had died. Immediately he rang Brown, and they arranged to meet in London the next day. The second person he rang was Cherie, who met him at Heathrow, determined – like Lady Macbeth – to screw her husband's courage to the sticking place. But Blair's mind was already made up. 'I have never been in the presence of a man so sure of his destiny,' one aide who saw him that day remembered.[34] If he had felt any doubts, the London *Evening Standard* was already declaring the contest over before it had begun:

> There is only one potential successor to John Smith who is streets ahead of all the other candidates. He is Tony Blair . . . an unabashed moderniser with the mission to make the party electable – whatever it takes.[35]

Alastair Campbell, interviewed on BBC TV's *Newsnight* that evening, said the same; and next morning the rest of the papers, from *The Times* and *Financial Times* to the *Daily Mail* and the *Sun*, followed the *Standard*'s lead. The almost universal view was that Blair's freshness, Englishness and freedom from ideological baggage could reach parts of the electorate – the very parts that Labour needed to win over – that would not be wooed by Brown's more traditional Labour image.

> Blair has the looks, style and message that could appeal to many disenchanted Tory voters. (*Sun*)

> Blair is the man the Conservatives most fear – a man of rare ability . . . and he has an unblemished reputation for honesty and integrity. (*Daily Mail*)[36]

A MORI poll published two days later confirmed that Blair was the clear public choice, with 32 per cent support. Brown actually trailed behind Prescott and Margaret Beckett with just 9 per cent.[37]

Brown did have support in the unions and in the constituencies, which together made up two-thirds of the electoral college. Afterwards his supporters insisted that with his deeper roots in the party he could still have twisted enough arms to win. It was said that Brown was slow to mobilise his support because he was genuinely shocked by Smith's death, spent most of the first day writing tributes and thought it indecent to start politicking until after the funeral, while Blair was quicker to seize the moment. Possibly Brown could have made a fight of it if he had announced immediately that he would be standing, and challenged Blair to oppose him, instead of the other way round. But such calculations would have counted for little in the face of Blair's overwhelming media endorsement. The truth is that Brown never stood a chance; and within a few days of Smith's death he knew it. On 15 May the pollster Philip Gould told him directly that he could not win. 'Gordon asked me why and I replied that Tony not only met the mood of the nation, he exemplified it. He would create for Labour and for Britain a sense of change, of a new beginning, which Gordon could not do.'[38] The next day

Peter Mandelson gave him the same message. This was hard for Mandelson, who had always assumed that Brown would be the next leader. But 'it was like standing in front of a herd coming towards you. It was inescapable.'[39] In a letter urging Brown to concede gracefully he tried to sugar the pill. Brown was 'the biggest intellectual force and strategic thinker the party has', he flattered; but Blair was already so far ahead that he could not withdraw. 'Nobody is saying that you are not capable/appropriate as leader,' he told Brown, though he did have 'presentational difficulties'; but the clinching argument was that 'because you would be appearing to come in as the second runner, you would be blamed for creating a split'. He would do better to stand aside 'with enhanced position, strength and respect'.[40] This indeed was the conclusion Brown himself soon reached; but he took Mandelson's defection as a personal betrayal which he could not forgive.

For some days Brown and his team weighed the possibility that he could still put together enough support to stop the Blair bandwagon. But he could have done so only by painting Blair as a closet Tory and appealing to the very sections of the party whose influence they had been striving together to reduce: he would have made himself the prisoner of the unions and the left. Alternatively if he stood as a rival moderniser he risked letting in Prescott or Beckett. Either way he would damage his own cause. In practice, once he had accepted that Blair was determined to stand, Brown's only course was to drive a hard bargain for his supposed 'sacrifice', in order to maximise his influence in the short and medium term and keep alive his prospects in the long term. He made two defiant speeches setting out his vision for the party which kept open the possibility that he might yet stand; and for another three weeks, over no fewer than ten meetings with Blair – in Edinburgh after Smith's funeral and later in London – he persistently refused to concede. These meetings were 'incredibly tense . . . incredibly emotional. There were moments when Gordon gained the upper hand. He made Tony feel like a younger brother.'[41] Blair felt guilty about supplanting his mentor and friend. 'I love Gordon,' he told Brown's brother Andrew. 'He's the best mind the Labour party has ever had' – not that he was qualified to judge.[42] He knew that he must keep Brown on board to prevent a damaging split. But he would not back down. Instead he suggested that they were both young enough to have a turn at being leader: if Brown would give him the first shot he might hand over after a few years. This was the origin of the famous deal finally concluded at an Islington restaurant on 31 May.

Like an international summit meeting, the Granita dinner was only the formalisation of an agreement tortuously negotiated over previous days. There were actually two agreements. The first concerned policy. If Blair was to be leader, Brown wanted control of economic and social policy – partly to secure his position in a future Labour government, but also because he still cared deeply about traditional Labour objectives – what he called 'the fairness agenda' – and was not sure that Blair fully shared his concern. After a good deal of wrangling, Mandelson drafted a document which set out how far Blair was willing to tie his hands.

> In his Wales and Luton speeches, Gordon has spelled out the fairness agenda – social justice, employment opportunities and skills – which he believes should be the centrepiece of Labour's programme and Tony is in full agreement with this, and that the party's economic and social policies should be further developed on this basis.

When this was faxed to Brown he tried to strengthen it by striking out the phrase 'Tony is in full agreement with this', substituting 'Tony has guaranteed this will be pursued'. But there was a big difference between agreement and a guarantee, and Blair rejected the new wording. When Brown pressed a second time, 'Tony thought about it for, oh, fifteen seconds, and said "no" again. What's interesting is the extent to which he was already thinking about what would be appropriate after the election.'[43] Nevertheless Brown acted as if Blair had agreed. He spun his version of the deal to the *Times* columnist Peter Riddell, who reported two days later that Blair had indeed 'guaranteed' the fairness agenda.[44] In practice Blair did concede Brown an unprecedented degree of autonomy over the whole field of domestic policy. But already there was ambiguity and mistrust about precisely what had been agreed.

There was still less clarity about the second part of the deal, on which most of the recrimination between Brownites and Blairites later centred. Brown believed that Blair had promised to stand down in his favour after seven years of a Labour government, or about midway through the second term if the government was re-elected. Blair's allies equally firmly denied it; but on this point nothing was written down. On the one hand it is unlikely that Blair – as a lawyer well aware of the unwisdom of guaranteeing anything – would have given such a categorical promise; it can be argued that it would have been improper, even unconstitutional, for him to have done so. On the other hand, seven years into a government that had not yet been elected was a long way in the future: Blair might well have imagined that after seven years he would be ready to move on. It is easy to see how he might have given Brown that impression, while Brown would interpret an understanding as a promise. Blair was admittedly feeling bad about Brown; he was genuinely anxious to retain his friendship; and he always had a knack of letting people think he had said more than he had. This is surely what happened at Granita.

There was a third element in the deal. Brown believed that as well as control of the domestic agenda he was also promised a say in government appointments, so that he would be able to look after his friends and protégés and protect his own position. This was another source of poison in the future, since nothing is more contentious than matters of promotion and ambition. Every Prime Minister must balance different factions in his cabinet; but at the same time patronage is a key prerogative which he cannot afford to share. As relations between the Prime Minister and Chancellor became increasingly tense after 1997 and the government split very obviously into warring camps, the question of whose followers were promoted and whose sacked became another focus of institutionalised rivalry and recrimination.

In the end it might have been better for Brown – and for New Labour altogether – if he had stood for the leadership in 1994. He would not have won, but he would not have been humiliated either, and he would have established his position in the party beyond argument. As it was, he continued to feel that he had been jockeyed out of a position which on grounds of merit and experience he had every reason to expect would be his. He could not forget that he had been the senior partner and was still the better-qualified politician who deserved to be Prime Minister ahead of his shallower but media-friendly friend. In fact by standing aside he won a pretty good deal for himself, while he recognised that Blair's presentational gifts were a vital part of New Labour's electoral success which he could not have matched. In the short run the Granita deal held and served both men and the party well. But Brown never got over the hurt of those few days and weeks. 'The change that came over him in that period,' wrote one journalist who saw a lot of him at the time, 'was startling. He became manifestly less relaxed . . . He retreated into himself and became duller.' [45] He also became intensely suspicious of old friends like Mandelson and Campbell who he felt had plotted to deny him his due. Like Lloyd George's replacement of Asquith, Bevan's defeat by Gaitskell, Macmillan's double knifing of Butler, or Mrs Thatcher's overthrow of Heath, Blair's snatching the Labour leadership ahead of Brown was one of those visceral moments in politics which left deep and lasting wounds. But Blair and Brown had to go on working closely together, first in opposition and then in government, for the next thirteen years. They managed it, more or less, but the bitter fallout of the Granita deal haunted the Blair government from its first day to its last.

Blair eventually won a comfortable majority of the electoral college – 57 per cent, against 24 per cent for Prescott and 19 per cent for Margaret Beckett. Yet this was not a landslide comparable to John Smith's 91 per cent against Bryan Gould. Blair gained a majority in all three sections, thanks to the OMOV voting system which put an end to the union leaders' block vote; yet even in his strongest section, the parliamentary party, nearly 40 per cent of Labour MPs – more than 100 – supported either Prescott or Beckett. These figures compounded Brown's agony that perhaps he should have stood: they also provided a bedrock of support for him in the future, when Blair's popularity began to wane. Nevertheless Blair quickly established his authority. At forty-one he was the same age as Neil Kinnock when he became leader – significantly younger than either Wilson (forty-seven) or Gaitskell (forty-nine), both of whom had cabinet experience; like Wilson, however, he had the good fortune to take over at a time when Labour was already riding high in the polls against an exhausted and accident-plagued Tory government. After fifteen years in the wilderness the party was willing to suppress whatever doubts it felt about him to make absolutely sure of victory at the next election.

At first Brown still imagined that he could dominate the new leader. At a policy seminar in Hampshire before the autumn conference he suggested to Mandelson that they could effectively 'run' Blair if they worked together. Mandelson replied that Blair was now the leader and his first loyalty must be to him. 'You make your choice,' Brown told him and stormed off.[46] From now on he divided everyone into friends or enemies. From his friends he expected – and received – total loyalty: Ed Balls, his policy adviser; Charlie Whelan, his press officer; Sue Nye, who ran his office; and Nick Brown (no relation), his chief parliamentary supporter, formed a tight group devoted to protecting and promoting his interests. Mandelson and Campbell – who became Blair's press officer that summer – he now regarded as Blair's creatures. He had to work with them; but he never trusted them again – or they him.

Blair lost no time in stamping his personal style on the party. For the 1994 conference Campbell came up with the slogan 'New Labour, New Britain' which was placarded behind the platform at Blackpool. From now on Blair always spoke of 'New Labour', as though he had called into being an entirely new party. It was noticeable that Brown, though equally committed to modernisation, rarely did. Then in his leader's speech Blair signalled that he intended finally to tackle Clause Four of the party's constitution – the old formula dating from 1918 which committed Labour to the wholesale nationalisation of the economy, which Gaitskell had tried to scrap in 1959 but which still hung about the party's neck as a symbol of unreconstructed socialism. He took immense trouble to win over John Prescott – now deputy leader and official 'keeper of the cloth cap' – and with his support and much arm-twisting behind the scenes managed to overcome the opposition of the unions. A special conference in London in April 1995 voted to substitute a much longer and less specific text which embraced the market economy, lauded the idea of 'community', and spoke of placing 'power, wealth and opportunity in the hands of the many, not the few' – soon to become a New Labour mantra. This was a huge victory for Blair; but it was one achieved almost entirely without support from Brown, who regarded it as a pointless diversion of energy and stood conspicuously aloof from the battle. Though he had long outgrown his youthful leftism and was fully committed to broadening the party's appeal, he was still sensitive to its history and symbols. Blair, by contrast, asserted his own commitment to Labour with a clever formula. 'I wasn't born in this party,' he boasted after the critical vote. 'I chose it'[47] – as if the party should be very grateful for its good fortune.

Blair still devoted a lot of energy between 1994 and 1997 to keeping Brown happy; but he did so mainly by allowing him his separate sphere. In accordance with the Granita agreement he left Brown a largely free hand in the development of policy, while he concentrated on developing the New Labour brand and selling it to the electorate via the media – above all winning the support of Rupert Murdoch. Thus Brown, with Balls and the maverick millionaire Geoffrey Robinson, beavered away on detailed plans to reform the tax and benefit system, offer new incentives to the young unemployed and, most daringly, to give the Bank of England independence to set interest rates without political interference – all of which they were able to implement within the first year after coming into office – while Blair was wary of making precise commitments. 'When I talk to Tony about these things, his eyes glaze over,' Brown complained.[48] 'What matters is what works,' Blair declared vaguely in March 1997, promising that 'I'm going to be a lot more radical in government than people think.'[49] While Brown had Balls, Blair never had an economic adviser of his own: Mandelson and Campbell were spin doctors, more concerned with presentation than with content. His focus was single-mindedly on winning the election. The result was that he came into office woefully unsure of what he wanted to do – beyond five quite narrow promises on class sizes, NHS waiting lists and the like – or how to do it. The one major demand he did make of Brown was a commitment not to raise the basic or top rates of income tax. This was a matter of electioneering, not policy. Remembering 1992, Brown agreed – but he made no promise not to raise the total tax burden, so that he could still do what he liked with other taxes. In practice Brown was allowed to develop his own economic policy.

One potentially important initiative that Blair pursued without reference to Brown was to engage in talks with the Liberal Democrat leader Paddy Ashdown with a view to including the Lib Dems in a coalition after the election. Under the influence of the former SDP leader Roy Jenkins – his latest mentor, who tried to make him read some history – Blair conceived an ambitious project to heal the Labour–Liberal 'schism' which had delivered most of the twentieth century to the Tories: he thought that by bringing Labour and the Lib Dems together he could consign the Tories to permanent opposition. The plan was mad. When Brown heard about it he told Blair: 'You're on your own. I'm having nothing to do with it.'[50] In fact not just Brown, but the whole Labour leadership with the exception of Robin Cook – Prescott, Margaret Beckett and Jack Straw, who all loathed the Lib Dems – were adamantly against it. Ashdown could never have delivered his party either. The notion was an astonishing mixture of naïvety, self-delusion and arrogance on Blair's part. In fact the scale of Labour's landslide rendered it obviously impracticable, as well as unnecessary. Yet Blair still persisted with his dream: he set up a joint consultative committee with the Lib Dems, which achieved nothing, and in his victory speech at the 1997 conference he dared to tell the party that his heroes included the Liberals Keynes and Beveridge as well as Attlee, Bevin and Bevan. Nothing better demonstrated Blair's free-floating detachment from the Labour party than this quixotic fantasy. Luckily for him it came to nothing. If there was one issue that might have provoked a party revolt in Brown's favour this was it.

Labour duly won the 1997 election with a huge majority of 179. Blair became the youngest Prime Minister since Lord Liverpool in 1812, swept into office on an enormous tide of goodwill and commensurate expectation. 'It is a new dawn, is it not?' he exulted as the sun rose on 2 May. 'We have been elected as New Labour, and we will govern as New Labour.'[51] What this meant in practice was a double-headed administration in which authority was unprecedentedly shared between Numbers 10 and 11 Downing Street. In accordance with the Granita agreement, Blair granted his Chancellor what no previous Prime Minister would ever have contemplated – control over the economy and by extension practically the whole of domestic policy, since the Treasury controlled spending. Civil servants had to get used to the strange idea of divided authority; instead of looking always to the Prime Minister, cabinet ministers had to serve two masters. At first it worked surprisingly well. Together the two friends had achieved the first objective they had been planning ever since 1983 and in the first flush of power they were still united. 'They used to spend hours closeted together discussing the key messages', often with no one else present, and Blair was careful to let no difference appear between them.[52] 'It is like a marriage,' one official told Andrew Rawnsley, 'a tempestuous marriage. The rows can be terrible. But if you're on the outside and you interfere, you won't be thanked for it afterwards. You come between them at your peril.'[53] But it was a marriage in which one partner was always trying to appease the other. 'Gordon has a much more developed political philosophy than me,' Blair once admitted. 'For all his faults, Gordon is crucial to me'; and he still instinctively deferred to him.[54] In bilateral meetings with other colleagues, Blair would say 'I've got to clear this with Gordon', or 'I'll square this with Gordon'.[55] Whereas Brown often treated the Prime Minister with 'open disdain', Blair would go to extraordinary lengths to manage his touchy Chancellor. 'He mediates, he negotiates, he defuses, he cajoles, he rails, he shouts, he hugs, he flatters,' a cabinet colleague told Rawnsley.[56] Brown could be 'uncooperative', Blair admitted, 'but he always comes back in the end'.[57]

Blair played little part in Brown's early decisions. His first bold initiative, which set the framework for his whole tenure at the Treasury, was to give the Bank of England independence to set interest rates, thus putting a crucial instrument of inflation control beyond political interference, as in Germany or the United States. This was something Brown had worked up in opposition, with Balls (who joined him in the Treasury as his special adviser) and

Robinson (who became Paymaster-General). He did not tell Blair his intention until election day; but Blair – once assured that it was indeed 'the right thing to do' – happily went along with it. When the Cabinet Secretary, Robin Butler, asked if there should not be a meeting of the cabinet before it was announced, Blair replied airily: 'Oh, they won't mind. We'll ring round.'⁵⁸ He did have to intervene, however, to dissuade the Governor of the Bank, Eddie George, from resigning over the new regulatory framework for the City which Brown announced, without consultation, a few days later.* 'Jesus,' Blair is said to have exclaimed, 'what has Gordon done?'⁵⁹ Brown was determined to impose his will on the Treasury from day one; Blair had to use all his charm to smooth a lot of ruffled feathers. He did not have much more knowledge of his Chancellor's other fully worked out plans: the merging of the tax and benefit systems – the biggest overhaul of welfare since 1948 – and a windfall tax on the utilities to fund a 'new deal' to get unemployed young people back to work. These were Brown's policies; Blair let him get on with them, but rarely highlighted them among the government's achievements. He also accepted Brown's decision – highly unpopular with the party and many of his colleagues – to stick to the Tories' spending plans for the first two years. Brown knew that every previous Labour government had come into office with a spending spree in the first two years and then had to cut back; he was resolved to do the opposite. He was determined to assert his sole authority in the economic field and quickly established his ownership of it, using his rumbustious press spokesman Charlie Whelan to ensure that he got the credit.

The one major issue over which Blair and his Chancellor differed in the first term, on the borderland where economics and foreign policy overlap, was the question of whether Britain should join the European single currency – the euro – and if so, when. Both were initially in favour, in principle. Labour's manifesto had promised a referendum on the subject. Blair, like other

---

*Whereas the independence of the Bank dominated the headlines and was generally seen as a brilliant success, the new regulatory arrangements attracted little attention until they were suddenly shown to be seriously flawed in 2008.

Prime Ministers before him, came into office keen to improve relations with Europe and hoped to be able to capitalise on his popularity to win a referendum in the first term. Brown, however, soon turned against early entry – mainly because he had learned the lesson of Major's débâcle over the ERM and did not want to risk his successful management of the economy, at a time when the pound was much stronger than the fledgling euro, but also because it gave him another hold over the Prime Minister. He envisaged a referendum early in the second term, and as early as October 1997 gave an interview to *The Times* ruling out entry in the first term. Blair was not pleased, but after several days of disarray he let Brown make a Commons statement postponing the issue by setting 'five tests' to determine when Britain would be ready. Blair, seeing entry primarily as a political matter, thought the tests were essentially cosmetic and intended that the government should declare them to have been met when the moment was right. In fact he had unwittingly devolved the decision to the Treasury. While still insisting that he wanted to join when conditions were right, Brown made himself the 'guardian' of the five tests, thus taking a central question of national policy out of the Prime Minister's hands. Once Brown had defined it as an economic decision Blair was helpless, as a Treasury official cruelly spelled out. 'He was never going to win the arguments against Brown; one because he was hopelessly understaffed in Number 10; two, Brown worked eighteen hours a day and, unlike Blair, was on top of the arguments; three, the Treasury didn't want it, period.'[60] Blair might have found support to help him override the Chancellor if he had ever taken it to cabinet; but the cabinet never discussed the euro at all.

In fact the cabinet never discussed anything very much: its weekly meeting rarely lasted more than half an hour and Blair used it purely to report what he with his advisers in Number 10 – primarily Jonathan Powell, his principal private secretary; Anji Hunter, his 'special assistant'; and the ubiquitous Campbell – had decided in bilateral meetings with individual ministers. Here was a paradox. Except where Brown was concerned, Blair ran an exceptionally centralised and presidential style of government, with a tame parliamentary majority and a quiescent cabinet. At the end of his first year one commentator judged him 'the most powerful Prime Minister since Churchill's wartime premiership'.[61] Yet the Treasury was effectively a fiefdom on its own. Blair took an interest in some domestic subjects – education, where he worked closely with David Blunkett on strategies to improve literacy and numeracy; the NHS, struggling to deliver Labour's promise to cut waiting lists; and crime – but only within the constraints of the Treasury's tight spending limits. Brown made it his business to micromanage every department by his control of spending. Blair's successes lay in other areas. He eloquently articulated the public's grief on the death of Princess Diana and averted a serious backlash against the monarchy by his skilful handling of the Queen. He devoted enormous time and energy to Northern Ireland, building on the progress already made under Major, and finally succeeded in bringing both sides to an historic agreement on Good Friday 1998. He also displayed an increasing interest and confidence in foreign affairs – first in Iraq, where he joined with President Clinton in bombing Saddam Hussein's supposed nuclear installations in December 1998; then in Kosovo, where he took the lead in persuading a reluctant Clinton of the need to commit ground troops, not just bombing, to stop Serbian atrocities.

All Prime Ministers develop a taste for the world stage, which allows them to rise above the parochial frustrations of domestic politics; Blair, having devolved so much of the domestic agenda, had more need of a bigger stage than most. In Kosovo he found a lofty moral cause which answered his quasi-messianic desire to save the world. 'It is a battle between good and evil; between civilisation and barbarity,' he declared;[62] 'a battle for humanity.'[63] In a speech in Chicago in April 1999 he set out a new 'doctrine of the international community' to justify humanitarian intervention around the world to prevent oppression and genocide, raising echoes of Gladstone's crusade against the Bulgarian massacres a century before. Brown was deeply sceptical. 'We must assume Tony knows what he is doing,' he confided privately;[64] in public he said nothing at all. One of Brown's aims was to cut defence spending. There could be more for education and health, he told Blair, 'if you didn't want to spend so much on defence'. But this was one issue on which Blair would not give way, insisting 'I am not going to be the first Prime Minister in a hundred years to lose a war.'[65]

Blair also used the Prime Minister's power of patronage to assert his authority. But part of the Granita agreement was that Brown should be consulted on appointments, so here again he had to tread carefully. In May 1997 he appointed a fair number of the Chancellor's particular friends and allies to key positions, including Doug Henderson as Minister for Europe (against the objection of the Foreign Secretary, Robin Cook) and Nick Brown to be Chief Whip, as well as Alastair Darling and Geoffrey Robinson within the Treasury. But after fourteen months he took the opportunity of his first reshuffle to sack several Brownites who had failed to make the grade, while moving both Nick Brown and Henderson and promoting some of his own supporters: Mandelson from the Cabinet Office to Trade and Industry, where he was bound to clash with Brown; Stephen Byers into the Treasury in place of Darling; and Jack Cunningham to be the so-called 'cabinet enforcer'. The *Daily Mail* headlined the reshuffle 'Blair's Scalpel Shows Brown Who Is The Boss';[66] Brown thought it a breach of their 1994 deal. But he fought successfully to save Robinson, whom Blair had been determined to remove, while Darling's switch to Social Security brought that department effectively under his control. Blair had actually resisted the urging of his own team to be more sweeping, as Alastair Campbell recorded in his diary:

> We were pressing him to be bold but he said 'I'm just telling you there is a case to be cautious if it all ends up with GB offside'. TB said you have to remember we are co-creators of New Labour . . . We have come this far together in part because of his nous and political skills and I want to keep them inside the operation. With PM [Mandelson] and others in, and 4 out, you are talking a big reshuffle and I do not want a war with GB out of it . . . The PLP will see it as a bit of a hit on GB. I do not want them to see it as an all out attack.[67]

The first serious breach in their relationship occurred early in 1998 when the publication of an authorised biography of Brown by the *Daily Mirror* journalist Paul Routledge infuriated Blair by telling Brown's side of the events of May 1994, revealing his enduring sense of grievance. Someone in Number Ten hit back in an interview with the *Observer*'s Andrew Rawnsley, letting slip a cutting phrase which in turn infuriated Brown: 'You know Gordon, he feels so vulnerable and so insecure. He has these psychological flaws.' Rawnsley described his source as 'someone who has an extremely good claim to know the mind of the Prime Minister'.[68] At the time it was assumed to be either Mandelson or Campbell; in fact it may well have been Blair himself. Brown brushed off the slur in public, but privately demanded that Blair investigate and punish the culprit. Blair denied that it was anyone in Number Ten, but told Brown that he had brought it on himself by authorising 'that bloody stupid book'.[69] The phrase 'psychologically flawed' was duly repeated every time Brown's fitness to succeed was discussed over the next few years. Brown blamed Campbell and never forgave him.

The next row was also precipitated by Routledge, who followed his sympathetic Brown biography with a hostile one of Mandelson a year later in which he revealed that Mandelson had taken a large undeclared loan from Geoffrey Robinson to help him buy a house in Notting Hill, at a time when his department was investigating Robinson's business affairs. After a painful few days, Blair was forced to yield to the press outcry and accept Mandelson's reluctant resignation. Routledge did not reveal his source for the disclosure; but it was widely assumed that Charlie Whelan had deliberately leaked the information to destroy Mandelson, in delayed revenge for his 'betrayal' in 1994. Blair was miserable at the loss of his *alter ego*; Brown correspondingly delighted by Mandelson's disgrace. The one compensation for Blair was that Robinson resigned as well; soon afterwards Brown was also forced to let Whelan go. Radice thought Whelan's departure 'a blessing in disguise for Gordon. Hopefully he may decide to stop being manipulative and rely on the fact that he is an excellent Chancellor to speak for itself.'[70]

All this spinning and counter-spinning by the rival camps reinforced a growing perception that the government was obsessed with 'spin' at the expense of content. The first damage to Blair's reputation for integrity had been dealt as early as November 1997 when the government appeared to exempt motor racing from restrictions on tobacco advertising after accepting a £1 million donation from the Formula One boss, Bernie Ecclestone. Labour was obliged to return the donation, and Blair had to go on television to plead that he was 'a pretty straight sort of guy' who would never do anything improper.[71] At that honeymoon stage of his premiership the press and public were willing to believe him. Earlier Brown had denied on the *Today* programme that he had known about the donation: he was furious to have been put in that position. 'I lied,' he raged to his staff. 'My credibility will be in shreds . . . If this gets out I'll be destroyed.'[72] Three years later when this story leaked, he again denied that he had known about the donation, or that he had lied. He felt that he had been stitched up by being made to answer for a blunder for which he was not responsible, while Blair had got away with it.

By now the Treasury and Number Ten were briefing compulsively against each other. Brown successfully presented himself as the serious man of government whose prudent management of the economy was responsible for all the government's real achievements – the magic combination of sustained growth with low inflation, low interest rates and full employment, as well as programmes to combat child poverty and youth unemployment – while Blair was merely the golden-tongued front man with little grasp of detailed policy. The Chancellor, it was slyly suggested, was the government's chief executive while the Prime Minister was merely the non-executive chairman.[73] This story infuriated Blair, but there was just enough truth in it to rankle. After a couple of years he began to be frustrated at his own relative impotence, feeling that the plethora of initiatives and announcements was not having the expected impact in improving services on the ground. So 1999 was declared 'the year of delivery'; but this only raised expectations which still were not fulfilled. In July that year Blair voiced his frustration in a speech to venture capitalists claiming that after two years in government 'I bear the scars on my back' from trying to drive forward reforms in public services against the opposition of the unions.[74] He portrayed himself as a radical, even a revolutionary, and Brown implicitly as the obstruction in his way. 'I can really only be Prime Minister of a transforming, radical government,' he announced in September. 'The modernising revolution has only just begun.'⁷⁵ But the impression persisted that, having successfully transformed the Labour party, he did not know how to go about transforming the country.

At Bournemouth later that month Blair was 'totally discombobulated', in Campbell's words, by Brown's conference speech in which he presented himself not just as Labour's most successful Chancellor but as leader-in-waiting with a clear vision combining economic growth with social justice, which he was not afraid to call 'Socialism, radical and credible'. 'Though in public he remains loyal to Tony and the New Labour project,' Radice noted, 'he continues to suggest that he understands the concerns of Labour's traditionalists.'⁷⁶ Blair thought it 'the best conference speech by someone other than a leader he had ever seen. His worry now was that if we didn't do something special, the TB/GB mischief could get out of hand.'⁷⁷ His response was a much more aggressive speech than his normal inclusive style, in which he tried to put some flesh on his rather nebulous philosophy of the 'Third Way', asserting the distinctiveness of New Labour by contrasting it with both the Tories and 'old' Labour. 'The Third Way is not a new way between progressive and conservative politics,' he insisted. 'It is progressive politics distinguishing itself from conservatism of left or right.' Seventeen times in the speech he vowed to combat 'the forces of conservatism' – a phrase which Brown had used, unnoticed, the day before.⁷⁸ In a scarcely coded dig at his Chancellor he told the conference, 'You've never had it so prudent.'⁷⁹

In January 2000 Blair tried to seize the initiative by forcing Brown's hand on health spending. That autumn there had been a spate of bad headlines about underfunding in the NHS – long waiting lists, cancelled operations and patients left for hours on trolleys in hospital corridors. Brown was planning to announce increased spending in his budget: he had always intended to let the brakes off before the election. But then Blair went on *Breakfast with Frost* on a Sunday morning to promise a rise far beyond what they had previously agreed to bring it up to the European Union average over five years – insisting that this was entirely possible 'if we run the economy properly'.⁸⁰ Brown was furious, telling Blair, 'You've stolen my fucking budget', and briefed the press that the Prime Minister's figure had been 'an aspiration, not a commitment'.[81] In fact he did boost NHS spending by 6 per cent over the next few years: the dispute between them was over which of them should get the credit for the increase.

Blair's anxiety to claim some achievement of his own was embarrassingly disclosed by a leaked memo in April. The Tories and their newspapers were generating a lot of concern about law and order, and Blair feared that the government was perceived as 'soft' on crime, 'weak' on asylum seekers and 'insufficiently assertive' about patriotism. 'All these things,' he wrote, 'add up to a sense that the government – and this even applies to me – are somehow out of touch with gut British instincts.' He wanted his aides to come up with 'two or three eye-catching initiatives'.

> We should think now of an initiative, e.g. locking up street muggers. Something tough, with immediate bite . . . This should be done soon and I, personally, should be associated with it.[82]

The result was a plan – announced by Blair incongruously in a speech in Germany – to impose on-the-spot fines on young trouble-makers by marching them to the nearest cashpoint. This was clearly unworkable and drew universal ridicule, not least from the police. The leaked memo only confirmed that the supposedly all-powerful Prime Minister was obsessed with headlines and was making up policy off the top of his head.

By now the tension at the top of the government was attracting intensive press coverage. Towards the end of the first term the broadcaster James Naughtie was writing the first detailed study of the Blair–Brown relationship; published in 2001, it was entitled *The Rivals*. At that stage it was still possible for him to portray their mutual dependence quite warmly, as it had been in the early days:

> When Blair and Brown are together, they behave like brothers or young friends, leaning into each other, Blair touching and Brown grinning, making natural eye contact, understanding each other's reactions as only a close couple can. The notion of an estranged

pair of battling ministers, each trying to outdo the other, is inconceivable. Their disputes and sulks don't undermine the closeness; they are the dark reflection of it.[83]

A couple of pages later, however, he quoted a contrary view from an unnamed colleague:

> It was a warm, bonded relationship. It really was. Now it is merely a professional relationship, not underpinned by warmth or much emotion any more. It's sustained simply by the need to exist.[84]

At the very end of his book Naughtie compared the Blair–Brown rivalry to another close political friendship which went sour – that between Roy Jenkins and Tony Crosland in the 1960s. Crosland, Labour's leading moderniser of the day, was a couple of years older than Jenkins and believed himself to be better qualified than his younger friend to be Chancellor when Jim Callaghan resigned after devaluation in 1967; he was outraged when Harold Wilson chose Jenkins ahead of him, and their relations cooled from that moment. According to Giles Radice, who was writing a book on the three-way rivalry between Jenkins, Crosland and Denis Healey, Blair and Brown were both 'fascinated' by this earlier relationship. 'You know Gordon and I were even closer than Roy and Tony,' Blair told him in February 2001. 'We lived in each other's rooms for over ten years.'[85] 'Tell me the Crosland story again,' he would ask Jenkins when they met.[86] Brown was alarmed when Radice jokingly suggested writing another book about himself and Blair, but promised: 'We are not going to end in failure like your heroes.'[87] That determination was what kept his sense of grievance within bounds. The fact was that each still needed the other. Brown knew that he had no choice but to bide his time, jealously guarding his own patch while signalling coded dissent from aspects of Blair's agenda. Blair was often frustrated by Brown's semi-detachment – particularly his 'disappearing acts' at several moments of crisis, notably the fuel protests which rocked the government in September 2000 and the foot-and-mouth outbreak in spring 2001, when he conspicuously failed to put his head above the parapet; but he 'accepted that part of GB's strategy was that he put himself in a slightly different position' to Blair himself, and told Campbell that 'even that was worth bearing to keep his input'.[88]

From the beginning both men had been obsessed with winning the next election – Blair because no previous Labour government had ever succeeded in winning two full terms, Brown because he expected to inherit the premiership during the second term. But as Blair became increasingly aware that he had not achieved enough in his first term, he was determined to take control of the agenda for the second. 'He was very concerned that the 2001 election should give him a personal mandate for radical reform,' one adviser recalled, 'but he was uncertain exactly what the radical reform should be.'[89] He was coming to believe that the answer lay in injecting more private money, competition and consumer choice into the public services; but too little detailed work had been done to include any definite proposals in the manifesto, and his aides were concerned that under the pressure of events he was still not getting his head round the problem. In February Alastair Campbell recorded a gloomy session with Blair, his PPS Bruce Grocott and his speechwriter Peter Hyman thrashing around for ideas.

> He wanted to do meritocracy as the big idea, both Bruce and I thought he was tilting at windmills . . . It was all geared to a right-wing prism so a bit depressing. PH said that while GB was powering ahead with a real values-based agenda, TB looked like he was the pragmatic manager of different day-to-day problems . . . GB was doing well on the economy, had a message on society and was delivering, had taken over debt and Africa. He looked like someone with vision and drive whereas TB looked and sounded destabilised, felt isolated re Peter M and let down by the Civil Service.[90]

Blair had been upset two weeks earlier by Mandelson's second resignation. Just nine months after his first embarrassment Blair had shown his undiminished faith in his friend – but arguably poor judgement – by bringing him back into the cabinet as Northern Ireland Secretary, only for Mandelson to crash a second time over allegations that he had tried to secure British citizenship for two Indian businessmen who helped fund the Millennium Dome. Once again, as Radice noted, Brown was 'the clear gainer from the Mandelson disaster'.[91] Paddy Ashdown thought that with his downfall 'you can begin to see the end of the Blair era and the beginning of the Brown one'.[92] As well as Northern Ireland, Mandelson had been in charge of planning for the election; now Brown was able to take over and impose a cautious strategy founded on the strength of the economy and his own responsibility as Labour's Iron Chancellor. His prescription for the second term was more of the same: the reward of his prudence was that there would be more to spend – money that Blair called 'Gordon's hoard'; but he had no time for Blair's ill-defined 'radicalism'. The result was a schizophrenic campaign reflecting the duality that had riven the government for the past four years. The Prime Minister and Chancellor fought 'parallel – and sometimes divergent – elections'.[93] Brown chaired the daily press conferences in London, doggedly promising more teachers, more doctors, more nurses and more police, while Blair was out on the road, on television and on the airwaves vaguely foreshadowing 'a different partnership between the public and private sector'[94] and still trying to sound positive about the euro. On one side the Blairites complained that 'Gordon is trying to run the campaign with himself and a few cronies and is excluding people close to Tony'.[95] On the other, 'it annoyed Gordon that even though he was running it at the centre the media would always want to follow Tony on to the road'.[96] On the rare occasions when they appeared together the atmosphere was plainly strained. 'The Brown body language . . . whenever Blair was speaking,' Robert Harris reported in the *Sunday Times,* 'yawning, consulting his watch, discovering hitherto unsuspected fluff on his jacket, was as obvious as semaphore.'[97] Even on election night at Labour's Millbank headquarters, with another landslide in the bag, 'observers noticed that they could barely bring themselves to shake hands and exchange a sentence in public'.[98]

After four years in government Labour had secured a second term with its 1997 majority shaved by just twelve, to 167. This was the historic achievement that both men had been working for. Blair was disappointed, however, that turnout was only 59 per cent (down from 71 per cent in 1997): this was not the ringing personal mandate he had been seeking. Brown, by contrast, was ebullient. 'The campaign was chaired by Gordon, fought to Gordon's agenda and on his record as Chancellor,' one of his team exulted. 'It was his victory. What particularly pleased him this time was to win it without any input from Mandelson.'[99] 'After long years of anguish', Anthony Seldon wrote, Brown felt 'fully vindicated. He felt that his moment had all but arrived.'[100] Blair, conversely, feared that his was slipping away. During the election he was persistently questioned about whether, if re-elected, he intended to serve a full term or would stand down after two or three years in accordance with their reputed 'deal'. He denied that there was any such arrangement. 'As Gordon and I both say whenever we're asked about this,' he insisted, 'there is no gentleman's agreement.'[101] But this was not what Brown said when asked about the succession. He could not say positively that there *was* a deal; but he would not say that there was *not*, since he still firmly believed there was, and he expected Blair to stick to it. If Blair did not, the tension between them could only get worse.

While waiting for the election results in Sedgefield on polling day, Blair told Campbell of his determination to make up for lost time. 'He kept emphasising that it was all going to be different second term, that he was older, wiser, more experienced, would deal with the crap better, would be more focused on the things he needed to focus on.'[102] The critical decision he had to make was what to do with Brown. Most of his kitchen cabinet urged him to move the Chancellor, possibly to the Foreign Office. 'There were endless discussions about moving Gordon, which went on and on and on and on.'[103] This was the moment when he might have done it. But Brown strongly resisted, and Blair did not feel able to sack him: it would have been hard to explain after an election in which Labour's central claim had been his successful stewardship of the Treasury. Instead Blair set up a forest of new units designed to claw back the initiative from Number 11 into Number 10. These included a Delivery Unit to set targets in the key departments and ensure delivery 'in a notionally "Brown-proof" manner';[104] a Forward Strategy Unit, an Office of Public Service Reform, and three new directorates headed by Jonathan Powell, Campbell and Anji Hunter (later replaced by Sally Morgan). Together they constituted a Prime Minister's department in all but name, intended to shake up the civil service, counter Brown's domination from the Treasury and enhance the Prime Minister's personal control. They never really worked because the competing units all got in each other's way. Blair had no previous experience of administering anything, and had no interest in sound management. ('His eyes glazed over and he looked out at the Number 10 garden whenever the word "management" was used.')[105] Nor had Brown, of course; but he was temperamentally more interested in detail, and after initial tensions had learned to harness the power of the Treasury to dominate every corner of Whitehall.

Blair also tried to gain control by appointing his own supporters to the key departments: Alan Milburn to Health, Stephen Byers to Transport, David Blunkett to the Home Office and Estelle Morris to Education. He told them he wanted them all to stay in place for the whole Parliament to deliver public service reform. 'There are Blair departments and there are Brown departments,' Morris told her team at Education. 'We are the former and we will be dealing with Downing Street.'[106] In addition Blair appointed Charles Clarke, a longstanding critic of the Chancellor, as party chairman; and Patricia Hewitt to the DTI. Though he did promote some Brownites in the junior ranks, the new cabinet had a much more Blairite allegiance. Alas for his hopes, all four of his key appointments fell by the wayside for one reason or another before the next election. Byers resigned in May 2002 after a series of blunders; in August Morris confessed she was not up to the job; Milburn retired hurt after losing too many battles with Brown in June 2003; while Blunkett was caught up in a sex scandal involving conflicts of interest in December 2004. The rapid turnover of ministers only reinforced Brown's commanding position at the Treasury. Meanwhile Blair, despite all his good intentions, became increasingly distracted by the international scene following the terrorist attack on New York and Washington in September 2001, the punitive war in Afghanistan and his fateful decision to join the Americans in invading Iraq in March 2003.

Brown first tried to get Blair to set a date for his departure in the autumn of 2001. He came back from his summer holiday in Massachusetts determined to force the issue: at several meetings with Blair he allegedly banged the table, demanding, 'When are you going to move off and give me a date?' and 'I want the job now,'[107] while his acolytes briefed the press that Blair was reneging on his promise to hand over. Number Ten responded by leaking that Brown was trying to push Blair out and reviving doubts about his fitness to be Prime Minister, especially in the wake of 9/11 in America. The press was encouraged to start speculating about alternative candidates, maybe 'skipping a generation' when the time came: Byers, Blunkett and Clarke were all mentioned, which fed Brown's paranoia. Campbell – whose published diaries carefully excised most of the worst rows – wrote in November that relations were at 'an all-time low'.

> TB was exercised about it, said it was bad anyway but also that the party really wouldn't like it if they felt that TB was going for GB. It was one thing for the guy at the top to be under attack but it would look bad for TB if it was reciprocated.[108]

But in December he fired a warning across Brown's bows.

> TB had dinner last night with GB and said he had been on best behaviour but it was still difficult . . . He told him he still believed he [Brown] was easily the best person to follow him but he was not going to support him in circumstances where he felt he was being forced out.[109]

After Christmas Blair was just screwing himself up for a showdown when human tragedy stayed his hand. By now even their family lives had become a source of rivalry. In August 2000 Brown had finally married a PR executive, Sarah Macaulay, amid cynical speculation that he was doing so only to improve his chances of the premiership. Three months earlier Blair had raised the stakes by becoming a father for the fourth time when Cherie produced the first baby born to a serving Prime Minister in 150 years, highlighting the Prime Minister's virility as well as his rare virtue as a faithful husband. Sarah Brown's pregnancy the following year was seen as Gordon's riposte; but the baby lived only a few days, which temporarily shamed the cynics. Briefly Jennifer Brown's death brought the two old friends together. Going back to Brown's home near Edinburgh after the funeral, Blair found him 'very warm . . .

it reminded him of the days when they had been genuinely close'. (At the same time he was 'quite shocked' to see so many journalists at the funeral.)[110] Happily, the Browns had a healthy boy in 2002. Fatherhood at the age of fifty-one was said by friends to have humanised the driven Chancellor, though there was little outward sign of it. The Downing Street neighbours both now had young children, but the improvement in their political relations did not last.

Their quarrel was not just about the timing of the handover. Just as real policy differences exacerbated Heath's jealousy of Mrs Thatcher, so the gap which had always existed between their political philosophies widened in the second term as Blair began to put flesh on his more market-oriented approach to public services. This fundamental clash of principles centred on two proposals in particular: 'foundation' hospitals and university 'top-up' fees. Milburn's promotion of the former, designed to be independent of the NHS bureaucracy and free to raise money on their own behalf, seemed to Brown to undermine the core principle of the NHS by introducing a two-tier service (besides weakening Treasury control). Variable university fees had been explicitly ruled out in the party's 2001 manifesto for similar reasons; now Charles Clarke (who succeeded Estelle Morris in 2002) was reviving them. In both cases Brown took the exceptional step of setting out his objections in memoranda circulated to the whole cabinet. During most of 2002–3 the government was paralysed over these two issues. While the Blairites resented Brown's blocking their pet policies, Brown bitterly resented the Blairite spin that now painted him as an 'Old Labour' dinosaur obstructing necessary reform – a 'consolidator' rather than a 'transformer'.[111] Instead of preparing to take over, he felt he was being marginalised, as he complained to Clare Short in November 2002: 'TB doesn't listen to him any more and was listening only to non-Labour voices and thinking about his reputation in history.'[112] In a speech to the Social Market Foundation in January 2003 Brown set out his view that markets had a part to play in delivering services, but were not the whole answer:

Markets are part of advancing the public interest and the left are wrong to say they are not; but also markets are not always in the public interest and the right is wrong to automatically equate the imposition of markets with the public interest.[113]

While distancing himself from the left, he was plainly identifying the Blairites as 'the right'.

Brown also leaked his opposition to Blair and Blunkett 'banging on about asylum and crime',[114] and his distaste for Blunkett's draconian anti-terrorist legislation in the wake of 9/11: he tried to obstruct the introduction of identity cards by warning colleagues that the cost would come out of their budgets. Most maddeningly so far as the Prime Minister was concerned, he continued to block progress towards joining the euro, which Blair still believed was Britain's 'destiny'. Blair still hoped for a referendum in 2003 or 2004 after which he could either step down with at least one historic legacy secured or go on with renewed momentum to a third election. The obstacle remained that he had abdicated the decision to Brown alone. 'I very much hope it will be both of us together,' he stated rather plaintively before the election. 'That would be the normal way of doing it.'[115] But Brown would not budge – even when Blair offered to accelerate his departure if Brown would only lift his veto. 'History will never forgive us for having that conversation,' Brown self-righteously declared. 'I'm not going to do it.' Blair repeated his offer at least twice in 2002, using Clare Short as intermediary. Brown still refused, saying first that 'such deals were not worth talking about because previous agreements had not been kept', and second that 'he would not contemplate recommending that we join the euro in order to advance his own position rather than advance the economic interest of the country'.[116]

His position was not so high-minded as it appeared, since it was plainly not in his interest to become Prime Minister only to face an immediate crisis – like that of the Tories' ERM in 1992 – caused by joining the euro at the wrong time. The fact was that Blair wanted to join primarily for political reasons and brushed aside the economic arguments against; but Brown – stiffened by Balls – knew too well the history of bad economic decisions taken for political reasons and would not be lured down that route. He dragged out the Treasury's judgement on the 'five tests' by commissioning eighteen separate studies which eventually concluded – in April 2003 – that a 'clear and unambiguous case' for entry had not been made. Blair still tried to have the verdict fudged. 'If you are not going to give me what I want,' he threatened, 'then you should consider your position.' 'I'll do just that,' Brown retorted and left the room.[117] For a moment it was not clear if he had resigned or had been sacked. But Blair could not afford to lose his Chancellor on this of all issues: losing Chancellors is never good for a Prime Minister, as Mrs Thatcher learned with Nigel Lawson. For the moment he was furious at having been once again outgunned; paradoxically, however, Brown's intransigence had got Blair off a hook, since he could never have won a referendum on the euro against the violent opposition of the Tory press – it is hard to see how he ever thought he could – and defeat would probably have forced him to step down earlier than he wanted. After this, joining the euro disappeared off the map of practical politics.

Instead, the overriding issue which dominated his second term was the invasion of Iraq. Blair trapped himself in this disaster through a combination of opposite qualities. On the one hand was his conviction – which went right back to the beginning of New Labour and was fully shared by Brown – that the party must never again let itself be cast as anti-American or weak on defence. This led him, from the moment he took office, to align Britain unswervingly as America's best friend and closest ally, even more closely than Mrs Thatcher had done with Ronald Reagan. His resolve was undented – in fact it was redoubled – when Bill Clinton was succeeded by the conservative Republican (and born-again Christian) George W. Bush. On the other, this essentially defensive electoral calculation chimed with his idealistic, quasi-religious ambition to save the world. From the moment the airliners smashed into the Twin Towers on 11 September 2001 Blair felt that he had found his transcendent cause. 'Sometimes things happen in politics,' he declared later, 'an event that is so cataclysmic that . . . all the doubt is removed. From the outset, I really felt very certain as to what had to be said and done.'[118] 'He knew what it meant, even then, in terms of a war on terrorism and . . . an invasion of Iraq. He knew that evening that this would be the defining issue of his premiership.'[119] The successful – as it appeared at the time – intervention in Kosovo had given him both confidence in his judgement and a belief in the beneficent use of force. With virtually no reference to the cabinet, he immediately threw Britain behind America's war to hunt down al-Qaeda – the perpetrators of 9/11 – and drive their fundamentalist allies the Taliban from power in Afghanistan. This too was initially successful; so when Bush moved on to the – entirely unconnected – resumption of his father's unfinished business with Saddam Hussein, inventing false evidence that Saddam was close to deploying nuclear weapons as a pretext to depose him, Blair signed up unhesitatingly for this too, painting the 'war on terror' as a global crusade of good against evil. Long before the charade of weapons inspections and the search for a UN resolution to legitimise invasion had been exhausted, Blair had committed himself to Bush's war. He genuinely expected the outcome to vindicate the dodgy means; and when Saddam was quickly toppled he seemed to be right.

Brown supported Blair's war. He did not in reality have much choice. He did not share Blair's messianic recklessness, but he believed equally in the centrality of the American alliance. Though most of the Labour party, and much of the public, were uneasy or actively opposed to military action without UN authority, the Tories – now briefly led by Iain Duncan Smith – were hawkish, and most of the press was stridently bellicose. On tax, on crime and on defence, the whole strategy of New Labour had always been to ensure that it could not be outflanked on the right. No more than any other member of the cabinet was Brown involved until the decision for war was virtually made: he was not brought into the military discussions until 11 March, just nine days before hostilities began. He was then said to be 'alarmed' that Blair 'presented no option other than all-out support for America.'[120] He was not keen on the war – no Chancellor is ever keen on the expense of war – but he was never going to rock the boat on such an issue. At first Blair's people were annoyed that Brown did not give more active support: they thought it was another of his 'disappearing acts' and suspected that he was positioning himself to benefit if it all went wrong, like Macmillan after Suez. But under the Granita deal foreign affairs were Blair's patch. Two cabinet ministers, Robin Cook and (eventually) Clare Short resigned, along with one or two junior ministers; but when it mattered Brown stayed loyal. Having failed to win a second UN resolution, Blair's survival was on the line. Had he lost the crucial Commons vote on 18 March, or had to depend on Tory votes to win, he would have resigned; had Brown equivocated now he could have brought him down. In fact he lobbied hard to limit the Labour rebellion. On the critical amendment 139 Labour MPs voted with the Liberal Democrats against the government. This was more than half the non-payroll vote; with Tory support, however, Blair still gained a comfortable majority of 396 to 217. He had got his war, with Brown tied to his chariot wheels.

Quickly, however, when no weapons of mass destruction were found, the invasion was seen to have been promoted on a false prospectus; Iraqi civil society collapsed as the invaders were revealed to have no plans to rebuild it, and the country slid into anarchy. British troops suffered fewer casualties than the Americans, but they found themselves caught in a trap from which there was no exit strategy. In the face of successive unsatisfactory inquiries – one prompted by the death of the weapons inspector David Kelly, hounded to suicide in July 2003; another into the misuse of intelligence – Blair continued to insist that it had been right to remove Saddam; but his credibility and popularity were permanently damaged. With his contentious reforms of hospitals and universities also foundering, there was a growing sense that the government had lost its way. Hugo Young wrote bluntly in the *Guardian* that Blair should go: 'His unique contribution to political renewal is already made . . . Someone else deserves a turn.'[121] Inside Number Ten, Brown was joined by Prescott in arguing that 'there was so much focus on reform that we were losing sight of values, that the messages were becoming too technocratic'. ('It was exactly what I had been saying,' Campbell agreed.)[122] Brown repeated this theme at the party conference in the autumn. Blatantly parodying Blair's claim the previous year that 'we are best when we are at our boldest', he proclaimed instead that 'We are best when we are Labour.' Altogether he mentioned 'Labour' forty times: 'New Labour' not at all.

What Gordon was saying to the world was 'I'm here, I'm ready. I've won' . . . He'd won on the battlefield of ideas, policy, personality and even publicity. He saw himself as palpably stronger than a shrunken and weakened Prime Minister. This was his moment.[123]

Another Brownite told Seldon:

Gordon's greatest worry was not that he wouldn't take over – he never doubted that – but that he would inherit a shell of a party that has effectively been destroyed by Blair . . . He was reaching out to the party's heartland, to the unions, and alerting them.[124]

Blair saw this as a direct challenge. He rewrote his own speech the next day, adding an emotional passage on Iraq and vowing to carry forward his public service reforms, asserting (in a conscious echo of Mrs Thatcher): 'I don't have a reverse gear.'[125] As he could always do when up against it, he had the conference eating out of his hand. Brown's challenge brought out the best in him. Blair had once again shown his overweening Chancellor who was boss; but still he was not strong enough to sack or move him. He merely denied him a place on Labour's National Executive – a petty humiliation which provoked 'the worst crisis in their long years of tension'.[126] But now, with matters getting out of hand, John Prescott used his authority as deputy leader to broker a truce. Over dinner at his flat in Admiralty House in early November he told them both: 'If you carry on like this you will destroy the Labour Party. And I won't let you do that.'[127] Both men knew that they still needed each other. Brown knew also that he needed Prescott's support if he was ever going to succeed. Blair admitted that he had lost public trust over Iraq; he still believed he would be vindicated in the end, but confirmed that he would stand down before the next election. 'I know I must leave,' he allegedly told Brown, 'but I need your help to get through the next year.'[128] For the moment the old understanding between them was renewed.

In January 2004 Brown did help Blair survive another rebellion, this time over top-up fees. No fewer than 160 Labour MPs led by Brown's faithful acolyte Nick Brown (whom Blair had sacked from the Department of Agriculture after his mishandling of the foot-and-mouth outbreak in 2001), had signed a motion refusing to back the policy. Clarke made substantial concessions; and at the last minute Nick Brown and one or two more – just enough to swing the result – fell into line. The government – with a notional majority of 161 – won by just five votes. This was another moment when Brown could possibly have brought Blair down but chose to throw his influence the other way. 'The Chancellor has shown that he is the only man who can save the Prime Minister in his hour of need,' *The Times* reported.[129] Blair was depressed by this latest evidence of his dependence. This was his lowest time. Battered by the continuing recriminations over Iraq, more unpopular than he had ever been and worried by the continuing effects of a minor heart scare the previous autumn, he seriously considered stepping down. Most of all 'it was the endless psychological drain of the warfare with Gordon that got him down. It went on and on, and it sucked his energy dry.'[130]

In March Blair actually floated with Brown the idea of 'pre-announcing' his intention to resign in September. But Brown feared this would only trigger a protracted leadership battle over the summer, giving time for another candidate – John Reid or Charles Clarke – to stand against him. He told Blair it would make him a lame duck for his last six months and throw the party into turmoil: it would be better to stand down in the autumn, when a quick contest would facilitate a smooth succession.[131] Brown soon regretted this advice, since Blair's temporary wobble quickly passed. The leading Blairites in the cabinet – Reid, Clarke, Blunkett, Tessa Jowell and Charlie Falconer – those who had most to fear from a Brown takeover – rallied round to dissuade him from stepping down; so did Jonathan Powell and Sally Morgan within his inner circle. Above all, Cherie was 'massively in favour of him staying on'.[132] 'She couldn't stand the neighbour,' a Downing Street official explained. 'She simply couldn't bear the prospect of Brown taking over.'[133] Political wives – Margot Asquith, Dora Gaitskell, Jennie Lee – are often more partisan than their husbands.

The local and European election results in June – pretty bad for Labour, but not quite so bad as predicted – confirmed Blair's determination to carry on. The Brown camp were furious when they realised he had changed his mind. Ed Miliband marched in to see Sally Morgan and demanded: 'Why haven't you packed up to go yet? There's a deal and he's got to go.' She replied coolly: 'I don't know anything of the sort.'[134] Brown himself stormed next door and allegedly demanded again: 'When are you going to F off and give me a date? I want the job now!'[135] The seven years were up: the next election was less than two years away. But when the story of Blair's wobble leaked at the beginning of July, it confirmed the impression of a weakened Prime Minister, limping from spring to autumn and on to Christmas. This was not the way Blair wanted to go. At another Prescott dinner on 18 July, the day after the Butler report criticised the use of flawed intelligence before the war, he told Brown: 'To go now would look like I've been defeated on Iraq. I need more time, I can't be bounced.'[136] If he was not going to go at once, the only way Blair could end the uncertainty was by announcing that he would fight a third election.

After an unusually long summer holiday (divided between Cliff Richard's house in Barbados, a visit to Silvio Berlusconi in Sardinia and a stay in a Tuscan palace), he signalled his renewed resolution at the beginning of September by bringing a somewhat reluctant Alan Milburn back into the cabinet as 'election co-ordinator' (replacing Brown's ally Douglas Alexander, who was demoted to make room for him). Brown saw this as yet another breach of the Granita deal. 'Why's Milburn coming back?' he demanded. 'Is it about cooking the manifesto against me? This is symptomatic of the way you behave.'[137] In a newspaper interview before the party conference he refused to say that he and Blair still trusted each other. 'I think the record speaks for itself: people must judge on the basis of what's been achieved . . . I've got my job to do and he's got his job to do. It's as simple as that.'[138] At Brighton, however, both men drew back from open confrontation. In his speech Brown repudiated the 'divisive and damaging policies' represented by Milburn (and implicitly by Blair) – asserting that 'there are values far beyond those of contracts, markets and exchange' – and presented himself as the unifier who embodied true Labour values. Blair responded by refusing to apologise for Iraq while insisting that his new buzzword 'choice' – 'not by virtue of your wealth, but your equal status as a citizen' – was 'precisely what the modern Labour Party should stand for'. But he offered an olive branch by calling Brown 'a personal friend for twenty years and the best Chancellor this country has ever had'.[139] When they met in Blair's hotel room the next day he charged Brown with undermining him, but half promised that if Brown would only co-operate with him to secure his legacy then he would step down. 'You've got to work with me,' he pleaded. Brown did not believe him; and he was right. Blair did not tell him that he planned to announce the next day his intention not just to fight the next election but to serve another full term as Prime Minister.[140] He did not even tell him directly the next day, but waited until Brown had left for an IMF meeting in Washington, then got one of his staff to tip off Brown's PPS before he made his announcement from Downing Street. Brown's camp likened this to 'an African coup' while his rival was out of the country.[141]

With this *démarche* Blair had finally torn up the Granita agreement. On his return from Washington Brown stormed into Blair's study to demand why he had not told him his intention in Brighton. It was now that he allegedly told Blair: 'There is nothing that you could ever say to me now that I could ever believe.' Three months later this line appeared in a book published by the journalist Robert Peston and serialised in the *Sunday Telegraph*. The gulf between the Prime Minister and the Chancellor, Peston wrote, was now 'a chasm'.[142] Both men tried to dismiss the embarrassing report, but neither actually denied the killer line, which was widely accepted as an accurate reflection of the state their relationship had now reached. Faced by an angry meeting of Labour MPs worried that the public bickering could cost them their seats, they made a show of papering over their differences. ('I think we've got the message,' Blair assured them.) Privately, however, both felt liberated by the acknowledgement that Granita was a dead letter. Having decided to carry on, Blair was determined finally to marginalise Brown, to win a mandate to push through his own agenda – academies and trust schools, breaking up the 'monolithic' NHS, and a tough line on crime, immigration and security – to secure his elusive 'legacy'. He had finally made up his mind to move Brown from the Treasury, as he had failed to do in 2001.

'I'm going to take no more shit from over the road,' he told his aides. 'I'm going to do it.'[143] Brown in turn felt released from any remaining obligation to Blair. 'If there's no point in waiting for Blair to anoint him as the successor,' Peston wrote, 'Brown can be truer to his own beliefs in words and deeds.'[144]

Yet they were still chained together, at least up to the election; and Brown still in some ways held the stronger hand. Blair's reputation had been tarnished by the war in Iraq, while Brown's stewardship of the economy was still Labour's trump card. Blair initially tried to freeze the Chancellor out of the campaign, until persuaded by Campbell and Philip Gould that he could not do without him: the electorate will always punish a divided party, and the Tories, now led by Michael Howard, were posing a serious challenge for the first time since 1997. But Brown agreed to help only on his own terms: first, that Milburn was sidelined and, second, that his own continuation at the Treasury was guaranteed. Once again Blair had to concede. On 6 April he announced that Brown was 'the most successful Chancellor in a hundred years. We would be crazy to put that at risk.'[145] Instead of marginalising Brown as intended, the election grid was redrawn so that the two men were seen together as much as possible. Anthony Minghella directed a broadcast portraying them as the best of friends, as in the old days; in one palpably contrived election stunt they were photographed eating ice-creams together; and at a joint press conference, with Blair still under heavy criticism over Iraq, Brown explicitly backed both the Prime Minister personally and his decision to go to war: 'I not only trust Tony Blair but I respect Tony Blair for the way he went about that decision.' 'For a few seconds,' wrote Anthony Seldon, 'Brown held Blair's political future, and credibility, in the palm of his hand.'[146] Blair was hugely relieved to have Brown back on side, and for a few days both men seem to have believed that this latest *rapprochement* might lead on to a final constructive period of co-operation until Blair stood down.

By any normal historical standard, Labour won the 2005 election comfortably; but 47 seats were lost, cutting the government's majority to 66. To Blair it felt like a defeat. In so far as he had won, the victory was widely credited to Brown. Doubts immediately arose about whether Blair would really be able to serve another full term; at the first party meeting of the new Parliament a number of MPs called for him to go quickly, saying that he had become 'a negative factor'.[147] The truce with Brown failed even to survive the post-election reshuffle; Brown thought it another breach of faith when Blair replaced several more of his allies with his own loyalists. 'Gordon,' Blair reminded him: 'It's got to be my reshuffle. I am the Prime Minister.'[148] Brown did succeed in blocking some appointments and advancing others; but the acrimonious bargaining revealed a party more split than ever between Blairite and Brownite factions. The knowledge that Brown was likely to take over sooner rather than later only heightened tension between the two groups.

The third term actually started well for Blair. First the French and Dutch electorates voted in referenda against the proposed new European constitution. Blair had unwisely promised a referendum in Britain too; he would almost certainly have lost it, which would have increased the pressure on him to go. Suddenly he was saved from that elephant trap and could look forward more confidently to another three or four years. Then London unexpectedly beat Paris to win the 2012 Olympics, which was seen as a triumph for the Prime Minister's energetic lobbying of IOC delegates in Singapore. He hosted a successful G8 summit at Gleneagles which seemed to mark a new beginning in tackling climate change and poverty in Africa. Finally he was seen to react firmly to a clutch of Islamic terrorist bombings in London on 7 July 2005, which helped to vindicate his insistence on the need for tough security measures (though they also confirmed the warnings of anti-war campaigners that slavishly following American policy in Iraq would make Britain a target). All these events boosted the sense that Blair had regained his old touch. At conference that autumn he made a confident speech which seemed to re-establish his authority.

But then it waned again. An unprecedented breakdown of cabinet discipline over banning smoking was followed by the loss of yet another of the Prime Minister's key allies when David Blunkett, whom he had brought back into the cabinet after the election, was forced to resign again over a share scandal; then the government was defeated in the Commons over Charles Clarke's attempt to allow the detention of suspected terrorists without trial for ninety days. (Instead, the maximum period was doubled to twenty-eight days.) In March another part of the Prime Minister's personal agenda – city academies with the power to select pupils – provoked such strong opposition (even John Prescott voiced his concern) that it was carried only with Tory support. Then it emerged that Labour had evaded its own new rules on party funding by taking 'loans' instead of gifts from wealthy donors, allegedly in exchange for honours: this led to a police investigation which overhung the rest of Blair's time in office. Finally at the end of March the government suffered triple humiliation on a single day when Clarke had to admit the failure of the Home Office to deport convicted foreign criminals (making a farce of Blair's claim to be tough on crime); Health Secretary Patricia Hewitt was jeered by nurses angry at threatened job cuts; and Prescott was revealed to have been having an affair with his diary secretary. The government – like Major's government after 1992 or Macmillan's in 1963 – appeared to be falling apart in a welter of sleaze, incompetence and ridicule.

In all these embarrassments the Blairites detected the hand of Brown and his allies either actively stirring up difficulties or failing to give much support. Brownite briefing certainly encouraged the idea that only a change of Prime Minister could restore the government's integrity and sense of purpose; there was growing talk of a leadership challenge. Some of Blair's supporters thought he might gain time by announcing a date for his departure: he remained determined to keep his options open. The Brown camp was likewise torn between those who thought he should still work for a 'smooth and orderly transition' and others who wanted him to capitalise on Blair's weakness. After Labour trailed third in the local elections in May – the party's worst result since 1983 – Blair carried out yet another reshuffle but bungled it, pleasing no one. Egged on by his militants – primarily Ed Balls and Nick Brown – Brown went on the *Today* programme and declared solemnly: 'We have got to renew ourselves . . . It has got to start now.' But as so often when he had the chance to do real damage, he drew back. 'You bottled it,' Balls reportedly raged at him. Even Number

Ten admitted that if Brown had only drawn the parallel of Mrs Thatcher staying on too long after 1987 'it could have been fatal'. Others compared Brown's missed opportunity to Rab Butler's famous refusal to fire the 'loaded gun' given him by Enoch Powell and Iain Macleod in 1963.[149] Three days later Blair made a significant concession: instead of repeating that he would serve a full term he promised a tense meeting of Labour MPs that he would leave his successor 'ample time' before the next election. But at the same time Number Ten warned that 'if Tony was deposed, he and his supporters would not support Gordon as the next leader'.[150] The Blairites began to build up John Reid – who had just replaced Clarke at the Home Office – as a possible alternative.

A showdown finally occurred in September, in the run-up to the party conference. Blair's refusal to condemn Israel's punitive incursion into Lebanon in pursuit of Palestinian terrorists in July – widely seen as dragging Britain once again shamefully at George Bush's heels – had further swelled the number of Labour MPs – not all confirmed Brownites – demanding that he should go at once. Realising that he could not prevaricate for ever, Blair authorised David Miliband – chosen as a rising younger minister not too closely identified with either faction – to go on *Today* to confirm the 'conventional wisdom' that he would carry on 'for about another twelve months'. The effect of this was undercut, however, by the embarrassing leak of a document proposing that he should orchestrate his 'final phase' with farewell tours, television appearances and other populist stunts: 'He needs to go with the crowds wanting more. He should be the star . . . The more successful we are, the more it will agitate and possibly de-stabilise [Brown].'[151] The next day the two men met for two hours in Number Ten. Neither would admit responsibility for the machinations of their respective supporters. Brown demanded 'bankable' public pledges on Blair's departure date and 'a clear run' for the succession: he also wanted a period of 'joint premiership' up to the handover. Blair told him: 'I can't do that. I can't stop people standing.' Brown allegedly threatened: 'If you don't do what I ask there'll be big trouble.'[152] That afternoon one junior minister and seven PPSs resigned from the government. But several senior party figures called for Blair to be allowed to go in his own time. Once again both men realised that they must close down the media frenzy. At a second meeting the same day Blair finally promised Brown that he would go next summer. As he left Number Ten Brown was photographed uncharacteristically grinning broadly. The next day he made a statement in Glasgow pledging his continued loyalty; an hour later at a London school Blair confirmed – without setting a precise date – that the coming conference would be his last. But he still did not endorse a successor.

This attempted coup rebounded against Brown. Admittedly Blair was forced to set a date for his departure earlier than he would have liked; but he gained himself another year and still managed to retain some freedom of manoeuvre to set his own timetable. Brown, on the other hand, had once again seemed greedy to grasp the crown without the ruthlessness to seize it. Compared with Lloyd George in 1916, Macmillan in 1957 or Mrs Thatcher in 1975 he seemed to lack an essential quality that successful Prime Ministers need. The BBC reported that the question at Westminster was no longer 'How long can Tony Blair hang on?' but instead 'Is Gordon Brown fit to be Prime Minister?'[153] Over the weekend Charles Clarke – something of a loose cannon after his sacking from the Home Office – revived the old canard of 'psychological' issues, calling Brown a 'control freak' and 'totally uncollegiate', and spoke of Milburn's 'leadership potential'. Monday's *Daily Mail* proclaimed: 'Now the Crusade to Stop Gordon'.[154]

Blair, with typical chutzpah, managed to turn his valedictory conference into a triumphant swan-song. Brown did his best to make a loyal speech, declaring that it had been 'a privilege to work with the most successful Labour Prime Minister'. Unfortunately Cherie Blair, watching on television outside the hall, was heard to exclaim 'Well, that's a lie', which naturally stole the next day's headlines.[155] In his speech Blair made a joke of it: 'At least I don't have to worry about her running off with the bloke next door.' He went out of his way to praise Brown, reminding the conference that 'New Labour would never have happened, and three election victories would never have been secured, without Gordon Brown. He is a remarkable man. A remarkable servant to this country. And that is the truth.' But still he stopped short of anointing Brown as his preferred successor. He warned the party, if it wanted to win a fourth election, not to abandon his agenda, and ended with an extraordinary, almost Christ-like, peroration, reminiscent of Mrs Thatcher's promise to be a 'backseat driver': 'Whatever you do, I'm always with you . . . Next year I won't be making this speech. But in the years to come, wherever I am, whatever I do, I'm with you.'[156]

They did manage a smooth handover in the end, largely on Blair's terms. He used his final year to set up a series of policy reviews – five chaired by Blair; only one, on the economy, by Brown – to try to bind Brown's hands after he had gone: as well as pressing on with school and hospital reforms he deliberately brought forward a number of big decisions on long-term questions like nuclear energy and renewing Trident which could quite well have been left to the new Prime Minister. At first Brown tried to obstruct this process. But more than anything else he still wanted Blair's endorsement. The Blairites were openly promoting other candidates: first John Reid, then Alan Johnson, finally David Miliband. Blair flirted with all of them, thinking a contest might be healthier for the party than an unopposed succession; but in the end he did not really want a challenger to beat Brown. 'Tony's ultimate loyalty was to Gordon. He wanted Gordon to be Prime Minister, but in a way that was consistent with the project.'[157] In March Brown made a last attempt to pressure Blair to go before the local elections; but when Blair held firm he decided to support Blair's policy reviews after all, rather than be painted as an obstacle to change. In April Miliband ended months of speculation by announcing that he would not stand; Reid and Johnson had already done the same, so finally there was no serious alternative to Brown's succession. One last time he and Blair stage-managed a public and reciprocal *rapprochement* on the eve of the elections: Brown, writing in the *Sun*, praised Blair's 'social and economic achievements, and his leadership in the world', calling him 'my oldest friend in politics'; and the next day Blair, speaking appropriately in Edinburgh, finally endorsed Brown – though still not by name – as his successor: 'In all probability, a Scot will become Prime Minister . . . someone who has built one of the strongest economies in the world and who, as I've always said, will make a great Prime Minister for Britain.'[158]

On 10 May Blair finally announced that he would step down on 27 June 2007, after a long farewell very much on the lines of the leaked memo the previous year, milking every opportunity for emotional grandstanding with a world tour and valedictory G8 and EU summits. Secure at last, Brown worked closely with Blair over the last few weeks, seeking his advice as never before. 'In the build-up to the handover,' one Blair aide reported, 'Gordon and he were probably working more closely together than virtually at any point in the history of the government.'[159] 'If only they could have worked together for the previous ten years as they did in the last four weeks,' another reflected, 'so much more would have been achieved.'[160] But Brown would not co-operate until he knew that Blair was really going.

Brown at last came into what he regarded as his long-denied entitlement on a mixed tide of hope and apprehension. Plenty of people around New Labour had long doubted whether he had the qualities to make a good Prime Minister: as in 1994, he was still too driven, too secretive, too obsessive; insufficiently outgoing, lacking in human warmth. On the other hand many in the party and beyond had become disillusioned with Blair's shallow charm and saw Brown's solid Scots seriousness as a welcome contrast, hoping that he would restore integrity and old-fashioned standards to the conduct of government. Labour's first poster after the handover made a virtue of his lack of charisma: 'Not flash. Just Gordon.' Helped by a series of events – floods, failed terrorist attacks in London and Glasgow, a new outbreak of foot-and-mouth disease – which he handled firmly but without fuss, he was seen to make a good start. He promoted some of his own loyalists – Alistair Darling to be Chancellor, Balls Minister for Schools, Yvette Cooper Chief Secretary – but kept on some core Blairites, and made Miliband Foreign Secretary, raising the hope that the old factionalism might be healed. Labour's poll ratings – which under Blair had been trailing David Cameron's rejuvenated Tories – soared. By modelling himself on Blair, Cameron suddenly seemed to have misjudged the national mood. Although there was no need for an election only two years after the last one, Brown was widely expected to seize the opportunity to seek his own mandate – like Eden on finally succeeding Churchill in 1955. The media were all geared up for it: the Tories, while outwardly confident, were privately resigned to a fourth defeat. But, as so often at crucial moments in his life, Brown hesitated. He was afraid of looking opportunist; he was also afraid that if he failed to win, his premiership – after his long wait – would be the briefest in modern history: shorter even than Canning's four months in 1819. So – like Callaghan in 1978 – he raised the expectation and then dashed it.

From that moment everything in his premiership went wrong. The Tories crowed, and the opinion polls swung dramatically into reverse. The reassuringly calm Prime Minister of July was suddenly portrayed as a panicky ditherer who could not make up his mind. Then the economic weather suddenly turned nasty. In September Northern Rock – a medium-sized regional bank based in Newcastle and a major employer in the North-East – failed, leading to the first run on a British bank in living memory. Worse was to come, as banks in America and all round the world crashed like ninepins, taking hitherto healthy businesses with them, and the whole international economy slipped rapidly into meltdown. The so-called 'credit crunch' may have originated in America, caused by the reckless selling of 'sub-prime' mortgages: but British banks were equally heavily compromised and the failure of the Bank of England and the City regulators to spot the trouble and intervene in time was widely blamed on Brown's reform of the regulatory system back in 1997. For ten years Brown as Chancellor had taken the credit for the strength of the economy, boasting that he had eliminated the Tory cycle of 'boom and bust'. Now, by a cruel irony, just as he inherited the premiership that he had coveted so long, his luck ran out. It was the worst possible time to become Prime Minister. For a decade he had built a reputation for economic mastery which made up for his dour personality: now suddenly he seemed merely clumsy and inept, mouthing dreary platitudes with no spark of hope or inspiration, vindicating those who had always said he was unfitted for the job.

In the autumn of 2008 he staged a temporary recovery. As once-powerful financial institutions all round the world turned to their governments for help, Brown's unmatched experience as a finance minister over the past decade seemed after all to make him the man of the hour. The multi-million-pound rescue package he put together to recapitalise British banks was widely copied in other countries – even by the outgoing Bush administration in America – and the newly elected President Obama promised an even bigger economic stimulus. At the Labour conference in September Brown was able to brush off both Tory leader David Cameron and a half-baked challenge to his leadership from David Miliband with the confident assertion that the greatest economic hurricane since the 1930s was 'no time for a novice'.[161] He then stunned the political world by bringing Peter Mandelson back into the government as Business Secretary in a bold bid to silence the grumbling Blairites and heal the rift that had poisoned New Labour ever since 1994. The unprecedented scale of the crisis seemed to revitalise him. It was after all Thatcherite free-market economics that had so spectacularly failed: if the ideological pendulum was now swinging back towards greater government intervention, even public owner-ship, then Labour – headed by the former editor of *The Red Paper on Scotland* – should be better adapted to handle the new condi-tions than the Tories. But by the end of the year it appeared that all the billions of pounds poured into the banks, together with a large cut in VAT and interest rates reduced almost to zero, were having no effect. As more high street shops closed, unemployment soared, and the pound fell against both the euro and the dollar, the view gained hold that the crash had not after all been wholly made in America but was substantially caused by New Labour's uncritical embrace of the wealthy and 'light-touch' regulation of the very banks whose recklessness it now demonised; moreover that Brown's imprudent spending in his latter years as Chancellor had left the British economy in a weaker state to survive the downturn than many others. He could not blame his predecessor, since everyone knew that he had been the unchallenged master of the Treasury for the past decade. Instead he doggedly refused to admit any mistakes, while insisting that he was still the man to steer Britain and the world out of catastrophe. But his dour manner and robotic language still failed to carry any sort of inspiration, while other countries – notably Germany and France – seemed decreasingly willing to follow his lead. The painful truth was – as the press and the party had recognised in 1994 – that he was by nature simply not a leader. By the spring of 2009 – while

Blair floated free of the whole mess, blithely reinventing himself as a 'peace envoy' in the Middle East – the Government's poll ratings had plunged again and Brown's plight appeared to be terminal. He had just over a year to try to recover before the election that must be held in 2010, hoping desperately that the upturn would come in time for him to claim the credit.

By the crudest measure of political success, Tony Blair clearly 'won' his duel with Gordon Brown. After coming from behind to beat his best friend to the Labour leadership in 1994 he went on to win three general elections and became the second-longest-serving Prime Minister of the century before stepping down at a time more or less of his own choosing in 2007. The turn of the Millennium was thus Blair's decade, as the long Edwardian summer was Asquith's, the late 1950s were Macmillan's and the 1980s belonged to Margaret Thatcher. Yet the way he attained the leadership obliged him to cede his rival unprecedented autonomy in key areas of policy, so that he was less the master of his own government than any Prime Minister since MacDonald in the early 1930s. As a result he achieved much less in office than he should have done, disappointing the high hopes of 1997. Moreover much of what his government did achieve – ten years of uninterrupted growth, allowing unprecedented amounts of money to be poured into the NHS and other public services; the minimum wage, and some progress in reducing child poverty – was widely credited to Brown as Chancellor; while Blair's own reputation was overshadowed by the disastrously botched invasion of Iraq. He did finally – if it endures – bring peace to Northern Ireland, a historic achievement which had eluded Gladstone and Lloyd George. He also delivered (without much enthusiasm) devolution to Scotland and Wales, a mayor for London and half-hearted reform of the House of Lords, as well as some important social changes like the introduction of civil partnerships for same-sex couples (and some less successful, like the banning of fox-hunting, and of smoking in pubs). But he failed in most of his big ambitions: he backed away from electoral reform which might have delivered his dream of healing the 'schism' on the centre-left of British politics; he failed to take Britain into the euro; and once he had discovered how he wanted to reform the provision of public services he was unable to deliver significant progress on that front either. In all these areas he was thwarted by Brown.

The Granita deal of 1994 – both what was agreed and what was not – hobbled the Blair government from the beginning. No previous administration in the past two hundred years – not even the wartime coalitions – was so institutionally divided as Blair's between antagonistic factions. The nearest equivalent was the suspicion that persisted between former Bevanites and former Gaitskellites in Wilson's government in the 1960s: but their quarrels were largely in the past, while the Blairites and Brownites were fighting over the future. In the circumstances it is remarkable that the government functioned so well as it did; and not surprising that it lacked coherence. The problem was partly that Blair was never politically strong enough to confront Brown directly, move him from the Treasury or curb his insubordinate power. He needed Brown too much. They were the joint architects of the New Labour project, and Brown's deeper roots in the party gave him a legitimacy which Blair knew he lacked. But there was also honour involved, and the memory of close friendship which – on Blair's side at least – never entirely faded. He never quite stopped feeling guilty for the way he had stolen the leadership from his friend: he did feel that he owed Brown his turn in Number Ten. In the end he always wanted Brown to succeed him. But he was increasingly angered by Brown's secrecy, factionalism and obstructiveness. Had Brown been more willing to work with him to lay the foundations of a joint legacy, he might have been ready to step down earlier. Instead Brown's jealous determination – as it seemed to the Blairites – to block any reform until he could take the credit for it himself, drove Blair eventually to tear up the Granita agreement by deciding to stay on into a third term – which confirmed Brown's sense of betrayal.

Brown had some reason to feel hard done by in 1994. He had worked hard, even brilliantly, since his student days to reach the point where he was universally seen as a future leader, only to be gazumped by a latecomer with far less developed ideas but a winning smile, who also happened to be his best friend and protégé. But that is politics: crown princes rarely succeed (and when they do the results are often disappointing). Blair's light ideological baggage was precisely what made him the ideal front man for the New Labour project. His cross-party appeal almost certainly gained Labour a bigger majority in 1997 than Brown as leader could have won. Moreover Blair honoured the first part of the Granita deal by granting Brown, in the first term, the unprecedented independence to pursue his 'fairness agenda' that he had promised. Had Brown been satisfied with that, and been prepared to work with Blair, the greater prize might well have fallen into his hands sooner than it did. Barely had the 2001 election been won, however, than he started badgering Blair to honour the second part of the deal. It was his obsessive determination to keep hold of the domestic agenda – even when it was becoming clear that money alone was not going to deliver the sort of improved services they had promised – that drove Blair to follow his own instinct to develop more market-oriented solutions. At one level Brown had good reasons for thinking that trust schools and foundation hospitals threatened the deepest values which he had come into politics to promote; but he gave the impression of obstructing them as much because they were being pushed by Blair as from real conviction. Just as Blair was unwilling to confront him, however, so Brown could never bring himself to force an open breach with Blair, even when the Prime Minister was at his weakest. Above everything, he still wanted to be Prime Minister himself, and he did not want to jeopardise his hope of a smooth succession. So he griped and grumbled, but never made a decisive move. The longer Blair stayed on, the more negative Brown became; so that by the time Blair finally went in 2007 he seemed to have forgotten why he had wanted to be Prime Minister in the first place. Once famed for his powerful intellect and assumed to have an alternative vision which he had been waiting ten years for the opportunity to pursue, he no longer seemed to know what he believed in or what to do with power now he had it. Instead of the return to the serious, principled and competent government rooted in Labour values that so many had hoped for after the years of Blairite hype and spin, the new Prime Minister took on practically the whole of his predecessor's neo-Conservative agenda – including identity cards and the extended detention of terrorist suspects without trial which he had previously opposed – but with none of his predecessor's disarming flair. Having finally achieved his lifetime's goal he seemed paralysed by indecision as the strong economy he thought he had bequeathed himself slid into recession.

There is tragedy, but also a certain poetic justice, in Brown's fate. It recalls the legend of King Midas, who wished that everything he touched might turn to gold – except that everything Gordon Brown touched after he became Prime Minister turned to ashes. Like Ted Heath, whom he increasingly resembled – the same well-intentioned clumsiness, the same leaden inability to communicate – he seemed destined to be an unlucky Prime Minister; whereas Blair, like Mrs Thatcher, was for most of the time an extraordinarily lucky one. But the best politicians – like Pitt, Gladstone, Lloyd George, Churchill, Macmillan and Thatcher – make their own luck. They seize their moment and go on to embody their age. The less sure-footed – like Butler, Heath and Brown – miss their moment and never quite recover. Brown's fear, as he waited for his chance, was that he would turn out to be a 'tail-end' Prime Minister like Eden after Churchill, Home after Macmillan, Callaghan after Wilson or Major after Thatcher (even though he lasted seven years), doomed to the ranks of the also-rans. Unless he can belatedly recover his sense of vision and direction that seems all too likely.

The story of Blair and Brown bears out more cruelly than any other Lloyd George's bleak dictum that there is 'no friendship at the top'. The other pairs in this book were rivals, sometimes colleagues but never friends. Brown and Blair were, and it was their early friendship that made them ultimately incompatible. On paper, they could have made an exceptional team, their qualities perfectly complementing one another. But in politics, as Thomas Grenville put it in 1812, 'When two men ride a horse, one must ride behind.'[162] Brown could never accept that; but neither could Blair push Brown off the horse. For ten years they obstructed one another: as a result they wasted the great opportunity they had created and achieved less than they should have done. The deal they made in 1994 to try to share the spoils was a devil's pact which ultimately did neither of them – nor the country – much good.

Acknowledgements

I have incurred fewer debts than usual in writing this book. It is largely based on published sources, so I have not carried out my customary wide range of interviews even for the contemporary chapters. Three of the eight, in fact, draw heavily on my own previously published work on Lloyd George, Nye Bevan, Edward Heath and Margaret Thatcher. For the rest, it will be clear that I am indebted to the work of others whose work is listed in the bibliography. In particular, I must single out Richard Aldous's lively account of the Gladstone and Disraeli relationship, *The Lion and the Unicorn*, which appeared just as I was starting my chapter on the same subject. On the other hand, Giles Hunt's *The Duel*, the fullest examination yet written of the Canning – Castlereagh affair, appeared only after I had written my chapter. Above all, it will be obvious that my chapter on Blair and Brown relies substantially on the work of the corps of indefatigable journalists who nowadays reveal the intimate secrets of government – reflecting the spin and counterspin of the protagonists – while they are still warm. In this genre I am particularly grateful to James Naughtie, Andrew Rawnsley, John Rentoul, Robert Peston and – in a rather different category – Anthony Seldon. Between them they make it possible to write confidently about recent events far sooner than was imaginable even twenty years ago.

I am also deeply grateful to Peter Catterall for making available to me the still unpublished parts of Harold Macmillan's diaries, which he is editing, and to Philippa Blake-Roberts of the Macmillan Book Trust for allowing me to quote from them.

As always I am grateful to Dan Franklin of Jonathan Cape for his continuing faith and unwavering support; to Alex Bowler for picture research; and to my agent Bruce Hunter of David Higham Associates for his support and tenacity. Finally this book, like its predecessor, is dedicated to Kirsty Hogarth in gratitude for her love and encouragement over the past five years – and also for suggesting the title.

John Campbell
March 2009

Notes

Introduction

1. Shakespeare, *Julius Caesar*, IV, iii, 218–21.

Charles James Fox and William Pitt

1. R. Ellis Roberts, *Samuel Rogers and his Circle*, p.209.
2. Horace Walpole to Sir Horace Mann, 30 March 1771, in Paget Toynbee (ed.), *The Letters of Horace Walpole* , Vol.VIII, p.26.
3. Lord John Russell (ed.), *Memorials and Correspondence of Charles James Fox* Vol I, p.25.
4. H. J. Nicoll, *Great Orators: Burke, Fox, Sheridan, Pitt*, p.209.
5. Edward Gibbon, *Letters* Vol. III, pp.313–21, quoted in Stanley Ayling, *Fox: The Life of Charles James Fox*, p.185.
6. T. Copeland (ed.), *Correspondence of Edmund Burke*, Vol. III, p.385.
7. Ayling, p.185.
8. L. G. Mitchell, *Charles James Fox*, p.38.
9. Nicoll, p.227.
10. Walpole to Revd William Mason, 4 February 1778, in Toynbee, Vol.X, p.182.
11. House of Commons, 11 February 1780, quoted in Loren Reid, *Charles James Fox: A Man for the People*, p.107.
12. Russell, Vol. II, p.81.
13. Ayling, p.91.
14. Ibid., pp.91–2.
15. Russell, Vol. I, p.262.
16. Walpole to Sir Horace Mann, 3 June 1781, in Toynbee, Vol. XII, p.6.
17. J. Holland Rose, *Pitt and the National Revival*, p.88.
18. Walpole to Mann, 29 November 1781, in Toynbee, Vol. XII, p.109.
19. Horace Walpole, *Last Journals*, pp.389–90 (4 December 1781).
20. S. Romilly, *Memoirs of the Life of Sir Samuel Romilly*, Vol. I, p.192.
21. House of Commons, 8 March 1782, quoted in John Ehrman, *The Younger Pitt*, Vol. I, p.80.

22. Walpole, p.416 (8 March 1782).
23. Walpole to Mann, 5 May 1782, in Toynbee, Vol. XII, pp.244–5.
24. Walpole, p.443.
25. House of Commons, 7 May 1782, as quoted in Nicoll, pp.220–1.
26. Ibid., 19 June 1782.
27. William Hague, *William Pitt the Younger,* p.90, citing Bishop Tomline.
28. George III to Robert Jenkinson, 13 July 1782, in Reid, p.158.
29. Russell, Vol. I, p.447.
30. House of Commons, 10 July 1782, quoted in Hague, p.99.
31. Ibid., 5 December 1782.
32. Nicoll, p.254.
33. Mitchell, p.85, Robin Reilly, *Pitt the Younger,* p.101.
34. Ayling, p.140.
35. J. Grieg (ed.), *The Farington Diary,* Vol. III, p.260.
36. Reid, p.339.
37. Roberts, p.112.
38. Hague, p.223.
39. Quoted in I. M. Davis, *The Harlot and the Statesman,* p.74.
40. Hague, p.109, citing Tomline, p.68; Nicoll p.224.
41. House of Commons, 17 February 1783.
42. Ibid., 21 February 1783.
43. Hague, p.113.
44. Ibid., p.123.
45. Fox to Lord Northington, in Nicoll, p.101.
46. Reilly, p.88.
47. Ayling, p.119.
48. Hague, p.140.
49. House of Commons, 18 November 1783.
50. Ibid., 27 November 1783.
51. Ayling, p.120.
52. House of Commons, 1 December 1783.
53. Ibid., 18 November 1783.
54. Ibid., 27 November 1783.
55. Ibid.
56. Ibid., 1 December 1783.
57. Walpole to Sir Horace Mann, 2 December 1783, in Toynbee, Vol. XIII, p.96.
58. Hague, p.144.
59. Ibid.
60. House of Commons, 17 December 1783.
61. Hague, p.143.
62. House of Commons, 17 December 1783.
63. Hague, pp.145–6.
64. Ibid., p.152.
65. Mitchell, p.67.
66. Russell, Vol. II, p.224, in Ayling, p.124.
67. Nicoll, p.229.
68. See M. D. George, *English Political Caricature: A Study of Opinion and Propaganda.*
69. Hague, p.154.

70. Ayling, p.125.
71. House of Commons, 12 January 1784.
72. John Cannon, *The Fox–North Coalition: Crisis of the Constitution, 1782–4*, p.165, quoted with evident agreement by Hague, p.157.
73. House of Commons, 12 January 1784.
74. Walpole to Hon. Thomas Walpole, 1 February 1782, in Toynbee, Vol. XIII, pp.119–20.
75. House of Commons, 12 January 1784.
76. Ibid., 1 February 1784.
77. Ayling, p.127, citing Earl Stanhope, *The Life of the Right Honourable William Pitt*, Vol. I, Appendix vi–viii.
78. House of Commons, 20 January 1784.
79. Ayling, p.127.
80. House of Commons, 18 February 1784.
81. Hague, p.168.
82. Ayling, p.131; Cannon, p.222.
83. J. Debrett, *History of the Westminster Election.*
84. Nicoll, p.105.
85. Ibid.
86. Pitt to Portland, 24 May 1784 in Reid, p.206.
87. House of Commons, 24 May 1784. (Some texts give 'the extremest corner of the island'.)
88. House of Commons, 8 June 1784.
89. Mitchell, p.72.
90. Speech, 27 February 1786, in Mitchell, p.75.
91. House of Commons, 10 December 1788, in Nicoll, pp.109–10, Hague, p.259.
92. Lord Sheffield to William Eden, 12 December 1788, in W. Auckland, *The Journal and Correspondence of William Eden Auckland, First Lord Auckland*, Vol. II, p.257.
93. Ibid., 17 December 1788.
94. Nicoll, p.111.
95. Hague, pp.260–1.
96. Reilly, p.164.
97. House of Commons, 5 February 1790, in Hague, p. 272.
98. Fox to Grenville, August 1789, in Mitchell, p.108. He wrote a slightly different wording of the same thought to Richard Fitzpatrick on 30 July 1789 (Russell, Vol. XI, p.361).
99. House of Commons, 15 April 1791, in Mitchell, p.108.
100. Hague, p.325.
101. Portland to Fitzwilliam, 30 November 1792, in Mitchell, pp.129–30.
102. Fox to Lord Holland, November 1792, in Russell, Vol. II, p.376, in Mitchell, pp.124–5.
103. House of Commons, 1 February 1793, in Reid, p.298.
104. Russell, Vol. II, p.369, 3 February 1792.
105. Ibid., in Nicoll, pp.117–18.
106. House of Commons, 10 February 1794.
107. Ibid., 13 December 1792.
108. Speech at the Whig Club, 4 December 1792, in Mitchell, p.127.

109. 12 February 1792, Malmesbury Vol. II, pp.475–6, in Reid, p.292.
110. Fox to Lord Holland, in Russell, Vol. III, pp.60–2.
111. House of Commons, 17 May 1794.
112. Nicoll, p.121.
113. Hague, pp.389–90.
114. *The Rolliad*, ibid., p.203.
115. House of Commons, 10 November 1795.
116. Mitchell, p.140.
117. Fox to Lord Holland, 15 November 1795, in Mitchell, p.140.
118. *The Gazetteer,* 13 June 1796, in Reid, p.322.
119. House of Commons, 26 May 1797.
120. Ibid., 30 May 1797.
121. Fox to Denis O'Bryen, 19 March 1798, in Mitchell, p.145.
122. Reilly, p.279.
123. *The Times*, 11 November 1798
124. Lord Holland, *Memoirs of the Whig Party*, Vol. I, p.92.
125. Malmesbury, Vol. III, p.355, in Hague, p.406.
126. House of Commons, 3 February 1800.
127. Ibid., 17 February 1800.
128. Fox to O'Bryen, 16 February 1801, in Hague, p.477.
129. Fox to Grey, February 1801, in Russell, Vol. III, p.324.
130. Ibid.
131. Ibid., 15 March 1803, p.404.
132. Fox to Lauderdale, 24 February 1804, in Mitchell, p.202.
133. Thomas Creevey, 24 May 1803, in Hague, p.513.
134. House of Commons, 24 May 1803, in Eyck, p.347, and Ayling, p.216.
135. Ibid., 27 May 1803, in Ayling, p.217.
136. L. V. Harcourt (ed.), George Rose, *The Diaries and Correspondence of George Rose,* Vol. I, p.508.
137. Fox to Grey, 15 March 1803, in Russell, Vol. III, p.406.
138. Pitt to Dundas, 29 March 1804, in Hague, p.524.
139. Russell, Vol. III, pp.455, 452, 464.
140. Hague, pp.527–8.
141. Fox to Coutts, 31 December 1805, in Hague p.531.
142. House of Commons, 18 June 1804.
143. Fox to Holland, 24 July 1804, in Reid, p.402.
144. William Eden to Lord Auckland, 19 June 1804, in Auckland Vol. IV, p.199.
145. Rose, Vol. II, pp.156–7, in Reid, p.403.
146. Fox to Grey, 28 August 1805, in Russell, Vol. IV, p.105.
147. Rose, Vol. II, p.110.
148. Fox to Holland, 7 November 1805, in Russell, p.121.
149. Ibid., 2 January 1806, in Russell Vol. IV, p.130.
150. Fox to Lauderdale, 17 December 1805, in Mitchell, p.215.
151. Dorothy M. Stuart, *Dearest Bess: The Life and Times of Lady Elizabeth Foster, afterwards Duchess of Devonshire* pp.133–4.
152. Lady Bessborough to Lord Bessborough, 23 January 1806, in Hague, p.579.
153. Stuart, p.134.
154. House of Commons, 27 January 1806.
155. Holland, *Memoirs of the Whig Party*, Vol. I, pp.249–50, in Ayling, p.227.

156. Walter Scott, *Patriotism: Nelson, Pitt, Fox* in Sir Arthur Quiller-Couch (ed.), *The Oxford Book of English Verse, 1250–1900*.
157. G. M. Trevelyan, *Lord Grey of the Reform Bill*, p.107, in Ayling, p.238.
158. G. M. Trevelyan, *British History in the 19th Century*, p.69, quoted by Ayling, p.233.

Viscount Castlereagh and George Canning

1. H. Reeve (ed.), *The Greville Memoirs*, Vol. I, pp.52–3.
2. Peter Dixon, *Canning: Politician and Statesman*, p.162.
3. Francis Bickley (ed.), *The Diaries of Sylvester Douglas, Lord Glenbervie*, Vol. I, p.209.
4. Dixon, p.77.
5. Sir H. Maxwell (ed.), *The Creevey Papers*, Vol. I, p.9 (25 November 1802).
6. Dorothy Marshall, *The Rise of George Canning*, pp.269–70.
7. Ibid., p.270.
8. Dixon, pp.98–9.
9. Dennis Gray, *Spencer Perceval: The Evangelical Prime Minister*, p.96.
10. Sir Charles Petrie, *George Canning*, pp.95–6.
11. Wendy Hinde, *George Canning*, p.209.
12. Ibid., p.218.
13. Gray, p.219.
14. Dixon, p.133.
15. Wendy Hinde, *Castlereagh*, p.164.
16. Hinde, *George Canning*, p.226.
17. Dixon, p.134.
18. Gray, p.231.
19. Lewis Melville (ed.), *The Huskisson Papers*, p.62 (12 September 1809).
20. Hinde, *Castlereagh*, p.165.
21. *Annual Register*, 1809, pp.562–3.
22. Marquess of Londonderry (ed.), *Memoir and Correspondence of Viscount Castlereagh, Second Marquess of Londonderry*, pp.38–9.
23. *Annual Register*, pp.564–6.
24. Gray, p.243.
25. *Annual Register*, pp.562–3.
26. Hinde, *Canning*, p.226; Dixon, pp.136–7.
27. L. Jennings (ed.), *The Croker Papers*, Vol. II, pp.20–1.
28. Creevey, ed. Maxwell, Vol. I, p.97.
29. Elizabeth Longford, *Wellington: The Years of the Sword*, p.258.
30. Hinde, *Canning*, p.227.
31. *The Times*, 22 September 1809.
32. *Morning Chronicle*, 24 September 1809.
33. Creevey, ed. Maxwell, Vol. I. p.97.
34. Lord Colchester (ed.), *The Diary and Correspondence of Charles Abbott, First Lord Colchester* Vol. II, p.209.
35. Hinde, *Canning*, p.228.
36. W. Auckland, *The Journal and Correspondence of William Eden Auckland, First Lord Auckland*, Vol. IV, p.322.
37. Ibid., p.327.
38. Petrie, p.107.

39. Philip Ziegler, *Addington*, p.286.
40. Hinde, *Castlereagh*, p.170.
41. Creevey, ed. Maxwell, Vol. I, p.287.
42. Gray, p.227.
43. Dixon, p.143.
44. Ibid., p.144.
45. Grenville, 15 December 1809
46. Hinde, *Castlereagh*, p.173.
47. Hinde, *Canning*, p.236.
48. Hinde, *Castlereagh*, p.175.
49. Hinde, *Canning*, p.250.
50. Hinde, *Castlereagh*, p.183.
51. Hinde, *Canning*, p.253.
52. Ibid.
53. Hinde, *Castlereagh*, p.184.
54. Hinde, *Canning*, p.255.
55. Ibid., p.256.
56. Hinde, *Castlereagh*, p.184.
57. Hinde, *Canning*, p.267.
58. Dixon, p.164.
59. Ibid.
60. Ibid., p.175 (30 July 1813).
61. Ibid. (9 August 1813).
62. Ibid., p.182.
63. Ibid., p.184.
64. J. E. Cookson, *Lord Liverpool's Administration: The Crucial Years, 1815–22*, p.287.
65. Francis Bamford and the Duke of Wellington (eds), *The Journal of Mrs Arbuthnot, 1820–1832*, Vol. I, p.25.
66. Cookson, p.293.
67. Hinde, *Canning*, p.305.
68. Dixon, p.205.
69. Cookson, p.310.
70. H. Montgomery Hyde, *The Strange Death of Lord Castlereagh*, p.103.
71. Ibid., p.104.
72. Hinde, *Canning*, p.314.
73. Ibid.
74. See Giles Hunt, *The Duel: Castlereagh, Canning and Deadly Cabinet Rivalry* for a suggestion that Castlereagh's mental illness was caused by venereal disease contracted at Cambridge, as well as for the fullest account of the duel.
75. Creevey, ed. Maxwell, Vol. II, p.43.
76. Dixon, p.209.
77. Hinde, *Canning*, p.316.
78. Dixon, p.209.
79. Ibid., p.211.
80. Hinde, *Castlereagh*, p.258.
81. Dixon, p.252.
82. Henry Kissinger, *A World Restored: Metternich, Castlereagh and the Problems of Peace, 1812–1822*, p.314.

Notes

Benjamin Disraeli and William Gladstone

1. Roy Jenkins, *Gladstone*, p.53.
2. W. F. Monypenny and G. E. Buckle, *The Life of Benjamin Disraeli, Earl of Beaconsfield*, Vol. V, p.549.
3. For the coded homoeroticism of Disraeli's novels see William Kuhn, *The Politics of Pleasure: A Portrait of Benjamin Disraeli*.
4. Monypenny and Buckle Vol. I, pp.112, 127; John Morley, *The Life of Gladstone* Vol. I, p.122.
5. Richard Aldous, *The Lion and the Unicorn: Gladstone v. Disraeli*, p.34.
6. Disraeli to Sarah Disraeli, 6 February 1845, in John Matthews (ed.), *The Letters of Benjamin Disraeli*, Vol. III, p. 156.
7. Ibid., 6 September 1841, in Matthews, Vol. III, p.357.
8. Albert memorandum, 28 November 1852, in Matthews, Vol. VI, p.190 n.1.
9. W. S. Churchill, *Thoughts and Adventures*, p.213.
10. Richard Shannon, *Gladstone: 1809–1865*, p.213.
11. Aldous, p.61; Disraeli to Lord Stanley, 7 December 1850, in Matthews, Vol. V, p.383.
12. Shannon, *Gladstone, 1809–1865*, p.257.
13. Monypenny and Buckle, Vol. III, p.344.
14. Gladstone to Catherine Gladstone, 23 February 1852, in Morley Vol. I, pp.416–17.
15. Gladstone to Lord Aberdeen, 30 July 1852, in Morley, Vol. I, p.429.
16. Robert Blake, 'Gladstone and Disraeli', in Peter J. Jagger (ed.), *Gladstone*, p.58.
17. Gladstone to Catherine Gladstone, 6 December 1852, in Morley, Vol. I, p.437.
18. Ibid., 8 December 1852, in Morley, Vol. I, p.438.
19. House of Commons, 16 December 1852 [Vol. 123, cols 1629–66].
20. Shannon, *Gladstone, 1809–1865*, p.259.
21. Gladstone to Catherine Gladstone, 18 December 1852, in Morley, Vol. I, p.438.
22. Shannon, *Gladstone, 1809–1865*, p.260.
23. Gladstone to Catherine Gladstone, 18 December 1852, in Morley, Vol. I, p.438.
24. House of Commons, 16 December 1852 [Vol. 123, cols 1666–93].
25. *The Times*, 18 December 1852.
26. Robert Blake, *Disraeli*, p.346.
27. Gladstone to Catherine Gladstone, 18 December 1852, in Morley, Vol. I, p.439.
28. Aldous, pp.73–4; Jenkins, pp.143–4.
29. Disraeli to Lord Henry Lennox, 18 July 1852, in Matthews, Vol. VI, p.94.
30. Disraeli to the Marchioness of Londonderry, 31 December 1852, in Monypenny and Buckle, Vol. III, p.476.
31. Monypenny & Buckle, Vol. III, pp.476–80.
32. H. Reeve (ed.), *The Greville Memoirs*, 21 April 1853 (Vol. VII, p.59).
33. *The Press*, 4 June 1853, in Matthews, Vol. VI, p.241, n.1.
34. Blake, p.159.
35. Aldous, p.91; Philip Magnus, *Gladstone*, p.119.
36. Matthews, Vol. VI, p.430 n.2.
37. Blake, p.363.
38. Morley, Vol. I, pp.427–8.

39. Ibid., p.428.
40. A. R. Ashwell and Reginald G.Wilberforce, *The Life of Samuel Wilberforce*, Vol. II, p.349.
41. Shannon, *Gladstone, 1809–1865*, p.315.
42. Jenkins, p.187.
43. Shannon, *Gladstone, 1809–1865*, p.356.
44. Ibid., p.357.
45. Disraeli to Gladstone, 25 May 1858, in Monypenny and Buckle, Vol. III, pp.157–8.
46. Gladstone to Disraeli, 25 May 1858, ibid., pp.158–9.
47. Ashwell and Wilberforce, Vol. III, p.70.
48. Disraeli to John Delane, 22 January 1858, in Matthews, Vol. VII, p.122.
49. Edward Bulwer-Lytton to Disraeli, 23 September 1858, in ibid., p.162.
50. Travis L. Crosby, *The Two Mr Gladstones*, pp.90 and 241 n.88.
51. Gladstone diary, 13 June 1859, in Shannon, p.382.
52. Gladstone to Catherine Gladstone, 22 July 1859, in Morley, Vol. II, p.19.
53. *Greville Memoirs*, 26 February 1860 (Reeve, Vol. VIII, p.298).
54. Gladstone to Lady Mildred Hope, 18 October 1859, in Shannon, p.261.
55. *Greville Memoirs*, 26 February 1860 (Reeve, Vol. VIII, p.298).
56. Monypenny and Buckle, Vol. IV, p.278.
57. House of Commons, 8 June 1860 [Vol. 158, cols 957–66].
58. Disraeli to Mrs Brydgeman Williams, n.d., in Monypenny and Buckle, Vol. II, pp.33–6.
59. Gladstone diary, 31 May 1861, in Shannon, p.441.
60. Sir John Trelawney diary, p.105, in Aldous, p.127.
61. House of Commons, 11 May 1864.
62. Philip Guedalla, *Palmerston*, p.455.
63. Speech at Manchester, 18 July 1865, in Morley, Vol. II, p.146.
64. Guedalla, p.453.
65. Aldous, p.146.
66. Derby diary, ibid., p.148.
67. Monypenny and Buckle, Vol. II, pp.149–51.
68. W. S. Gilbert, *Iolanthe* (1882), Act 2.
69. House of Commons, 27 April 1866 [Vol. 183, cols 74–113].
70. Ibid.
71. Ibid. [Vol. 183, cols 113–52].
72. F. B. Smith, *The Making of the Second Reform Bill*, p.133.
73. Morley, Vol. I, p.223.
74. Aldous, p.176.
75. Monypenny and Buckle, Vol. IV, p.527.
76. Smith, pp.172–3.
77. Ibid., p.173.
78. Aldous, p.178.
79. House of Commons, 12 April 1867 [Vol. 186, cols 1675–88].
80. Jenkins, p.272.
81. Blake, p.467.
82. Ibid., p.471.
83. Smith, p.209.
84. Lord Houghton, May 1867, in Morley, Vol. II, p.230.

85. Morley, Vol. I, p.864.
86. Aldous, p.185.
87. Blake, p.487.
88. Ibid.
89. Morley, Vol. I, p.613.
90. Monypenny and Buckle, Vol. V, p.11.
91. Richard Shannon, *Gladstone: Heroic Minister, 1865–1898*, pp.48–9.
92. House of Commons, 3 April 1868 [Vol. 191, cols 893–924].
93. Ibid. [cols 924–41].
94. Jenkins, p.284.
95. Shannon, *Gladstone: Heroic Minister, 1865–1898*, p.52.
96. Aldous, p.198.
97. Ibid., p.200.
98. Blake, p.487; Shannon, p.63.
99. Lewis Carroll, *Through the Looking-Glass*, Chapter 7.
100. Derby diary, Vol. I p.341, in Aldous, pp.206–7.
101. Monypenny and Buckle, Vol. V, p.132.
102. Trelawney diary, p.419, in Shannon, p.94.
103. Monypenny and Buckle, Vol. II, pp.475–6.
104. Shannon, *Gladstone: Heroic Minister, 1865–1898*, p.94.
105. Ibid.
106. Ibid., p. 97.
107. Sir William Fraser, *Disraeli and his Day*, pp.375–6.
108. Speech in Manchester, 3 April 1872, in Blake, p.523.
109. Shannon, *Gladstone: Heroic Minister, 1865–1898*, p.102.
110. Ibid., p.113.
111. Monypenny and Buckle, Vol. V, p.211.
112. Trelawney diary, p.480, in Aldous, p.236.
113. Aldous, p.233.
114. Shannon, *Gladstone: Heroic Minister, 1865–1898*, p.126.
115. Moneypenny and Buckle, Vol. V p.275.
116. Speech in Aylesbury, 31 January 1874, in Aldous, p.243.
117. *The Times,* 2 February 1874.
118. Ibid., 3 February 1874.
119. Ibid., 9 February 1874.
120. Disraeli to Lady Bradford, 2 February 1875, in Marquess of Zetland (ed.), *The Letters of Disraeli to Lady Bradford and Lady Chesterfield*, Vol. I, pp.195–6.
121. Monypenny and Buckle, Vol. V, p.299.
122. Blake, p.538.
123. Aldous, p.254.
124. Morley, Vol. II, p.498.
125. G.W. E. Russell, *Collections and Recollections*, Chapter 14.
126. E.g. Disraeli to Lady Bradford, 20 December 1876, in Zetland Vol. II, p.95.
127. Aldous, pp.244–5.
128. Ibid., p.249.
129. Jonathan Parry, 'Benjamin Disraeli', in *Dictionary of National Biography*, p.23.
130. Disraeli to Lady Chesterfield, 29 June 1875, in Zetland, Vol. I, p.260.
131. Aldous, p.264.

132. Disraeli to Lady Bradford, 21 March 1876, in Zetland, Vol. II, p.26.
133. Magnus, p.244.
134. Disraeli to Lady Chesterfield, 14 July 1874, in Zetland, Vol. I, p.116.
135. Blake, p.569.
136. *The Times*, 11 July 1876.
137. Shannon, *Gladstone: Heroic Minister, 1865–1898*, pp.169–70.
138. Gladstone to Granville, 29 August 1876, in Agatha Ramm (ed.), *The Political Correspondence of Mr Gladstone and Lord Granville*, Vol. II, p.3.
139. Gladstone diary, 28 December 1879, in Shannon, p.24.
140. W. E. Gladstone, *Bulgarian Horrors and the Question of the East*, pp.61–2.
141. Jenkins, p.404.
142. Disraeli to Lady Bradford, 9 and 11 September 1876, in Zetland, Vol. II, pp.73–4.
143. Disraeli to Derby, 8 September 1876, in Monypenny and Buckle, Vol. VI, p.60.
144. Disraeli to Lady Bradford, 31 August 1876 (ibid. Vol. II, p.69).
145. House of Commons, 31 July 1876 [Vol. 231, cols. 202–16].
146. *The Times*, 11 September 1876.
147. Ibid., 21 September 1876.
148. Ibid.
149. Disraeli to Lady Bradford, 25 September 1876, in Zetland, Vol. II, p.76.
150. Disraeli to Lady Chesterfield, 12 October 1876, in Zetland Vol. II, p.79.
151. Ibid., 20 October 1876, (ibid. p.83).
152. *The Times*, 10 November 1876.
153. Gladstone to Granville, 26 November 1876. (Ramm, Vol. I, p.24)
154. Ibid., 6 December 1876.
155. Blake, p.613.
156. *The Times*, 10 December 1876.
157. G. W. Hunt, 'We Don't Want to Fight . . .' (1878).
158. *The Times*, 31 January 1878.
159. Ibid.
160. Disraeli to Lady Bradford, 1 February 1878, in Zetland, Vol.II, p.158.
161. House of Commons, 4 February 1878.
162. Monypenny and Buckle, Vol. VI, p.347.
163. Aldous, p.286.
164. Morley, Vol.II, p.575.
165. House of Commons, 30 July 1878.
166. *Nineteenth Century*, July 1878, in Shannon, p.221.
167. Gladstone to Granville, 26 November 1876 (Ramm, Vol.I, p.24).
168. Morley, Vol.II, p.551.
169. Shannon, *Gladstone: Heroic Minister, 1865–1898*, p.221.
170. Speech in Southwark, 21 July 1878, ibid., p.223.
171. Monypenny and Buckle, Vol.VI, pp.356–7.
172. Magnus, p.253; Monypenny and Buckle, Vol.VI, pp.357–8.
173. Granville to Queen Victoria, 21 April 1880 in Morley, Vol.II, p.253.
174. Disraeli to Derby, October 1876, in Monypenny and Buckle, Vol.VI, p.67.
175. Disraeli to Lady Bradford, 3 October 1879, ibid., Vol.VI, p.181.
176. Magnus, p.265.
177. Shannon, p.237.

178. Ibid., pp.237–8.
179. Ibid., p.236.
180. Magnus, p.265.
181. Aldous, p.303.
182. Gladstone to the Duke of Argyll, 12 April 1880, in Morley, Vol. II p.615.
183. Aldous, p.306.
184. Disraeli to Lady Chesterfield, 4 April 1880, in Zetland, Vol. II, p.267.
185. Disraeli to Lady Bradford, 10 September 1880, (ibid., p.290).
186. Ibid., 29 September 1880, (p.293).
187. Ibid.
188. Ibid., 2 November 1880, in Blake, p.740.
189. The fragment is printed in Monypenny and Buckle, Vol. V, pp.530–60.
190. Aldous, p.317.
191. Ibid., p.318.
192. ibid.
193. Aldous, p.7; Magnus, p.281.
194. Aldous, p.6.
195. *The Times*, 9 May 1881.
196. Gladstone to Harry Gladstone, 21 April 1881, in Aldous, p.2.
197. Magnus, p.244.
198. Morley, Vol. III, p.475.
199. Blake, p.607.

H. H. Asquith and David Lloyd George

1. R. B. Haldane, *An Autobiography*, p.103.
2. H. C. G. Matthew, 'Asquith' in *Dictionary of National Biography*, p.3.
3. John Grigg, *The Young Lloyd George*, p.67.
4. LG to Uncle Lloyd, 20 June 1890, in W. R. P. George, *Lloyd George: Backbencher*, p.32.
5. Peter Rowland, *Lloyd George*, p.101.
6. Ibid., p.87.
7. LG to Margaret, 15 February 1895, in K. O. Morgan, (ed.), *Lloyd George Family Letters, 1885–1936*, pp.80–1.
8. W. R. P. George, p.239.
9. Earl of Oxford and Asquith, *Fifty Years of Parliament*, Vol. I, p.230.
10. Asquith to Tom Ellis, 20 November 1895, in W. R. P. George, p.173.
11. Rowland, p.153, quoting Keith Robbins, *Sir Edward Grey*, pp.90–1.
12. Rowland, p.153.
13. LG to Maggie, 16 May 1902, in Morgan (ed.), *Family Letters*, p.135.
14. Ibid., 6 July 1905, p.142.
15. Ibid., 11 January 1904, p.140.
16. Roy Jenkins, *Asquith*, p.201.
17. Asquith to LG, 8 April 1908, in Jenkins, p.202; Grigg, *Lloyd George : The People's Champion, 1902–1911*, p.133.
18. LG to Asquith, 11 April 1908, in Jenkins, p.202; Grigg, p.134.
19. Jenkins, p.202.
20. Grigg, John, *Lloyd George: The People's Champion, 1902–1911*, pp.139–40.
21. Asquith to Venetia Stanley, 17 April 1914, in Michael and Eleanor Brock (eds.), *H. H. Asquith: Letters to Venetia Stanley*, p.66.

22. Ibid., 18 April 1914 (p.66).
23. Ibid., 13 January 1915 (p.378).
24. Ibid., 27 February 1915 (p.452).
25. Hobhouse diary, 20 February 1910, in Edward David (ed.), *Inside Asquith's Cabinet: From the Diaries of Charles Hobhouse*, p.87.
26. Jenkins, p.221.
27. Grigg, *Lloyd George: The People's Champion 1902–1911*, p.178.
28. Hobhouse diary, 17 June 1909, ed. David, p.78.
29. Asquith to LG, August 1909, in *Grigg, Lloyd George: The People's Champion 1902–1911*, pp.208–9.
30. Ibid., 20 August 1911, in ibid., p.293.
31. LG to Elizabeth Asquith, 22 August 1911, in Grigg, p.293.
32. Harold Nicolson, *King George V: His Life and Reign*, p.284.
33. House of Commons, 19 June 1913 [Vol. 54, cols 548–60].
34. Jenkins, p.282.
35. Austen Chamberlain, 9 March 1913, *Politics from Inside*, p.533.
36. Riddell diary, 19 July 1913, in Lord Riddell, *More Pages from my Diary, 1908–14*, p.171.
37. Asquith to Venetia Stanley, 2 March 1914, in Jenkins, p.302.
38. Asquith to Margot, 3 June and 4 June 1914, in John Grigg, *Lloyd George: From Peace to War, 1912–1916*, p.106.
39. Jenkins, p.357.
40. Asquith to Venetia Stanley, 22 July 1914 in Brock, p.109.
41. W. S. Churchill, *The World Crisis* (1938 edn), p.155.
42. LG to Churchill, 27 August 1911, in Frank Owen, *Tempestuous Journey: Lloyd George, His Life and Times*, p.212.
43. Asquith to Venetia Stanley, 1 August 1914 in Brock, p.140.
44. Ibid., 2 August 1914 (p.146).
45. LG to Margaret, 3 August 1914, in Morgan (ed.), *Family Letters*, p.167.
46. Asquith to Venetia Stanley, 9 August 1914 in Brock, p.162.
47. LG to Margaret, 3 August 1914, in Morgan, (ed.), *Family Letters*, p.167.
48. Riddell diary, 11 October 1914, in *Lord Riddell's War Diary, 1914–18*, p.34.
49. LG to Asquith, 31 December 1914, in Jenkins, p.390.
50. Riddell diary, 7 March 1914, in *Lord Riddell's War Diary* (p.65).
51. Asquith to Venetia Stanley, 29 March 1915 in Brock, p.519.
52. A. J. P. Taylor (ed.), *Lloyd George: A Diary by Frances Stevenson*, p.42 (8 April 1915).
53. Riddell diary, 30 March 1915, in *Lord Riddell's War Diary*, p.70.
54. Asquith to Venetia Stanley, 25 March 1915 in Brock, p.508.
55. Ibid., 31 March 1915 (pp.525–6).
56. Ibid., 14 April 1915 (p.541).
57. Stevenson diary, ed. Taylor, 4 April 1915 in Brock, (p.39).
58. Asquith to Venetia Stanley, 25 March 1915 in Brock, p.508.
59. Ibid., 16 April 1915 (p.544).
60. Jenkins, p.403.
61. Asquith to Venetia Stanley, 23 March 1914 in Brock, p.60.
62. Stevenson diary, ed. Taylor, 18 May 1915 (p.51).
63. LG to Margaret, 21 May 1915, in Morgan (ed.), *Family Letters*, p.177.
64. Asquith to LG, 25 May 1915, in Grigg, *From Peace to War*, p.255.

65. D. Lloyd George, *War Memoirs*, Vol. I, p.145.
66. LG to Margaret, 26 May 1915, in Morgan (ed.), *Family Letters*, p.178.
67. Asquith to Venetia Stanley, 3 June 1915, in Jenkins, p.409.
68. Hobhouse diary, ed. Taylor, 23 May 1915 (p.247).
69. Ibid., 22 June 1915 (p.249).
70. Jenkins, p.416.
71. Ibid., p.419.
72. Stevenson diary, ed. Taylor, 12 October 1915 (pp.67–8).
73. Jenkins, p.423n., citing Magnus, *Kitchener: Portrait of an Imperialist*, pp.352–3.
74. Ibid., p.427.
75. LG to Margaret, 27 December 1915, in Morgan (ed.), *Family Letters*, p.180.
76. Stevenson diary, ed. Taylor, 31 January 1916 (pp.89–90).
77. LG to Margaret, 28 December 1915 in Morgan, p.181.
78. House of Commons, 5 January 1916 [Vol. 77, cols 949–62].
79. Scott to Hobhouse, 30 December 1915, in Hobhouse, p.166.
80. Asquith to Kathleen Scott, in Jenkins, p.440.
81. Stevenson diary, ed. Taylor, 18 April 1916 (pp.106–7).
82. Hankey diary, cited in H. C. G. Matthew, 'Asquith', in *DNB*.
83. Grigg, John, *Lloyd George: from Peace to War, 1912–1916*, p.339.
84. Asquith to LG, in Jenkins, p.448.
85. Kathleen Scott diary, 24 May 1916, ibid.
86. Ibid., 16 June 1916, in Jenkins, pp.457–8.
87. Jenkins, p.461.
88. Ibid., p.469.
89. Stevenson diary, 11 March 1916 (p.102).
90. Jenkins, p.480.
91. Ibid., p.483.
92. Ibid., p.484.
93. Ibid., pp. 485, 487.
94. Hankey diary, 2 December 1916 (pp. 323–4).
95. Jenkins, p.498.
96. Asquith to Pamela McKenna, 3 December 1916, in Jenkins, pp.499–500.
97. Jenkins, p.503.
98. Trevor Wilson (ed.), *The Political Diaries of C. P. Scott, 1911–1928*, pp.247–8 (5 December 1916).
99. Jenkins, p.505.
100. Stevenson diary, ed. Taylor, 5 December 1916 (p.133).
101. Jenkins, pp.507–9.
102. Ibid., p.510.
103. Ibid., pp.510–11.
104. Lady Cynthia Asquith, *Diaries, 1915–18*, pp.241–2 (5 December 1916).
105. Sir Austen Chamberlain, *Down the Years*, p.124.
106. Lloyd George, *War Memoirs*, Vol. I, p.596.
107. Riddell diary, 6 December 1916 (p.228).
108. Jenkins, p.519.
109. Ibid., p.521.
110. Grigg, John, *Lloyd George: from Peace to War, 1912–1916*, p.466.
111. Stevenson diary, ed. Taylor, 6 December 1916 (p.134).

112. House of Commons, 19 December 1916 [Vol. 88, cols 1356–7].
113. Ibid. [Vol. 88, col. 1358].
114. Stevenson diary, ed. Taylor, 7 February 1917 (p.141).
115. Ibid., 14 February 1917 (p.144).
116. Asquith memorandum, 28 May 1917, in Trevor Wilson, *The Downfall of the Liberal Party, 1914–35*, p.123.
117. Scott diary, 15 May 1917, in Jenkins, p.292.
118. Ibid., 16–19 December 1917, in Jenkins, p.322.
119. LG to Margaret, 5 January 1918 in Morgan, (ed.) p.185.
120. Grigg, John, *Lloyd George: War Leader*, p.380.
121. House of Commons, 9 May 1918 [Vol. 105, cols 2355–73].
122. Riddell diary, 11 May 1918 (p.328).
123. Hankey diary, 18 November 1918 (p.631).
124. *The Times*, 25 November 1918.
125. Roy Douglas, *The History of the Liberal Party, 1895–1970*, p.122.
126. *The Times*, 25 November 1918.
127. Asquith to Hilda Harrisson, 25 November 1918, in Earl of Oxford and Asquith, *Letters to a Friend*, Vol. I, pp.85–6.
128. *The Times*, 29 November 1918.
129. Earl of Oxford and Asquith, *Memories and Reflections*, Vol. II, p.172.
130. Margot Asquith, *Autobiography*, Vol. II, p.292.
131. LG to Margaret, 13 December 1918, in Morgan, (ed.) pp.188–9.
132. Stevenson diary, ed. Taylor, 17 November 1935 (p.320).
133. H. H. Asquith, *The Paisley Policy*.
134. Stevenson diary, ed. Taylor, 8 February 1920 (p.200).
135. Riddell diary, 15 February 1920, in *Lord Riddell's Diary of the Peace Conference and After*, p.171.
136. Jenkins, pp.549–51.
137. *The Times*, 2 March 1920.
138. Jenkins, p.551; Stevenson diary, ed. Taylor, 1 March 1920 (p.205).
139. Stevenson diary, 15 March 1920 (p.205).
140. Asquith, *Memories and Reflections*, Vol. II, p.239.
141. Jenkins, p.554.
142. Stevenson diary, ed. Taylor, 18 March 1920 (p.206).
143. Scott diary, 9 August 1921, in Jenkins, p.400.
144. Ibid., 16–17 March 1920 (p.383).
145. Stephen Koss, *Asquith*, p.250.
146. Asquith to Hilda Harrisson, 27 June 1922, in *Letters to a Friend*, Vol. II, p.9.
147. Scott diary, 8 November 1922, in Jenkins, p.432.
148. Jenkins, p.563.
149. Asquith, *Memories and Reflections*, Vol. II, p.205.
150. Asquith to Hilda Harrisson, 28 November 1922, in *Letters to a Friend*, Vol. II, pp.39–40.
151. Robert Blake, *Bonar Law: The Unknown Prime Minister*, p.465.
152. Koss, p.250.
153. Scott diary, 1 July 1923, in Jenkins, p.440.
154. Asquith to Hilda Harrisson, 25 November 1923, in *Letters to a Friend*, Vol. II, pp.84–5.
155. Jenkins, p.564 n.1.

156. Ibid.
157. LG to Margaret, 11 December 1923, in Morgan, (ed.) p.202.
158. Ibid., 17 December 1923.
159. Asquith, *Memories and Reflections*, Vol. II, p.208.
160. H. A. L. Fisher diary, 9 December 1923, in John Campbell, *Lloyd George: The Goat in the Wilderness*, p.81.
161. Jenkins, p.566.
162. *Daily Chronicle*, 15 December 1923, in Campbell, p.81.
163. Scott diary, 5 January 1924, in Jenkins, p.450.
164. Maclean to Gladstone, 29 December 1923, in Campbell, p.92.
165. LG to Margaret, 19 December 1924, in Morgan, (ed.) pp.204–5.
166. Ibid., 15 January 1925, in Morgan, p.205.
167. Jenkins, p.572.
168. Tom Jones diary, 27 April 1924, in Keith Middlemas (ed.), *Thomas Jones: Whitehall Diary*, Vol. I, p.278.
169. LG to Frances, 12 August 1925, in A. J. P. Taylor (ed.), *My Darling Pussy: The Letters of Lloyd George and Frances Stevenson, 1913–1941*, p. 86.
170. LG to Godfrey Collins, 10 May 1926, in Campbell, p.139.
171. Lucy Masterman, *C. F. G. Masterman*, p.361.
172. Asquith to Hilda Harrisson, 11 May 1926, in *Letters to a Friend*, Vol. II, p.171.
173. Asquith to LG, 20 May 1926, in Campbell, p.141.
174. Maclean to Gladstone, 20 May 1926, ibid.
175. Stevenson diary, ed. Taylor, 21 May 1926 (p.246).
176. Scott diary, undated, in Jenkins, p.487.
177. LG to Frances, 24 May 1926, in *My Darling Pussy*, p.101.
178. *The Times*, 1 June 1926.
179. Asquith to Hilda Harrisson, 3 June 1926, in *Letters to a Friend*, Vol. II, pp.172–3.
180. Ibid., 9 June 1926 (p.175).
181. Ibid., 11 June 1926 (p.177).
182. Jenkins, p.585.
183. Asquith, *Memories and Reflections*, Vol. II, pp.240–1.
184. Masterman, p.346.
185. House of Commons, 16 February 1928 [Vol. 213, cols 1078–9].

Aneurin Bevan and Hugh Gaitskell

1. Philip Williams, *Hugh Gaitskell*, p.15.
2. Ibid., p.131.
3. Philip Williams (ed.), *The Diary of Hugh Gaitskell, 1945–1956*, pp.24–5 (12 August 1947).
4. Ibid.
5. Ibid., 18 June 1948 (p.72).
6. Ibid., 28 October 1948 (pp.90–1).
7. Ibid., 18 June 1948 (p.72).
8. Gaitskell diary, 17 March 1949, quoted in Williams, *Gaitskell*, p.183.
9. Williams, *The Diary of Hugh Gaitskell*, 21 November 1949 (p.158).
10. Ibid., 1 February 1950 (pp.164–5).
11. Ibid., 21 March 1950 (p.174).
12. Ibid., 11 August 1950 (p.214).

13. Ibid., 26 May 1950 (p.188).
14. Ibid., 21 March 1950 (p.174).
15. John Strachey's obituary of Gaitskell, *Sunday Times*, 20 January 1963, in Williams, *Gaitskell*, p.215.
16. *Daily Telegraph*, 2 October 1950, in Williams, *Gaitskell*, p.237.
17. Woodrow Wyatt, *Turn Again, Westminster*, p.148n.
18. Williams, *Gaitskell*, p.238.
19. Michael Foot, *Aneurin Bevan, 1945–1960* (Paladin edn), p.297.
20. Ben Pimlott (ed.), *The Political Diary of Hugh Dalton*, p.498 (18 January 1951).
21. Foot, pp.297–8.
22. Gaitskell diary, ed. Williams, 3 November 1950 (p.216).
23. Ibid., 5 January 1951 (p.221).
24. Ibid., 10 January 1951 (pp.226–7).
25. John Campbell, *Nye Bevan and the Mirage of British Socialism*, p.220.
26. Tony Benn, *Years of Hope: Diaries, Papers and Letters, 1940–1962*, p.142 (15 February 1951).
27. Gaitskell diary, ed. Williams, 16 February 1951 (pp.237–8).
28. *Evening Standard*, 12 February 1962 in Williams, *Gaitskell*, pp.836–7.
29. *The Times*, 4 April 1951.
30. Dalton diary, ed. Pimlott, 5 April 1951.
31. Ibid., 9 April 1951 (pp.521–2).
32. Ibid.
33. Douglas Jay in William Rodgers (ed.), *Hugh Gaitskell, 1906–1963*, p.100.
34. James Callaghan, *Time and Chance*, p.110.
35. Williams, *Gaitskell*, p.253; Brian Brivati, *Hugh Gaitskell*, p.121.
36. House of Commons, 10 April 1951 [Vol. 486, cols 867–8].
37. Robert Rhodes James (ed.), *'Chips': The Diaries of Sir Henry Channon*, p.458 (10 April 1951).
38. Benn diary, 11 April 1951 (p.146).
39. Williams, *Gaitskell*, p.256; Benn diary, 11 April 1951 (p.147).
40. Dalton diary, ed. Pimlott, 9 April 1951 (p.533).
41. Gaitskell diary, ed. Williams, 4 May 1951 (p.255).
42. House of Commons, 23 April 1951 [Vol. 487, cols. 34–43].
43. Benn diary, 23 April 1951 (p.149).
44. ibid., 24 April 1951 (p.149).
45. Dalton diary, ed. Pimlott, 23 April 1951 (pp.536–7).
46. Benn diary, 24 April 1951 (pp.151–2).
47. Gaitskell diary, ed. Williams, 4 May 1951 (p.256).
48. Callaghan, p.113.
49. Gaitskell diary, ed. Williams, 4 May 1951 (p.257).
50. Ibid., 10 August 1951 (p.271).
51. Jennie Lee, *Tomorrow is a New Day*, p.151.
52. Ian Mikardo, *Back-Bencher*, pp.108–9.
53. Campbell, p.257.
54. Dalton diary, ed. Pimlott, 3 February 1952 (p.580).
55. ibid., 11 March 1952 (p.582).
56. Gaitskell diary, ed. Williams, 21 March 1952 (p.313).
57. Dalton diary, ed. Pimlott, 17 July 1952 (p.594).
58. Williams, *Gaitskell*, p.301.

59. Janet Morgan (ed.), *The Backbench Diaries of Richard Crossman,* p.132 (1 August 1952).
60. Dalton diary, ed. Pimlott, 30 September 1952 (p.598); Foot, p.376.
61. Williams, *Gaitskell,* p.305.
62. *The Times,* 13 October 1952.
63. Crossman diary, ed. Morgan, 14 October 1952 (p.157).
64. Ibid., 3 December 1952 (p.186).
65. Dalton diary, ed. Pimlott, 25 November 1953 (pp.618–19).
66. Benn diary, 31 October 1951 (p.160).
67. Ibid., 24 September 1953 (p.171).
68. Crossman diary, ed. Morgan, 21 April 1954 (p.311).
69. Ibid. (p.315).
70. Ibid., 6 May 1954 (p.323).
71. Rodgers, p.110.
72. Foot, p.447.
73. Brivati, p.197; Williams, *Gaitskell,* pp.332–3 and n.
74. Gaitskell diary, ed. Williams, 19 March 1955 (p.368).
75. Williams, *Gaitskell,* p.340.
76. Dalton diary, ed. Pimlott, 16 March 1955 (pp.651–2).
77. Ibid. (p.653).
78. Crossman diary, ed. Morgan, 24 March 1955 (p.410).
79. Ibid., p.412.
80. Gaitskell diary, ed. Williams, 2 April 1955 (p.398).
81. Ibid. (p.401).
82. *Tribune,* 2 June 1955.
83. Ibid., 21 June 1955.
84. Ibid., 3 December 1954.
85. Leslie Hunter, *The Road to Brighton Pier,* pp.143–4.
86. Williams, *Gaitskell,* p.363.
87. Crossman diary, ed. Morgan 16 November 1955 (pp.452–3).
88. Williams, *Gaitskell,* p.371.
89. Crossman diary, ed. Morgan, 16 March 1955 (p.406).
90. Henry Fairlie, *The Life of Politics,* p.168.
91. Williams, *Gaitskell,* p.370.
92. Ibid.
93. Ibid., p.474.
94. Crossman diary, ed. Morgan, 22 June 1956 (p.498).
95. Dalton diary, ed. Pimlott, 27 October 1956 (p.679).
96. *The Times,* 6 February 1956.
97. Gaitskell diary, ed. Williams 14 February 1956 (p.438).
98. Ibid., (pp.442–3).
99. Ibid., 14 July 1956 (p.540).
100. Ibid., 12 March 1956 (p.467).
101. Ibid., 26 July 1956 (p.556).
102. Benn diary, 5 November 1956 (p.204).
103. Williams, *Gaitskell,* p.415.
104. House of Commons, 16. 5.57 [Vol. 570, cols. 679–89]
105. Gaitskell diary, ed. Williams, 22 August 1956 (p.581).
106. Williams, *Gaitskell,* p.433; Campbell, p.322.

107. House of Commons, 6 December 1956 [Vol. 561, col. 1570].
108. Crossman diary, ed. Morgan, 15 December 1956 (p.556).
109. Gaitskell diary, ed. Williams, 9 October 1956 (p.617).
110. Benn diary, 29 November 1956 (p.216).
111. Campbell, p.328.
112. *Tribune*, 23 August 1957.
113. Williams, *Gaitskell*, pp.447–8.
114. Ian Mikardo, *Back-bencher*, p. 159.
115. Campbell, p.337.
116. *News Chronicle*, 4 October 1957.
117. Crossman diary, ed. Morgan, 4 October 1957 (pp.615–16).
118. Ibid., 24 October 1957 (p.621).
119. Ibid., 18 December 1958 (p.726).
120. Ibid., 25 March 1959 (p.743).
121. Roy Jenkins, *A Life at the Centre*, p.114.
122. Crossman diary, ed. Morgan 11 July 1958 (p.687).
123. Rodgers, pp.124–5.
124. Crossman diary, ed. Morgan, 24 June 1959 (p.762).
125. Ibid., 17 July 1959 (pp.767–8).
126. Ibid., 13 August 1959 (p.769).
127. Campbell, p.354.
128. Foot, pp.622–6, quoting Geoffrey Goodman's 1959 diary.
129. Crossman diary, ed. Morgan, 22 September 1959 (p.779).
130. Geoffrey Goodman, *The Awkward Warrior: Frank Cousins: His Life and Times,* p.237.
131. Crossman diary, ed. Morgan, 30 September 1959 (p.782).
132. Foot, p.629.
133. Crossman diary, ed. Morgan, 19 October 1959 (pp.789–90).
134. Williams, *Gaitskell*, p.551.
135. Aneurin Bevan, *In Place of Fear*, p.118.
136. Williams, *Gaitskell*, p.554.
137. Ibid., p.556.
138. Campbell, pp.361–2.
139. Benn diary, 28 November 1959 (p.321).
140. *Evening Standard,* 30 November 1959.
141. Mikardo, p.163.
142. House of Commons, 7 July 1960 [Vol. 626, cols. 704–8].
143. Williams, *Gaitskell*, p.612.

Harold Macmillan and R. A. Butler

1. Harold Macmillan, *Winds of Change, 1914–1939*, p.99.
2. Alistair Horne, *Macmillan, 1894–1956*, p.441.
3. Robert Rhodes James (ed.), *'Chips': the Diaries of Sir Henry Channon,* p.156 (13 May 1938).
4. *The Times*, 27 May 1930.
5. Ibid., 28 May 1930.
6. Lord Butler, *The Art of the Possible*, p.27.
7. Anthony Howard, *RAB: The Life of R. A. Butler*, p.64.
8. Channon diary, ed. Rhodes James, p.69 (8 July 1936).

9. Edward Pearce, *The Lost Leaders*, p.5.
10. 'Watchman', *Right Honourable Gentlemen*, p.221.
11. Channon diary, ed. Rhodes James, p.147 (28 February 1938).
12. Ibid., p.151 (12 March 1938).
13. Ibid., p.178 (23 November 1938).
14. Ibid., p.197 (9 May 1939).
15. Alistair Horne, *Macmillan*, Vol. I, p.297.
16. John Colville, *The Fringes of Power: Downing Street Diaries, 1939–1955*, p.122 (10 May 1940).
17. Shakespeare, *Henry V*, IV.iii.64–7.
18. Channon diary, ed. Rhodes Janes, p.155 (29 May 1940).
19. Howard, p.109.
20. Harold Nicolson, *Diaries and Letters, 1945–62*, p.32 (16 September 1945).
21. Harold Nicolson, *Diaries and Letters, 1939–1945*, p.251 (23 October 1942).
22. Channon diary, ed. Rhodes James, p.393 (6 September 1944).
23. Harold Macmillan, *Tides of Fortune, 1945–1955*, pp. 304–5.
24. Butler, p.144.
25. Macmillan, *Tides of Fortune*, p.305.
26. Peter Catterall (ed.), *The Macmillan Diaries: The Cabinet Years, 1950–57*, p.114 (28 October 1951).
27. Ibid., p.127 (30 December 1951).
28. Ibid., pp.132, 135 (10 and 24 January 1952).
29. Ibid., pp.170–1 (11 and 14 July 1952).
30. Ibid., pp.174–5 (17 July 1952).
31. Ibid., p.187 (27 September 1952).
32. Ibid., p.226 (23 April 1953).
33. Roy Jenkins, *Churchill*, p.865.
34. Catterall (ed.), *Macmillan Diaries*, p.242 (4 July 1953).
35. Ibid., p.243 (6 July 1953).
36. Ibid., p.244 (14 July 1953).
37. Ibid., p.413 (6 April 1955).
38. Ibid., p.498 (27 October 1955).
39. Ibid., p.500 (30 October 1955).
40. Ibid, p.520 (22 December 1955).
41. Macmillan to Eden, 24 October 1955 (ibid. p.494).
42. Macmillan, *Tides of Fortune*, pp.693–4.
43. Howard, p.221.
44. *New Statesman*, 5 November 1955, in Anthony Sampson, *Macmillan: A Study in Ambiguity*, p.111.
45. Catterall (ed.), *Macmillan Diaries*, p.514 (7 December 1955).
46. Ibid., p.516 (13 December 1955).
47. Howard, p.221.
48. Butler, p.182.
49. William Clark, *From Three Worlds: Memoirs*, p.155.
50. Howard, p.222.
51. Catterall (ed.), *Macmillan Diaries*, p.524 (12 January 1956).
52. Ibid., p.529 (23 January 1956).
53. Ibid., p.530 (24 January 1956).
54. Ibid., p.531 (31 January 1956).

55. Ibid., p.537 (15 February 1956).
56. Ibid., p.547 (28 March 1956).
57. Clark, p.164.
58. Catterall (ed.), *Macmillan Diaries*, p.587 (18 August 1956).
59. Ibid., p.590 (24 August 1956).
60. Ibid., p.598 (13 September 1956).
61. Horne, Vol. I, p.447.
62. Clark, p.209.
63. Nicholas Henderson, *The Private Office Revisited*, p.116.
64. Howard, p.245.
65. Butler, p.195.
66. John Ramsden, *The Age of Churchill and Eden, 1940–1957*, p.322.
67. Peter Rawlinson, *A Price Too High*, p.71.
68. Tony Benn, *Years of Hope: Diaries, Papers and Letters, 1940–1962*, p.213 (22 November 1956).
69. Horne, Vol. I, p.455.
70. Howard, p.241.
71. Nigel Fisher, *Harold Macmillan*, p.170.
72. *Economist*, 22 December 1956, in Howard, p.243.
73. Howard, p.247.
74. Richard Cockett (ed.), *My Dear Max: The Letters of Brendan Bracken to Lord Beaverbrook, 1925–1958*, p.199.
75. *The Times*, 10 January 1957.
76. Earl of Kilmuir, *Political Adventure*, p.285.
77. Ben Pimlott, *The Queen: A Biography of Elizabeth II*, p.189.
78. D. R. Thorpe, *Sir Alec Douglas-Home*, p.189.
79. Janet Morgan (ed.), *The Backbench Diaries of Richard Crossman*, p.564 (11 January 1957).
80. Alistair Horne, *Macmillan, 1957–1986*, p.4.
81. Edward Heath, *The Course of my Life*, p.179.
82. Butler. p.196.
83. Heath, p.179.
84. Thorpe, p.189.
85. Howard, pp.248–9.
86. Pearce, p.99.
87. Horne, *Macmillan 1894–1956*, p.457.
88. Nigel to Harold Nicolson, 22 January 1957, in Nicolson, *Diaries and Letters, 1945–1962*, p.302.
89. Ibid., p.301 (10 January 1957).
90. 'Watchman', p.221.
91. Charles Lysaght, 'Dear Brendan and Master Harold', in Richard Aldous and Sabine Lee; *Harold Macmillan: Aspects of a Political Life*, p.158.
92. *The Times*, 11 January 1957.
93. Catterall (ed.), *Macmillan Diaries*, pp.613–14 (3 February 1957).
94. Butler, pp.31, 196.
95. Heath, p.180.
96. *Daily Express*, 11 January 1957, in Howard, p.250.
97. Butler, pp.197–8.
98. Shakespeare, *Twelfth Night*, II.iii.112.

99. Ibid., p.200.
100. Peter Catterall (ed.), *The Macmillan Diaries: Prime Minister and After, 1957–1966* (14 November 1957).
101. Ibid., 18 November 1958.
102. Ibid., 8 February 1959.
103. Howard, p.258.
104. Roy Jenkins, *A Life at the Centre*, p.123.
105. Benn diary, p.261 (10 January 1958).
106. *Bristol Evening World*, 7 January 1958, reprinted in Benn diary, p.259.
107. Macmillan at Bedford, in Horne, *Macmillan 1956–1986*, 21 July 1957.
108. Catterall (ed.) *Macmillan Diaries* (18 October 1959).
109. Ibid.
110. Macmillan, *Pointing the Way, 1959–1961*, p.17.
111. Catterall (ed.), *Macmillan Diaries*, (11 June 1960).
112. Howard, p.279n.
113. Catterall (ed.), *Macmillian Diaries*, (5 July 1960).
114. Harold Macmillan, *At the End of the Day*, p.41.
115. Howard, p.285.
116. Harold Evans, *Downing Street Diary: The Macmillan Years, 1957–63*, p.166 (14 October 1961)
117. Howard, p.285.
118. Catterall (ed.), *Macmillan Diaries* (13 October 1961).
119. Ibid., 21 August 1962.
120. Ibid., 9 October 1962 and 9 March 1963.
121. Horne, *Macmillan, 1894–1956*, Vol. II, p.410.
122. Butler, p.210.
123. Evans, p.209.
124. Howard, p.292.
125. Butler, p.234.
126. Catterall (ed.), *Macmillan Diaries*, (17 February 1963).
127. Dennis Walters, *Not Always with the Pack*, p.111.
128. Sampson, p.241.
129. Howard, p.304.
130. *Listener*, 28 July 1966, in Sampson, p.242.
131. Benn diary, pp.6–7 (20 February 1963).
132. *The Times*, 15 July 1963.
133. Catterall (ed.), *Macmillan Diaries*, (18 July 1963).
134. Ibid., 11 September 1963.
135. Ibid., 30 September 1963.
136. Ibid., 7 October 1963.
137. *The Times*, 17 October 1963.
138. Butler, pp.243–5.
139. Heath, p.255.
140. Howard, p.315.
141. *The Times*, 2 October 1963.
142. Catterall (ed.), *Macmillan Diaries*, (14 October 1963).
143. Ibid., 17 October 1963.
144. Pimlott, p.333.
145. Alan Thompson, *The Day before Yesterday*, p.219.

146. Walters, p.133.
147. Catterall (ed.), *Macmillan Diaries*, (18 October 1963).
148. Howard, p.332.
149. John Ramsden, *Winds of Change: Macmillan to Heath, 1957–1975*, p.207.
150. *The Times*, 10 October 1963.
151. Thorpe, p.319; Horne, *Macmillan 1894–1956*, Vol. II, p.582.
152. Howard, p.370.
153. Catterall (ed.), *Macmillan Diaries*, (19 October 1963).
154. Walters, p.138, quoting Lord Poole.
155. Catterall (ed.), *Macmillan Diaries*, (20 October 1963).
156. John Boyd-Carpenter, *Way of Life*, pp.178–9.
157. Henderson, p.311.
158. Butler, pp.250, 29.
159. Henderson, p.111.
160. Butler, p.xi.
161. Ibid., p.31.
162. Pearce, p.14.
163. Butler, p.31.

Edward Heath and Margaret Thatcher

1. Phillip Whitehead, *The Writing on the Wall: Britain in the Seventies*, p.327.
2. Patrick Cosgrave, *Margaret Thatcher: A Tory and her Party*, p.72.
3. *Daily Mail*, 28 June 1949.
4. Margaret Thatcher, *The Path to Power*, p.68.
5. Edward Heath, *The Course of my Life*, p.136.
6. Ibid., p.153.
7. John Campbell, *Margaret Thatcher: The Grocer's Daughter*, p.78.
8. Ibid., p.93.
9. John Campbell, *Edward Heath*, p.94.
10. *Sunday Graphic*, 17 February 1952.
11. Campbell, *Margaret Thatcher: The Grocer's Daughter*, p.87.
12. *Finchley Press*, 25 October 1963.
13. *Economist*, 12 October 1963.
14. Campbell, *Margaret Thatcher: The Grocer's Daughter*, p.133.
15. Ibid., p.134.
16. Ibid.
17. *Finchley Press*, 13 August 1965.
18. James Prior, *A Balance of Power*, p.42.
19. Peter Rawlinson, *A Price Too High*, p.247.
20. *Sunday Express*, 30 June 1968.
21. Campbell, *Margaret Thatcher: The Grocer's Daughter*, p.144.
22. Heath, p.302.
23. *Financial Times*, 22 October 1969.
24. *Sunday Times*, 5 March 1967.
25. *Sun*, 10 April 1970.
26. *Sunday Times*, 5 March 1967.
27. *Finchley Press*, 26 June 1970.
28. Heath, p.311.
29. Andrew Roth, *Heath and the Heathmen*, p. xiii.

30. Heath, p.317.
31. *People*, 12 July 1970.
32. Campbell, *Margaret Thatcher: The Grocer's Daughter*, p.189.
33. Rawlinson, p.248.
34. *The Times*, 20 June 1972.
35. Heath, pp.447–8, 417.
36. Campbell, *Margaret Thatcher: The Grocer's Daughter*, p.221.
37. Ibid., p.207.
38. Ibid., p.233.
39. John Ramsden, *Winds of Change: Macmillan to Heath, 1957–1975*, p.359.
40. Campbell, *Margaret Thatcher: The Grocer's Daughter*, p.195.
41. Ibid., p.266.
42. Heath, p.523.
43. Campbell, *Margaret Thatcher: The Grocer's Daughter*, p.249.
44. Ibid., p.260.
45. BBC Radio 4, *Any Questions?* 4 October 1974.
46. *Sunday Times*, 13 October 1974.
47. *The Times*, 16 October 1974.
48. Ibid., 11 September 1974.
49. *Any Questions?* 4 October 1974.
50. Campbell, *Margaret Thatcher: The Grocer's Daughter*, p.261.
51. Ibid., p.266.
52. *Economist*, 30 November 1974.
53. *The Times*, 16 October 1974.
54. Campbell, *Margaret Thatcher: The Grocer's Daughter*, p.267.
55. Heath, p.530.
56. Ibid., p.529.
57. Nicholas Ridley, *'My Style of Government': The Thatcher Years*, p.9.
58. *The Times*, 23 January 1975.
59. *Daily Telegraph*, 30 January 1975.
60. Speech in Finchley, 31 January 1975, in *The Times*, 1 February 1975.
61. *Daily Telegraph*, 3 February 1975.
62. Francis Pym, *The Politics of Consent*, p.5.
63. *Daily Telegraph*, 4 February 1975.
64. *The Times*, 1 February 1975.
65. Ibid., 31 January 1975.
66. Nigel Fisher, *The Tory Leaders: Their Struggle for Power*, p.169.
67. Tam Dalyell, *Misrule: How Mrs Thatcher Misled Parliament from the Sinking of the* Belgrano *to the Wright Affair*, p.xx.
68. Peter Jenkins, *Mrs Thatcher's Revolution: The Ending of the Socialist Era*, p.64.
69. Norman Tebbit, *Upwardly Mobile*, p.142.
70. *Sun*, 12 February 1975.
71. Campbell, *Margaret Thatcher: The Grocer's Daughter*, p.306.
72. Tony Benn, *Against the Tide: Diaries, 1973–76*, p.319 (18 February 1975).
73. *The Times*, 12 February 1975.
74. Ernle Money, *Margaret Thatcher: First Lady of the House*, p.95; Campbell, *Margaret Thatcher: The Grocer's Daughter*, p.283.
75. Heath, pp.536–7.
76. Speech at St Ermin's Hotel, 16 April 1975.

77. Heath, p.546.
78. *The Times*, 4 June 1975.
79. House of Commons, 9 June 1975 [Vol. 893, col. 32].
80. *The Times*, 13 June 1975.
81. Barbara Castle, *The Castle Diaries, 1974–76*, p.473 (22 July 1975).
82. *The Times*, 23 September 1975.
83. Ibid., 9 October 1975.
84. Ibid., 9 October 1976.
85. Ibid., 7 October 1976.
86. Ibid., 12 October 1978.
87. Ibid.
88. Campbell, *Edward Heath*, p.711.
89. Bernard Donoughue, *Prime Minister: The Conduct of Politics under Harold Wilson and James Callaghan*, p.191.
90. *Observer*, 25 February 1979; Heath, pp.571–2.
91. Campbell, *Edward Heath*, p.713.
92. Heath, p.573.
93. Ronald Millar, *A View from the Wings*, p.262.
94. Campbell, *Margaret Thatcher: The Grocer's Daughter*, p.456.
95. Millar, p.262.
96. Ibid., p.268.
97. Heath, p.574.
98. *Daily Telegraph*, 19 May 1979.
99. BBC Radio 4, 28 January 1988, in Campbell, *Edward Heath*, p.715.
100. Speech at Conservative party conference, Brighton, 10 October 1980.
101. *The Times*, 11 June 1980.
102. Ibid.
103. House of Commons, 27 April 1980 [Vol. 994, cols 602–6].
104. *The Times*, 29 November 1980.
105. ITN interview, 13 April 1981, in John Campbell, *Margaret Thatcher: The Iron Lady*, p.114; *The Times*, 2 July 1981.
106. *The Times*, 4 July 1981.
107. Ibid., 7 October 1981.
108. Ibid.
109. Ibid.
110. Ibid., 17 October 1981.
111. House of Commons, 15 March 1982 [Vol. 20, cols. 36–43]
112. *The Times*, 16 May 1988.
113. Heath, p.699.
114. Ibid., p.387.
115. Speech at Bruges, 20 September 1988, in *The Times*, 21 September 1988.
116. Heath, p.707.
117. *The Times*, 30 May 1989.
118. *Daily Telegraph*, 31 May 1989.
119. Campbell, *Edward Heath*, pp.756, 758.
120. Ibid., p.787.
121. *The Times*, 15 March and 26 February 1991.
122. *Daily Mail*, 19 June 1991.
123. *The Times*, 19 June 1991.

124. *Daily Mail,* 19 June 1991.
125. Campbell, *Edward Heath,* p.798.
126. *Daily Mail,* 20 June 1991.
127. *The Times,* 21 June 1991.
128. *The Times,* 12 October 1991.
129. House of Commons, 20 November 1991 [Vol. 199, cols 290–8].
130. Ibid., 21 November 1991 [Vol. 199, cols 457–85]
131. *The Times,* 25 November 1991.
132. *Newsweek,* 17 April 1992.
133. *Sunday Telegraph,* 16 March 1997.
134. *Daily Telegraph,* 18 July 2005.

Gordon Brown and Tony Blair

1. James Naughtie, *The Rivals: The Intimate Story of a Political Marriage* (2002 ed), p.17.
2. Gordon Brown (ed.), *The Red Paper on Scotland,* pp.7–19, quoted in Francis Beckett, *Gordon Brown: Past, Present and Future,* p.30.
3. House of Commons, 27 July 1983 [Vol. 46, cols 1239–44, 1256].
4. Ibid., 6 July 1983 [Vol. 45, cols 313–16, 319].
5. Anthony Seldon, *Blair,* p.659.
6. John Rentoul, *Tony Blair: Prime Minister,* p.151.
7. Seldon, *Blair,* p.659.
8. Andrew Rawnsley, *Servants of the People: The Inside Story of New Labour,* p.xv.
9. Seldon, *Blair,* p.159.
10. *Sunday Mirror,* 11 September 2008, in Seldon, *Blair,* p.298.
11. Naughtie, p.28.
12. Giles Radice, *Diaries, 1980–2001,* p.164 (2 August 1987).
13. Seldon, *Blair,* p.101.
14. Radice, p.187 (21 November 1988).
15. Seldon, *Blair,* p.107.
16. Radice, p.214 (2 March 1990).
17. Ibid., p.225 (1 October 1990).
18. Naughtie, p.44.
19. Radice, p.271 (12 April 1992).
20. Robert Peston, *Brown's Britain,* p.40.
21. *Sunday Times,* 19 July 1992; *Evening Standard,* 21 July 1992, in Tom Bower, *Gordon Brown,* p.93.
22. Seldon, *Blair,* p.179.
23. Ibid., p.180.
24. Naughtie, p.52.
25. *Sunday Telegraph,* 28 December 1993, in Seldon, *Blair,* p.182.
26. Seldon, *Blair,* p.184.
27. Anthony Seldon, *Major: A Political Life,* pp.461–2.
28. Seldon, *Blair,* p.186.
29. Radice, p.320 (18 May 1994).
30. Seldon, *Blair,* p.24.
31. Peston, p.49.

32. Alastair Campbell, *The Blair Years: Extracts from the Alastair Campbell Diaries*, p.10 (10 August 1994).
33. Seldon, *Blair*, p.144.
34. Ibid., p.413.
35. *Evening Standard*, 12 May 1994, in Seldon, *Blair*, p.186.
36. Bower, p.139; Seldon, *Blair*, p.187.
37. Seldon, *Blair*, p.188.
38. Naughtie, p.62
39. Seldon, *Blair*, p.189.
40. Naughtie, pp.63–4.
41. Seldon, *Blair*, p.193.
42. Peston, p.59.
43. Ibid. p.67; the document was leaked to the *Guardian* in June 2003.
44. *The Times*, 2 June 1994.
45. Peston, pp.22–3.
46. Seldon, *Blair*, p.162.
47. Ibid., p.227.
48. Ibid., p.666.
49. Rawnsley, pp.6–7.
50. Naughtie, p.158.
51. Seldon, *Blair*, p.260.
52. Ibid., p.673.
53. Rawnsley, p.147.
54. Ibid., p.144.
55. Naughtie, p.106.
56. Rawnsley, p.145.
57. Ibid., p.146.
58. Ibid., pp.32–3; Seldon, *Blair*, p.281.
59. Rawnsley, p. 42.
60. Seldon, *Blair*, p.331.
61. *New Statesman*, 1 May 1998, in Seldon, *Blair*, p.424.
62. *Sunday Telegraph*, 4 April 1999, in Rawnsley, p.263.
63. Speech in Kosovo, 3 May 1999, ibid., p.282.
64. Rawnsley, p.282.
65. Ibid., p.165.
66. Ibid., p.159.
67. Campbell, p.312 (23 July 1998).
68. Rawnsley, p.150.
69. Ibid., p.152.
70. Radice, p.436 (27 January 1999).
71. Seldon, *Blair*, p.535.
72. Rawnsley, p.98.
73. *The Times*, 28 January 1998.
74. Seldon, *Blair*, p.423.
75. *The Times*, 2 September 1999.
76. Radice, p.448 (27–29 September 1999).
77. Campbell, p.423 (27–29 September 1999).
78. Rawnsley, pp.320–1.
79. Naughtie, p. 268.

80. Rawnsley, p.337.
81. Ibid., pp.338–9.
82. Ibid., p.390.
83. Naughtie, p.282.
84. Ibid., p.284.
85. Radice, p.481.
86. Naughtie, p.370.
87. Radice, p.477.
88. Campbell, p.478 (8 November 2000).
89. Anthony Seldon, *Blair Unbound,* p.23.
90. Campbell, p.500 (5 February 2001).
91. Radice, p.479 (24 January 2001).
92. Ibid.
93. Rawnsley, p.495.
94. BBC Radio 2, 23 May 2001, in Rawnsley, p.496.
95. Ibid., p.487.
96. Seldon, *Blair Unbound,* p.28.
97. *Sunday Times,* 11 June 2001 in Seldon, *Blair,* p.462.
98. Seldon, *Blair,* p.467.
99. Ibid., p.677.
100. Ibid.
101. Rawnsley, p.488.
102. Campbell, p.539 (7 June 2001).
103. Seldon, *Blair Unbound,* p.33.
104. Seldon, *Blair,* p.630.
105. Ibid., p.629.
106. Ibid.
107. Ibid., p.678.
108. Campbell, p.588 (17 November 2001).
109. Ibid., p.592 (19 December 2001).
110. Ibid., p. 602 (11 January 2002).
111. *The Times,* 7 August 2002.
112. Peston, p.332.
113. Ibid., p.303.
114. Seldon, *Blair,* p.681.
115. Naughtie, p.141.
116. Peston, p.229.
117. Ibid., p.238.
118. Seldon, *Blair,* p.483.
119. Ibid., p.489.
120. Ibid., p.595.
121. *Guardian,* 8 July 2003, in Seldon, *Blair,* p.641.
122. Campbell, p.713 (3 July 2003).
123. Seldon, *Blair,* p. 684.
124. Ibid.
125. Seldon, *Blair Unbound,* p.227.
126. Seldon, *Blair,* p.685.
127. Ibid., p.645.
128. Peston, p.335.

129. *The Times*, 29 January 2004.
130. Seldon, *Blair Unbound*, p.271.
131. Peston, pp.337–8.
132. John Burton in Seldon, *Blair Unbound*, p.273.
133. Ibid.
134. Ibid., p.277.
135. Ibid.
136. Peston, p.343.
137. Seldon, *Blair Unbound*, p.296.
138. Peston, p.12.
139. Seldon, *Blair Unbound*, p.298.
140. Peston, p.347.
141. Seldon, *Blair Unbound*, p.301.
142. Peston, p.349.
143. Seldon, *Blair Unbound*, p.330.
144. Peston, p.22.
145. Seldon, *Blair Unbound*, p.337.
146. Ibid., p.341.
147. Ibid., p.349.
148. Ibid., p.347.
149. Ibid., pp.451–2.
150. Ibid., p.453.
151. Ibid., p.488.
152. Ibid., pp.490–1.
153. Ibid., p.493.
154. *Daily Mail*, 11 September 2006, ibid., p.494.
155. Ibid., p.496.
156. Ibid., p.497.
157. Ibid., p.546.
158. Ibid., p.550.
159. Ibid., p.552.
160. Ibid., p.574.
161. *The Week*, 24 September 2008.
162. Wendy Hinde, *Castlereagh*, p.184.

Sources and Bibliography

Fox and Pitt

W. Auckland, *The Journal and Correspondence of William Eden Auckland, First Lord Auckland* (Richard Bentley, 1861–62)

Stanley Ayling, *Fox: The Life of Charles James Fox* (John Murray, 1991)

John Cannon, *The Fox–North Coalition: Crisis of the Constitution, 1782–4* (Cambridge, 1969)

T. Copeland (ed.), *Correspondence of Edmund Burke* (Cambridge, 1958–78)

I. M. Davis, *The Harlot and the Statesman* (Kensal Press, 1986)

J. Debrett, *History of the Westminster Election* (1784)

John Ehrman, *The Younger Pitt*, 3 vols (Constable, 1969, 1986, 1996)

Eric Eyck, *Pitt versus Fox: Father and Son, 1735–1806* (London 1950)

M. D. George, *English Political Caricature: A Study of Opinion and Propaganda* (Oxford, 1959)

J. Grieg (ed.), *The Farington Diary* (Hutchinson 1923–28)

William Hague, *William Pitt the Younger* (HarperCollins, 2004)

L. V. Harcourt (ed.), *The Diaries and Correspondence of George Rose* (Richard Bentley, 1860)

Lord Holland, *Memoirs of the Whig Party* (Longman, 1852–54)

Earl of Malmesbury, *Diaries and Correspondence of James Harris, First Earl of Malmesbury* (Richard Bentley, 1845)

L. G. Mitchell, *Charles James Fox* (Oxford, 1992)

H. J. Nicoll, *Great Orators: Burke, Fox, Sheridan, Pitt* (Warne, n.d.)

Sir Arthur Quiller-Couch (ed.), *The Oxford Book of English Verse, 1250–1900* (Oxford, 1921)

Loren Reid, *Charles James Fox: A Man for the People* (Longman, 1969)

Robin Reilly, *Pitt the Younger* (Cassell, 1978)

R. Ellis Roberts, *Samuel Rogers and his Circle* (Methuen, 1910)

S. Romilly, *Memoirs of the Life of Sir Samuel Romilly* (John Murray, 1840)

J. Holland Rose, *Pitt and the National Revival* (George Bell, 1911)

Lord John Russell (ed.), *Memorials and Correspondence of Charles James Fox* (Richard Bentley, 1853–57)

Earl Stanhope, *The Life of the Right Honourable William Pitt* (John Murray, 1867)

Dorothy M. Stuart, *Dearest Bess: The Life and Times of Lady Elizabeth Foster, afterwards Duchess of Devonshire* (Methuen, 1955)

G. Tomline, *Memoirs of the Life of the Right Honourable William Pitt* (John Murray, 1821)

Paget Toynbee (ed.), *The Letters of Horace Walpole* (Oxford, 1903–05)

G. M. Trevelyan, *Lord Grey of the Reform Bill* (Longman, 1920)

G. M. Trevelyan, *British History in the 19th Century*, (Longman, 1944)

Horace Walpole, *Last Journals* (J. Lane, 1910)

Castlereagh and Canning

W. Auckland, *The Journal and Correspondence of William Eden Auckland, First Lord Auckland* (Richard Bentley, 1861–62)

Francis Bamford and the Duke of Wellington (eds) *The Journal of Mrs Arbuthnot, 1820–1832* (Macmillan 1950)

Francis Bickley (ed.), *The Diaries of Sylvester Douglas, Lord Glenbervie* (Constable, 1928).

Lord Colchester (ed.), *The Diary and Correspondence of Charles Abbott, First Lord Colchester* (John Murray, 1861)

J. E. Cookson, *Lord Liverpool's Administration: The Crucial Years, 1815–22* (Chatto & Windus, 1975)

Peter Dixon, *Canning: Politician and Statesman* (Weidenfeld & Nicolson, 1976)

Denis Gray, *Spencer Perceval: The Evangelical Prime Minister* (Manchester, 1963)

Wendy Hinde, *George Canning* (Collins, 1973)

—— *Castlereagh* (Collins, 1981)

Giles Hunt, *The Duel: Castlereagh, Canning and Deadly Cabinet Rivalry* (I. B Tauris, 2008).

H. Montgomery Hyde, *The Strange Death of Lord Castlereagh* (Heinemann, 1959)

L. J. Jennings (ed.), *The Croker Papers* (John Murray, 1884–85)

Henry Kissinger, *A World Restored: Metternich, Castlereagh and the Problems of Peace, 1812–1822* (Weidenfeld & Nicolson, 1957)

Marquess of Londonderry (ed.), *Memoir and Correspondence of Viscount Castlereagh, Second Marquiess of Londonderry* (Henry Colburn, 1848–50)

Elizabeth Longford, *Wellington: The Years of the Sword* (Weidenfeld & Nicolson, 1969)

Sir H. Maxwell (ed.), *The Creevey Papers* (John Murray, 1903)

Dorothy Marshall, *The Rise of George Canning* (Longman, 1938)

Lewis Melville, (ed.), *The Huskisson Papers* (1931)

Sir Charles Petrie, *George Canning* (Eyre & Spottiswoode, 1930)

H. Reeve (ed.), *The Greville Memoirs* (Longman, 1875)

Philip Ziegler, *Addington* (Collins, 1965)

Disraeli and Gladstone

Richard Aldous, *The Lion and the Unicorn: Gladstone v. Disraeli* (Hutchinson, 2006)

A. R. Ashwell and Reginald G. Wilberforce, *The Life of Samuel Wilberforce* (John Murray, 1880–82)

Sources and Bibliography

Robert Blake, *Disraeli* (Eyre & Spottiswoode, 1966)

Lewis Carroll, *Through the Looking-Glass* (Macmillan, 1871)

W. S. Churchill, *Thoughts and Adventures* (Thornton Butterworth, 1932)

Travis L. Crosby, *The Two Mr Gladstones* (Yale, 1997)

Sir William Fraser, *Disraeli and his Day* (Kegan Paul, 1891)

W. E. Gladstone, *Bulgarian Horrors and the Question of the East* (John Murray, 1876)

Philip Guedalla, *Palmerston* (Ernest Benn, 1926)

Peter J. Jagger (ed.), *Gladstone* (Hambledon Press, 1998)

Roy Jenkins, *Gladstone* (Macmillan, 1995)

William Kuhn, *The Politics of Pleasure: A Portrait of Benjamin Disraeli* (Free Press, 2006)

Philip Magnus, *Gladstone* (John Murray, 1954)

H. C. G. Matthew, *Gladstone 1809–1874* (Oxford, 1986)

—— *Gladstone 1875–1898* (Oxford, 1995)

John Matthews (ed.), *The Letters of Benjamin Disraeli* (University of Toronto, 1982–2004)

W. F. Monypenny and G. E. Buckle, *The Life of Benjamin Disraeli, Earl of Beaconsfield* (John Murray, 1910–20)

John Morley, *The Life of Gladstone* (Hodder & Stoughton, 1903)

Agatha Ramm (ed.), *The Political Correspondence of Mr Gladstone and Lord Granville* (Oxford, 1962)

H. Reeve (ed.), *The Greville Memoirs* (Longman, 1875)

G. W. E. Russell, *Collections and Recollections* (Smith Elder, 1898)

Richard Shannon, *Gladstone: 1809–1865* (Hamish Hamilton, 1982)

—— *Gladstone: Heroic Minister, 1865–1898* (Allen Lane, 1999)

F. B. Smith, *The Making of the Second Reform Bill* (Cambridge, 1966)

Marquess of Zetland (ed.), *The Letters of Disraeli to Lady Bradford and Lady Chesterfield* (Ernest Benn, 1929)

Asquith and Lloyd George

Lady Cynthia Asquith, *Diaries 1915–18* (Hutchinson, 1968)

H. H. Asquith, *The Paisley Policy* (Cassell, 1920)

Margot Asquith, *The Autobiography of Margot Asquith* (Thornton Butterworth, 1920–22)

Robert Blake, *Bonar Law: The Unknown Prime Minister: The Life and Times of Andrew Bonar Law* (Eyre & Spottiswoode, 1955)

Michael and Eleanor Brock (eds.), *H.H. Asquith: Letters to Venetia Stanley* (Oxford, 1982)

John Campbell, *Lloyd George: The Goat in the Wilderness* (Jonathan Cape, 1977)

Sir Austen Chamberlain, *Down the Years* (Cassell, 1935)

—— *Politics from Inside* (Cassell, 1936)

W. S. Churchill, *The World Crisis* (Thornton Butterworth, 1923–27;)

Edward David (ed.), *Inside Asquith's Cabinet: From the Diaries of Charles Hobhouse* (John Murray, 1977)

Roy Douglas, *The History of the Liberal Party, 1895–1970* (Sidgwick & Jackson, 1971)

W. R. P. George, *Lloyd George: Backbencher* (Gomer, 1983)

John Grigg, *The Young Lloyd George* (Eyre Methuen, 1973)
—— *Lloyd George : The People's Champion, 1902–1911* (Eyre Methuen, 1978)
—— *Lloyd George: From Peace to War, 1912–1916* (Eyre Methuen, 1985)
—— *Lloyd George: War Leader* (Eyre Methuen, 2002)
R. B. Haldane, *An Autobiography* (Hodder & Stoughton, 1929)
Cameron Hazlehurst, *Politicians at War, July 1914 to May 1915* (Jonathan Cape, 1971)
Roy Jenkins, *Asquith* (Collins, 1964)
Stephen Koss, *Asquith* (Allen Lane, 1976)
D. Lloyd George, *War Memoirs* (Odhams, 1938)
Philip Magnus, *Kitchener: Portrait of an Imperialist* (John Murray, 1958)
Lucy Masterman, *C. F. G. Masterman* (Frank Cass, 1939)
Keith Middlemas (ed.), *Thomas Jones: Whitehall Diary* (Oxford, 1969)
Kenneth O. Morgan (ed.), *Lloyd George Family Letters, 1885–1936*
Harold Nicolson, *King George V: His Life and Reign* (Constable, 1952)
Frank Owen, *Tempestuous Journey: Lloyd George, His Life and Times* (Hutchinson, 1954)
Earl of Oxford and Asquith, *Fifty Years of Parliament* (Cassell, 1926)
—— *Memories and Reflections* (Cassell, 1928)
—— *Letters to a Friend* (Geoffrey Bles 1933–34)
Lord Riddell, *Lord Riddell's War Diary, 1914–18* (Ivor Nicholson & Watson, 1933)
—— *Lord Riddell's Diary of the Peace Conference and After* (Gollancz, 1933)
—— *More Pages from my Diary, 1908–14* (Country Life, 1934)
Keith Robbins, *Sir Edward Grey* (Cassell, 1971)
Stephen Roskill, *Hankey: Man of Secrets* (Collins, 1970–74)
Peter Rowland, *Lloyd George* (Barrie & Jenkins, 1975)
A. J. P. Taylor (ed.), *Lloyd George: A Diary by Frances Stevenson* (Hutchinson, 1971)
—— *My Darling Pussy: The Letters of Lloyd George and Frances Stevenson, 1913–1941* (Weidenfeld & Nicolson, 1975)
Trevor Wilson, *The Downfall of the Liberal Party, 1914–35* (Collins, 1966)
—— (ed.), *The Political Diaries of C.P. Scott, 1911–1928* (Collins, 1970)

Bevan and Gaitskell

Tony Benn, *Years of Hope: Diaries, Papers and Letters, 1940–1962* (Hutchinson, 1994)
Aneurin Bevan, *In Place of Fear* (MacGibbon & Kee, 1952)
Brian Brivati, *Hugh Gaitskell* (Richard Cohen, 1996)
James Callaghan, *Time and Chance* (Collins, 1987)
John Campbell, *Nye Bevan and the Mirage of British Socialism* (Weidenfeld & Nicolson, 1987)
C. A. R. Crosland, *The Future of Socialism* (Jonathan Cape, 1956)
Henry Fairlie, *The Life of Politics* (Methuen, 1968)
Michael Foot, *Aneurin Bevan, 1945–1960* (Davis Poynter, 1973)
Geoffrey Goodman, *The Awkward Warrior: Frank Cousins: His Life and Times* (Davis Poynter, 1979)
Leslie Hunter, *The Road to Brighton Pier* (Arthur Barker, 1959)
Roy Jenkins, *A Life at the Centre* (Macmillan, 1991)
Jennie Lee, *Tomorrow is a New Day* (Cresset Press, 1939)

—— *My Life with Nye* (Jonathan Cape, 1980)

Ian Mikardo, *Back-Bencher* (Weidenfeld & Nicolson, 1988)

Janet Morgan (ed.), *The Backbench Diaries of Richard Crossman* (Hamish Hamilton & Jonathan Cape, 1981)

Kenneth O. Morgan, *Labour in Power, 1945–51* (Oxford, 1984)

Ben Pimlott (ed.), *The Political Diary of Hugh Dalton* (Jonathan Cape, 1986)

Robert Rhodes James (ed.), *'Chips': The Diaries of Sir Henry Channon* (Weidenfeld & Nicolson, 1967)

William Rodgers (ed.), *Hugh Gaitskell, 1906–1963* (Thames & Hudson, 1964)

Philip Williams, *Hugh Gaitskell* (Jonathan Cape, 1979)

—— (ed.), *The Diary of Hugh Gaitskell, 1945–1956* (Jonathan Cape, 1983)

Woodrow Wyatt, *Turn Again, Westminster* (Deutsch, 1973)

Macmillan and Butler

Richard Aldous and Sabine Lee, *Harold Macmillan: Aspects of a Political Life* (Macmillan, 1999)

Tony Benn, *Years of Hope: Diaries, Papers and Letters, 1940–1962* (Hutchinson, 1994)

John Boyd-Carpenter, *Way of Life* (Sidgwick & Jackson, 1980)

Lord Butler, *The Art of the Possible* (Hamish Hamilton, 1971)

Peter Catterall (ed.), *The Macmillan Diaries: The Cabinet Years, 1950–57* (Macmillan, 2003)

—— *The Macmillan Diaries: Prime Minister and After, 1957–1966* (Macmillan forthcoming)

William Clark, *From Three Worlds: Memoirs* (Sidgwick & Jackson, 1986)

Richard Cockett (ed.), *My Dear Max: The Letters of Brendan Bracken to Lord Beaverbrook, 1925–1958* (Historians' Press, 1990)

John Colville, *The Fringes of Power: Downing Street Diaries, 1939–1955* (Hodder & Stoughton, 1955)

Harold Evans, *Downing Street Diary: The Macmillan Years, 1957–63* (Hodder & Stoughton, 1981)

Nigel Fisher, *The Tory Leaders: Their Struggle for Power* (Weidenfeld & Nicolson, 1977)

—— *Harold Macmillan* (Weidenfeld & Nicolson, 1982)

Edward Heath, *The Course of my Life* (Hodder & Stoughton, 1998)

Nicholas Henderson, *The Private Office Revisited* (Profile Books, 2001)

Alistair Horne, *Macmillan, 1894–1956* (Macmillan, 1988)

—— *Macmillan, 1957–1986* (Macmillan, 1989)

Anthony Howard, *RAB: The Life of R. A. Butler* (Jonathan Cape, 1987)

Roy Jenkins, *A Life at the Centre* (Macmillan, 1991)

—— *Churchill* (Macmillan, 2001)

Earl of Kilmuir, *Political Adventure* (Weidenfeld & Nicolson, 1964)

Harold Macmillan, *Winds of Change, 1914–1939* (Macmillan, 1966)

—— *Tides of Fortune, 1945–1955* (Macmillan, 1969)

—— *Riding the Storm, 1956–1959* (Macmillan, 1971)

—— *Pointing the Way, 1959–1961* (Macmillan, 1972)

—— *At the End of the Day, 1961–1963* (Macmillan, 1973)

Janet Morgan (ed.), *The Backbench Diaries of Richard Crossman* (Hamish Hamilton & Jonathan Cape, 1981)

Harold Nicolson, *Diaries and Letters, 1939–1945* (Collins, 1967)
—— *Diaries and Letters, 1945–1962* (Collins, 1968)
Edward Pearce, *The Lost Leaders* (Little, Brown, 1997)
Ben Pimlott, *The Queen: A Biography of Elizabeth II* (HarperCollins, 1996)
John Ramsden, *The Age of Churchill and Eden, 1940–1957* (Longman, 1995)
—— *Winds of Change: Macmillan to Heath, 1957–1975* (Longman, 1996)
Peter Rawlinson, *A Price Too High* (Weidenfeld & Nicolson, 1989)
Robert Rhodes James, (ed); *'Chips': The Diaries of Sir Henry Channon* (Weidenfeld & Nicolson, 1967)
Anthony Sampson, *Macmillan: A Study in Ambiguity* (Allen Lane, 1967)
Alan Thompson, *The Day before Yesterday* (Panther Books/Sidgwick & Jackson, 1971)
D. R. Thorpe, *Sir Alec Douglas-Home* (Sinclair-Stevenson, 1996)
Dennis Walters, *Not Always with the Pack* (Constable, 1989)
'Watchman', *Right Honourable Gentlemen* (Right Book Club, 1940)

Heath and Thatcher

Tony Benn, *Against the Tide: Diaries, 1973–76* (Hutchinson, 1989)
John Campbell, *Edward Heath* (Jonathan Cape, 1993)
—— *Margaret Thatcher: The Grocer's Daughter* (Jonathan Cape, 2000)
—— *Margaret Thatcher: The Iron Lady* (Jonathan Cape, 2003)
Barbara Castle, *The Castle Diaries, 1974–76* (Weidenfeld & Nicolson, 1980)
Patrick Cosgrave, *Margaret Thatcher: A Tory and her Party* (Hutchinson, 1978)
Tam Dalyell, *Misrule: How Mrs Thatcher Misled Parliament from the Sinking of the Belgrano to the Wright Affair* (Hamish Hamilton, 1987)
Bernard Donoughue, *Prime Minister: The Conduct of Politics under Harold Wilson and James Callaghan* (Jonathan Cape, 1987)
Nigel Fisher, *The Tory Leaders: Their Struggle for Power* (Weidenfeld & Nicolson, 1977)
Edward Heath, *The Course of my Life* (Hodder & Stoughton, 1998)
Peter Jenkins, *Mrs Thatcher's Revolution: The Ending of the Socialist Era* (Jonathan Cape, 1987)
Ronald Millar, *A View from the Wings* (Weidenfeld & Nicolson, 1989)
Ernle Money, *Margaret Thatcher: First Lady of the House* (Leslie Frewin, 1975)
James Prior, *A Balance of Power* (Hamish Hamilton, 1986)
Francis Pym, *The Politics of Consent* (Hamish Hamilton, 1984)
John Ramsden, *Winds of Change: Macmillan to Heath, 1957–1975* (Longman, 1996)
Peter Rawlinson, *A Price Too High* (Weidenfeld & Nicolson, 1989)
Nicholas Ridley, *'My Style of Government': The Thatcher Years* (Hutchinson, 1991)
Andrew Roth, *Heath and the Heathmen* (Routledge & Kegan Paul, 1972)
Norman Tebbit, *Upwardly Mobile* (Weidenfeld & Nicolson, 1988)
Margaret Thatcher, *The Downing Street Years* (HarperCollins, 1993)
—— *The Path to Power* (HarperCollins, 1995)
Phillip Whitehead, *The Writing on the Wall: Britain in the Seventies* (Channel4/Michael Joseph, 1985)
Hugo Young, *One of Us: A Biography of Margaret Thatcher* (Macmillan, 1989, 1991).

Sources and Bibliography

Brown and Blair

Francis Beckett, *Gordon Brown: Past, Present and Future* (Haus, 2007)

Tom Bower, *Gordon Brown* (HarperCollins, 2004)

Gordon Brown (ed.), *The Red Paper on Scotland* (Edinburgh University Student Publications Board, 1975)

Alastair Campbell, *The Blair Years: Extracts from the Alastair Campbell Diaries* (Hutchinson, 2007)

Wendy Hinde, *Castlereagh* (Collins, 1981)

James Naughtie, *The Rivals: The Intimate Story of a Political Marriage* (Fourth Estate, 2001, 2002)

Robert Peston, *Brown's Britain* (Short Books, 2005, 2006)

Giles Radice, *Diaries, 1980–2001* (Weidenfeld & Nicolson, 2004)

Andrew Rawnsley, *Servants of the People: The Inside Story of New Labour* (Hamish Hamilton, 2000; Penguin, 2001)

John Rentoul, *Tony Blair: Prime Minister* (Little, Brown, 2001)

Anthony Seldon, *Major: A Political Life* (Weidenfeld & Nicolson, 1997)

—— *Blair* (Free Press, 2004)

—— *Blair Unbound* (Simon & Schuster, 2007)

Jon Sopel, *Tony Blair: The Moderniser* (Michael Joseph, 1995)

Dictionary of National Biography
Parliamentary Debates
Annual Register
The Times
and other newspapers

Index

Index

Munich crisis (1938), 251–2, 266, 272
Murdoch, Rupert, 367
Mussolini, Benito, 249–50, 265

Nasser, Colonel, 231–2
National Health Service (NHS), 1980–9,
  202, 207–10, 218, 371, 376–7, 384,
  392, 402
Naughtie, James, 377
Neave, Airey, 319, 321
Nehru, Jawaharlal, 234
Nelson, Horatio, 51, 54
Nenni, Pietro, 234
Newsnight, 361
New Statesman, 262
Newsweek, 342
Nicolson, Harold, 253
Nicolson, Nigel, 271
Norfolk, Duke of, 45
North, Lord, 12–13 & n., 14, 17, 19–21,
  24, 26–8, 30–1, 33, 236, 288
Northcliffe, Lord., 169–71
Northern Ireland, 372, 379–80, 402
Nott, John, 331, 333
Nuclear weapons, 205, 223–4, 236, 240–1,
  281, 387–8, 398, 401
Nye, Sue, 366

Obama, Barack, 401
Observer, 374
'One Nation', 301, 336

Paine, Thomas, 42 & n.
Pakenham, Frank, 202
Palmer, Thomas, 42 & n.
Parkinson, Cecil, 333
Parliamentary reform, 16–17, 44–5, 558, 80,
  93, 110–15, 138, 401
Patten, Chris, 336,
Pearce, Edward, 293
Peel, Robert, 55, 86, 89, 90–1, 93–4, 97,
  100, 115–16, 130, 138–9, 172, 247,
  279, 288
Peninsular war (1809–14), 65–6, 70
People, The, 308
Perceval, Spencer, 7, 62–4, 66, 68–70, 74–9
'Peterloo' massacre (1819), 82
Peyton, John, 322–3 & n.
Pike, Mervyn, 307n.
Pile, Sir William, 308
Pitt, Lady Hester, 10
Pitt, William, the Elder (Earl of Chatham), 9,
  12, 14, 28, 30
Pitt, William, 1, 2, 3, 7, 57–62, 73n., 75, 80,
  82, 85, 86, 88, 91, 93, 96, 99–100,
  125, 138, 172, 199, 244–5, 404;
  rivalry with Fox, 9–56; youth and

character, 10; on Fox, 12, 17, 21, 23,
  26, 34, 36, 38–9, 45; in Parliament,
  14–15, 17–18, 21, 25–6, 32–3, 38, 45,
  46, 50; and parliamentary reform,
  16–17, 44–5; as Chancellor, 17, 22;
  style of oratory, 19–19; becomes Prime
  Minister, 30–2; in Regency crisis, 37–9;
  and French revolution, 39; and security, 42–4, 47, 55; and Napoleonic
  war, 48–9, 55, 64; and slave trade, 47,
  53, 55; resigns, 47–8; Prime Minister
  again, 50–1; death, 51–2; legacy and
  reputation, 54–5
Pompidou, Georges, 312
Ponsonby, Sir Henry, 122
Porson, Richard, 18
Portland, Duke of, 17, 22, 30, 33, 37, 42–3,
  63–4, 66–9, 71–2, 74–5, 78
Powell, J. Enoch, 8, 255, 268, 280, 287,
  289, 301, 304–5, 311n., 312, 316 &
  n., 321, 396
Powell, Jonathan, 371, 381, 390
Prescott, John, 240, 281, 355, 357–9, 361–2,
  365–6, 368, 388–9, 391, 395
Prior, James, 307, 313–15, 320, 322 & n.,
  329, 331, 333
Private Eye, 280, 302n.
Profumo, John, 281, 293
Punch, 118–19
Pym, Francis, 321, 331
Pym, John, 35

Question Time, 354

Radice, Giles, 354–7, 359, 374, 376, 378–80
Ramsden, John, 268
Rawlinson, Peter, 307, 309
Rawnsley, Andrew, 369, 374
Reading, Lord, 163, 174
Reagan, Ronald, 355, 386
Redmayne, Martin, 286
Red Paper on Scotland, The (1975), 349–50
Redmond, John, 153, 165
Reid, John, 390, 396, 398
Rhodes, Cecil, 145
Richard, Cliff, 391
Riddell, Lord, 153, 155, 157, 172, 176–7,
  181
Riddell, Peter, 363
Ridley, Nicholas, 319–20
Right Approach, The (1976), 327
Rigby, Richard, 19
Rippon, Geoffrey, 308n.
Robens, Alf, 232
Roberts, Alfred, 297–8
Robertson, Sir William, 163, 166
Robinson, Geoffrey, 367, 370, 372, 374
Rockingham, Marquess of, 12, 14–15, 17
Romilly, Sir Samuel, 86

451